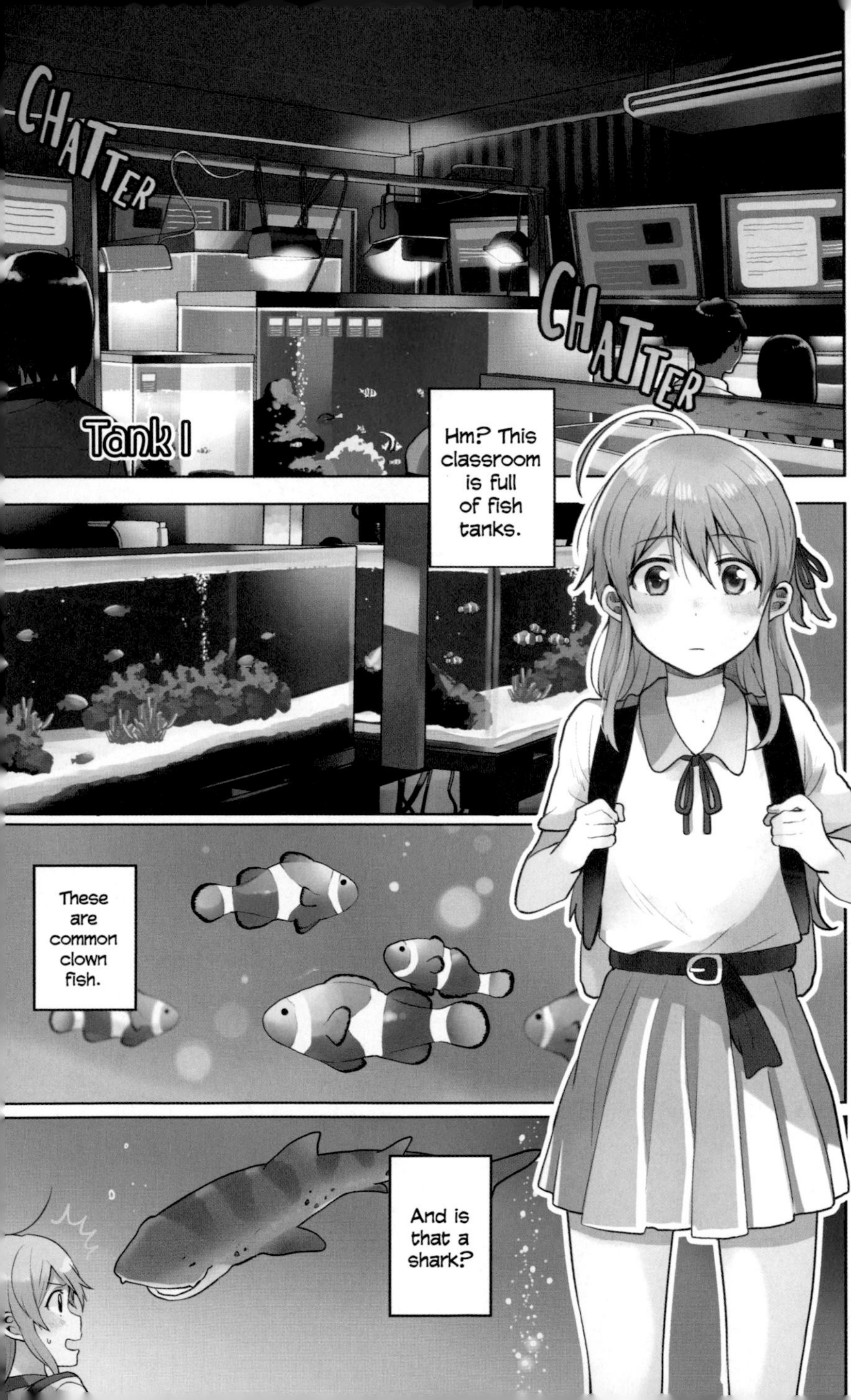
CHATTER
CHATTER
Tank 1
Hm? This classroom is full of fish tanks.
These are common clown fish.
And is that a shark?

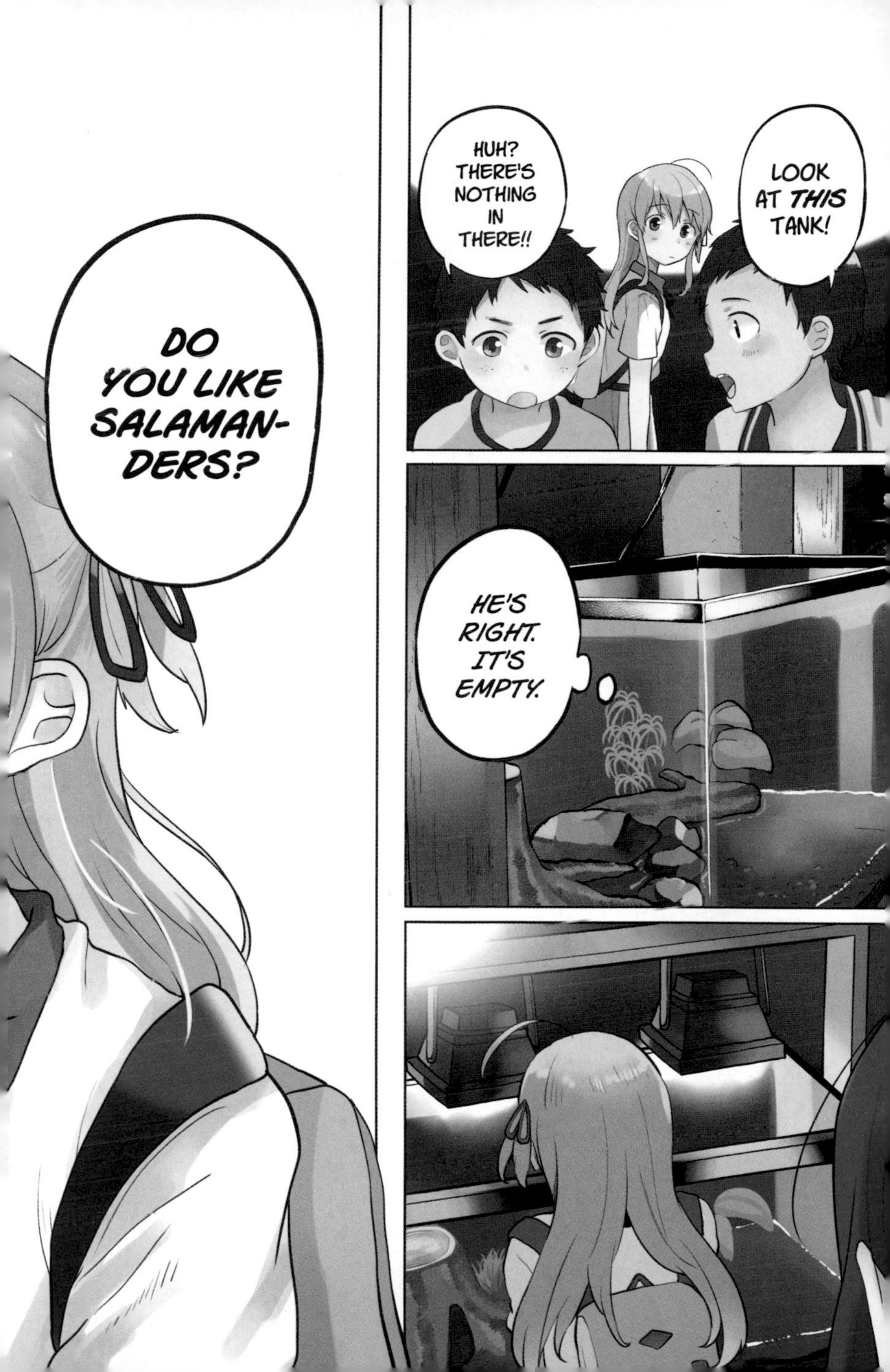
LOOK AT THIS TANK!
HUH? THERE'S NOTHING IN THERE!!
HE'S RIGHT. IT'S EMPTY.
DO YOU LIKE SALAMANDERS?

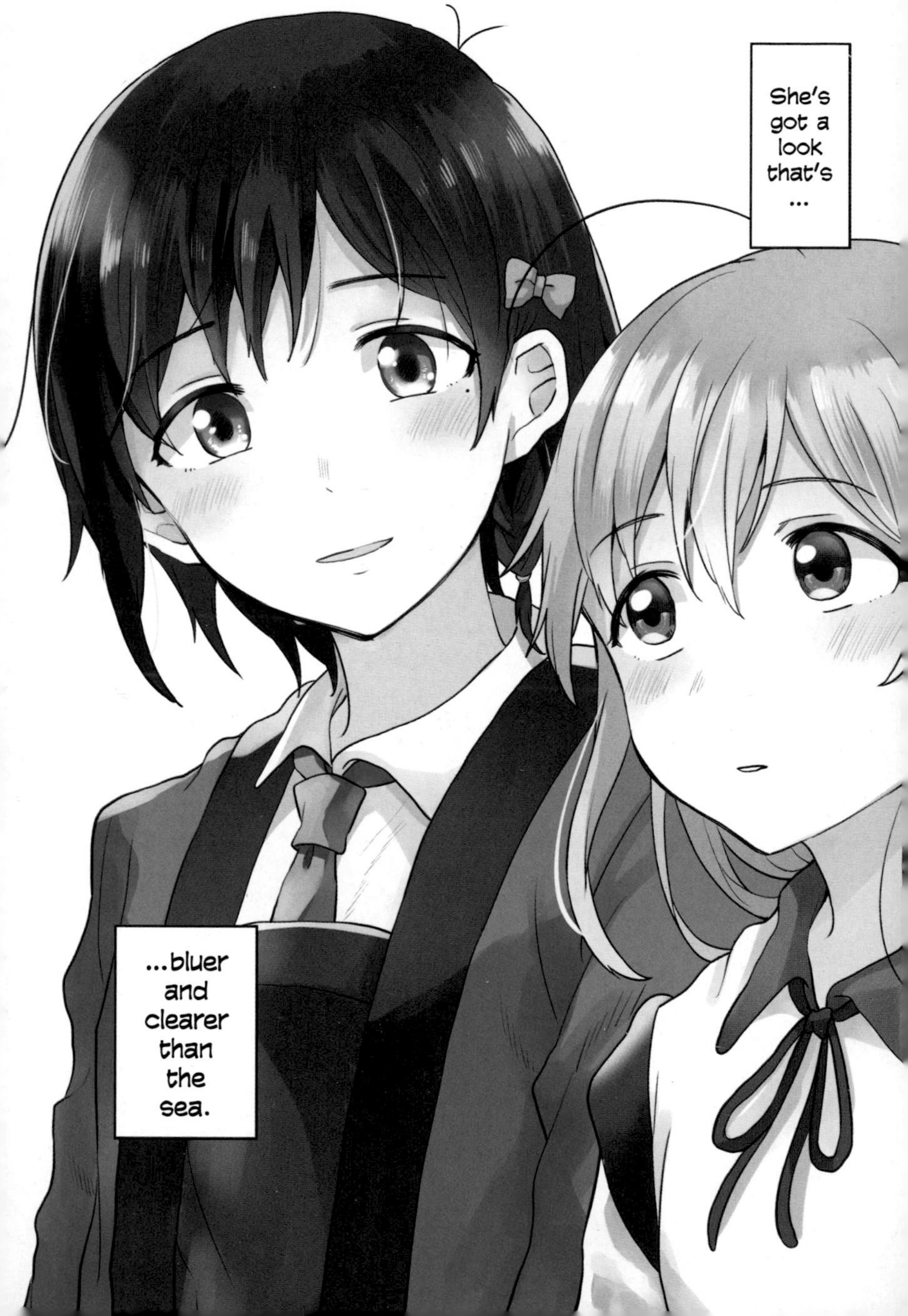
She's got a look that's ...
...bluer and clearer than the sea.

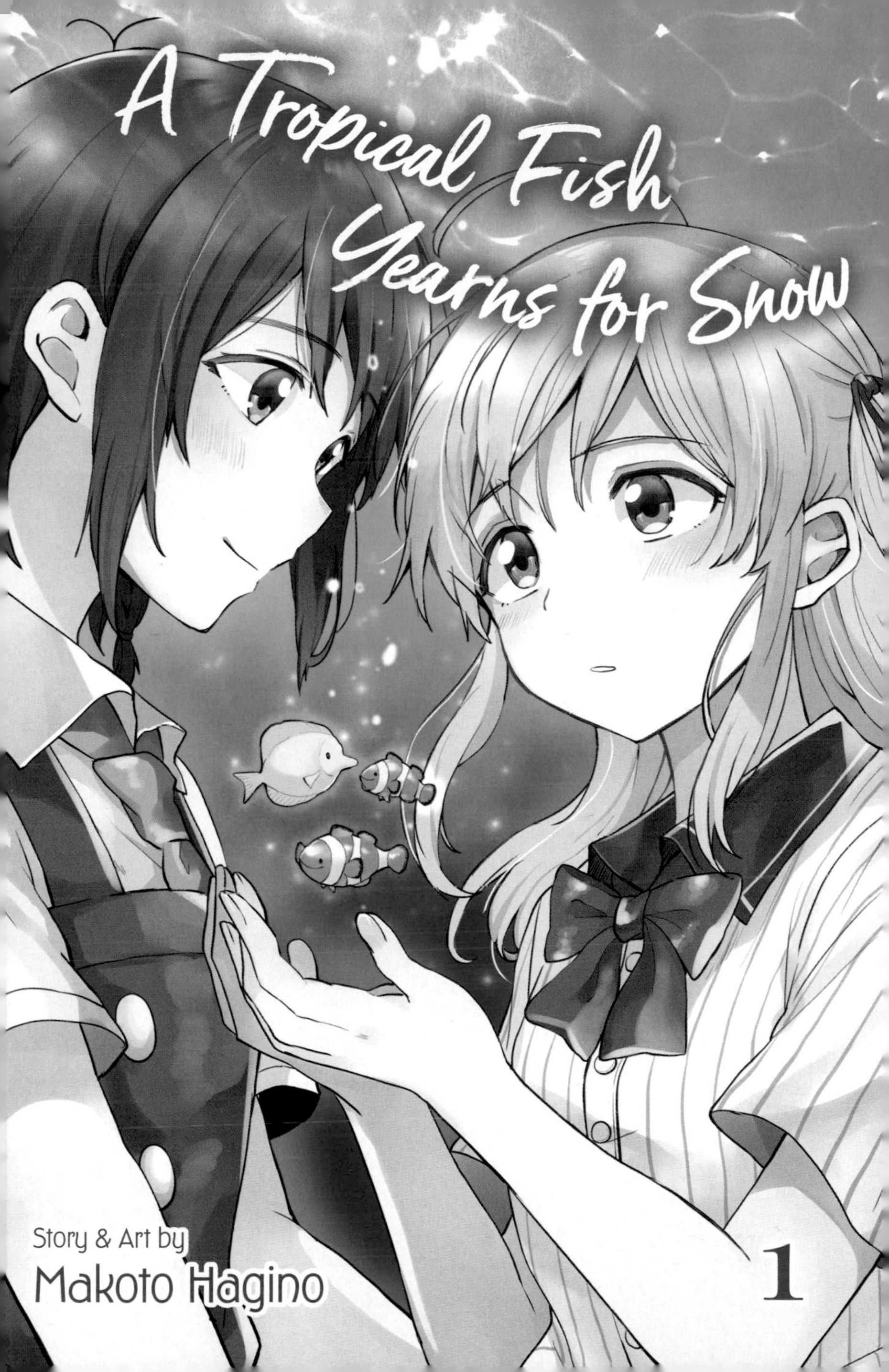
A Tropical Fish Yearns for Snow
Story & Art by
Makoto Hagino
1

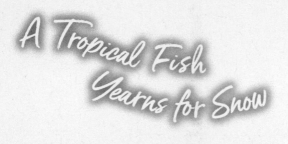

A Tropical Fish
Yearns for Snow

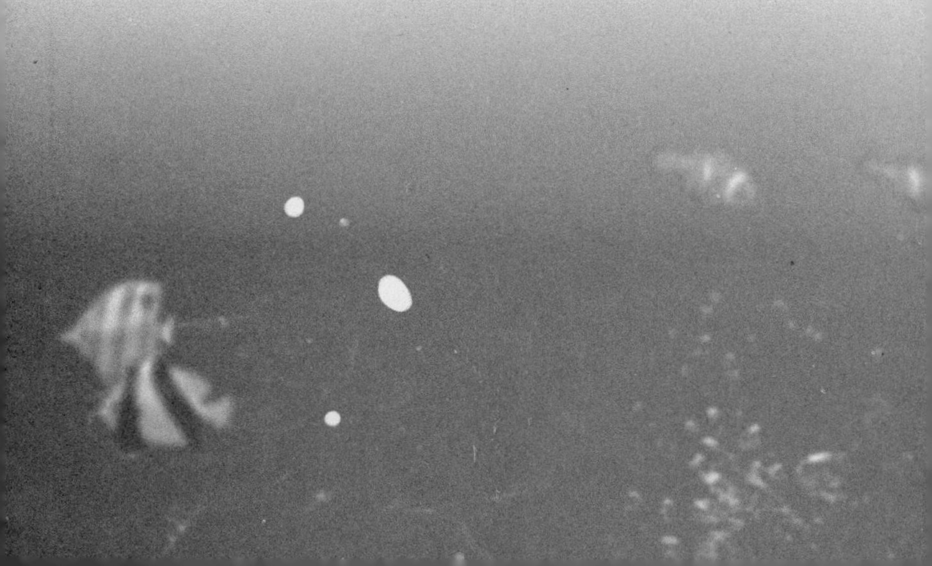

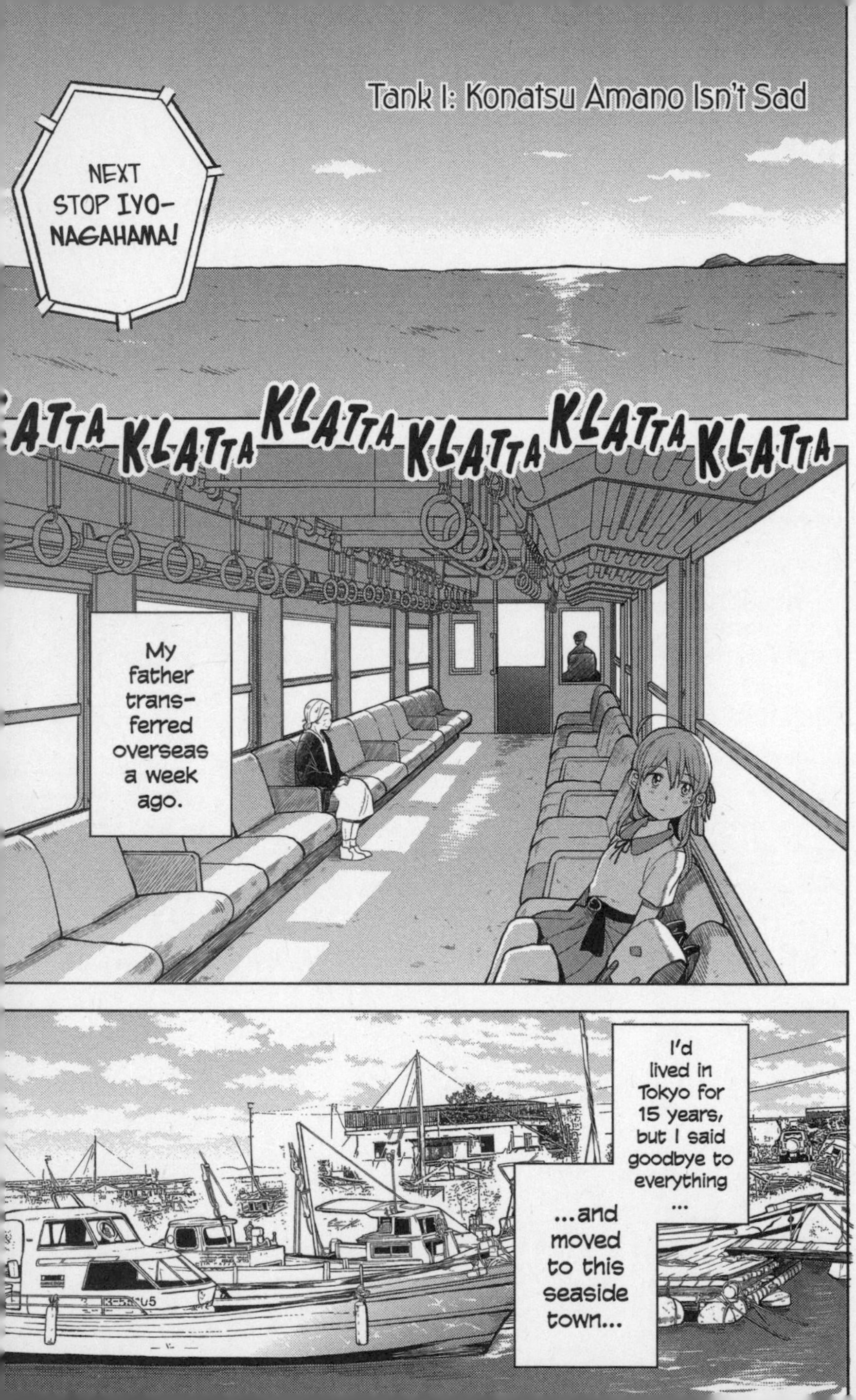
Tank 1: Konatsu Amano Isn't Sad
NEXT STOP IYO-NAGAHAMA!
ATTA KLATTA KLATTA KLATTA KLATTA KLATTA
My father trans-ferred overseas a week ago.
I'd lived in Tokyo for 15 years, but I said goodbye to everything ...
...and moved to this seaside town...

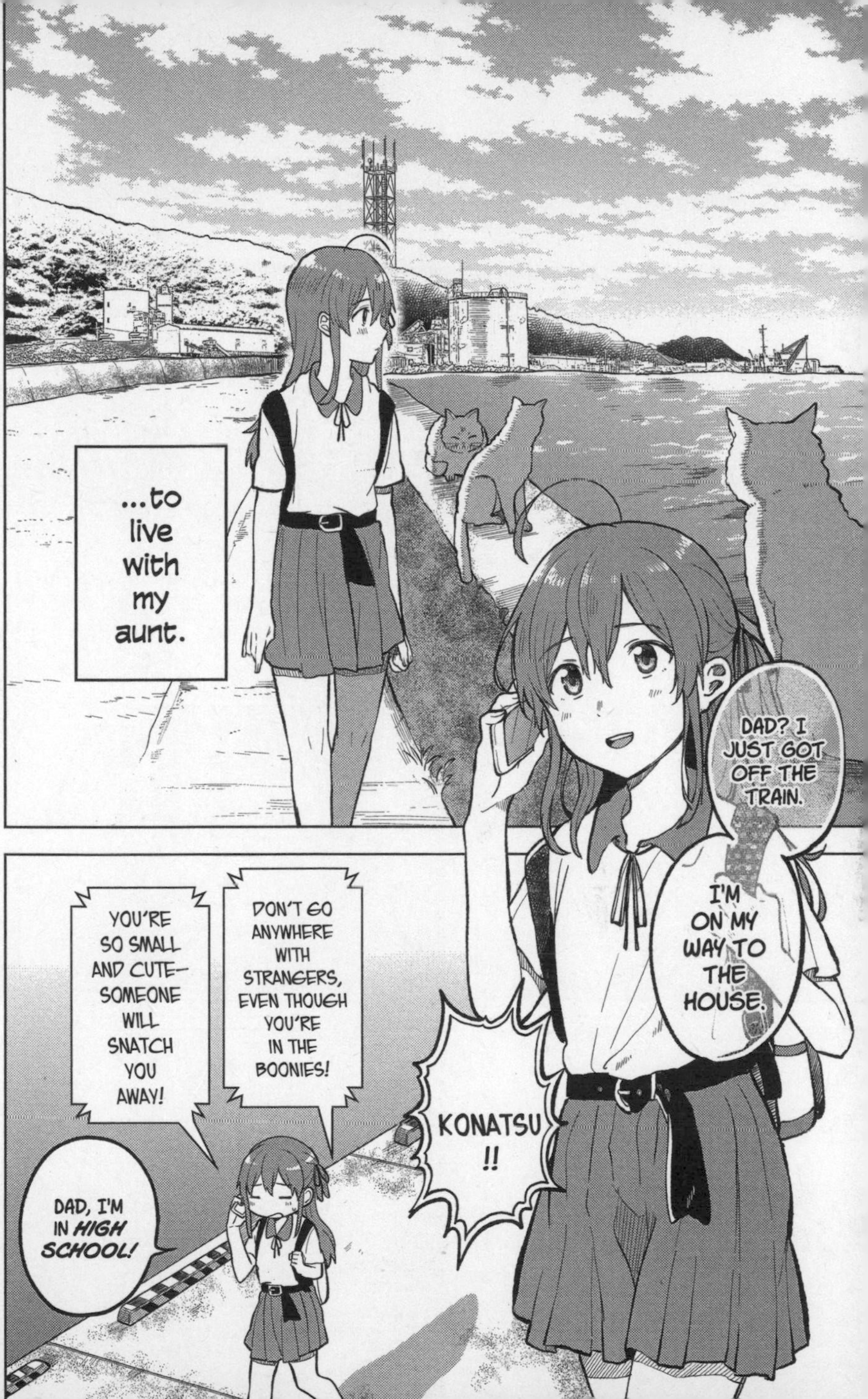
...to live with my aunt.
DAD? I JUST GOT OFF THE TRAIN.
I'M ON MY WAY TO THE HOUSE.
KONATSU!!
DON'T GO ANYWHERE WITH STRANGERS, EVEN THOUGH YOU'RE IN THE BOONIES!
YOU'RE SO SMALL AND CUTE-SOMEONE WILL SNATCH YOU AWAY!
DAD, I'M IN *HIGH SCHOOL!*

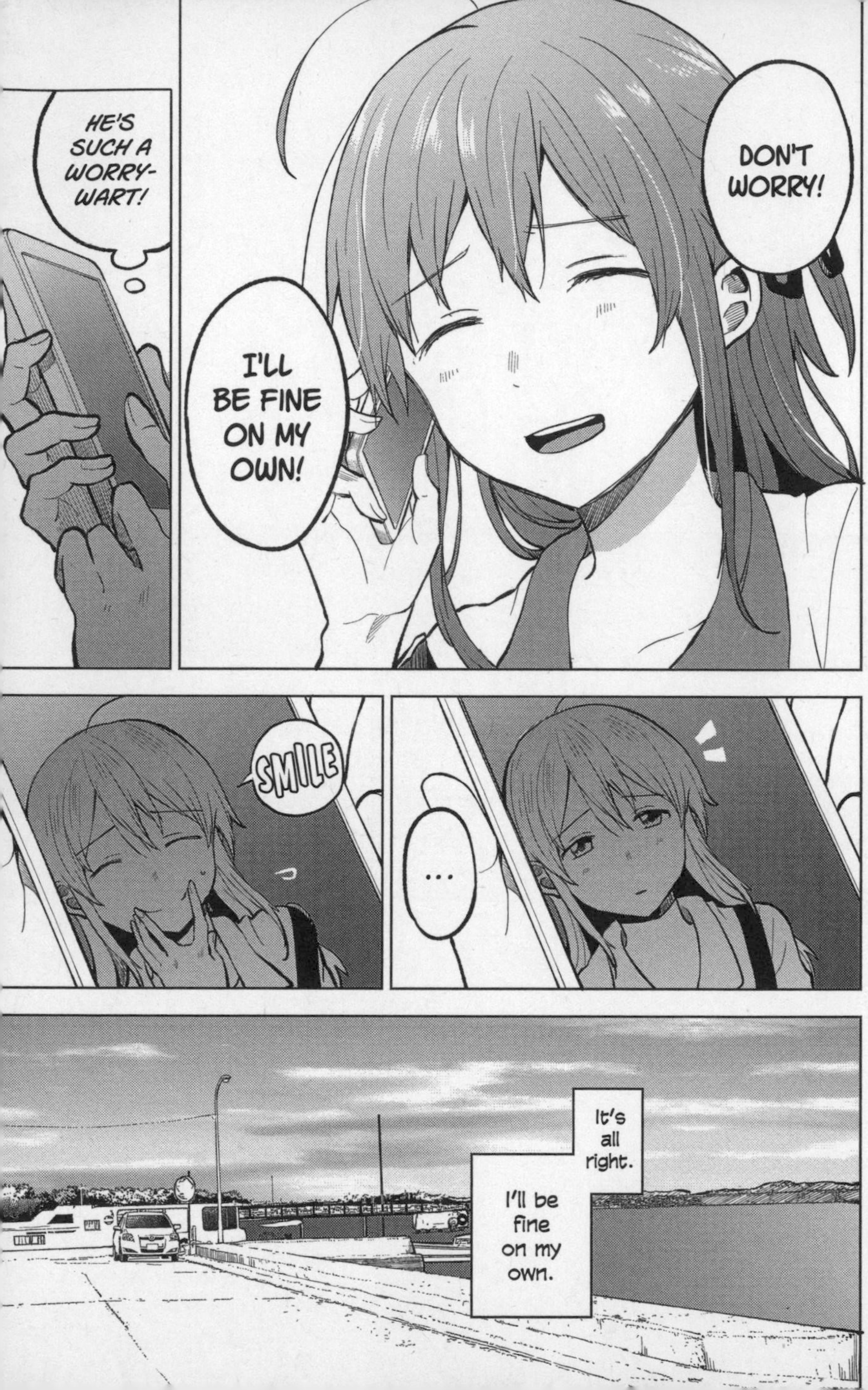
DON'T WORRY!
I'LL BE FINE ON MY OWN!
HE'S SUCH A WORRY-WART!
...
SMILE
It's all right.
I'll be fine on my own.

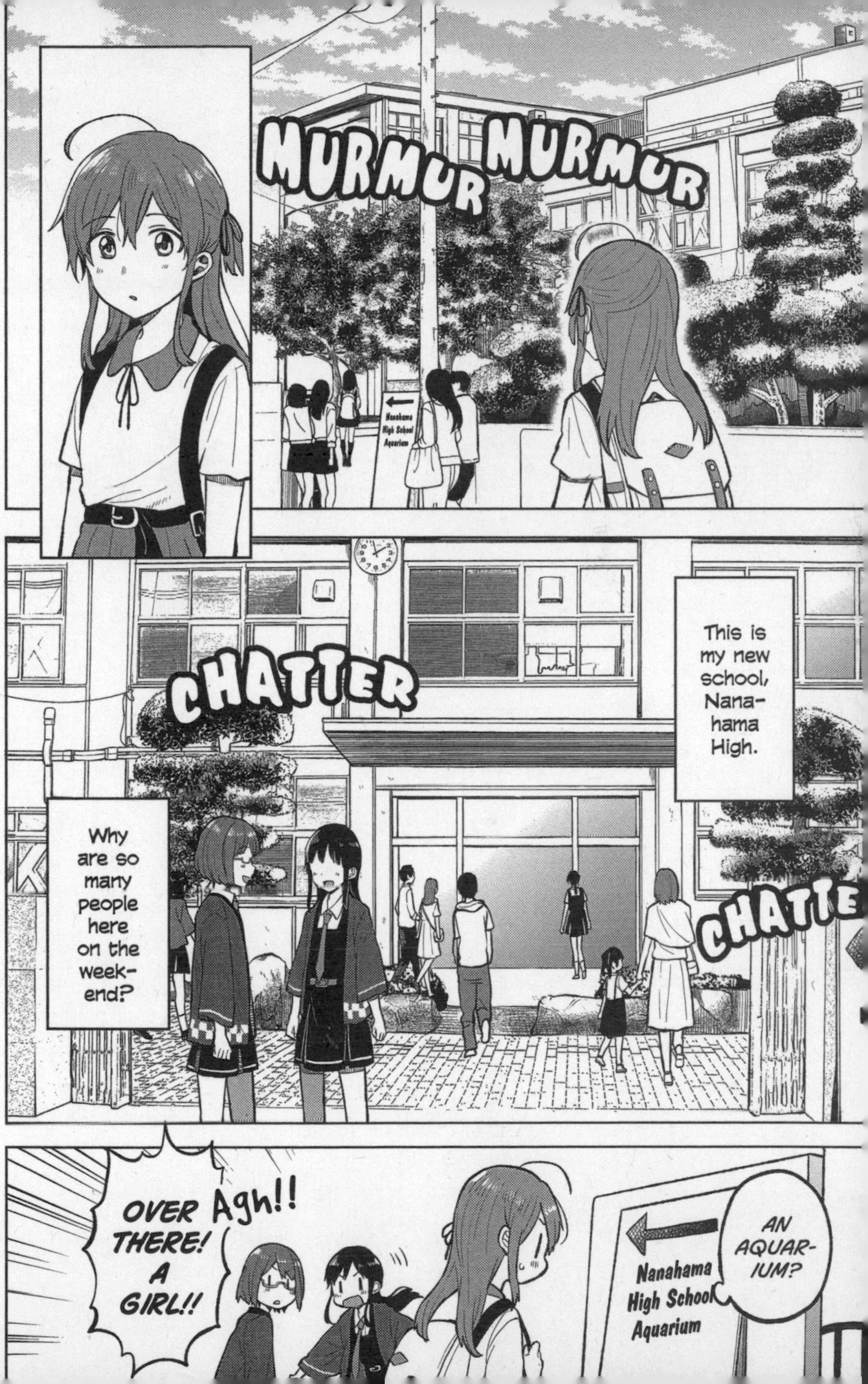
MURMUR MURMUR
Nanahama High School Aquarium
CHATTE
This is my new school, Nanahama High.
CHATTER
Why are so many people here on the weekend?
Nanahama High School Aquarium
AN AQUARIUM?
Agh!!
OVER THERE! A GIRL!!

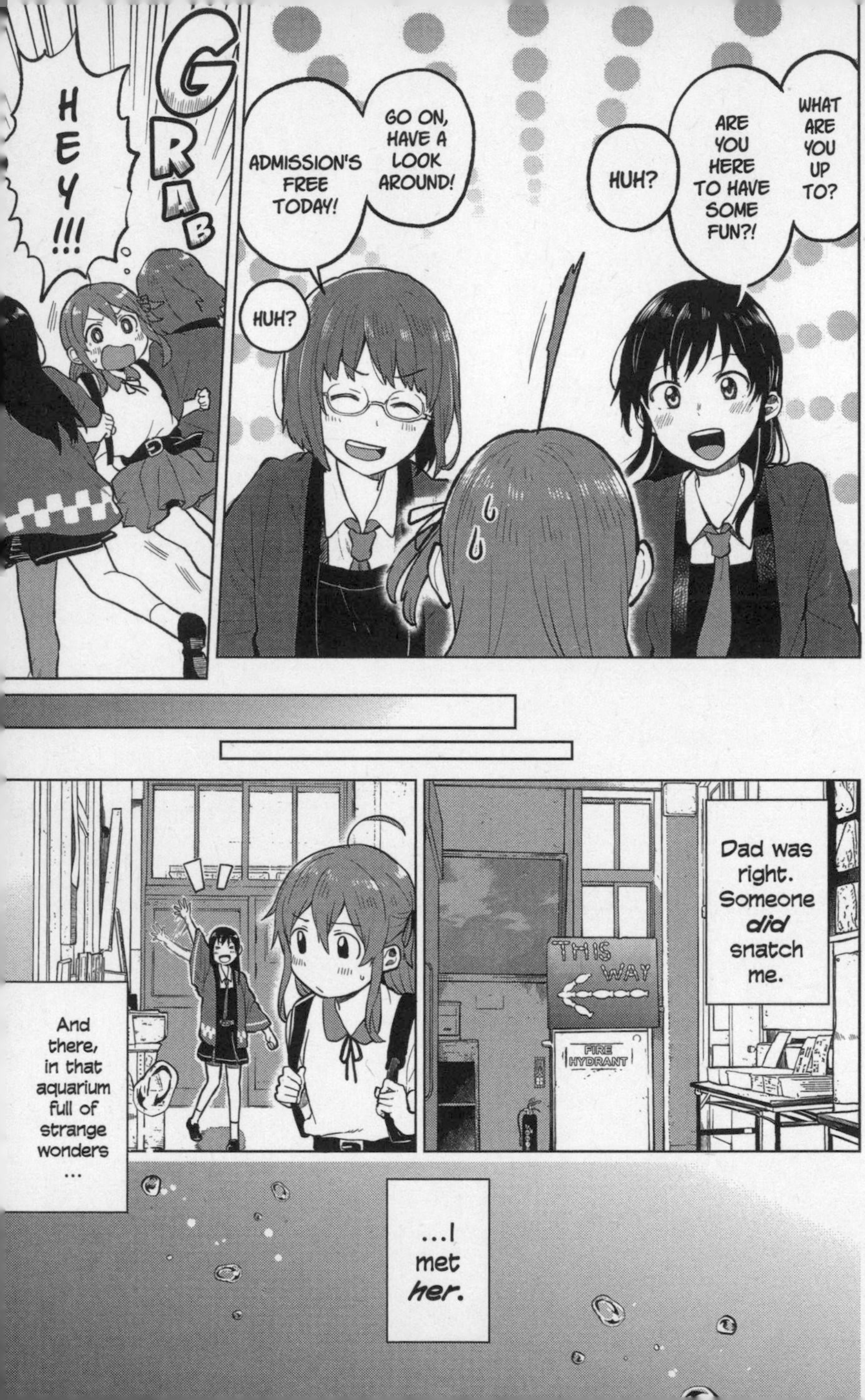
WHAT ARE YOU UP TO?
ARE YOU HERE TO HAVE SOME FUN?!
HUH?
GO ON, HAVE A LOOK AROUND!
ADMISSION'S FREE TODAY!
HUH?
GRAB
HEY!!!
Dad was right. Someone *did* snatch me.
THIS WAY
FIRE HYDRANT
And there, in that aquarium full of strange wonders...
...I met *her*.

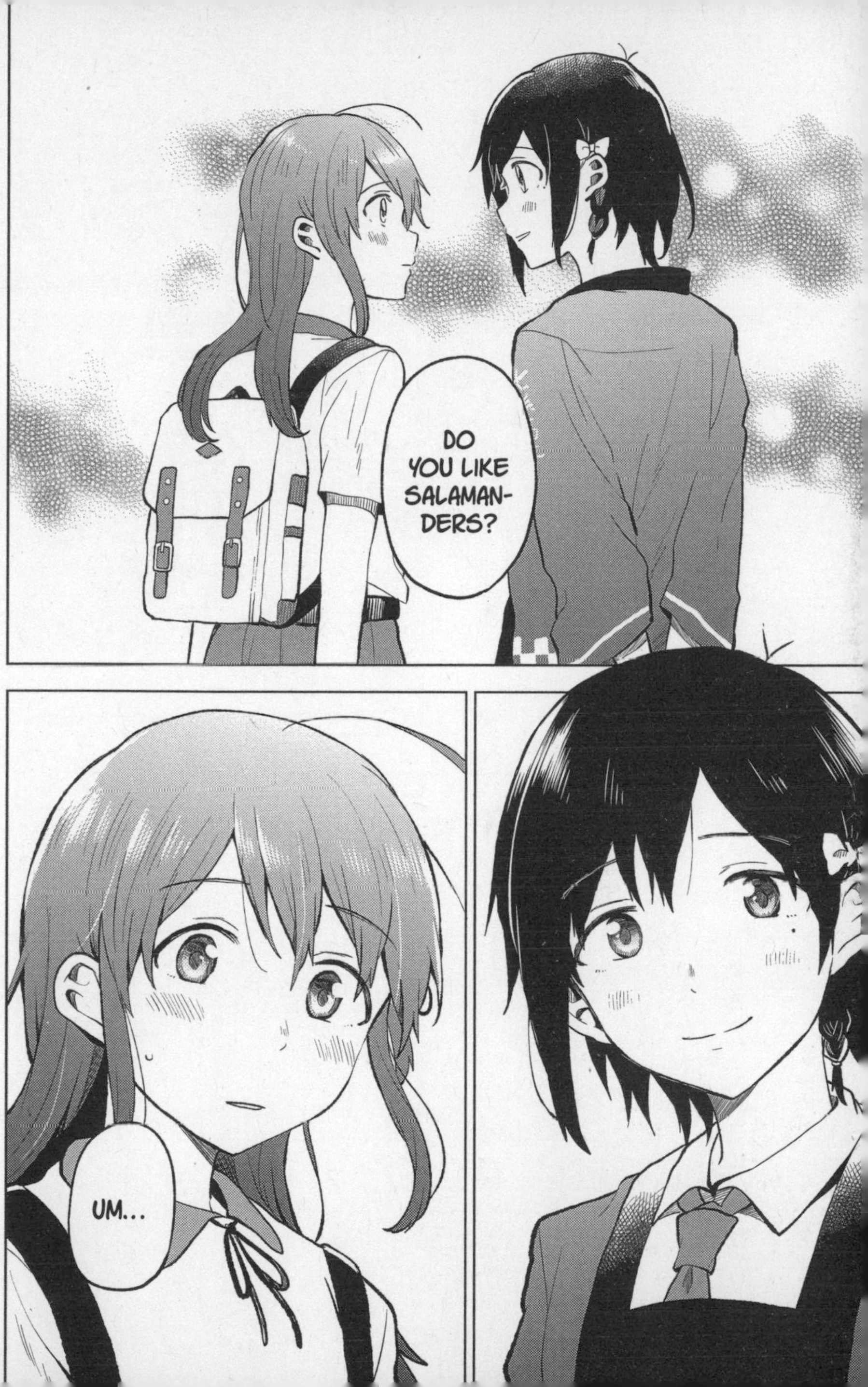
DO YOU LIKE SALAMANDERS?
UM...

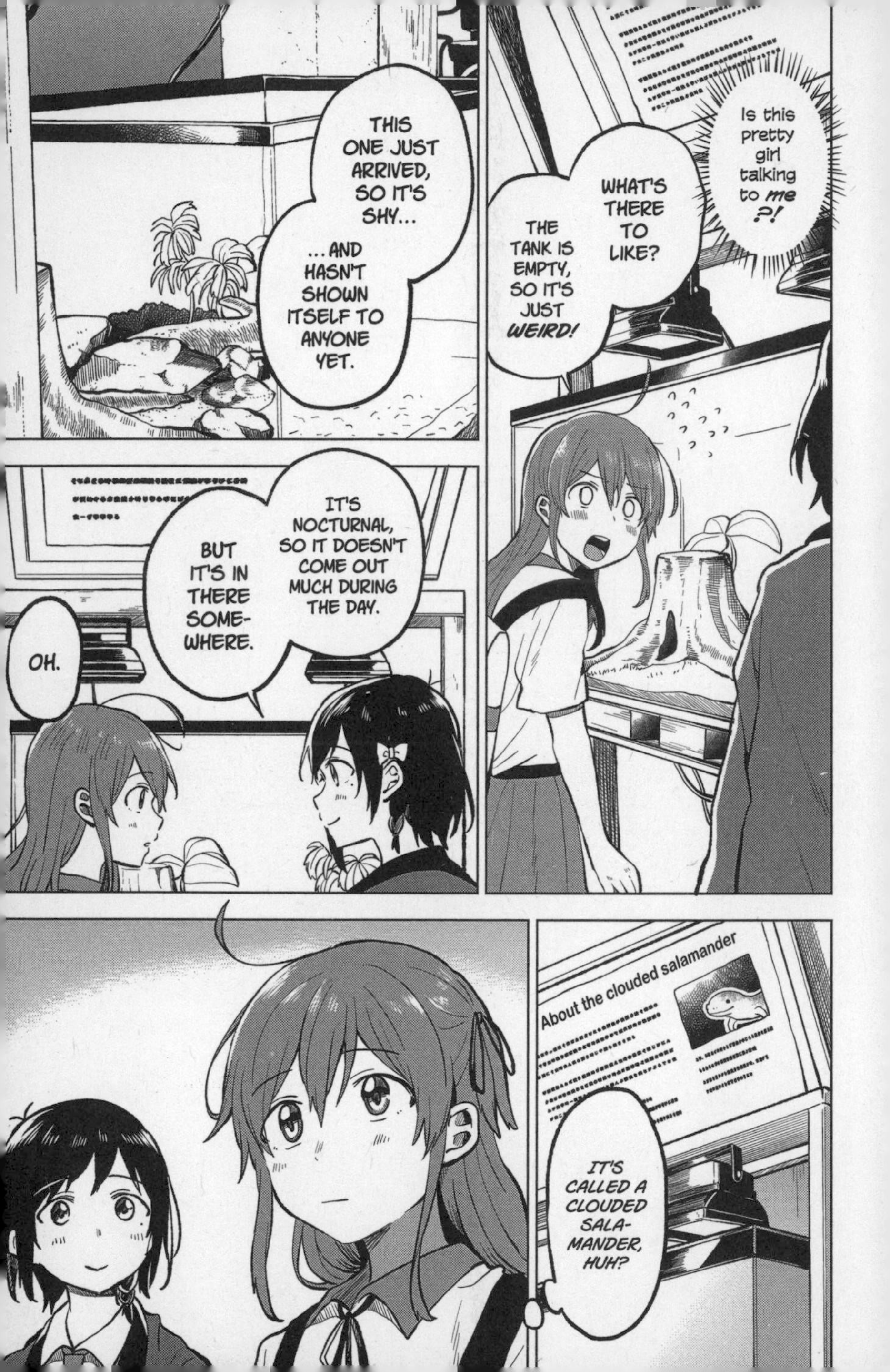
Is this pretty girl talking to *me* ?!
WHAT'S THERE TO LIKE?
THE TANK IS EMPTY, SO IT'S JUST *WEIRD!*
THIS ONE JUST ARRIVED, SO IT'S SHY...
...AND HASN'T SHOWN ITSELF TO ANYONE YET.
IT'S NOCTURNAL, SO IT DOESN'T COME OUT MUCH DURING THE DAY.
BUT IT'S IN THERE SOME-WHERE.
OH.
About the clouded salamander
IT'S CALLED A CLOUDED SALA-MANDER, HUH?

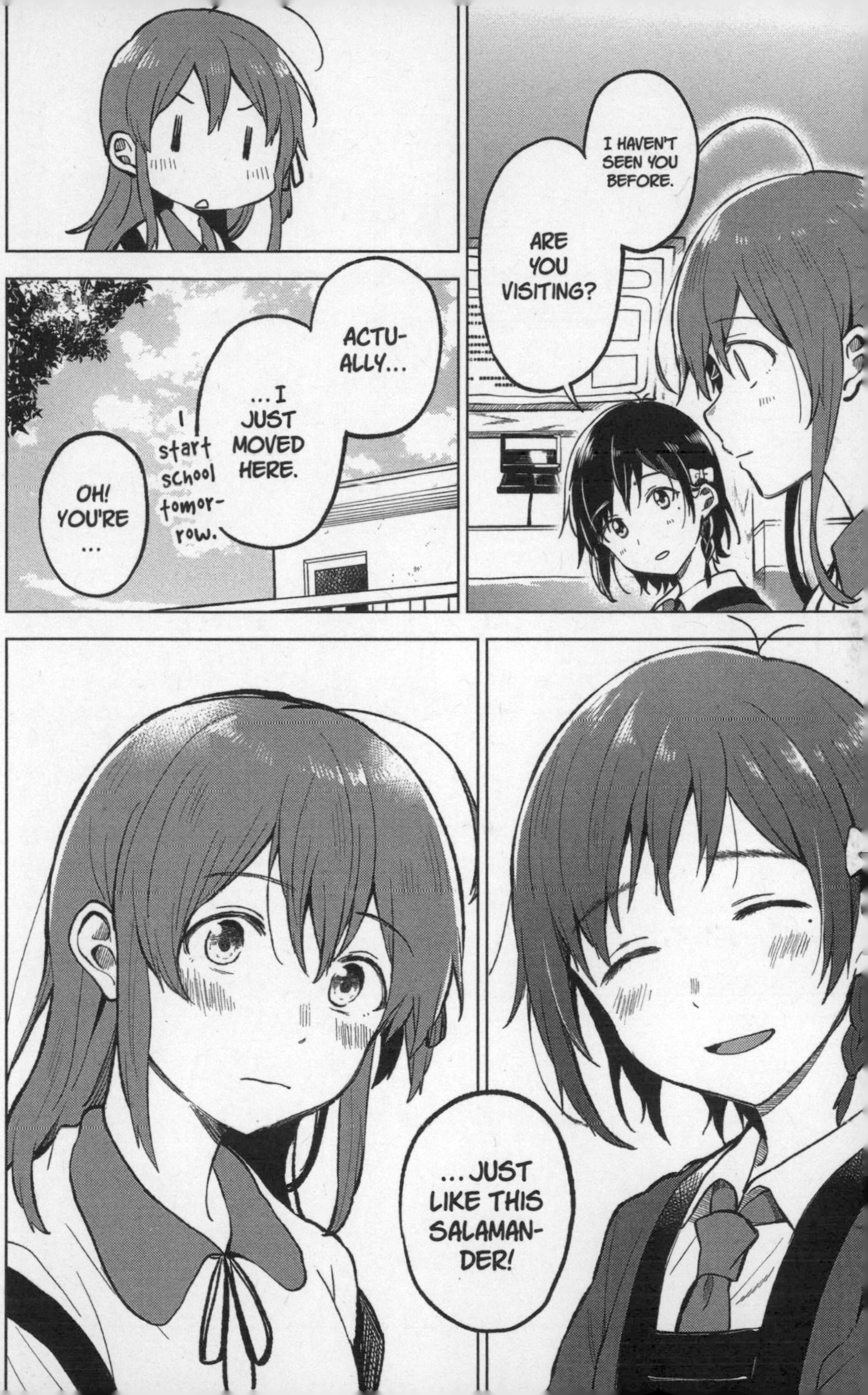
I HAVEN'T SEEN YOU BEFORE.
ARE YOU VISITING?
ACTU-ALLY...
...I JUST MOVED HERE.
I start school tomor-row.
OH! YOU'RE ...
...JUST LIKE THIS SALAMAN-DER!

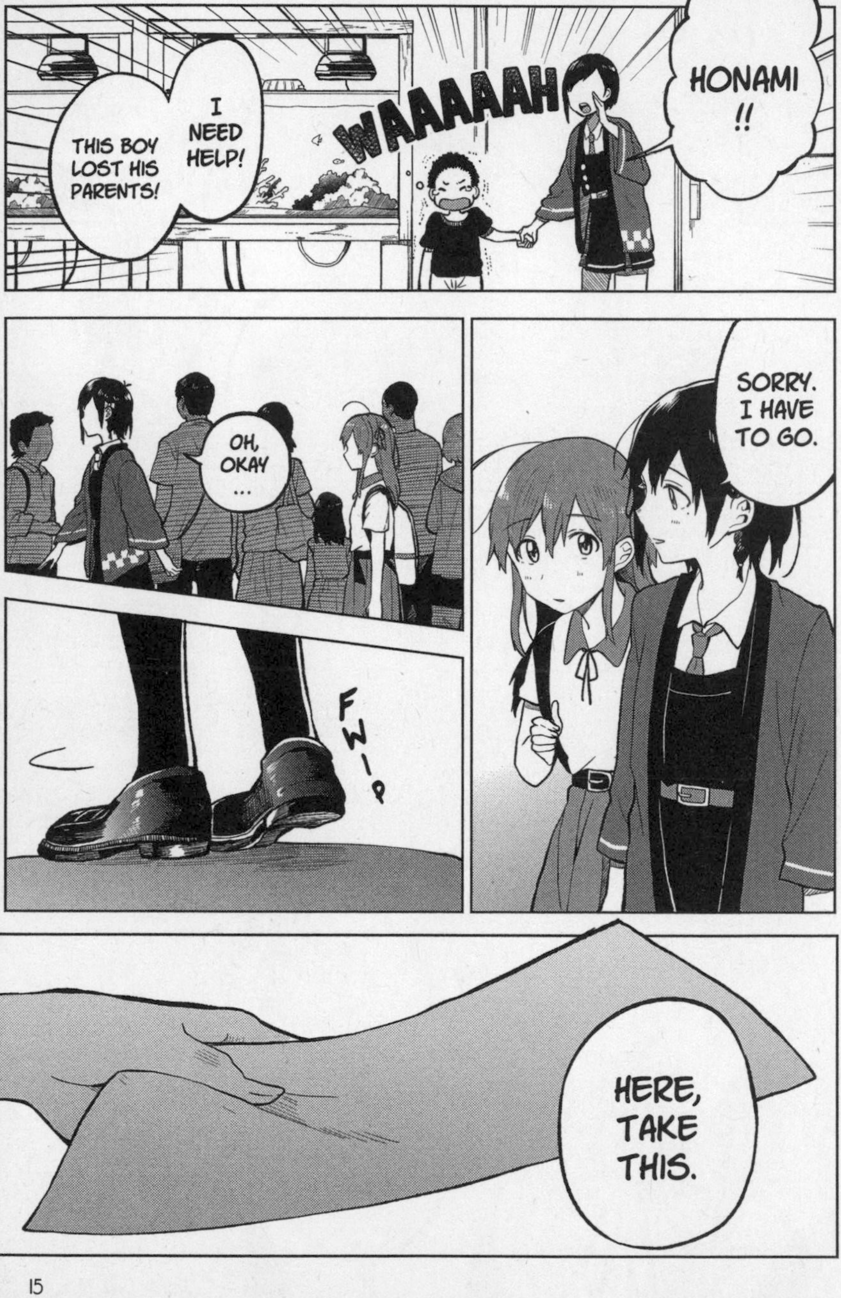
HONAMI !!
WAAAAAH
I NEED HELP!
THIS BOY LOST HIS PARENTS!
SORRY. I HAVE TO GO.
OH, OKAY ...
FWIP
HERE, TAKE THIS.

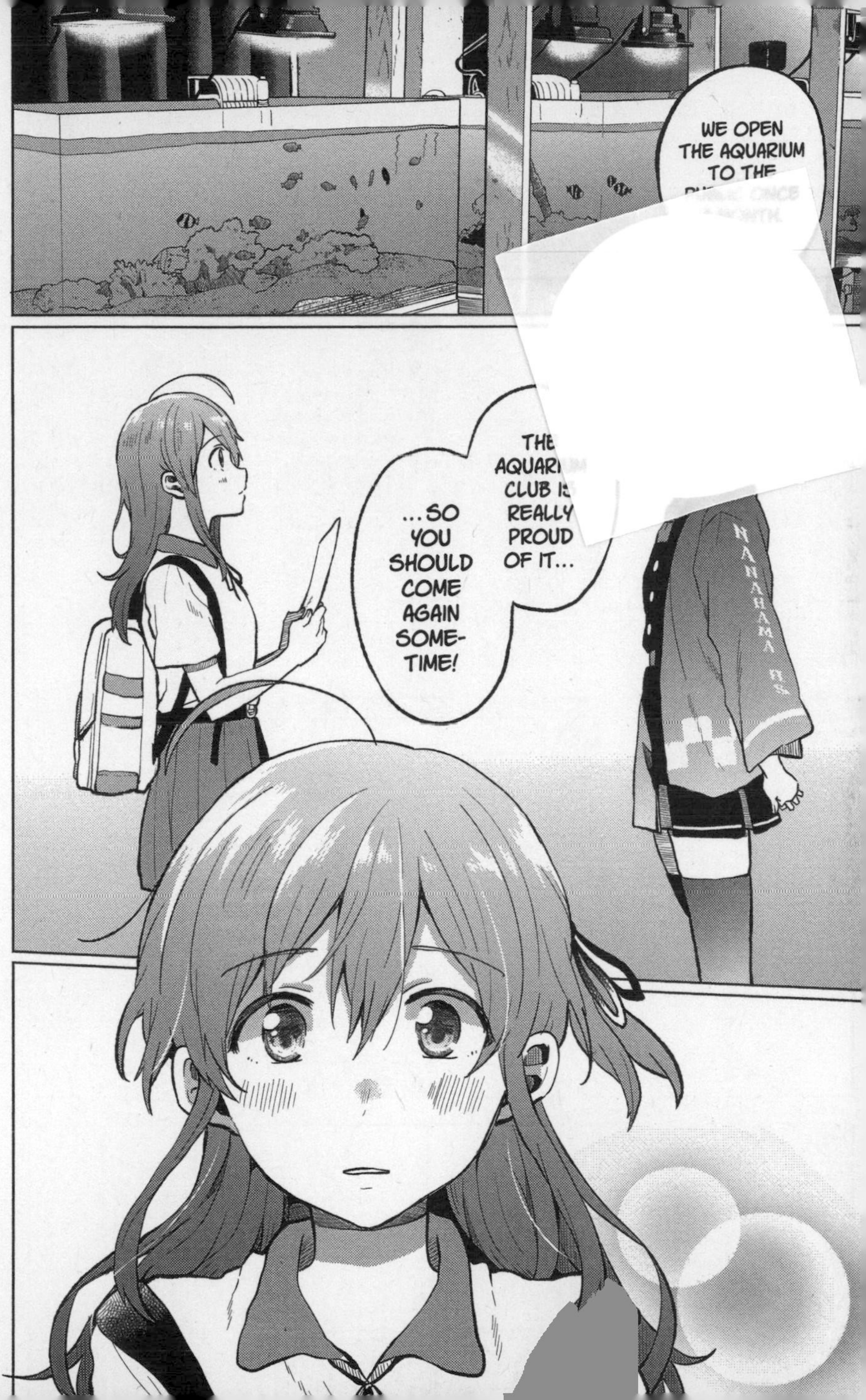
WE OPEN THE AQUARIUM TO THE
NANAHAMA H.S.
THE AQUARIUM CLUB IS REALLY PROUD OF IT...
...SO YOU SHOULD COME AGAIN SOME-TIME!

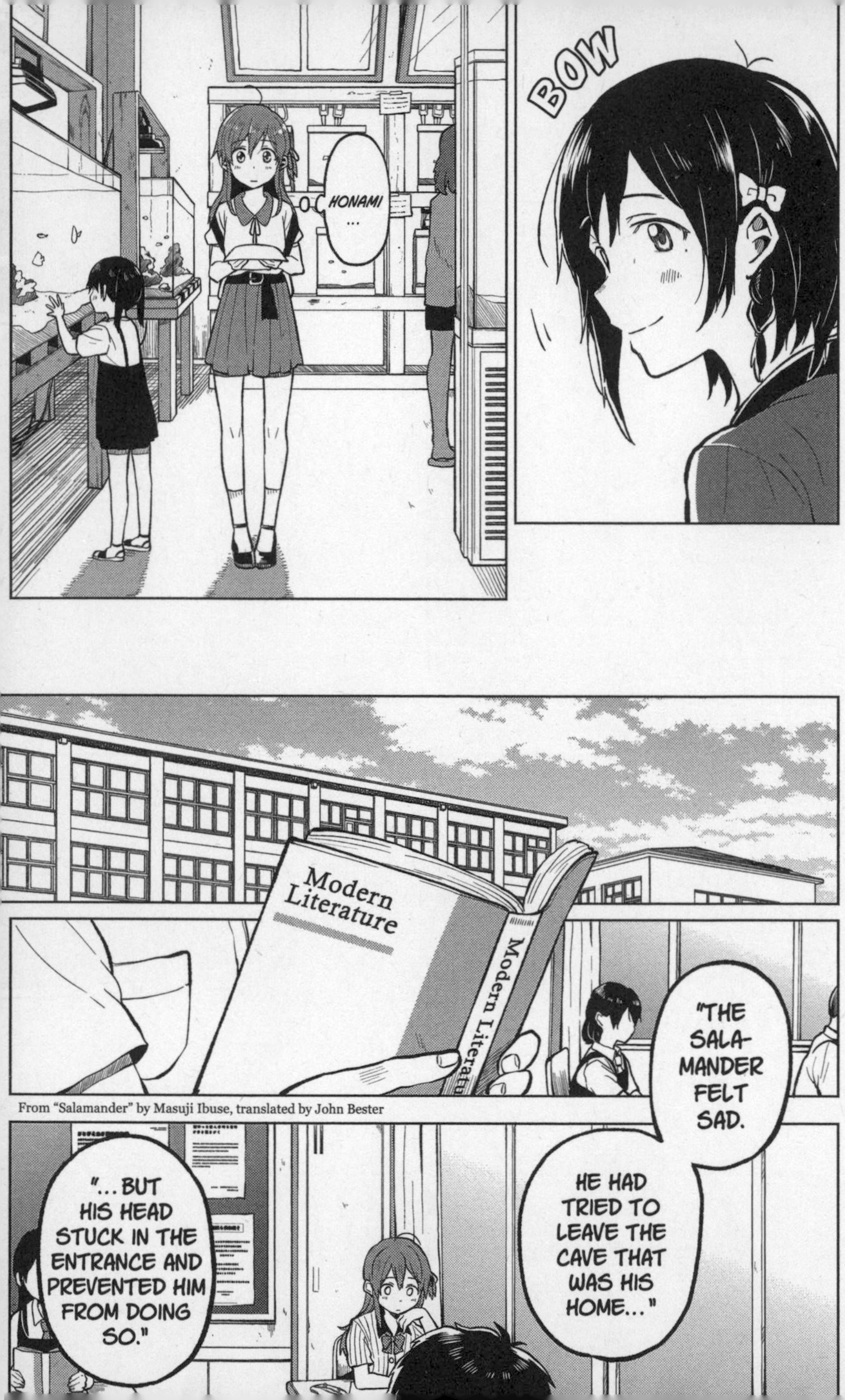
BOW
HONAMI ...
Modern Literature
Modern Literature
Modern Literatu
"THE SALAMANDER FELT SAD.
HE HAD TRIED TO LEAVE THE CAVE THAT WAS HIS HOME..."
"... BUT HIS HEAD STUCK IN THE ENTRANCE AND PREVENTED HIM FROM DOING SO."

From "Salamander" by Masuji Ibuse, translated by John Bester

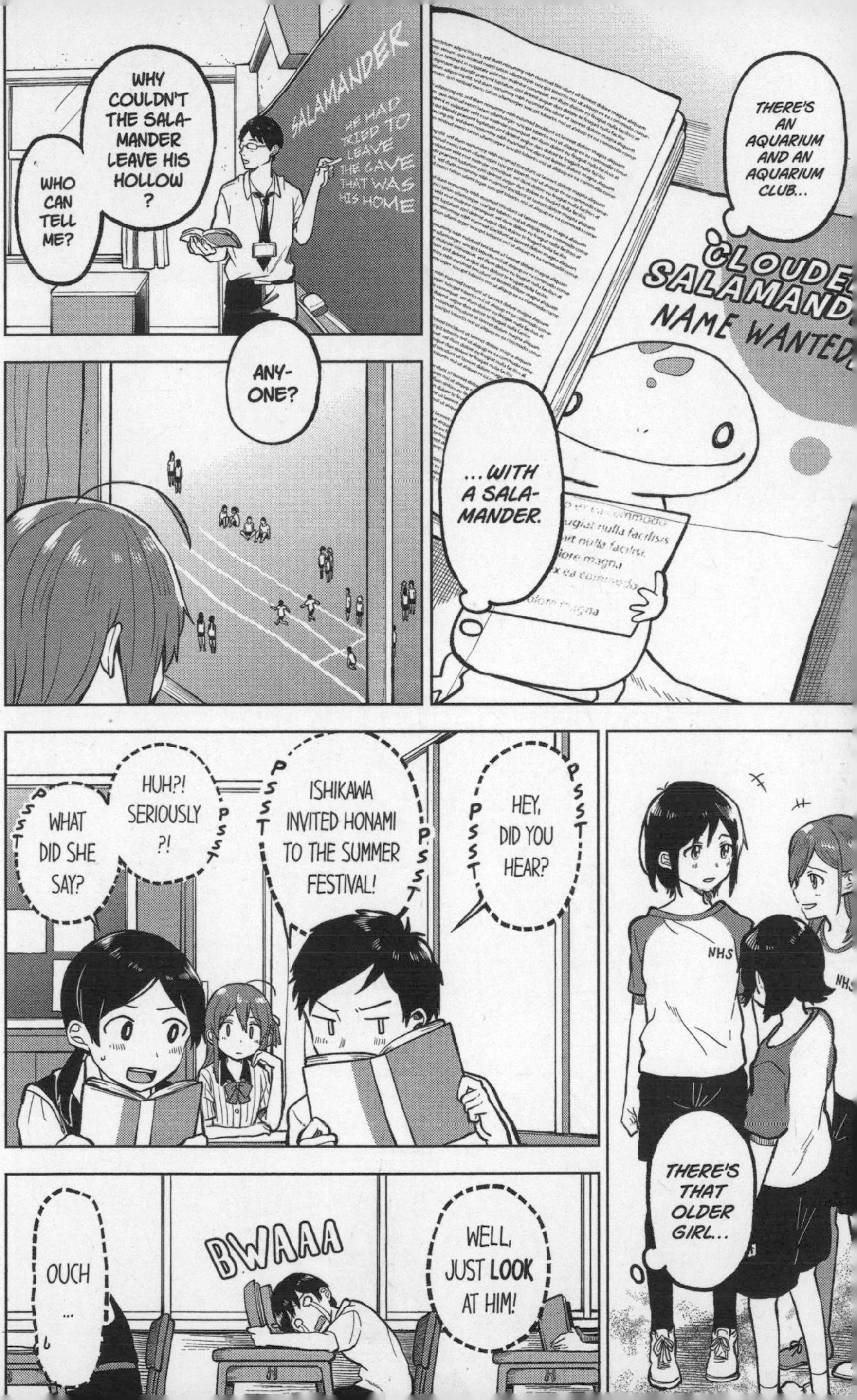

THERE'S AN AQUARIUM AND AN AQUARIUM CLUB...
CLOUDE
SALAMAND
NAME WANTED
...WITH A SALAMANDER.
SALAMANDER
HE HAD TRIED TO LEAVE THE CAVE THAT WAS HIS HOME
WHY COULDN'T THE SALAMANDER LEAVE HIS HOLLOW?
WHO CAN TELL ME?
ANYONE?
THERE'S THAT OLDER GIRL...
PSST
HEY, DID YOU HEAR?
PSST
ISHIKAWA INVITED HONAMI TO THE SUMMER FESTIVAL!
PSST
HUH?! SERIOUSLY?!
PSST
WHAT DID SHE SAY?
WELL, JUST **LOOK** AT HIM!
BWAAA
OUCH ...

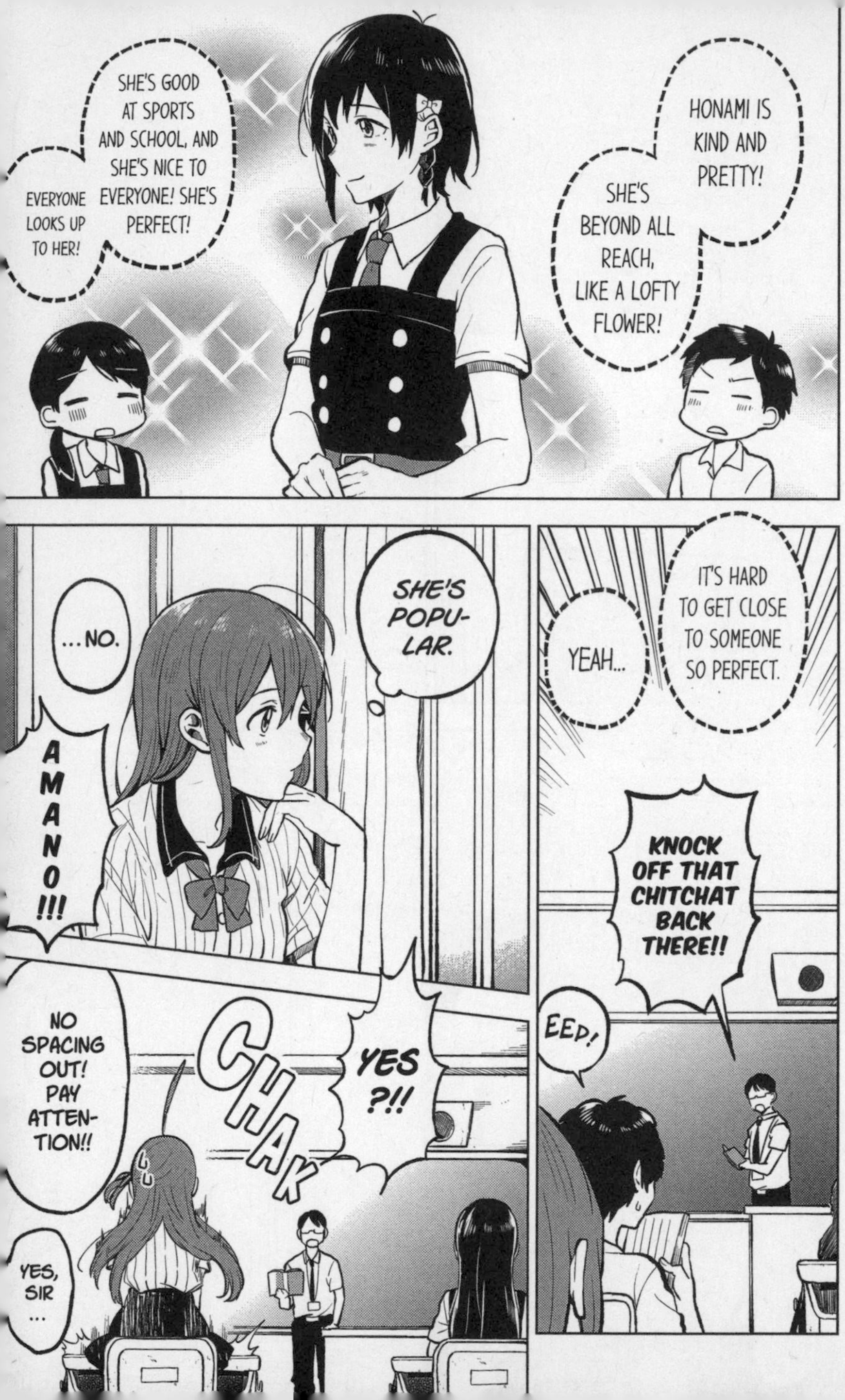
HONAMI IS KIND AND PRETTY!
SHE'S BEYOND ALL REACH, LIKE A LOFTY FLOWER!
SHE'S GOOD AT SPORTS AND SCHOOL, AND SHE'S NICE TO EVERYONE! SHE'S PERFECT!
EVERYONE LOOKS UP TO HER!
IT'S HARD TO GET CLOSE TO SOMEONE SO PERFECT.
YEAH...
KNOCK OFF THAT CHITCHAT BACK THERE!!
EEP!
SHE'S POPU-LAR.
...NO.
AMANO!!!
YES?!!
CHAK
NO SPACING OUT! PAY ATTEN-TION!!
YES, SIR...

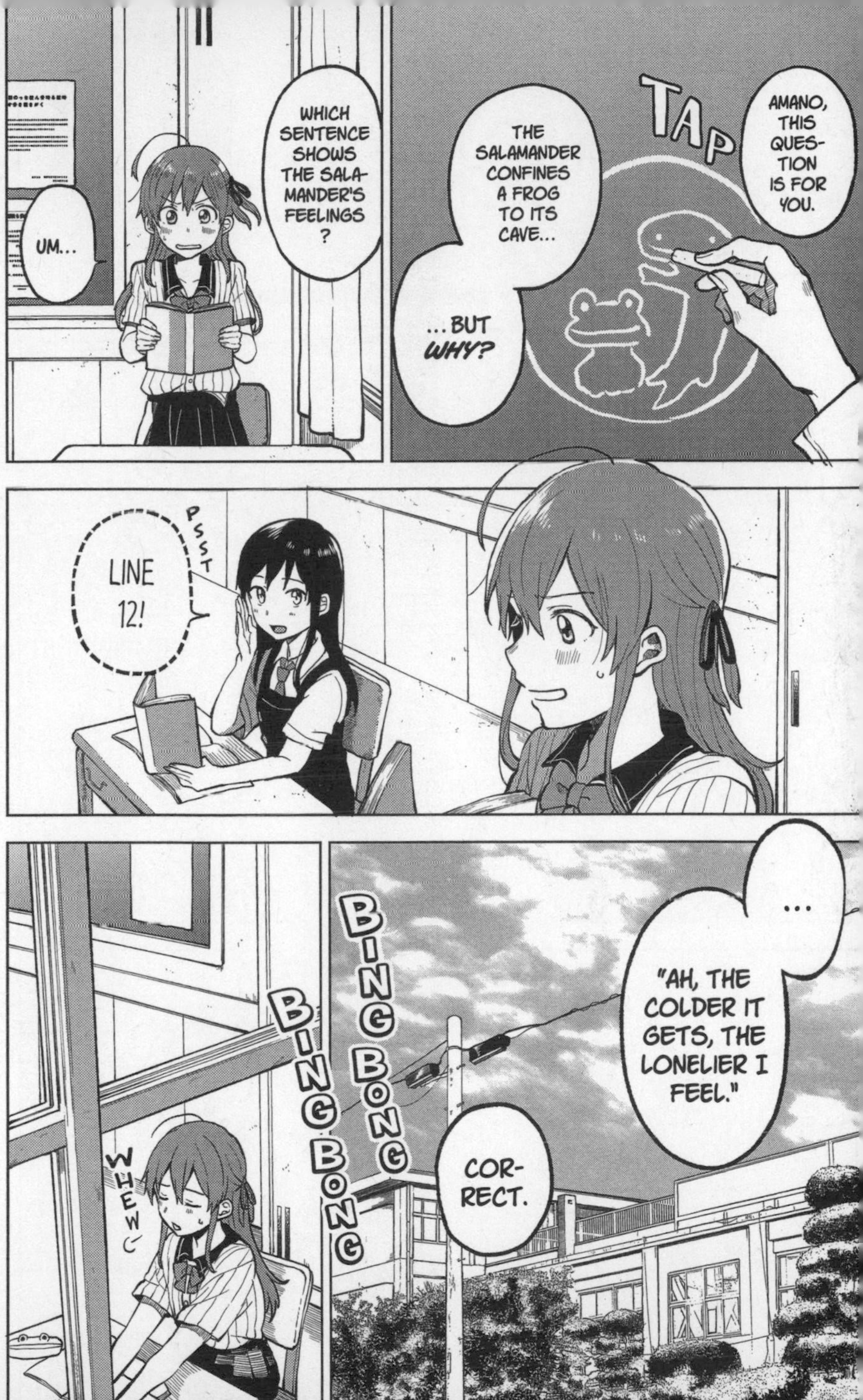
TAP
AMANO, THIS QUES-TION IS FOR YOU.
THE SALAMANDER CONFINES A FROG TO ITS CAVE...
...BUT *WHY?*
WHICH SENTENCE SHOWS THE SALA-MANDER'S FEELINGS?
UM...
PSSST
LINE 12!
...
"AH, THE COLDER IT GETS, THE LONELIER I FEEL."
COR-RECT.
BING BONG
BING BONG
WHEW

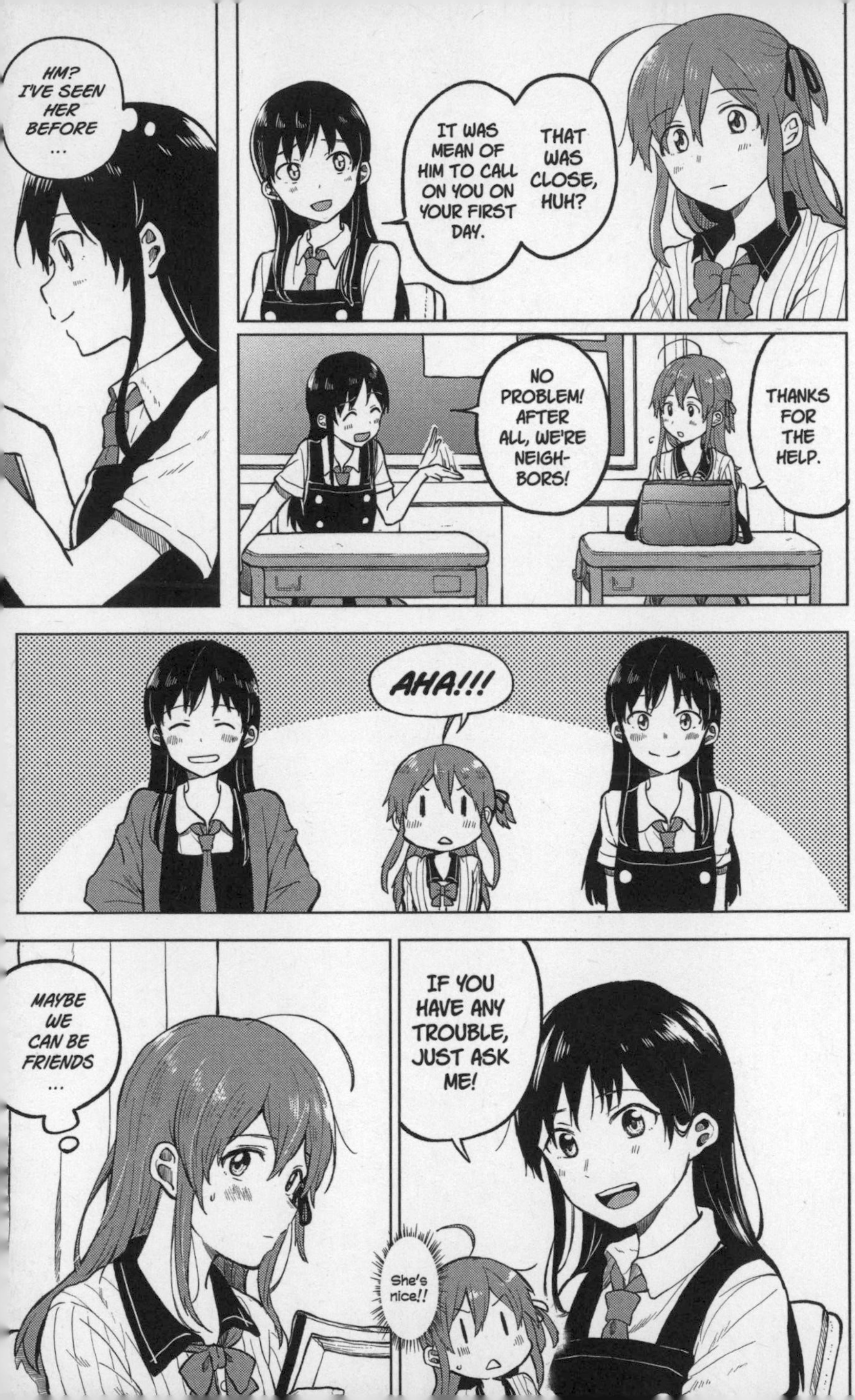
THAT WAS CLOSE, HUH?
IT WAS MEAN OF HIM TO CALL ON YOU ON YOUR FIRST DAY.
THANKS FOR THE HELP.
NO PROBLEM! AFTER ALL, WE'RE NEIGH-BORS!
HM? I'VE SEEN HER BEFORE ...
AHA!!!
IF YOU HAVE ANY TROUBLE, JUST ASK ME!
She's nice!!
MAYBE WE CAN BE FRIENDS ...

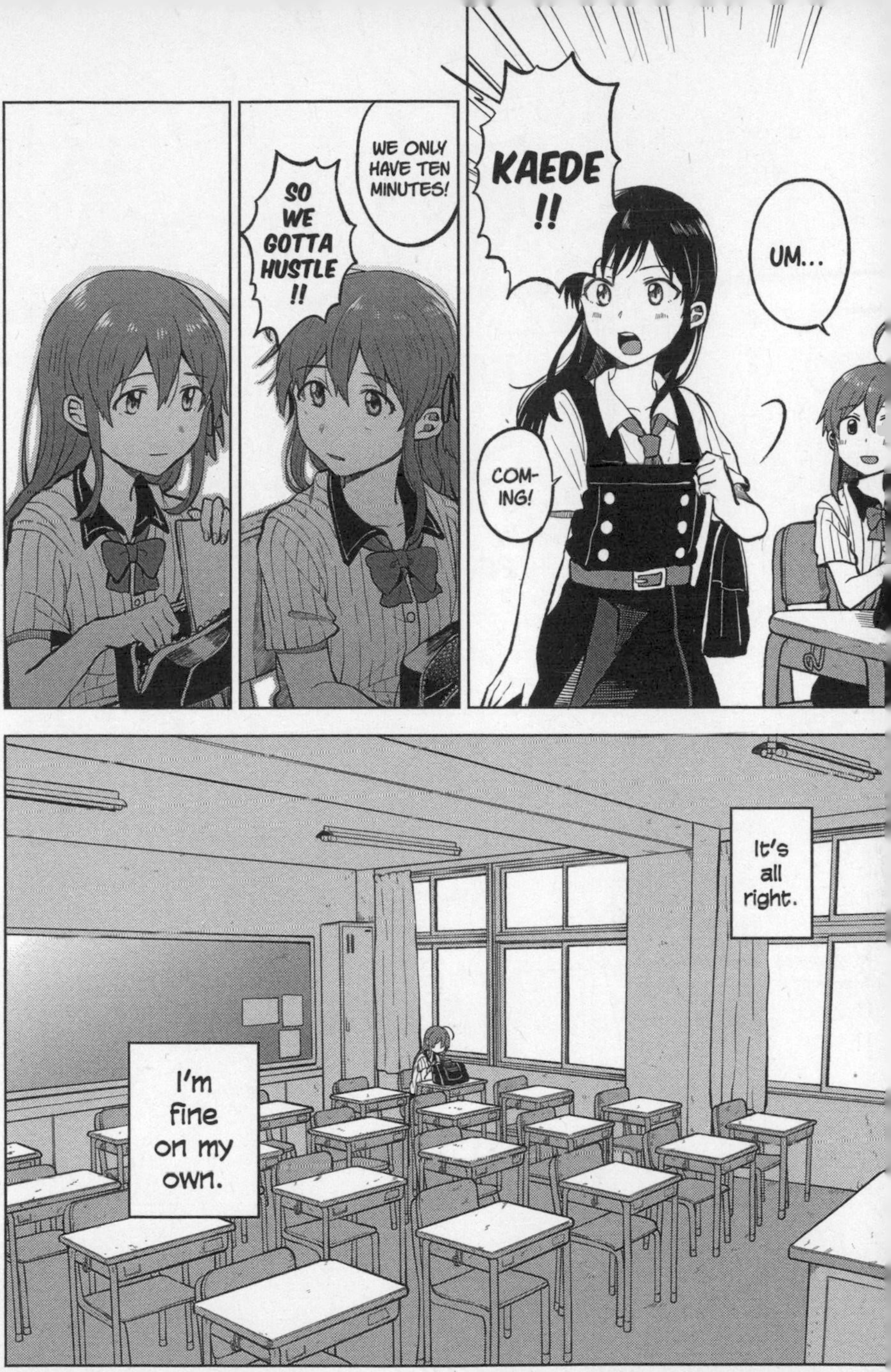
UM...
KAEDE !!
COM-ING!
WE ONLY HAVE TEN MINUTES!
SO WE GOTTA HUSTLE !!
It's all right.
I'm fine on my own.

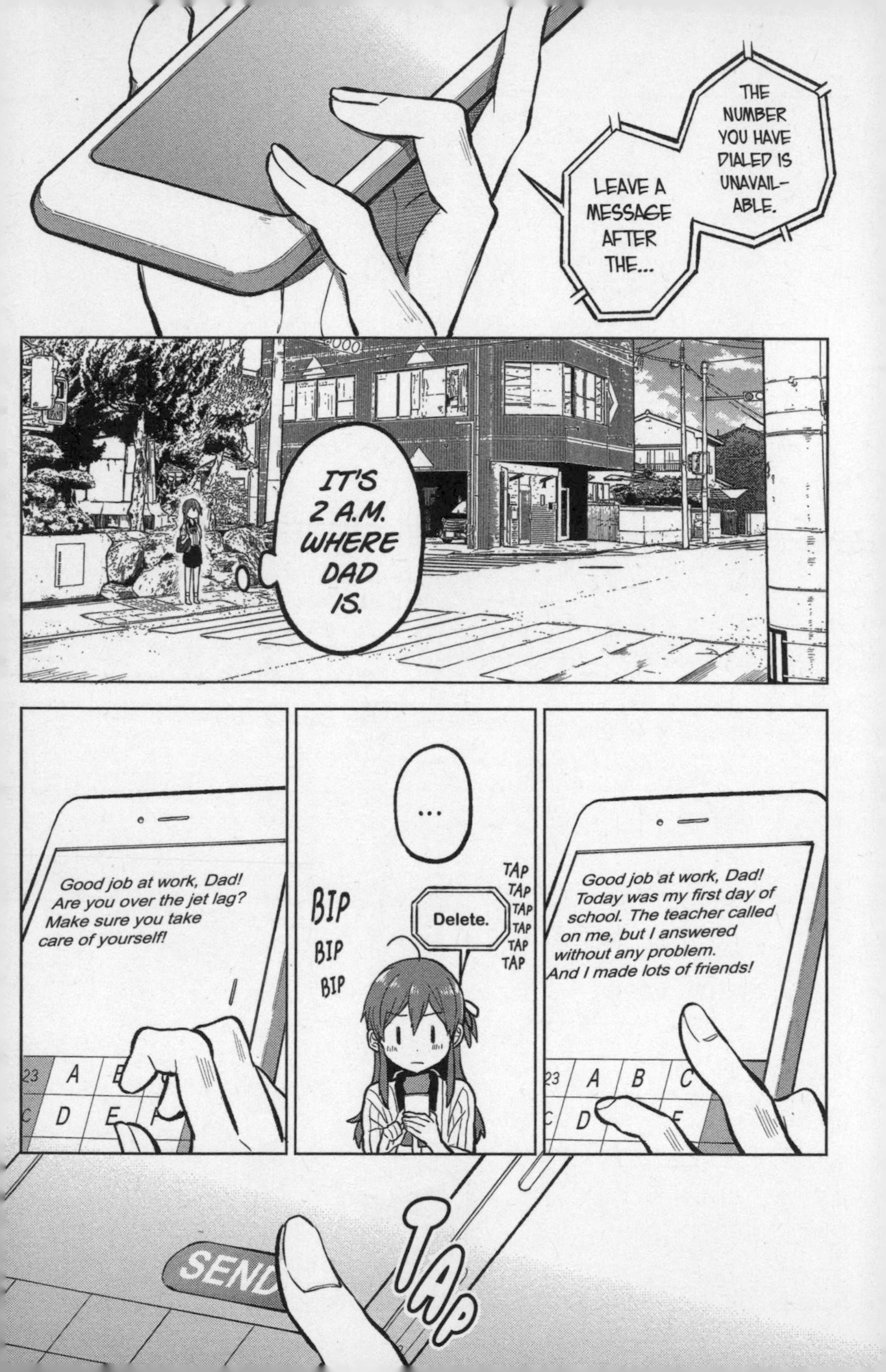
THE NUMBER YOU HAVE DIALED IS UNAVAIL-ABLE.
LEAVE A MESSAGE AFTER THE...
IT'S 2 A.M. WHERE DAD IS.
Good job at work, Dad! Today was my first day of school. The teacher called on me, but I answered without any problem. And I made lots of friends!
...
TAP TAP TAP TAP TAP TAP
Delete.
BIP BIP BIP
Good job at work, Dad! Are you over the jet lag? Make sure you take care of yourself!
SEND
TAP

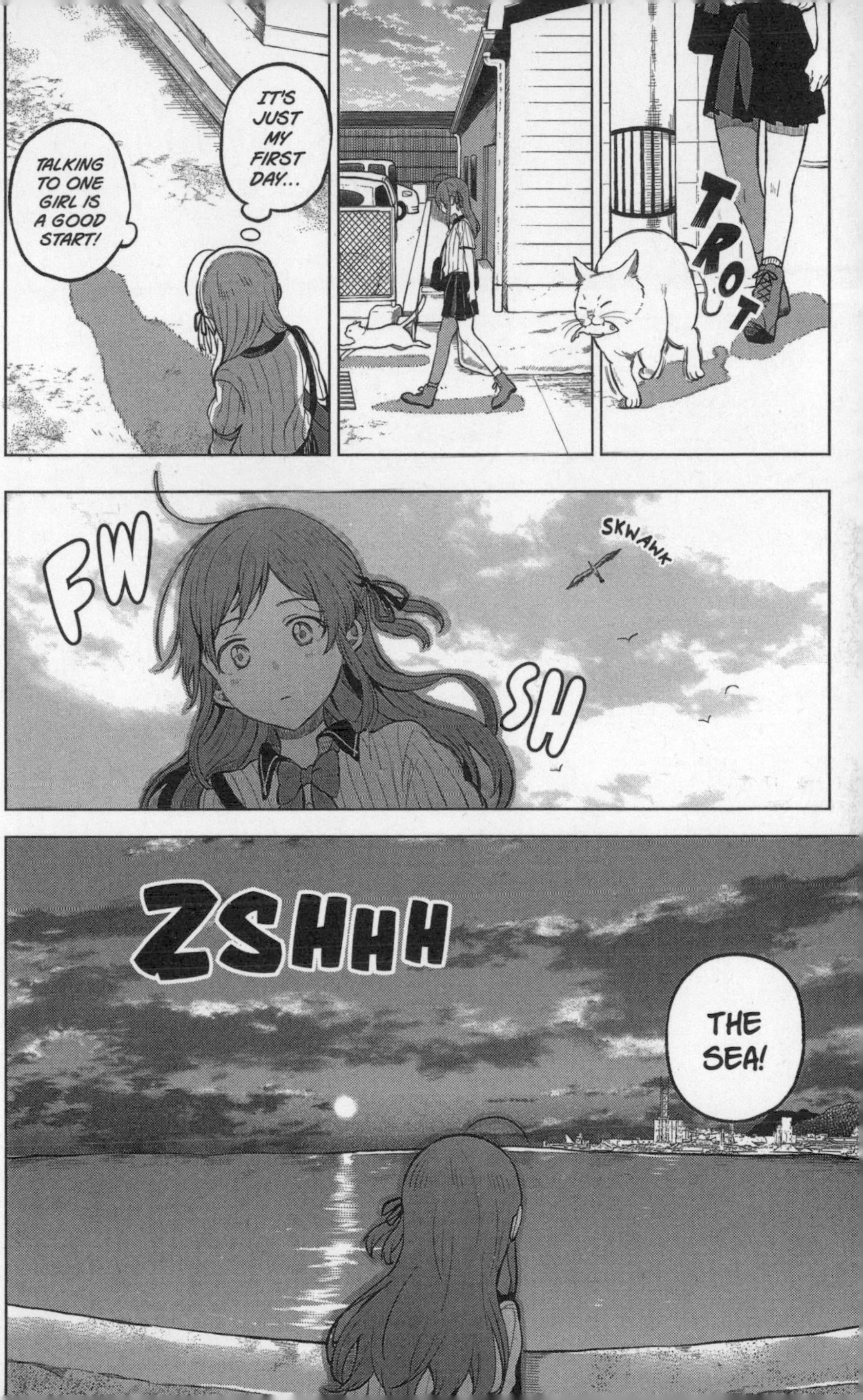
TROT
IT'S JUST MY FIRST DAY...
TALKING TO ONE GIRL IS A GOOD START!
SKWAWK
FW
SH
ZSHHH
THE SEA!

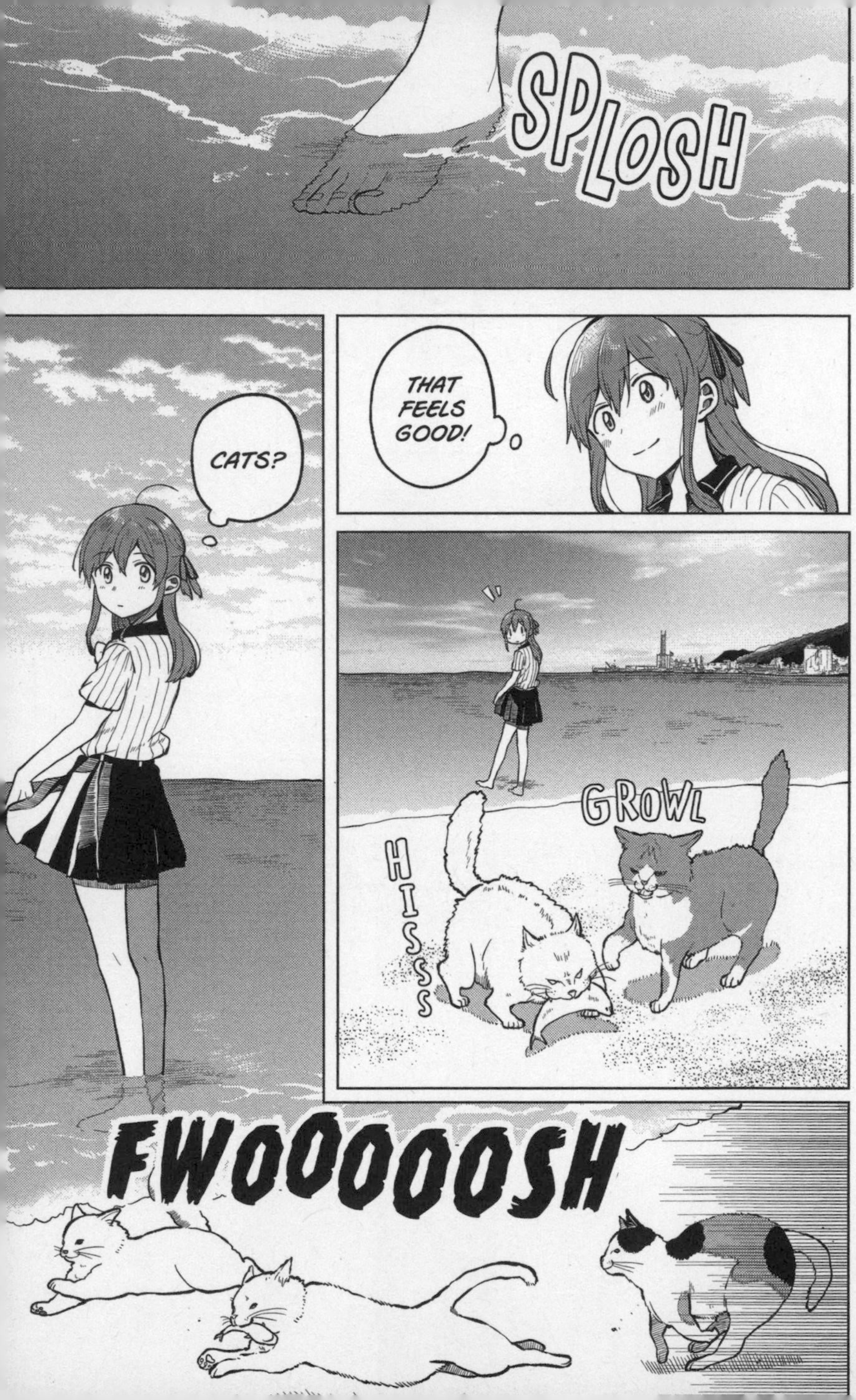
SPLOSH
THAT FEELS GOOD!
GROWL
HISS
CATS?
FWOOOOOSH

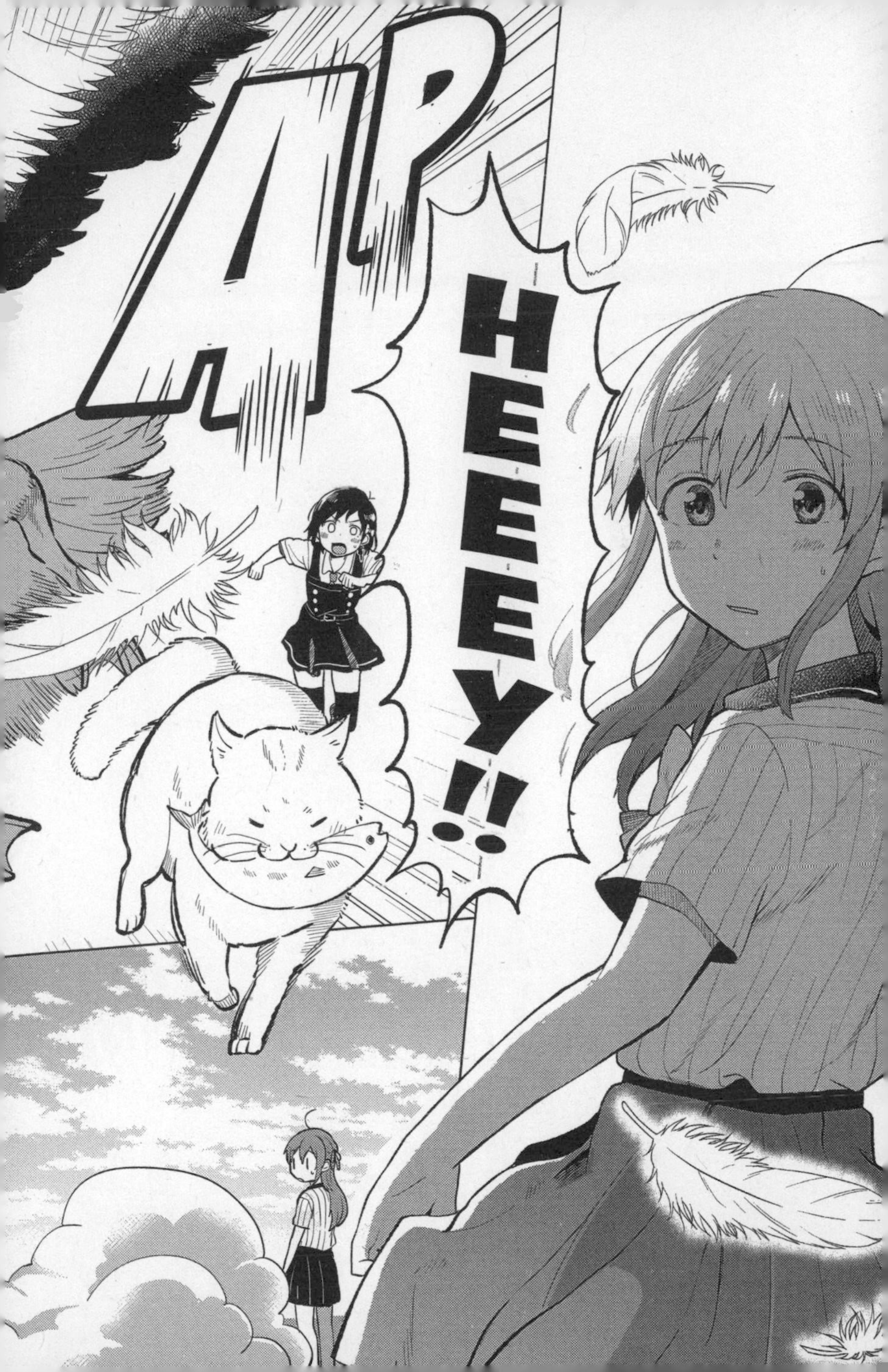
AP
HEEEY!!

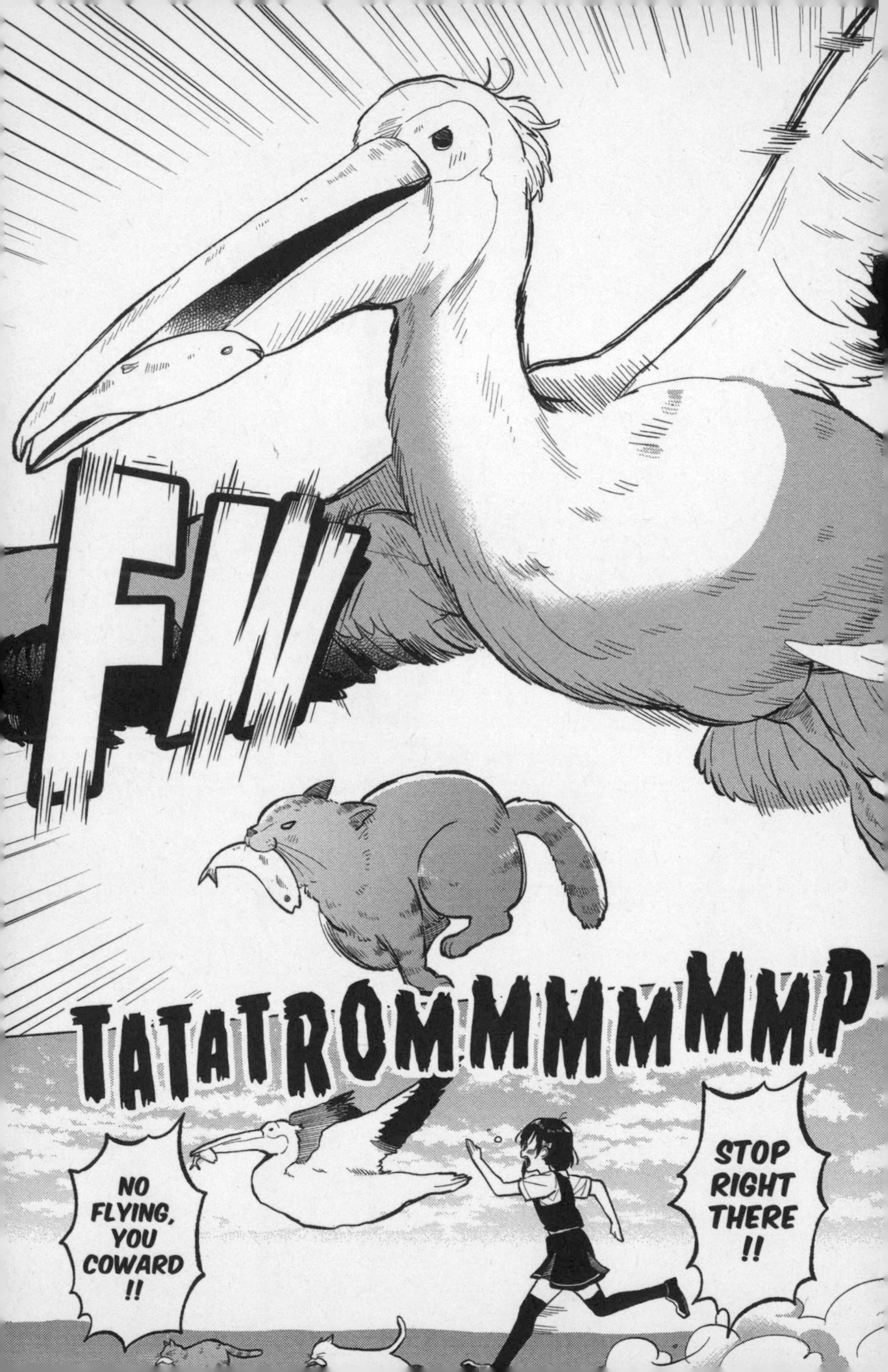
FW
TATATROMMMMMMMP
STOP RIGHT THERE!!
NO FLYING, YOU COWARD!!

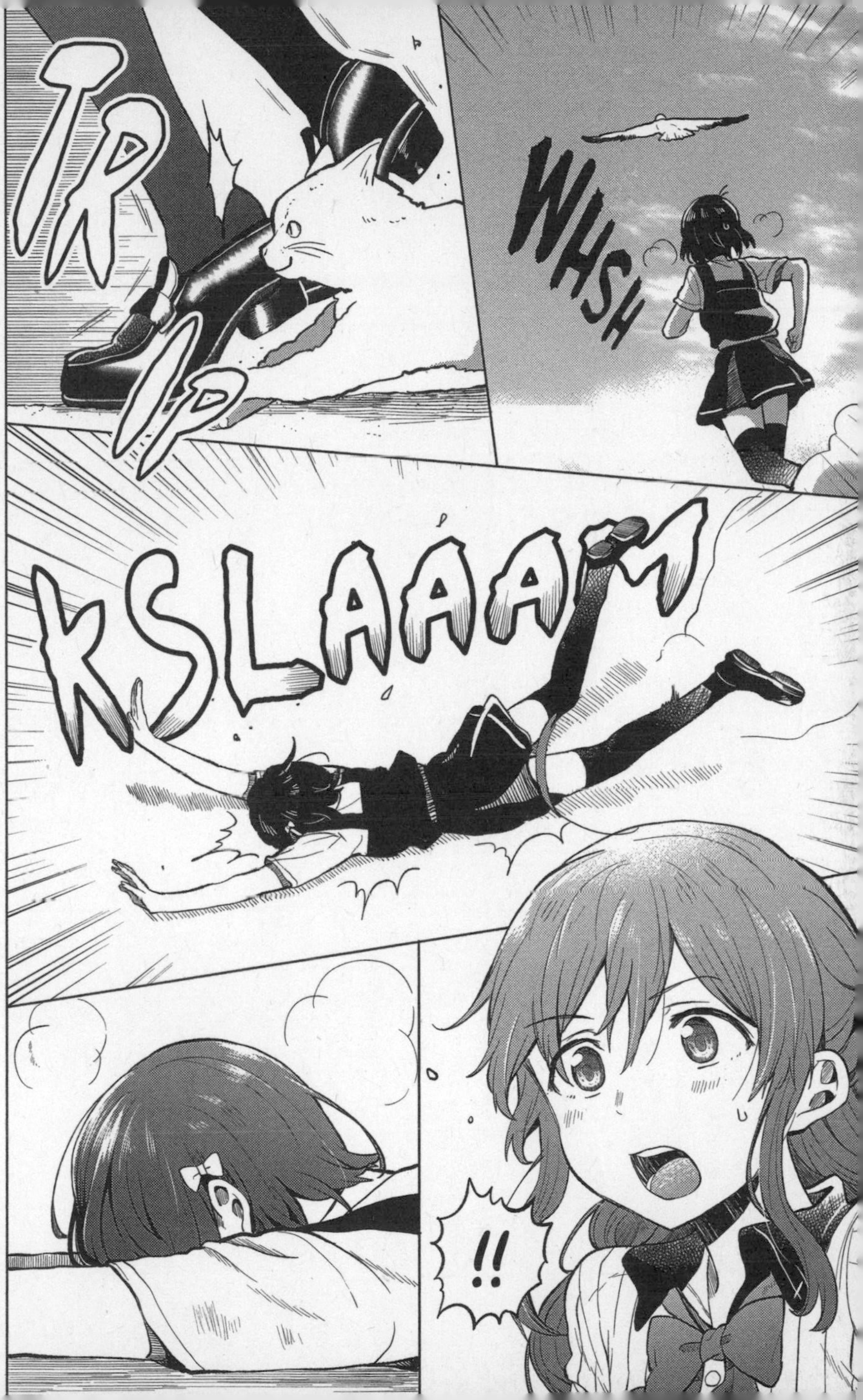
WHSH
TRIP
KSLAAAM
!!

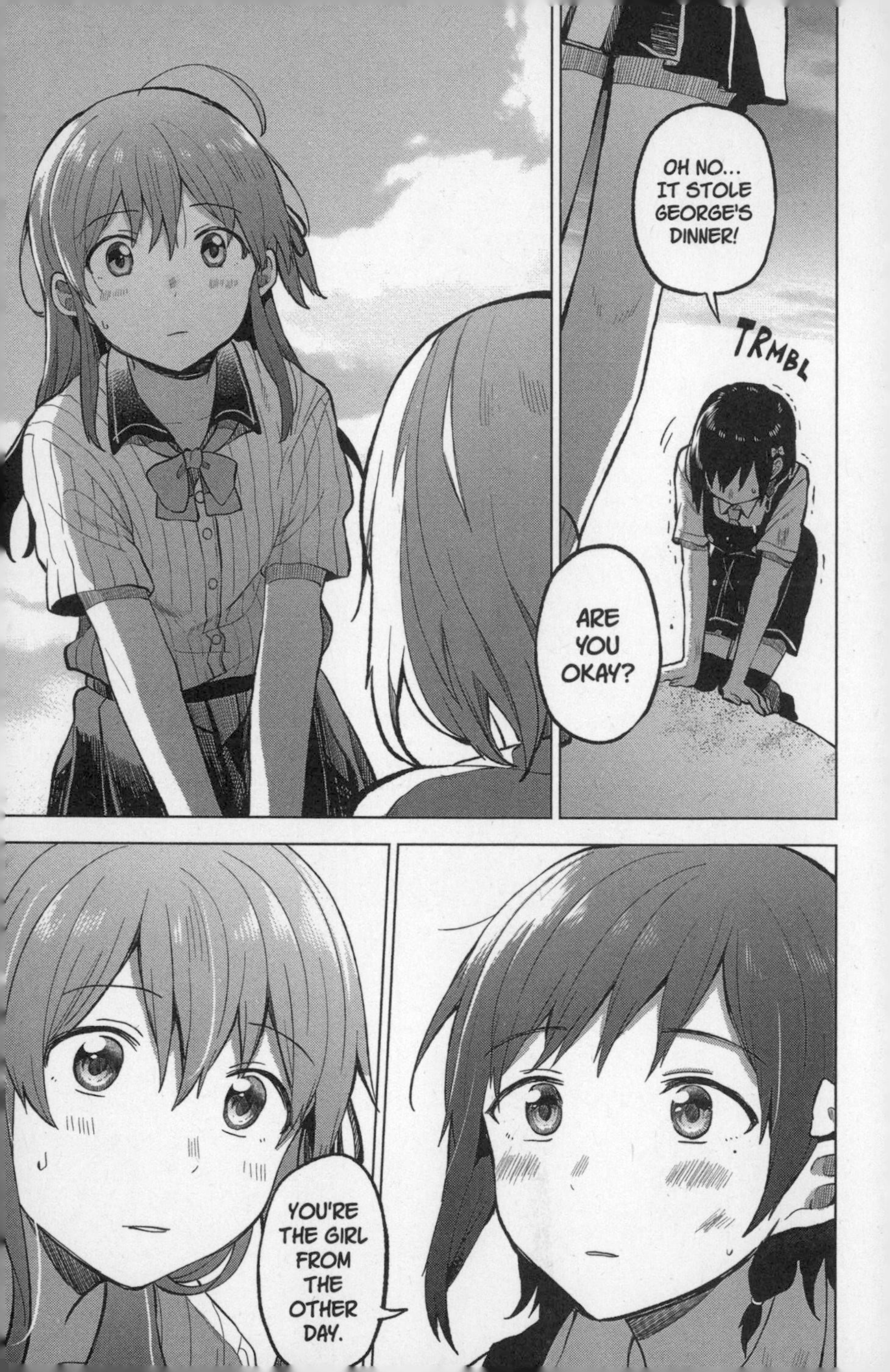
OH NO... IT STOLE GEORGE'S DINNER!
TRMBL
ARE YOU OKAY?
YOU'RE THE GIRL FROM THE OTHER DAY.

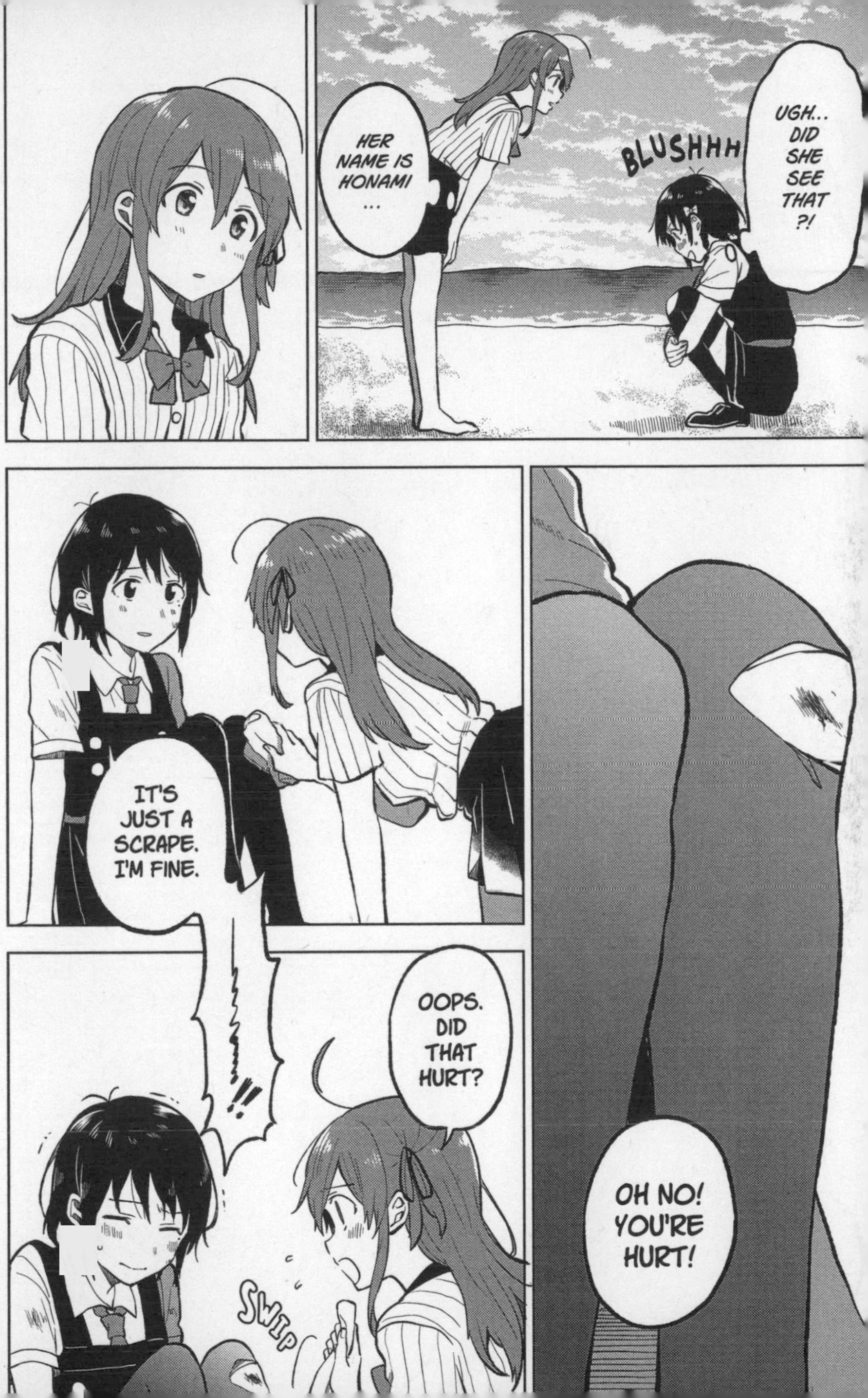
UGH... DID SHE SEE THAT?!
BLUSHHH
HER NAME IS HONAMI...
OH NO! YOU'RE HURT!
IT'S JUST A SCRAPE. I'M FINE.
OOPS. DID THAT HURT?
!!
SWIP

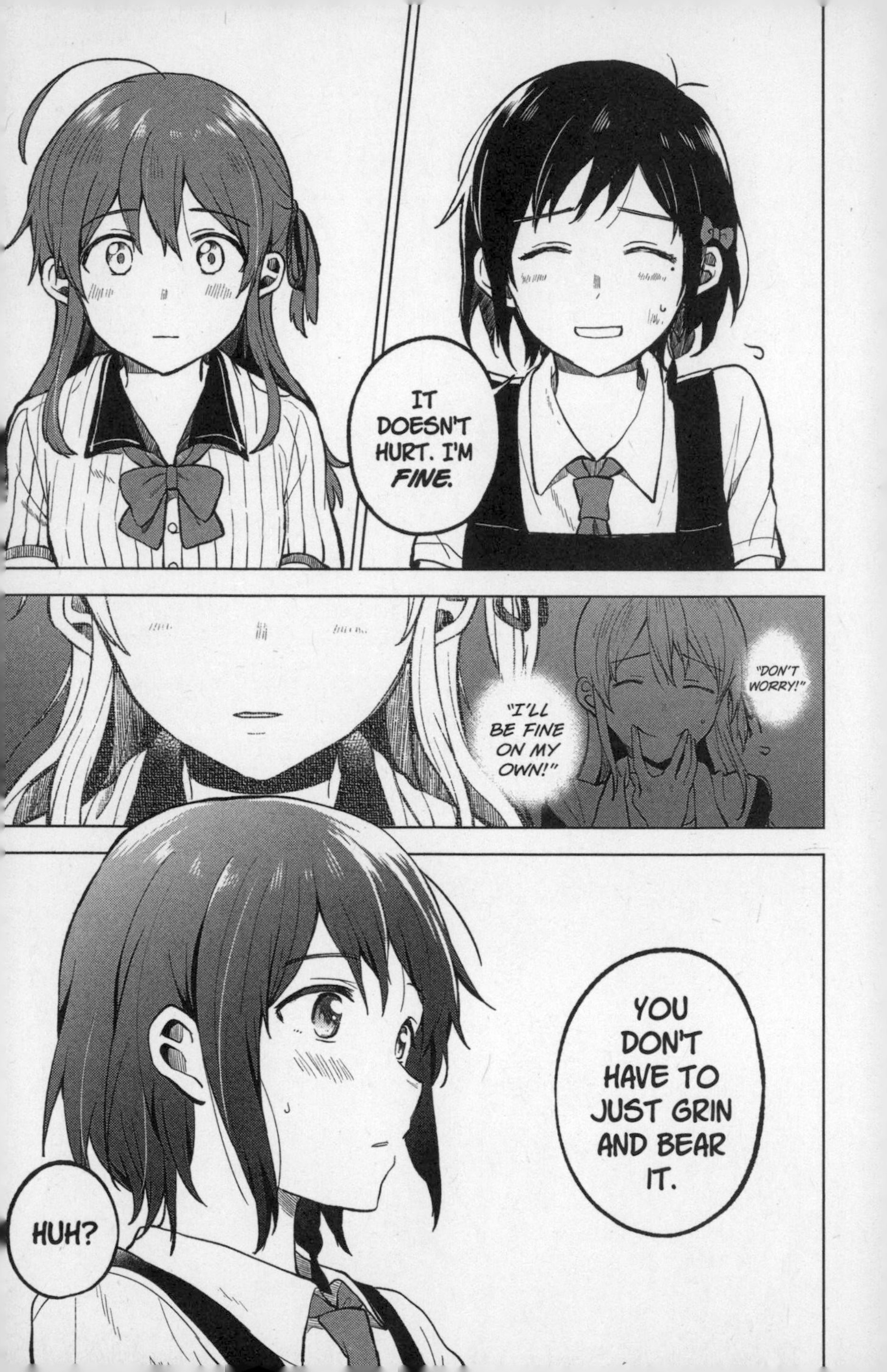
IT DOESN'T HURT. I'M *FINE.*
"DON'T WORRY!"
"I'LL BE FINE ON MY OWN!"
YOU DON'T HAVE TO JUST GRIN AND BEAR IT.
HUH?

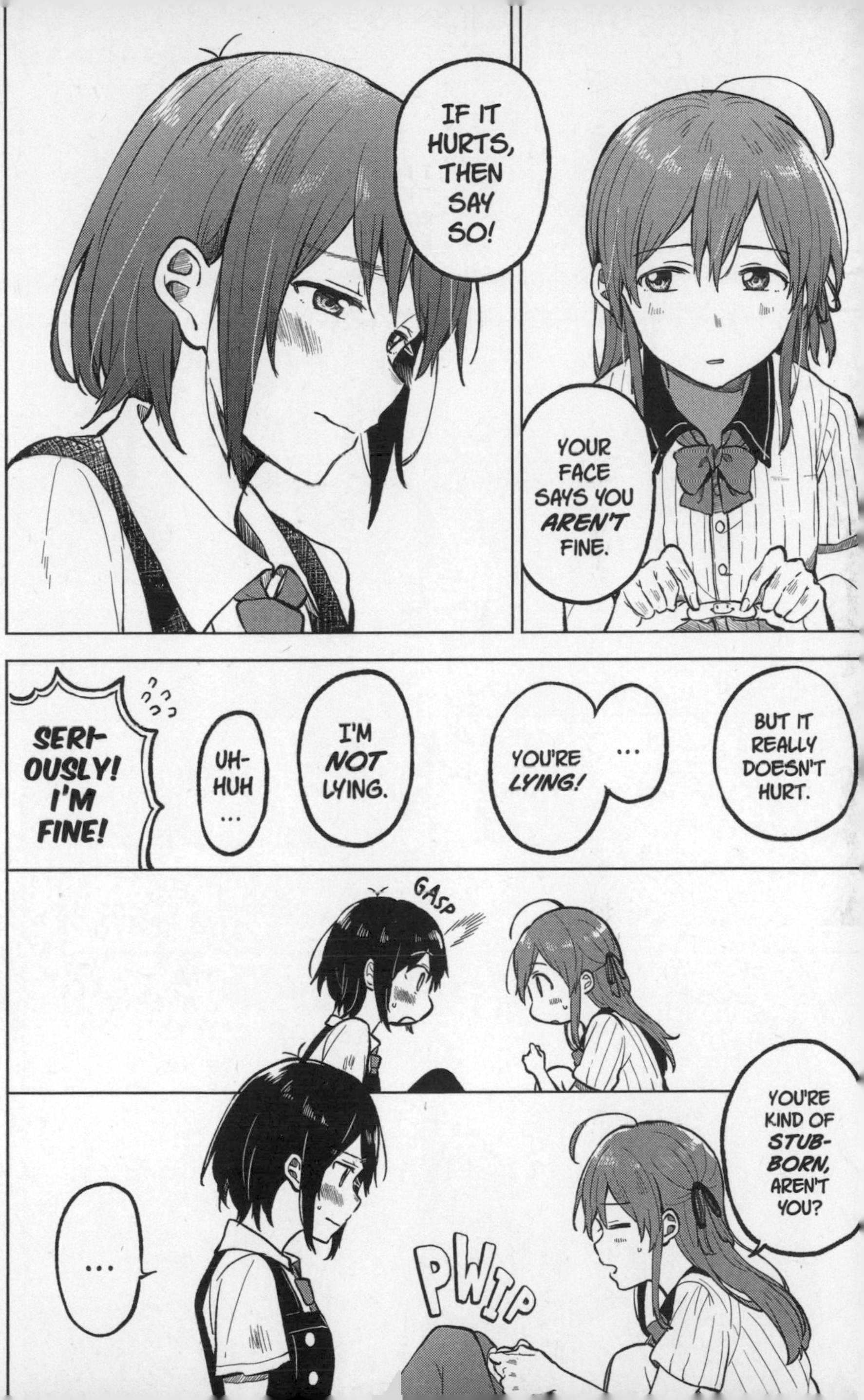
YOUR FACE SAYS YOU AREN'T FINE.
IF IT HURTS, THEN SAY SO!
BUT IT REALLY DOESN'T HURT.
...
YOU'RE LYING!
I'M NOT LYING.
UH-HUH ...
SERIOUSLY! I'M FINE!
GASP
YOU'RE KIND OF STUBBORN, AREN'T YOU?
PWIP
...

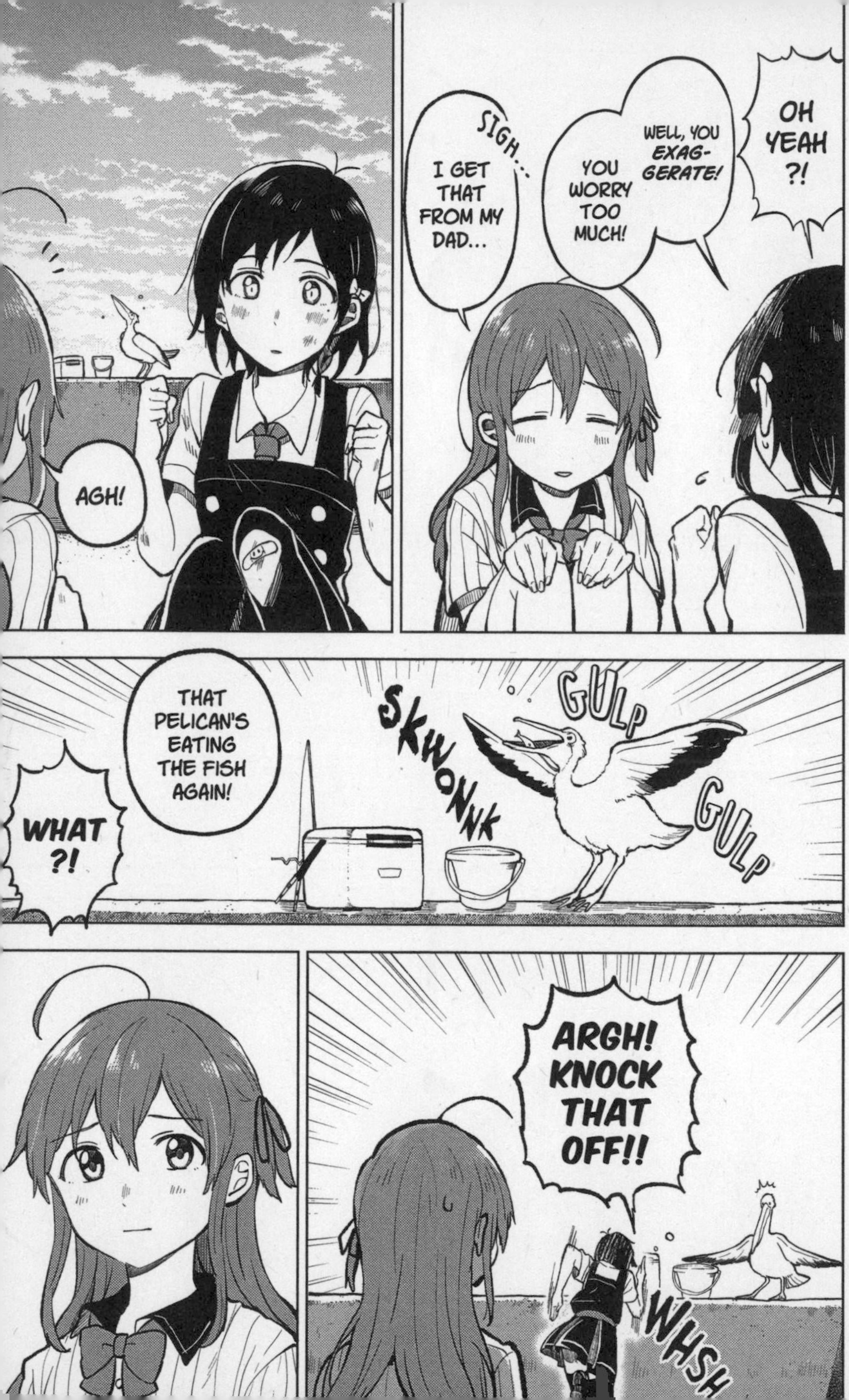
OH YEAH ?!
WELL, YOU EXAG-GERATE!
YOU WORRY TOO MUCH!
SIGH...
I GET THAT FROM MY DAD...
AGH!
GULP
GULP
SKWONNK
THAT PELICAN'S EATING THE FISH AGAIN!
WHAT ?!
ARGH! KNOCK THAT OFF!!
WHSH

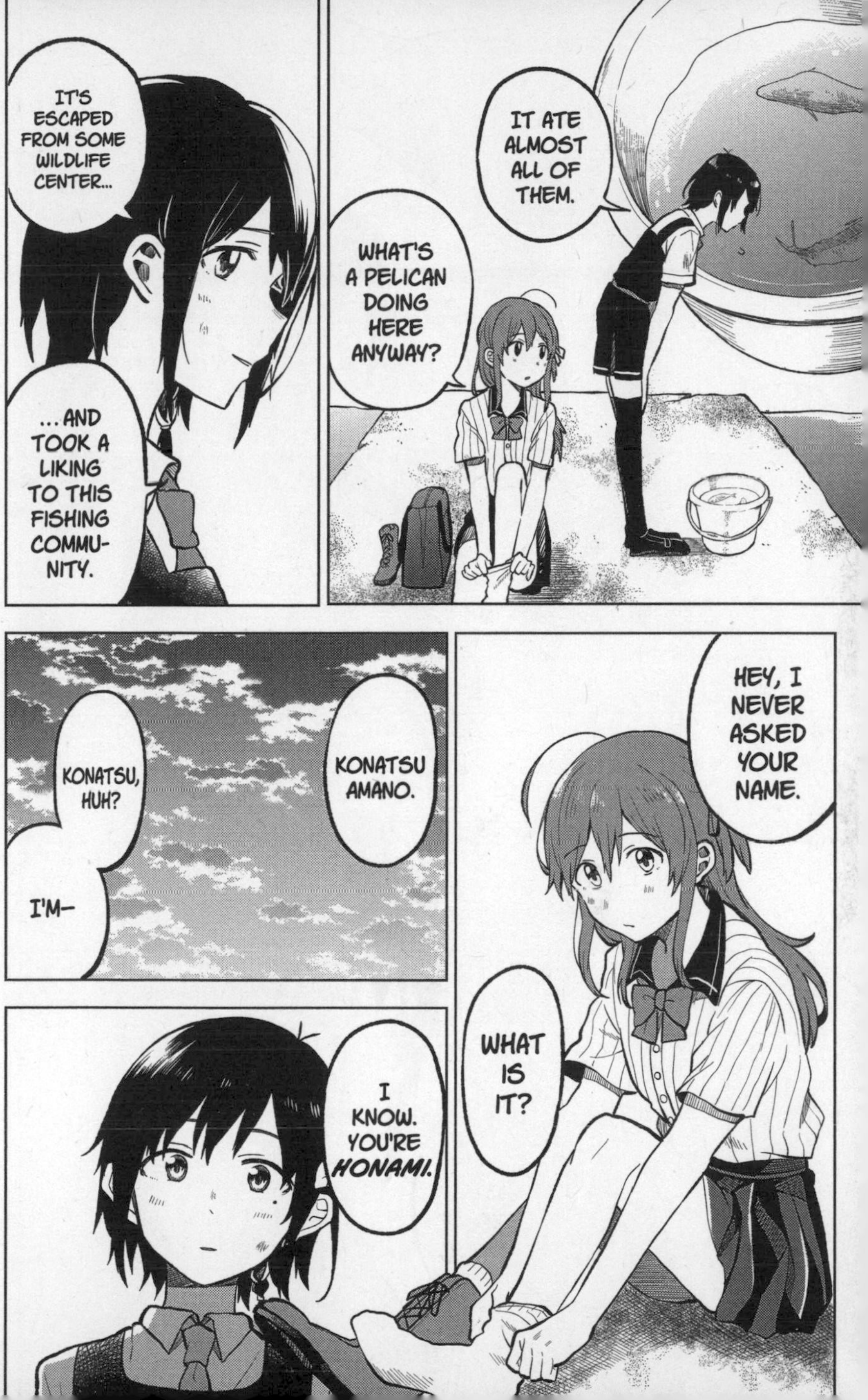
IT ATE ALMOST ALL OF THEM.
WHAT'S A PELICAN DOING HERE ANYWAY?
IT'S ESCAPED FROM SOME WILDLIFE CENTER...
...AND TOOK A LIKING TO THIS FISHING COMMUNITY.
HEY, I NEVER ASKED YOUR NAME.
WHAT IS IT?
KONATSU AMANO.
KONATSU, HUH?
I'M—
I KNOW. YOU'RE *HONAMI.*

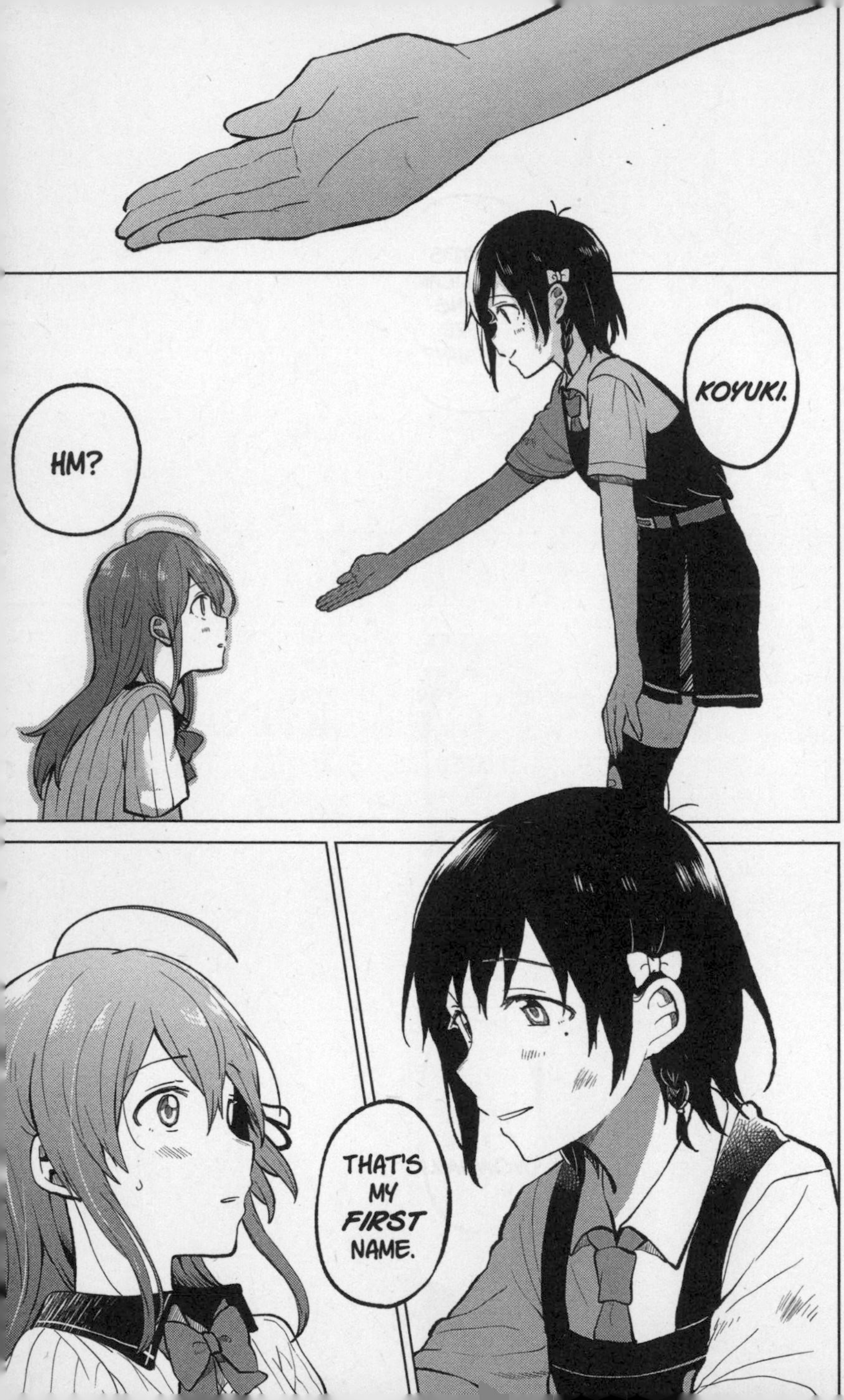
KOYUKI.
HM?
THAT'S MY FIRST NAME.

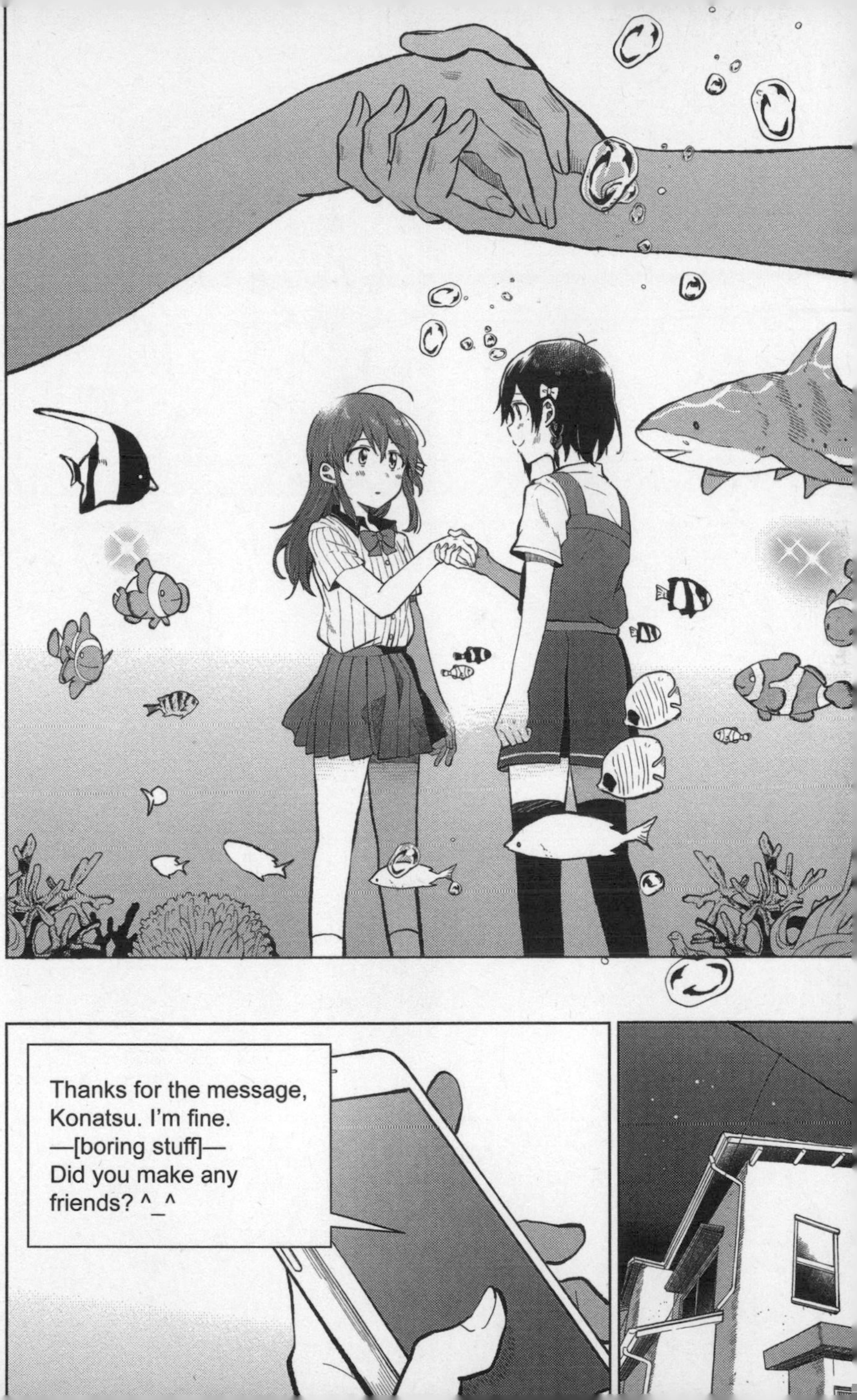
Thanks for the message, Konatsu. I'm fine. —[boring stuff]— Did you make any friends? ^_^

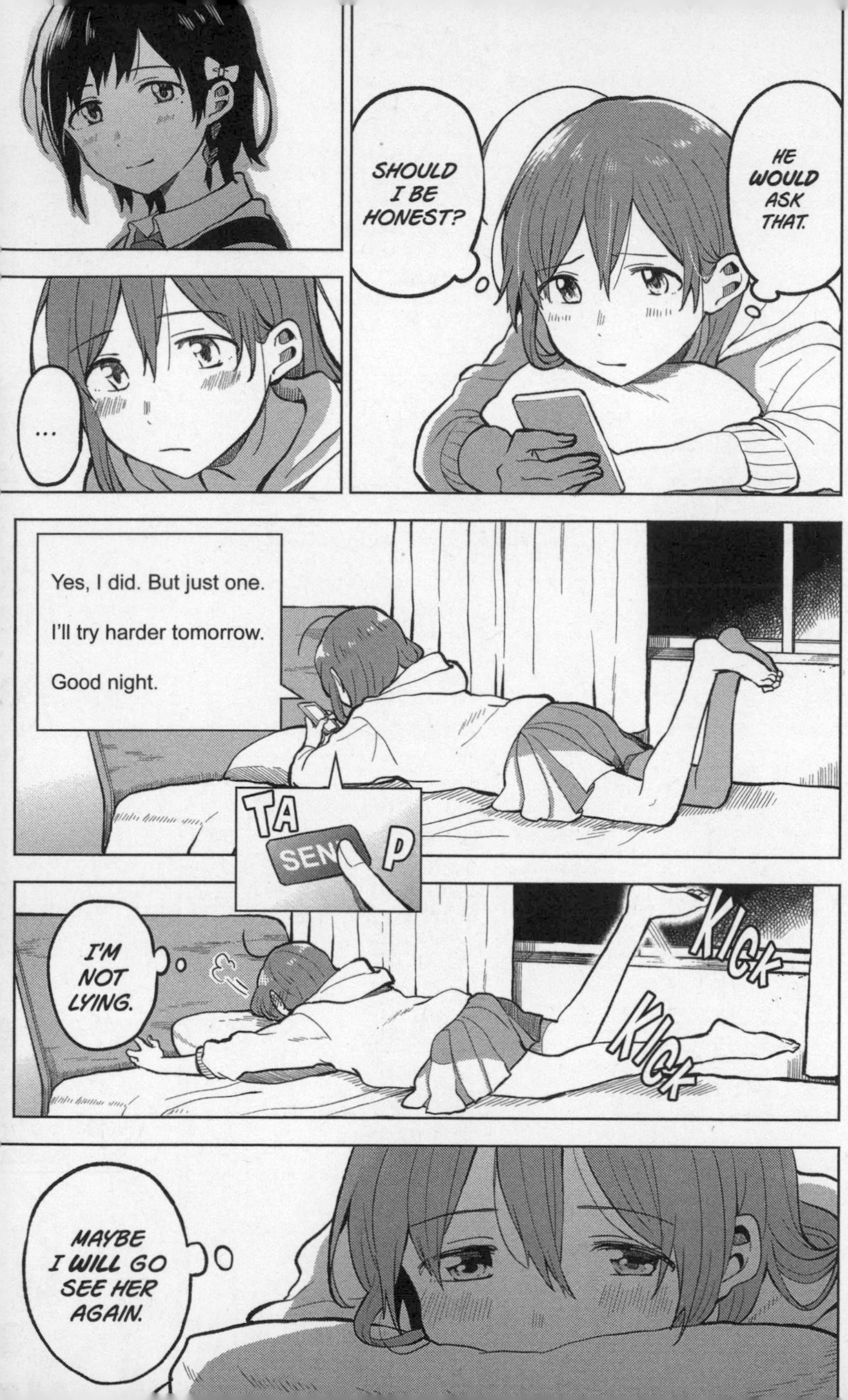
HE WOULD ASK THAT.
SHOULD I BE HONEST?
...
Yes, I did. But just one.
I'll try harder tomorrow.
Good night.
SEN
TAP
KICK
KICK
I'M NOT LYING.
MAYBE I WILL GO SEE HER AGAIN.

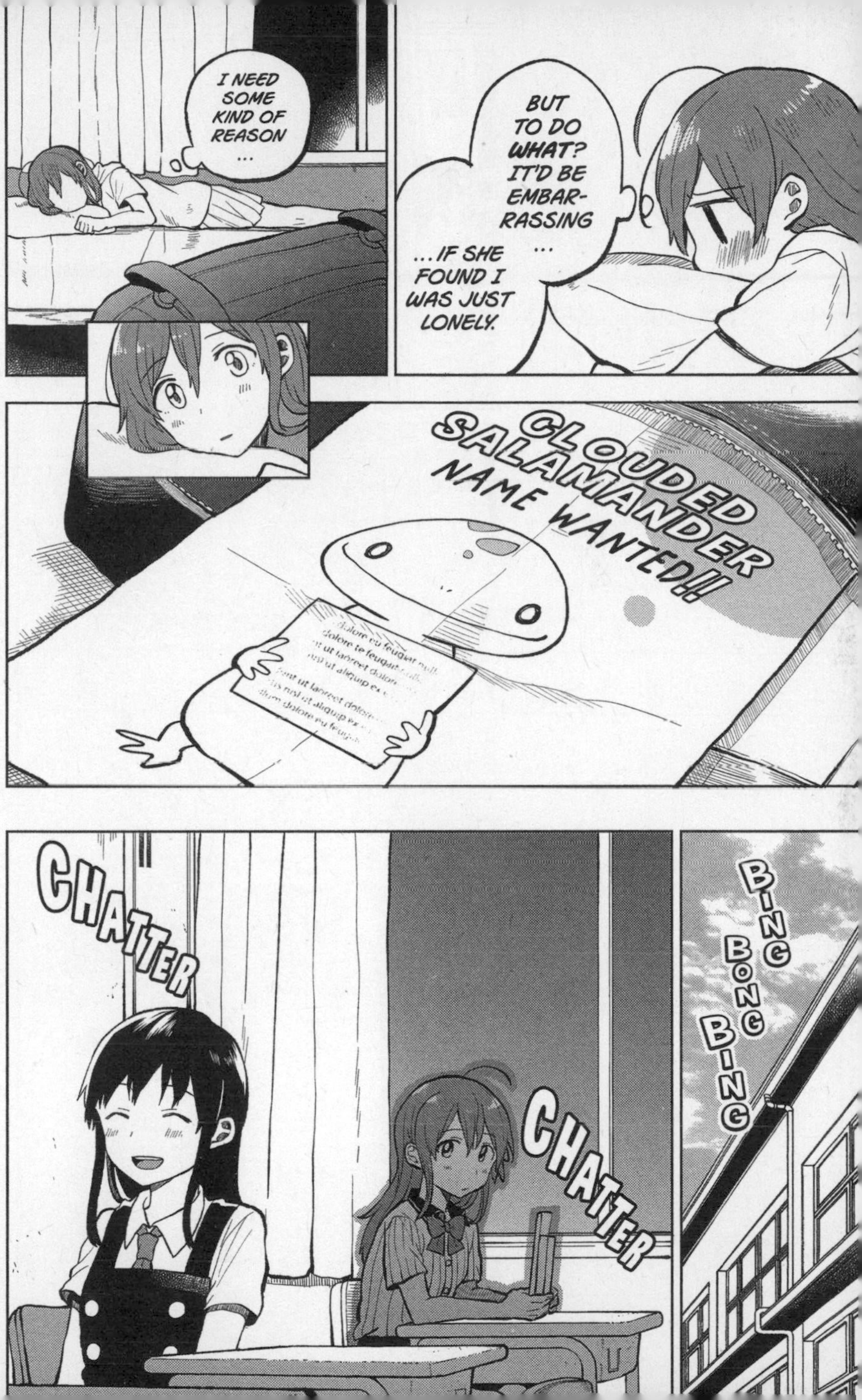
BUT TO DO WHAT? IT'D BE EMBARRASSING ...
...IF SHE FOUND I WAS JUST LONELY.
I NEED SOME KIND OF REASON ...
CLOUDED SALAMANDER
NAME WANTED!!
BING BONG BING BONG
CHATTER
CHATTER

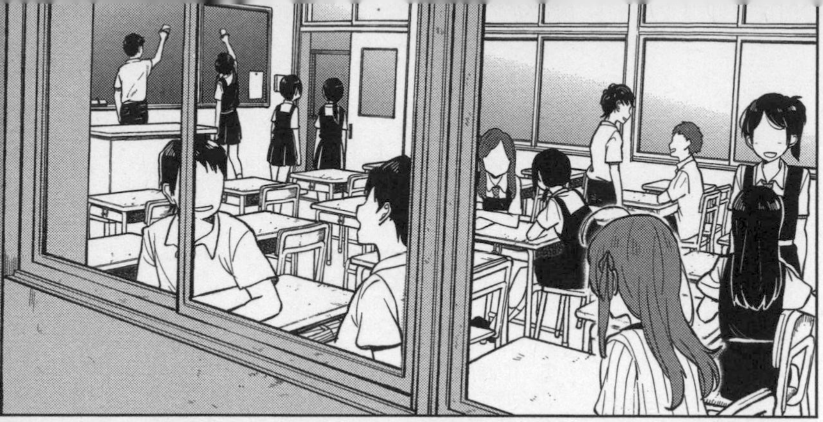

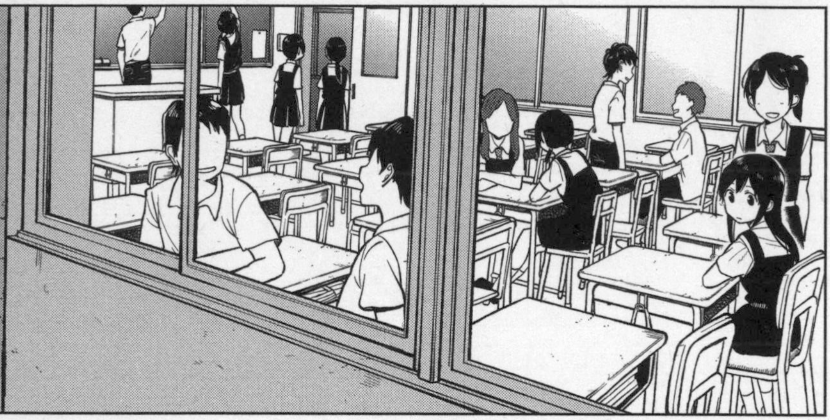

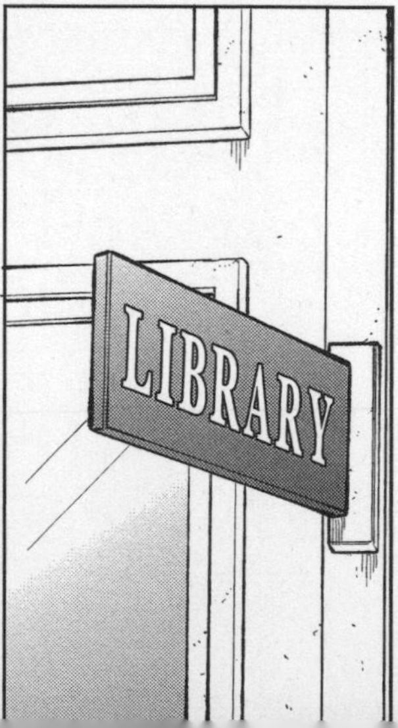
LIBRARY

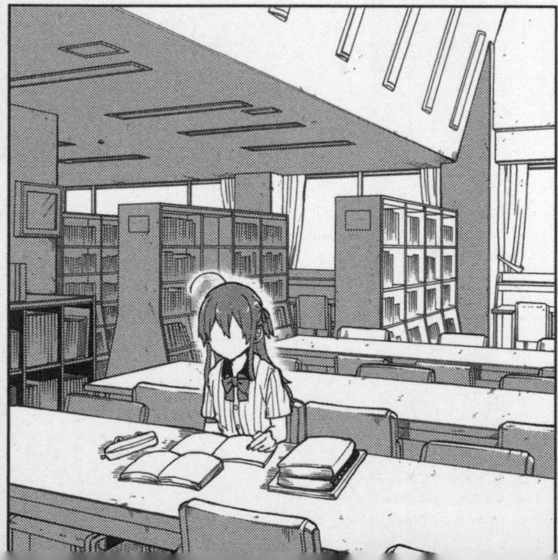

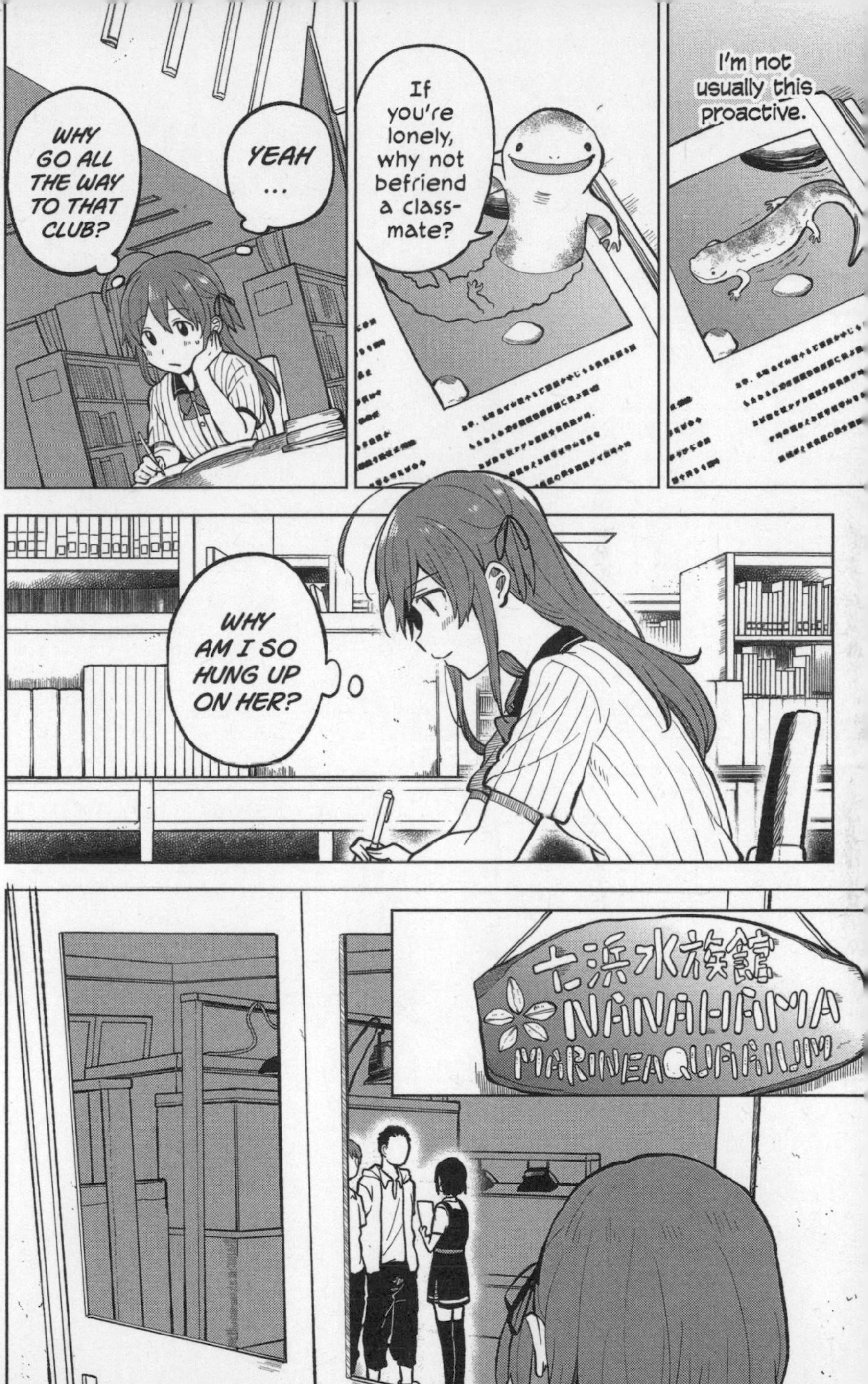
I'm not usually this proactive.
If you're lonely, why not befriend a classmate?
YEAH ...
WHY GO ALL THE WAY TO THAT CLUB?
WHY AM I SO HUNG UP ON HER?
七浜水族館
NANAHAMA
MARINEAQUARIUM

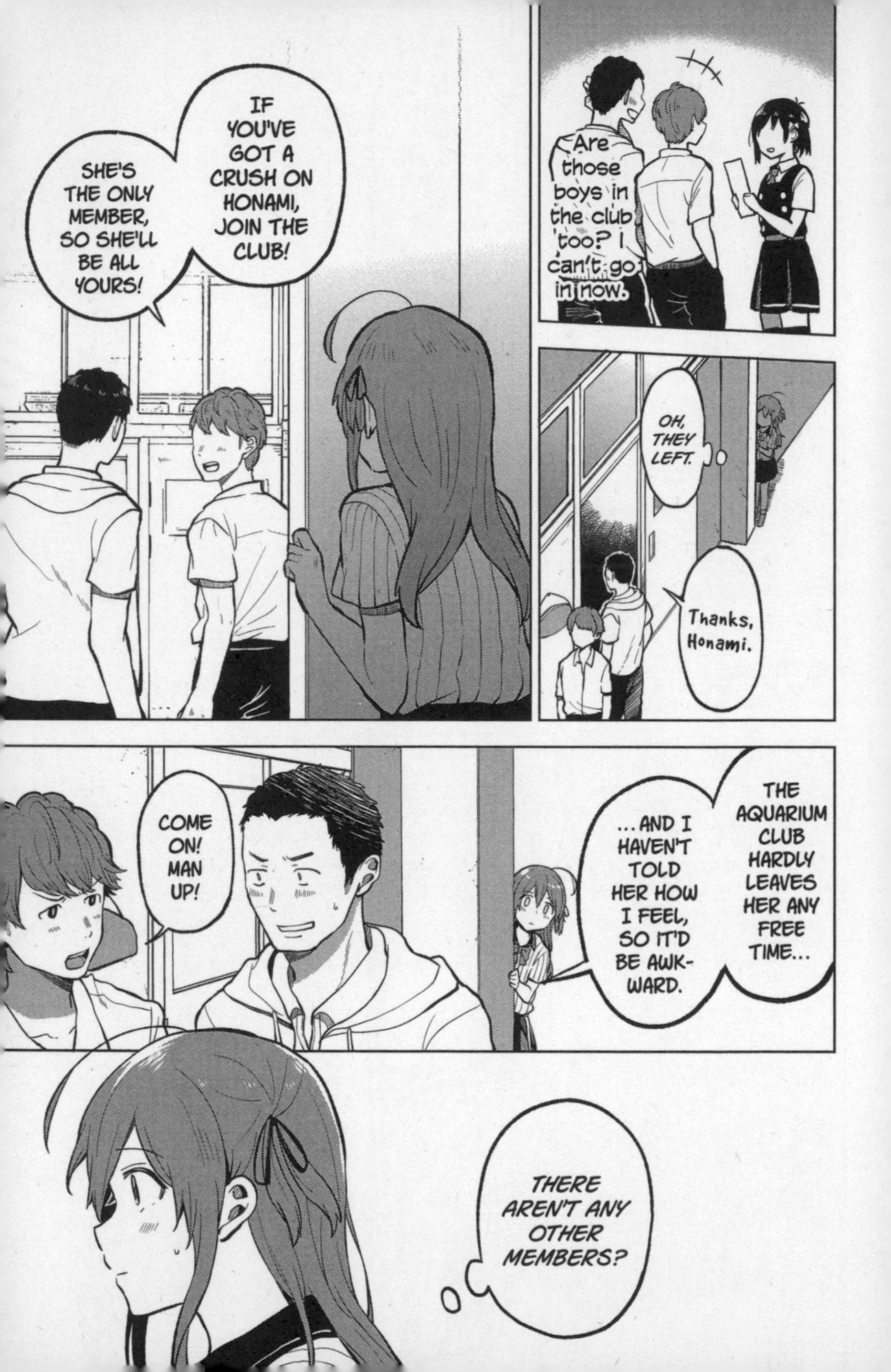
Are those boys in the club too? I can't go in now.
OH, THEY LEFT.
Thanks, Honami.
IF YOU'VE GOT A CRUSH ON HONAMI, JOIN THE CLUB!
SHE'S THE ONLY MEMBER, SO SHE'LL BE ALL YOURS!
THE AQUARIUM CLUB HARDLY LEAVES HER ANY FREE TIME...
...AND I HAVEN'T TOLD HER HOW I FEEL, SO IT'D BE AWK-WARD.
COME ON! MAN UP!
THERE AREN'T ANY OTHER MEMBERS?

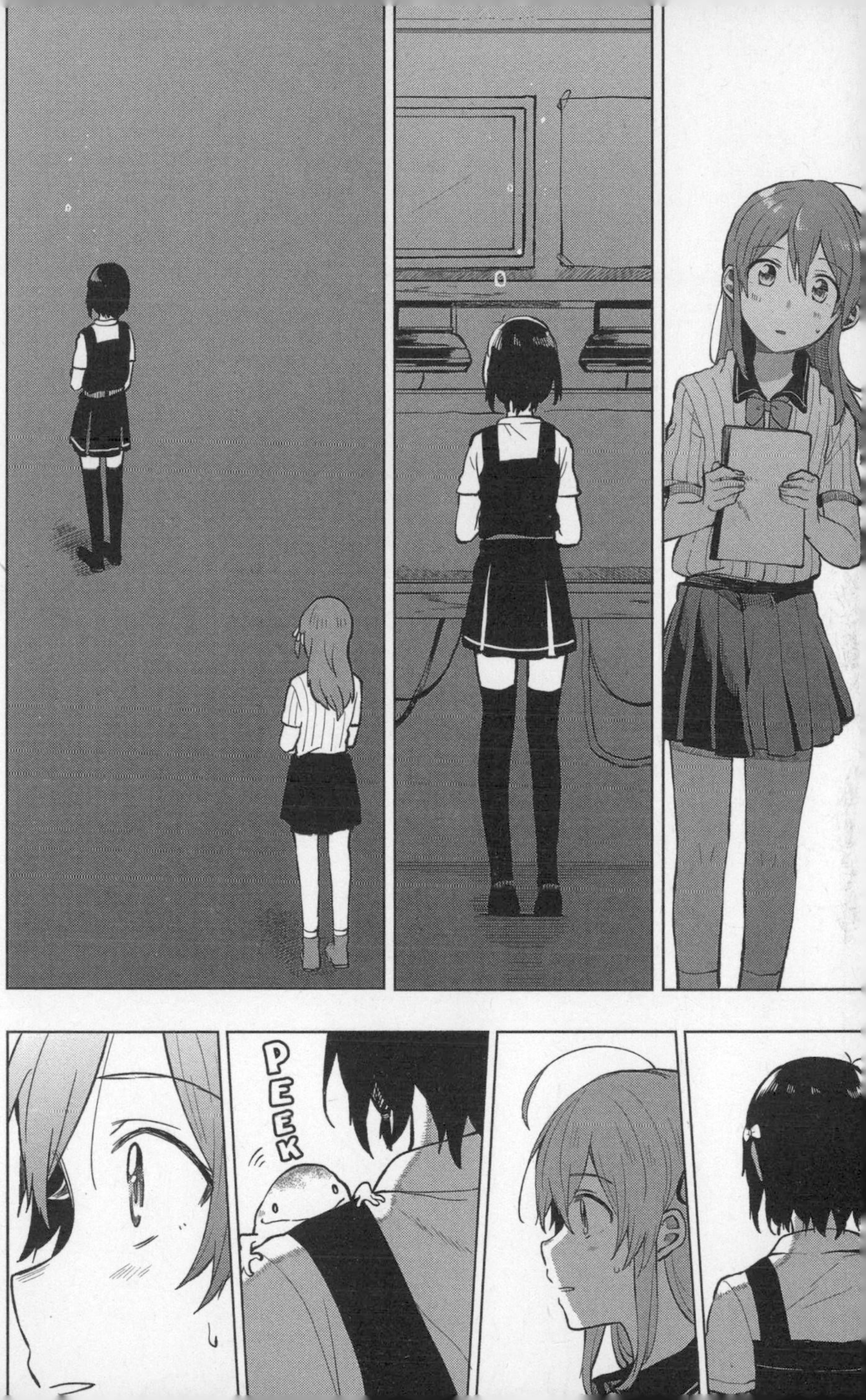
PEEK

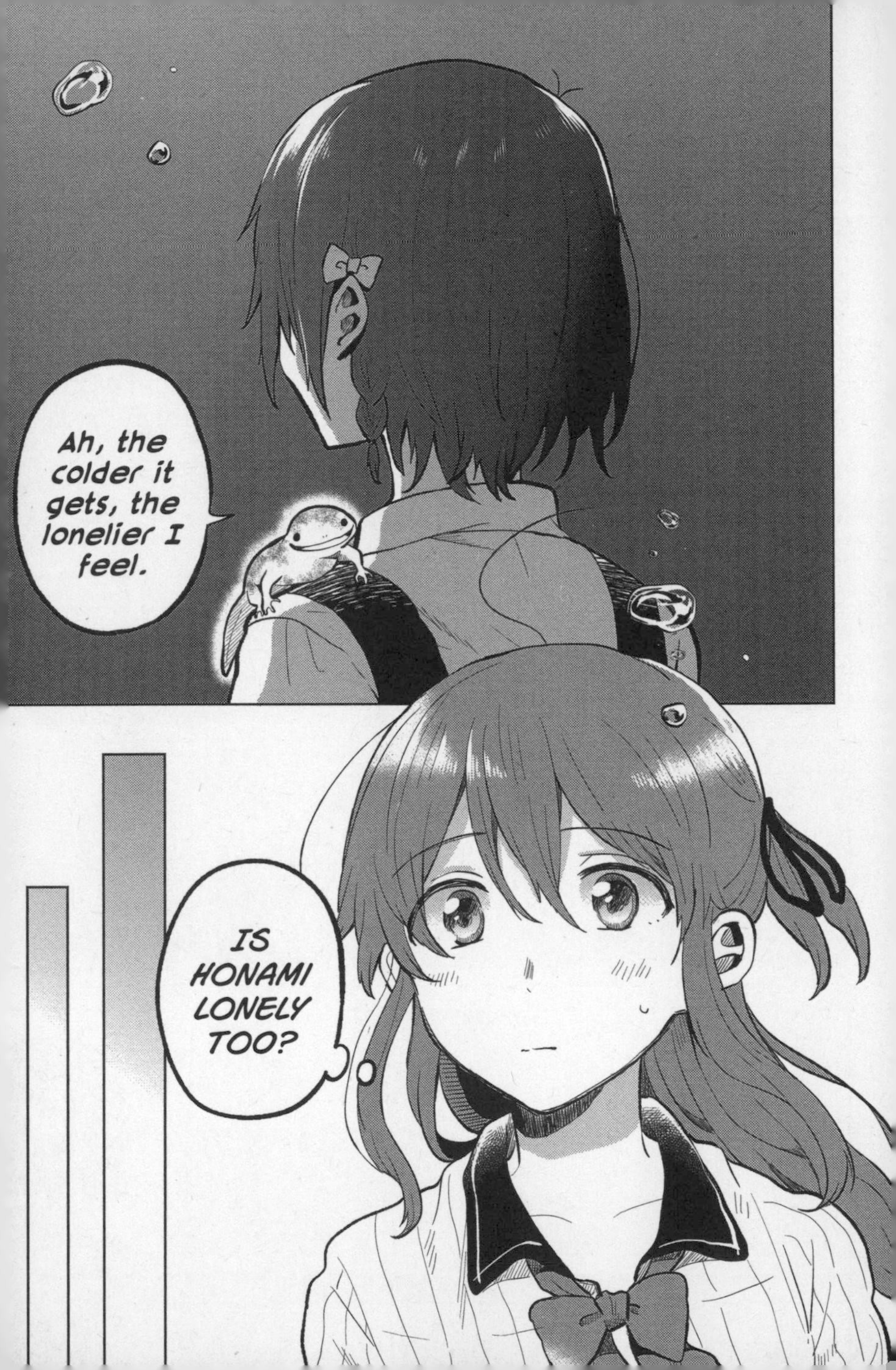
Ah, the colder it gets, the lonelier I feel.
IS HONAMI LONELY TOO?

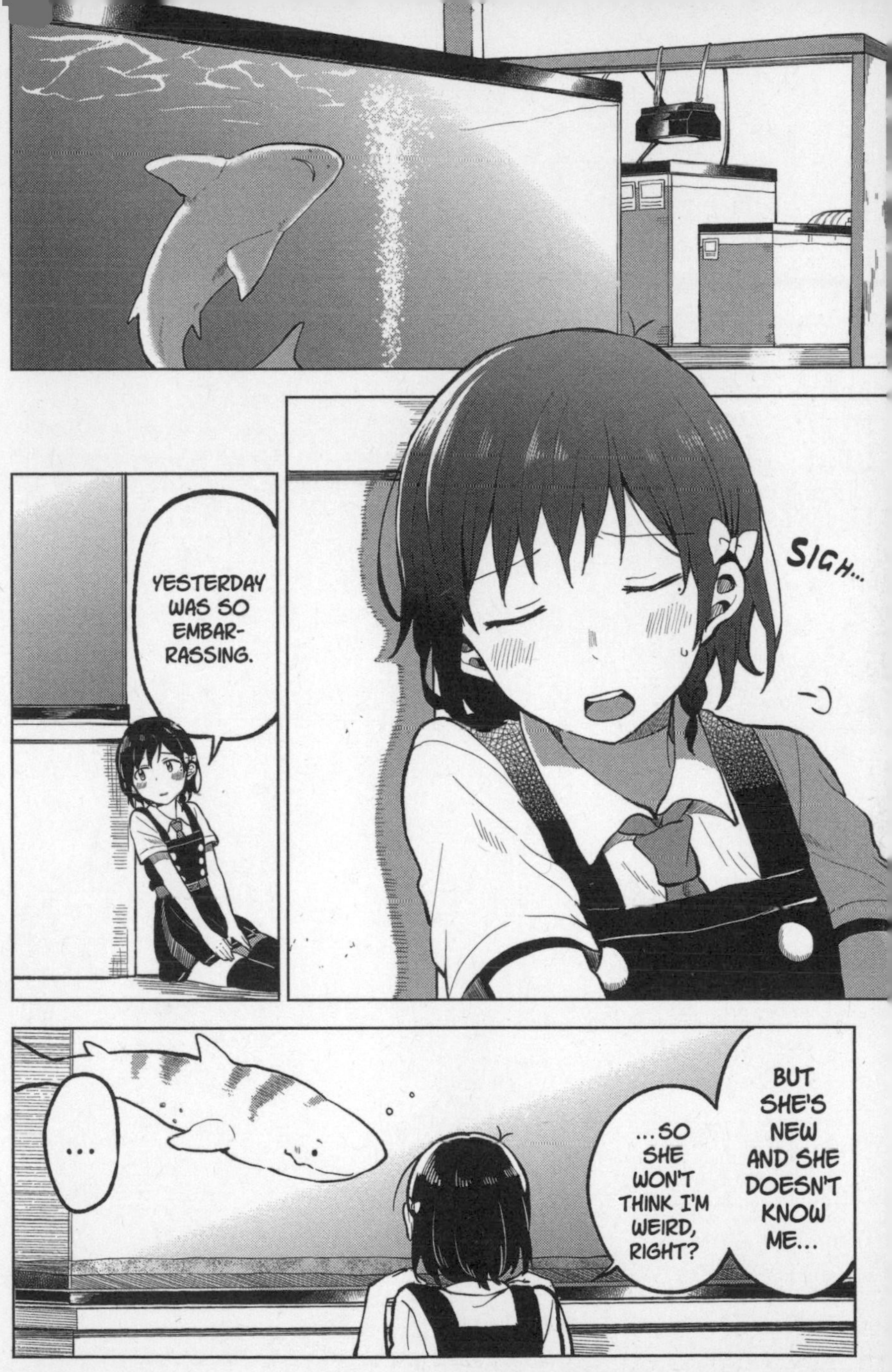
SIGH...
YESTERDAY WAS SO EMBAR-RASSING.
BUT SHE'S NEW AND SHE DOESN'T KNOW ME...
...SO SHE WON'T THINK I'M WEIRD, RIGHT?
...

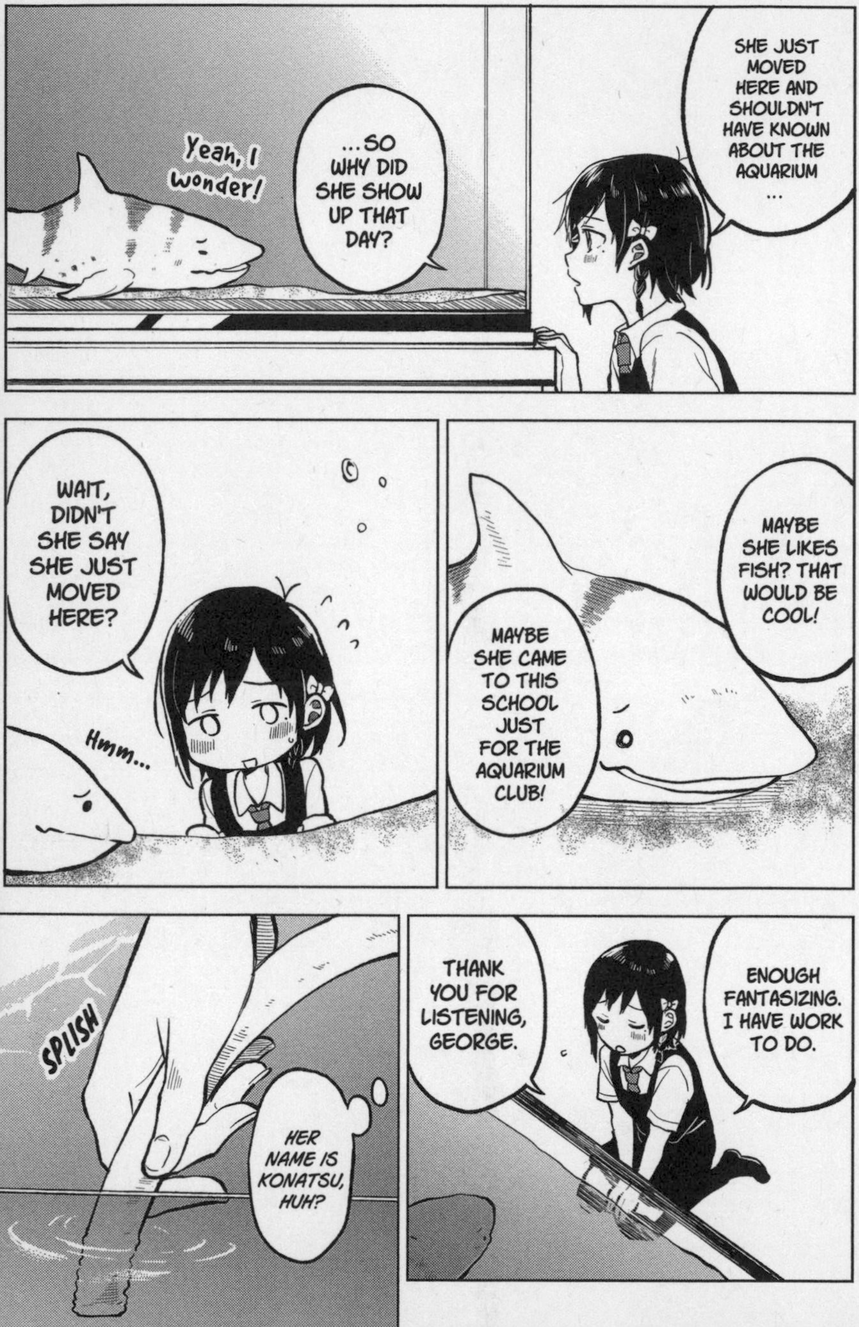
SHE JUST MOVED HERE AND SHOULDN'T HAVE KNOWN ABOUT THE AQUARIUM ...
...SO WHY DID SHE SHOW UP THAT DAY?
Yeah, I wonder!
MAYBE SHE LIKES FISH? THAT WOULD BE COOL!
MAYBE SHE CAME TO THIS SCHOOL JUST FOR THE AQUARIUM CLUB!
WAIT, DIDN'T SHE SAY SHE JUST MOVED HERE?
Hmm...
ENOUGH FANTASIZING. I HAVE WORK TO DO.
THANK YOU FOR LISTENING, GEORGE.
HER NAME IS KONATSU, HUH?
SPLISH

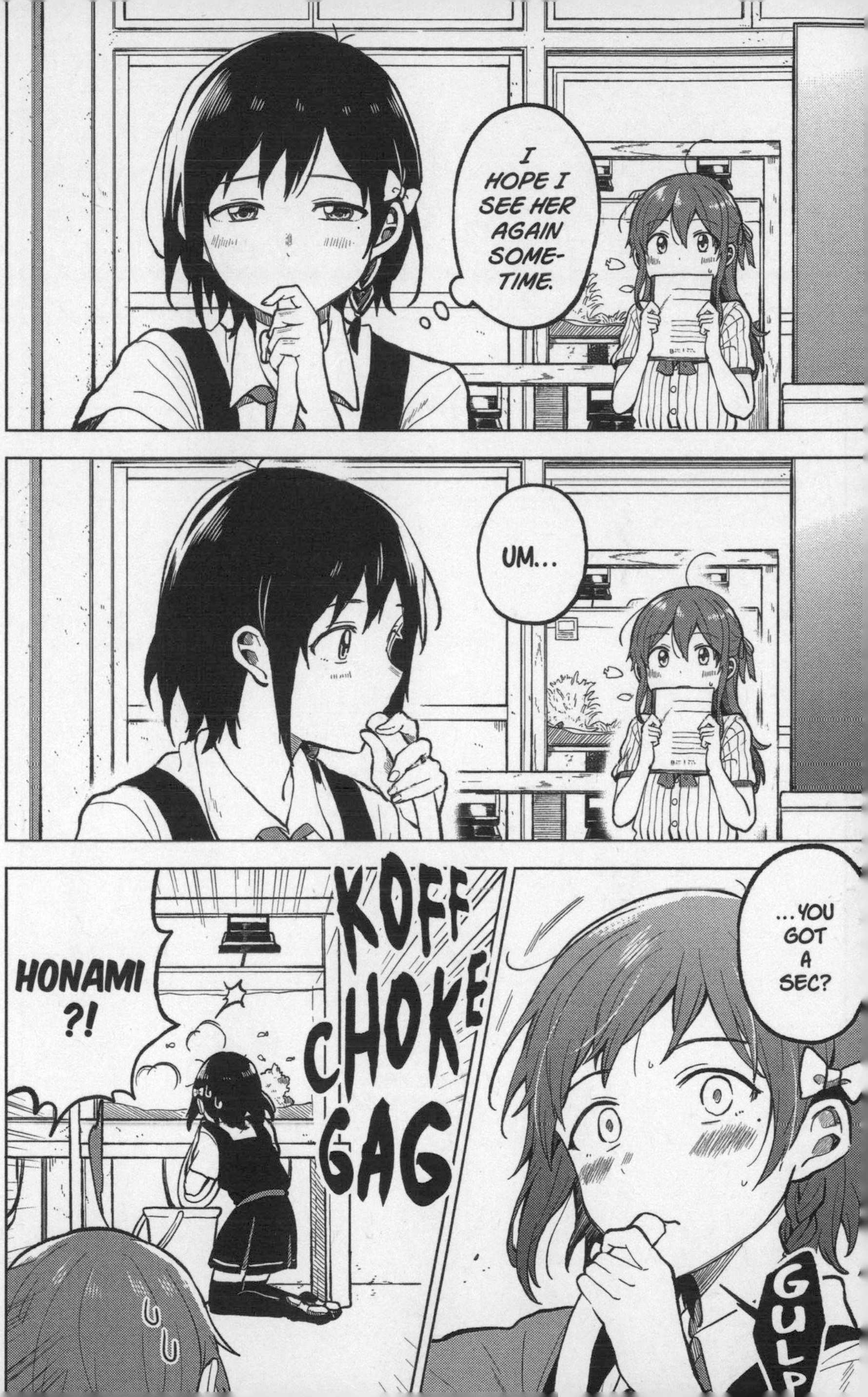
I HOPE I SEE HER AGAIN SOME-TIME.
UM...
...YOU GOT A SEC?
GULP
KOFF CHOKE GAG
HONAMI ?!

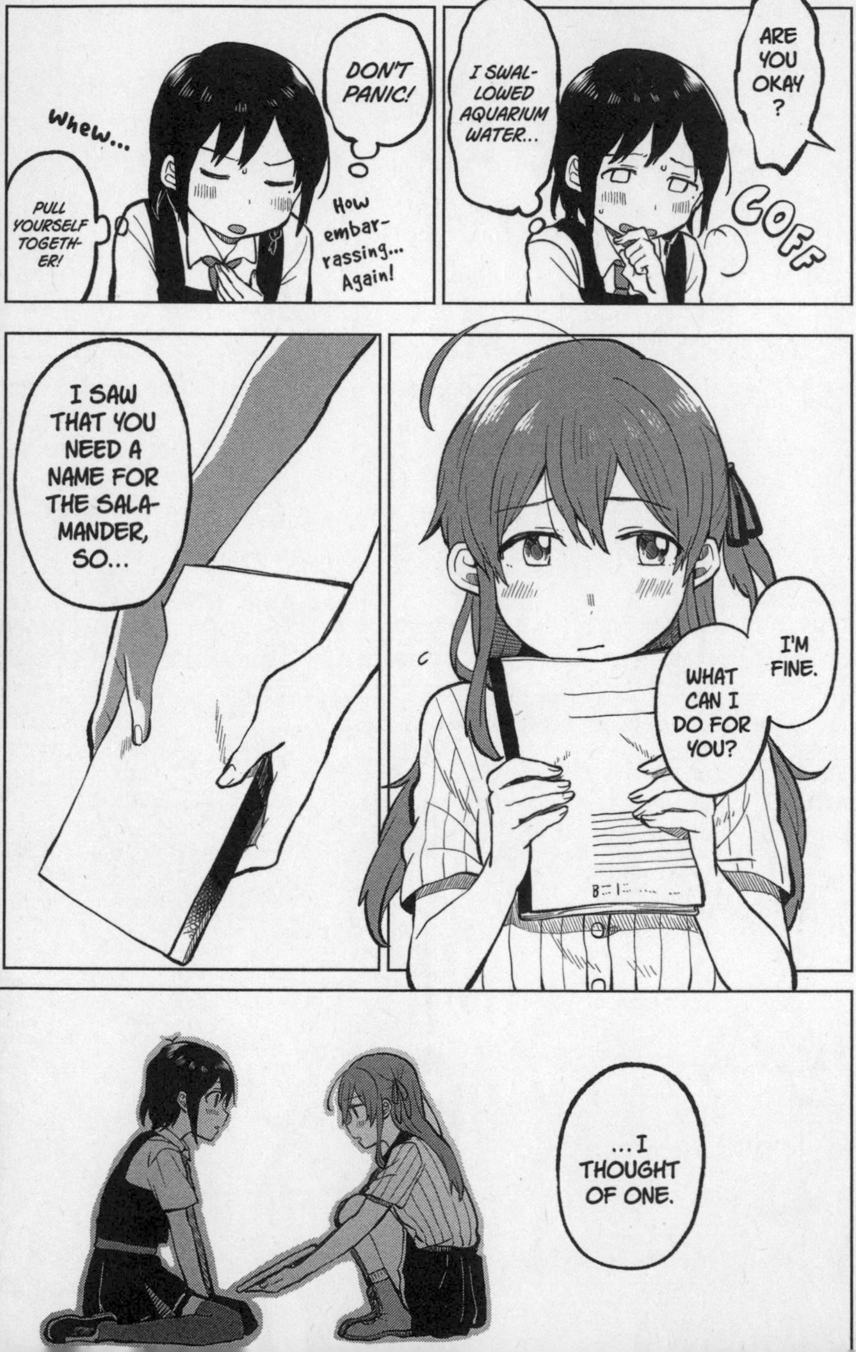
ARE YOU OKAY?
COFF
I SWAL-LOWED AQUARIUM WATER...
DON'T PANIC!
How embar-rassing... Again!
Whew...
PULL YOURSELF TOGETH-ER!
I'M FINE.
WHAT CAN I DO FOR YOU?
I SAW THAT YOU NEED A NAME FOR THE SALA-MANDER, SO...
...I THOUGHT OF ONE.

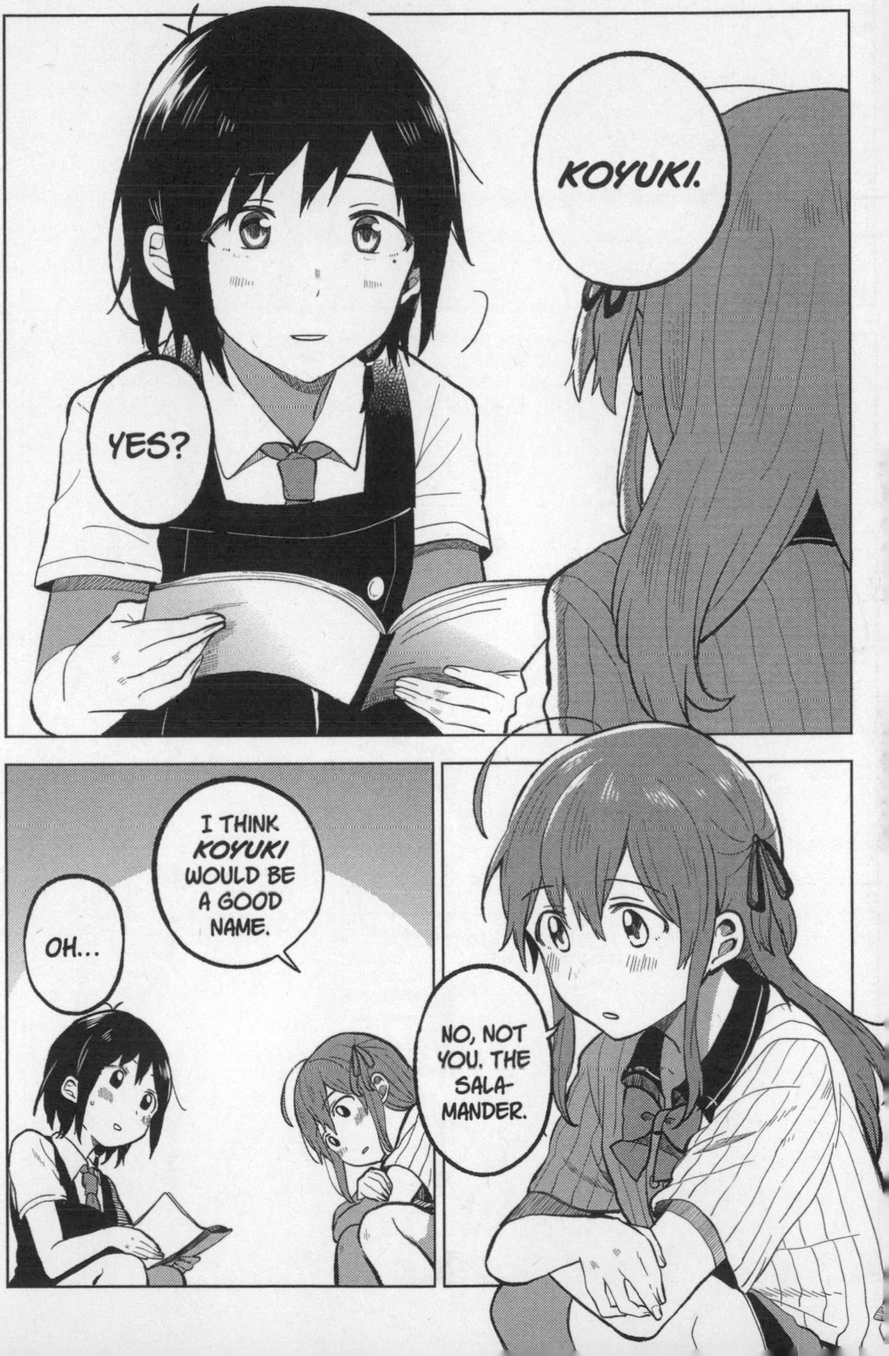
KOYUKI.
YES?
NO, NOT YOU. THE SALAMANDER.
I THINK *KOYUKI* WOULD BE A GOOD NAME.
OH...

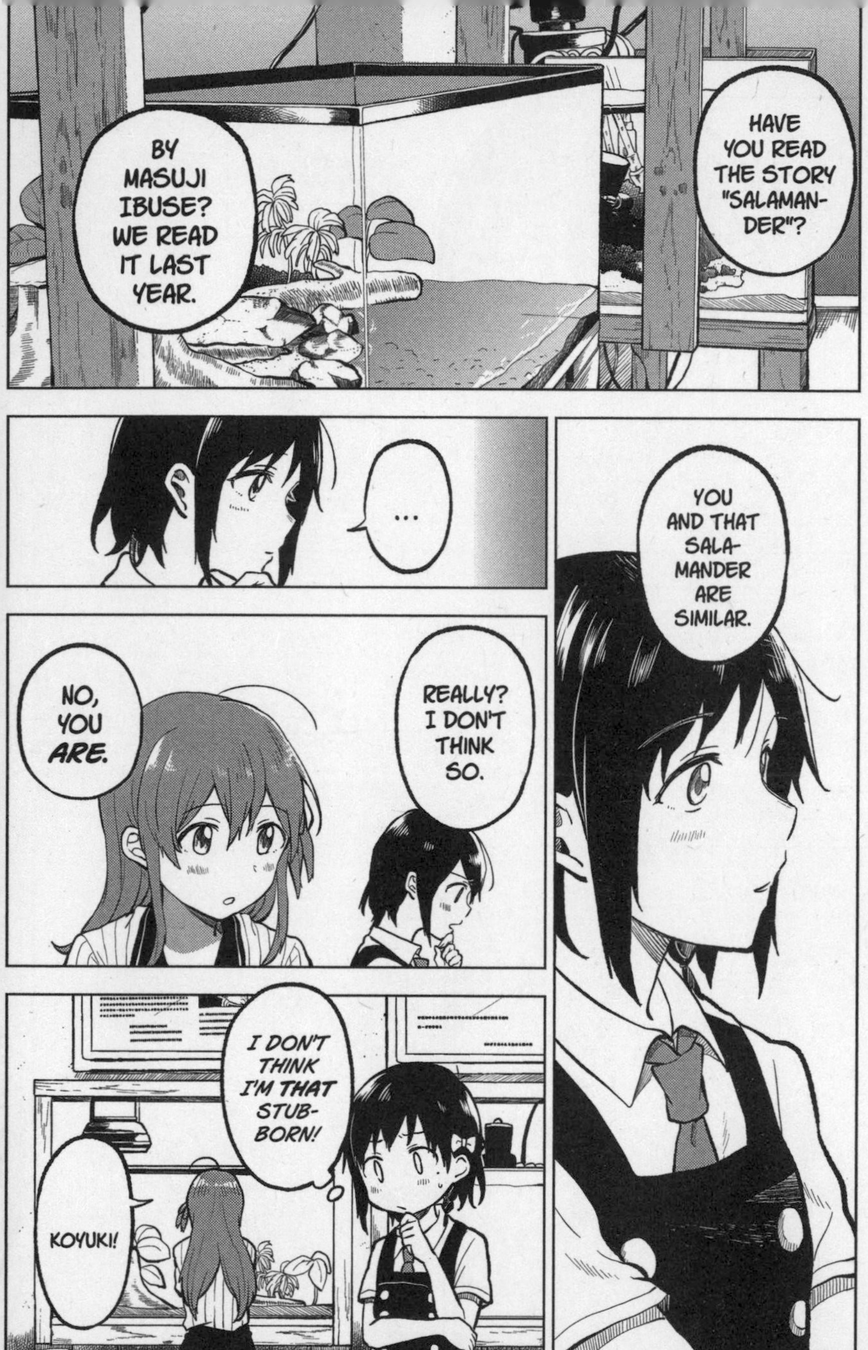
HAVE YOU READ THE STORY "SALAMANDER"?
BY MASUJI IBUSE? WE READ IT LAST YEAR.
YOU AND THAT SALAMANDER ARE SIMILAR.
...
REALLY? I DON'T THINK SO.
NO, YOU *ARE.*
I DON'T THINK I'M THAT STUBBORN!
KOYUKI!

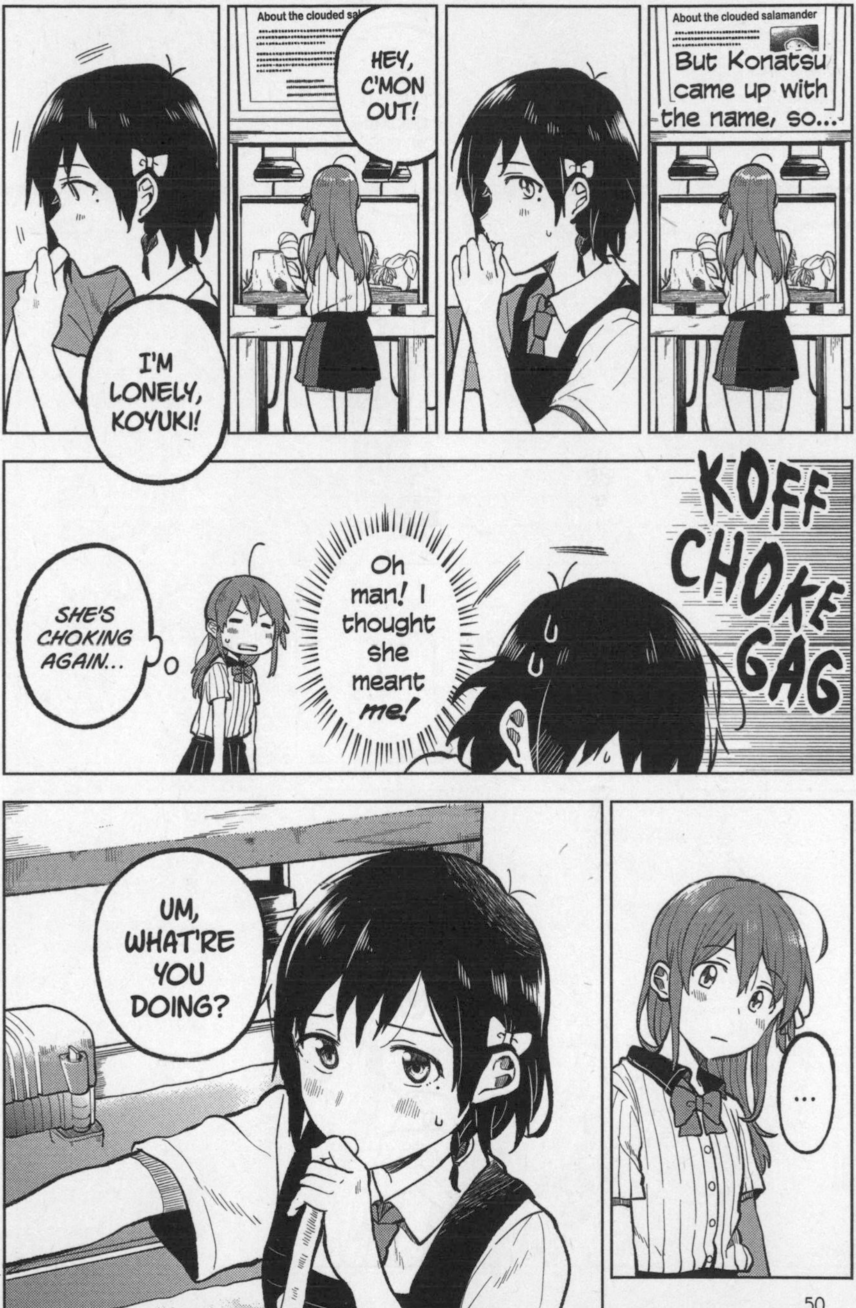
About the clouded salamander
But Konatsu came up with the name, so...
About the clouded sal
HEY, C'MON OUT!
I'M LONELY, KOYUKI!
KOFF CHOKE GAG
Oh man! I thought she meant me!
SHE'S CHOKING AGAIN...
...
UM, WHAT'RE YOU DOING?

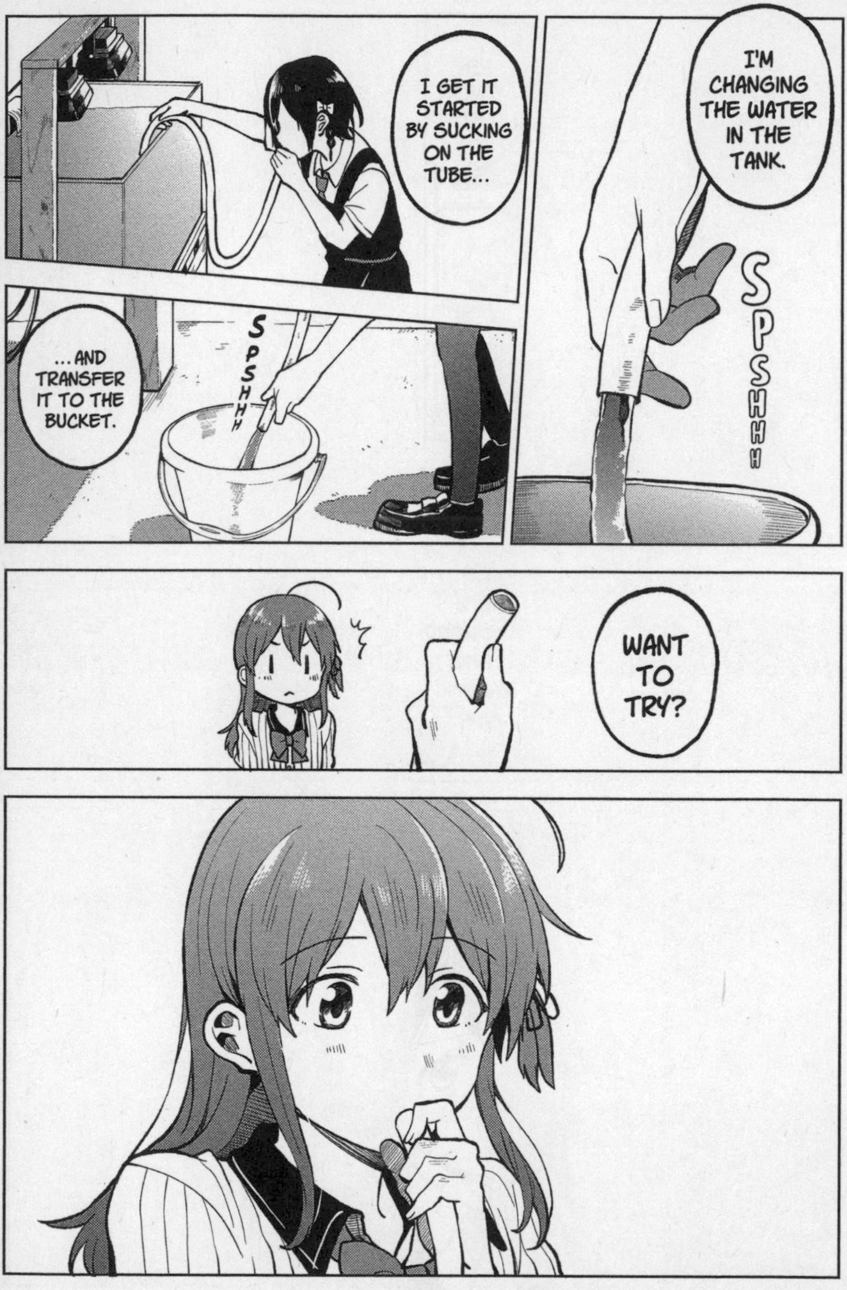
I'M CHANGING THE WATER IN THE TANK.
SPSHHH
I GET IT STARTED BY SUCKING ON THE TUBE...
...AND TRANSFER IT TO THE BUCKET.
SPSHHH
WANT TO TRY?

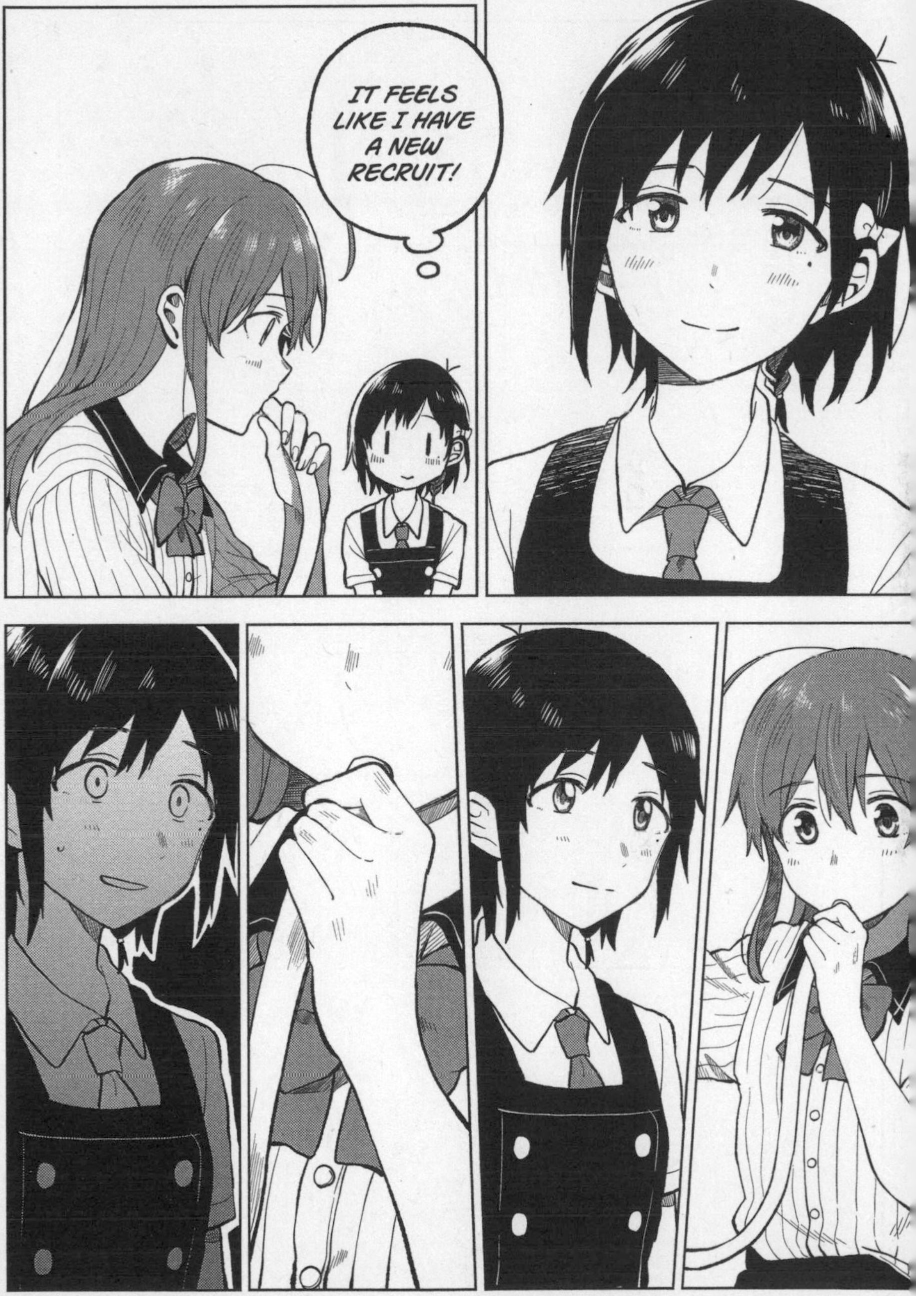
IT FEELS LIKE I HAVE A NEW RECRUIT!

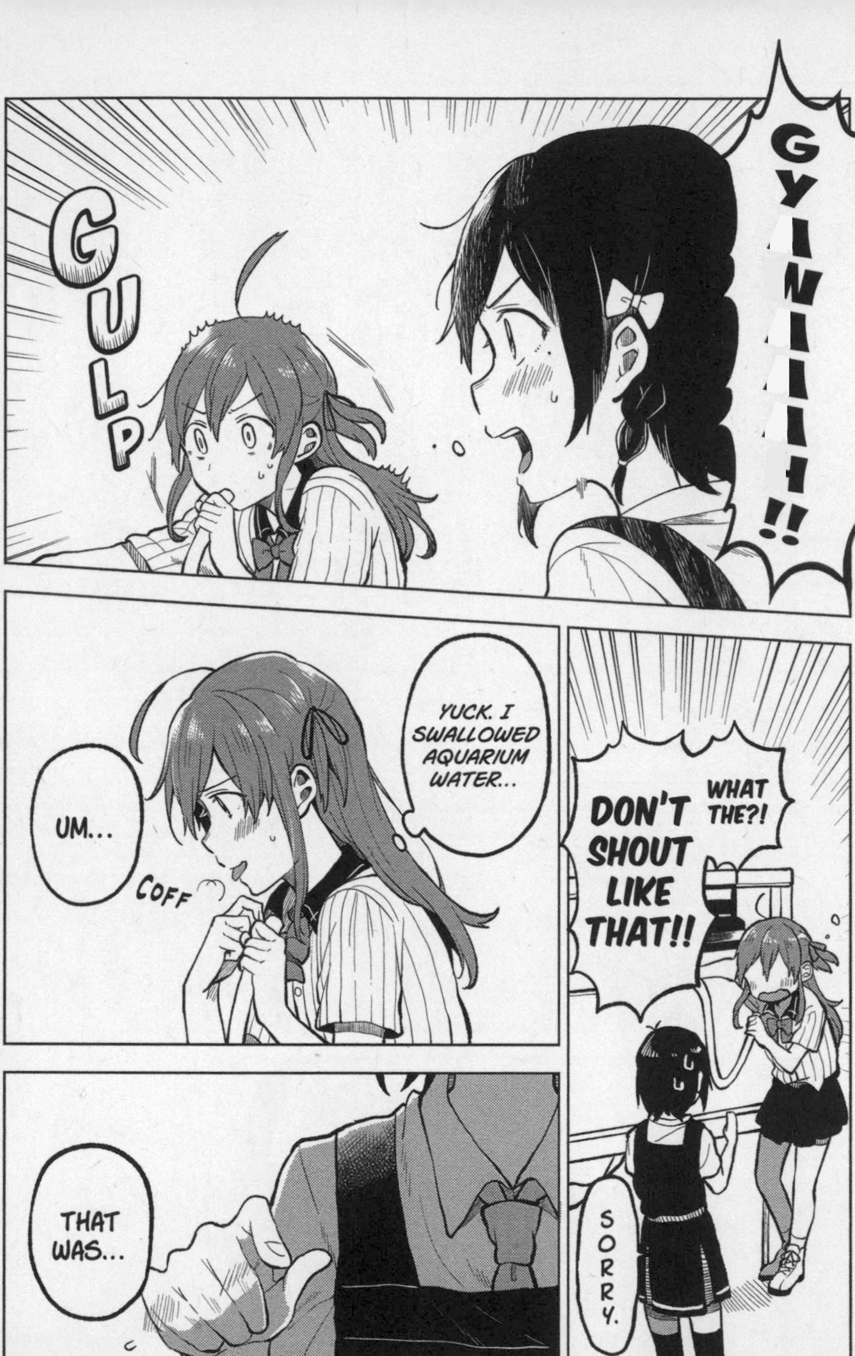
GYINIIII!!
GULP
WHAT THE?!
DON'T SHOUT LIKE THAT!!
SORRY.
YUCK. I SWALLOWED AQUARIUM WATER...
UM...
COFF
THAT WAS...

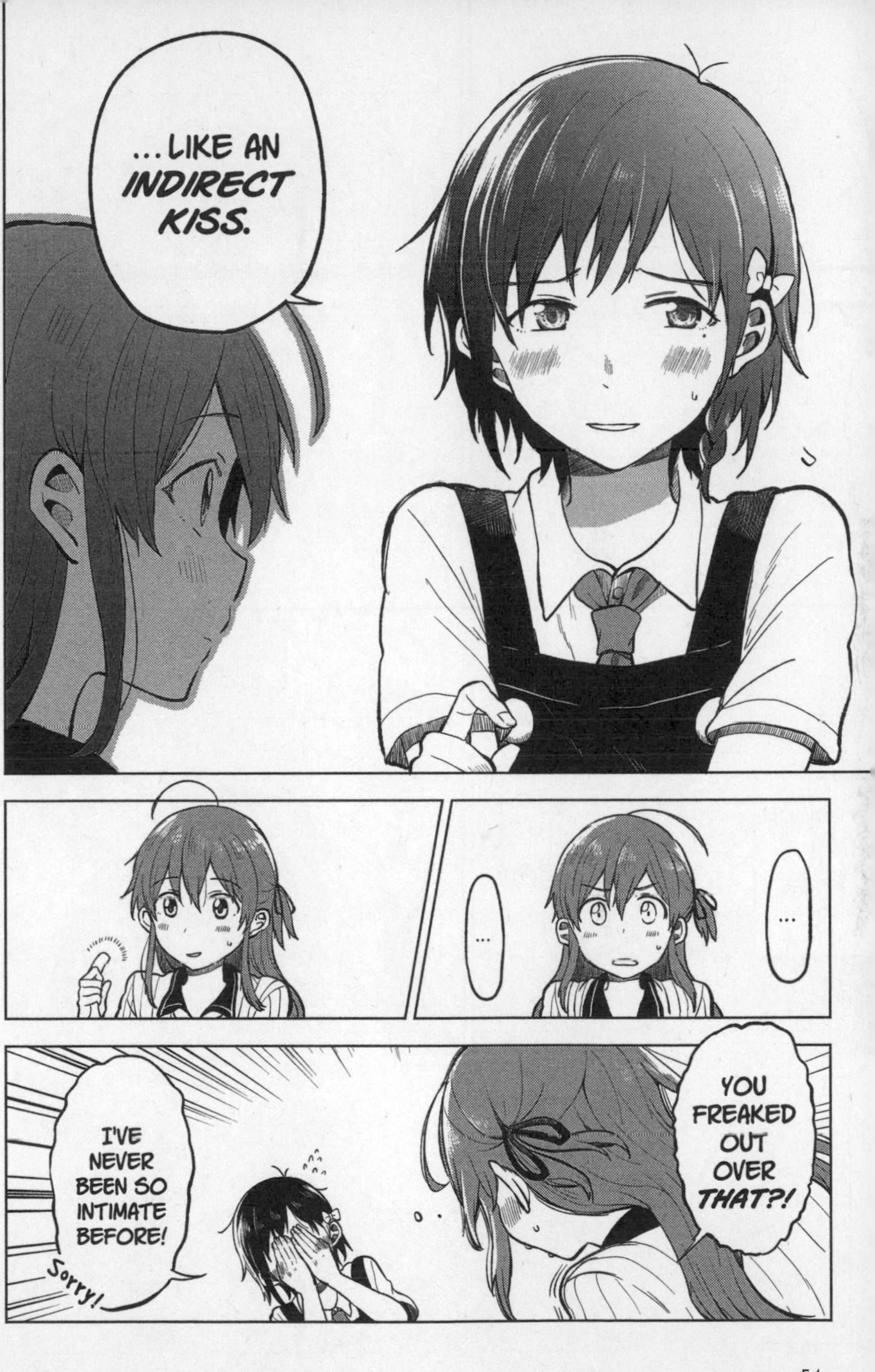
...LIKE AN *INDIRECT* KISS.
...
...
YOU FREAKED OUT OVER *THAT?!*
I'VE NEVER BEEN SO INTIMATE BEFORE!
Sorry!

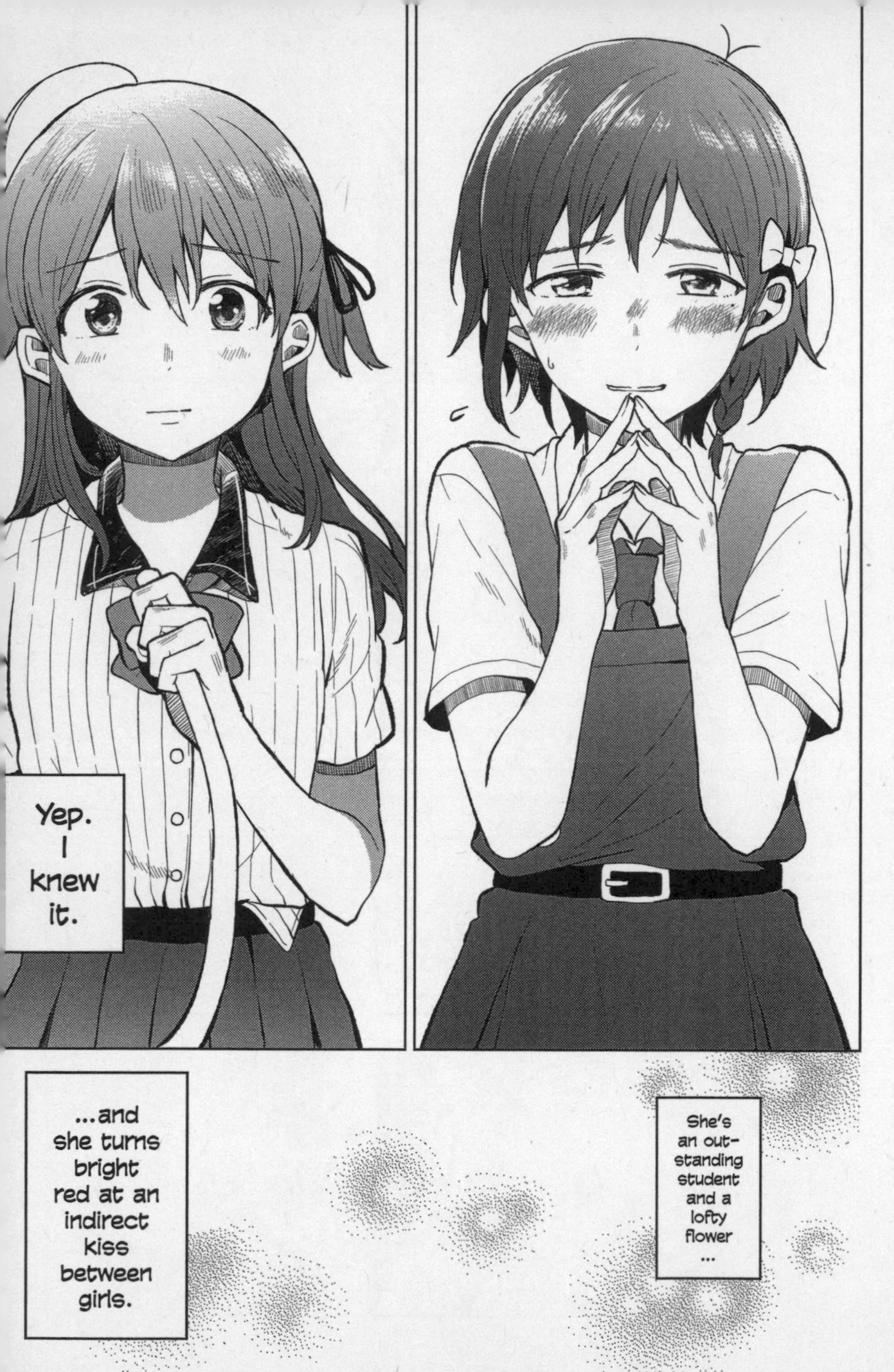
Yep. I knew it.
She's an out-standing student and a lofty flower ...
...and she turns bright red at an indirect kiss between girls.

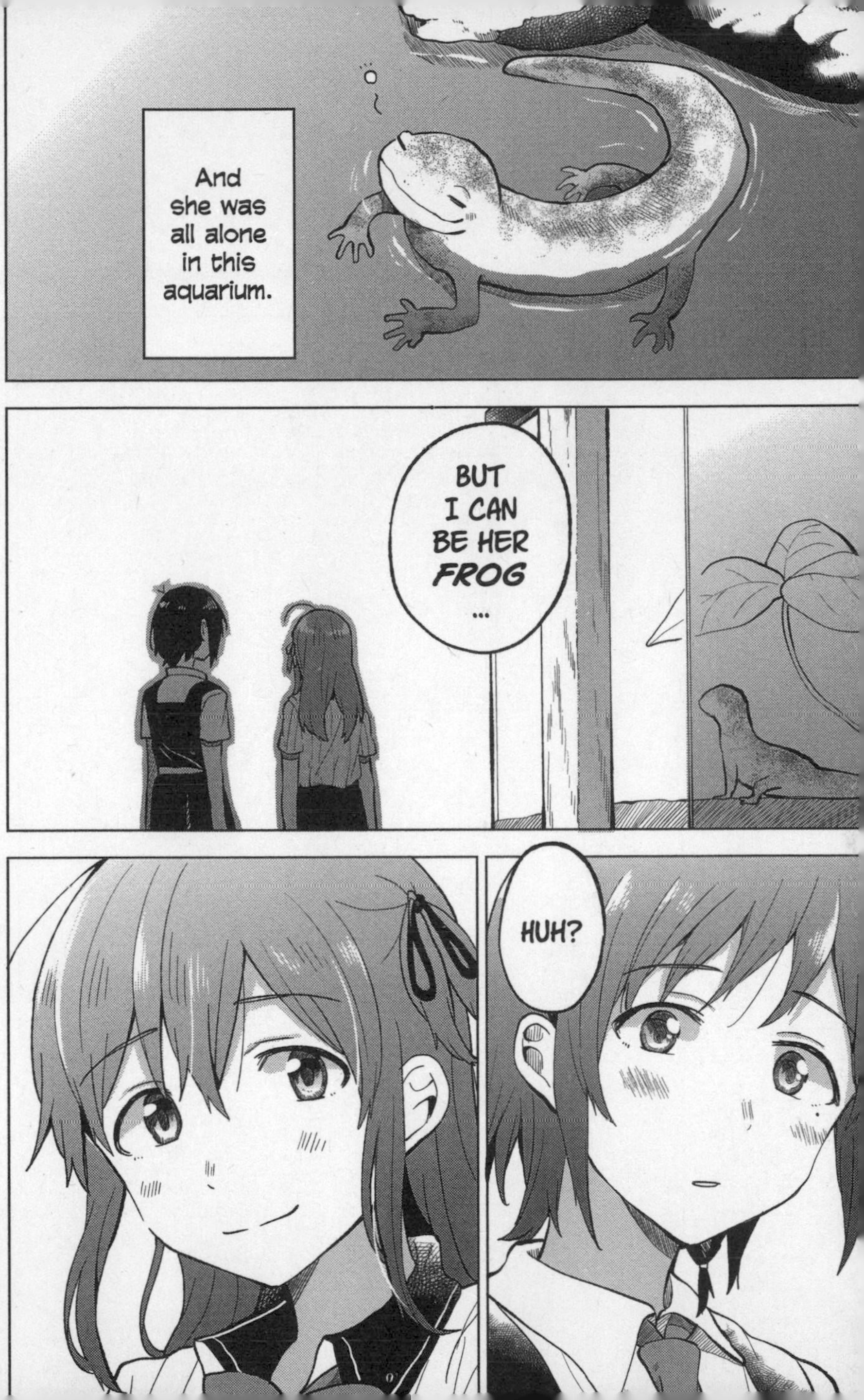
And she was all alone in this aquarium.
BUT I CAN BE HER *FROG* ...
HUH?

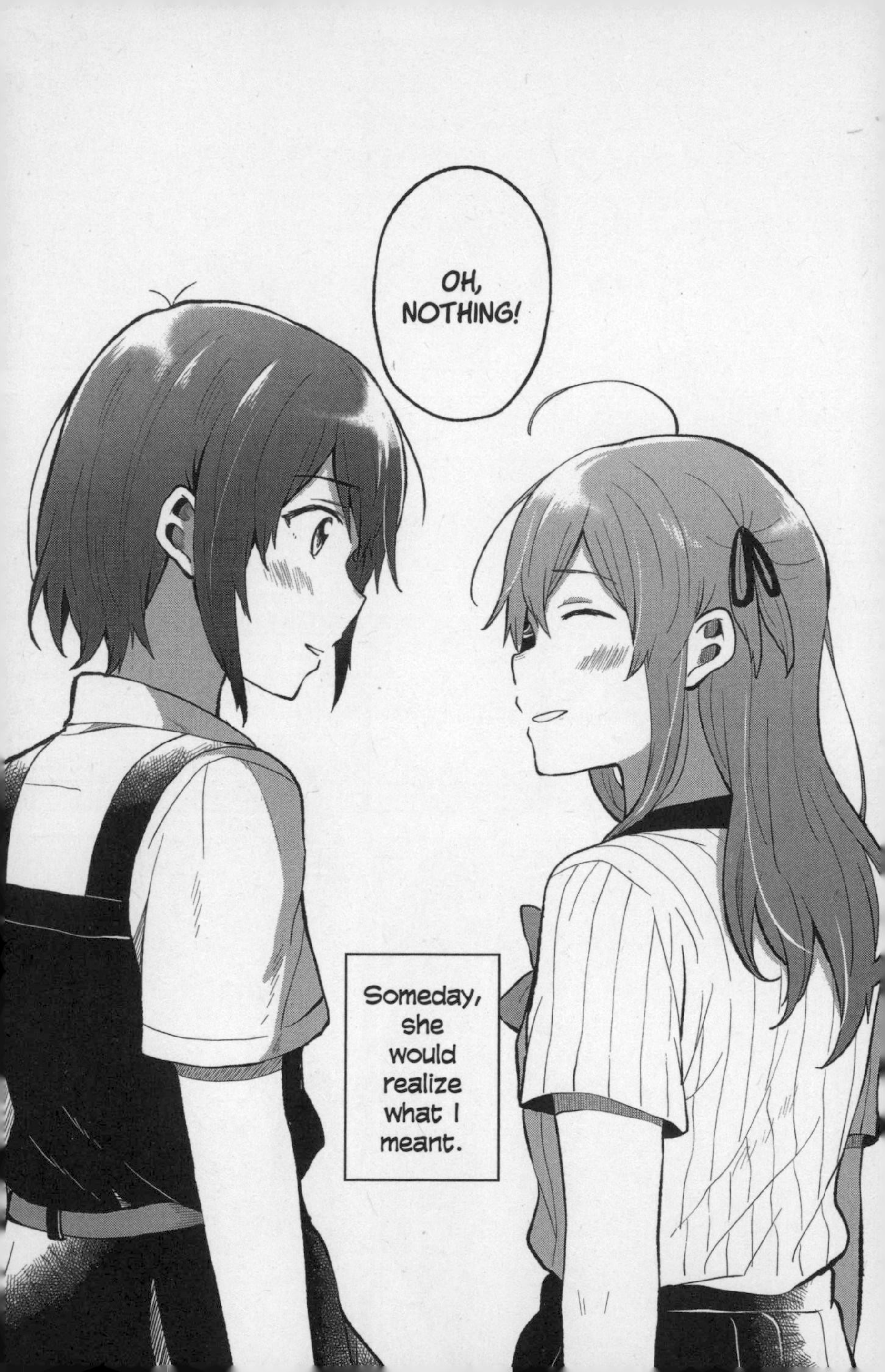
OH, NOTHING!
Someday, she would realize what I meant.

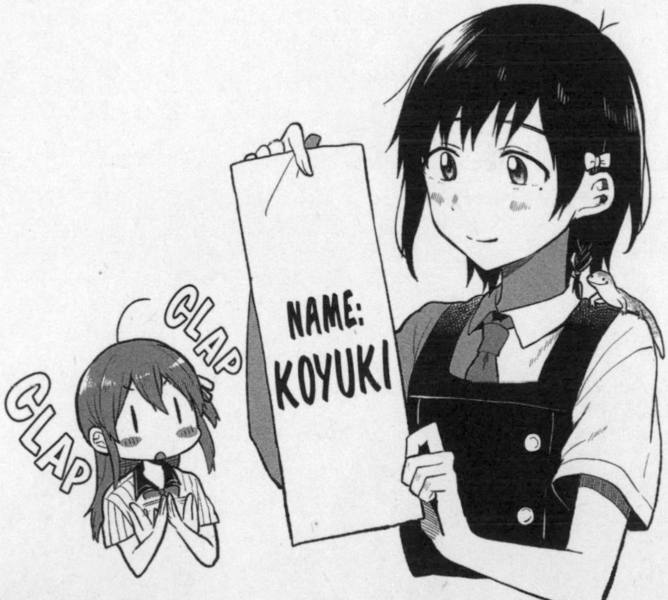
NAME:
KOYUKI
CLAP
CLAP

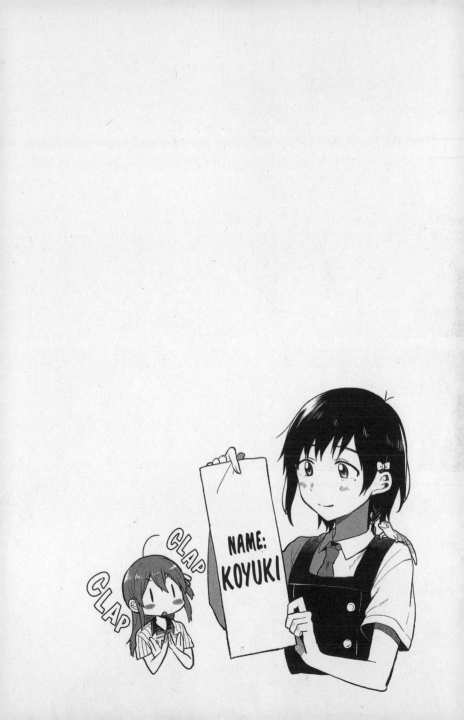

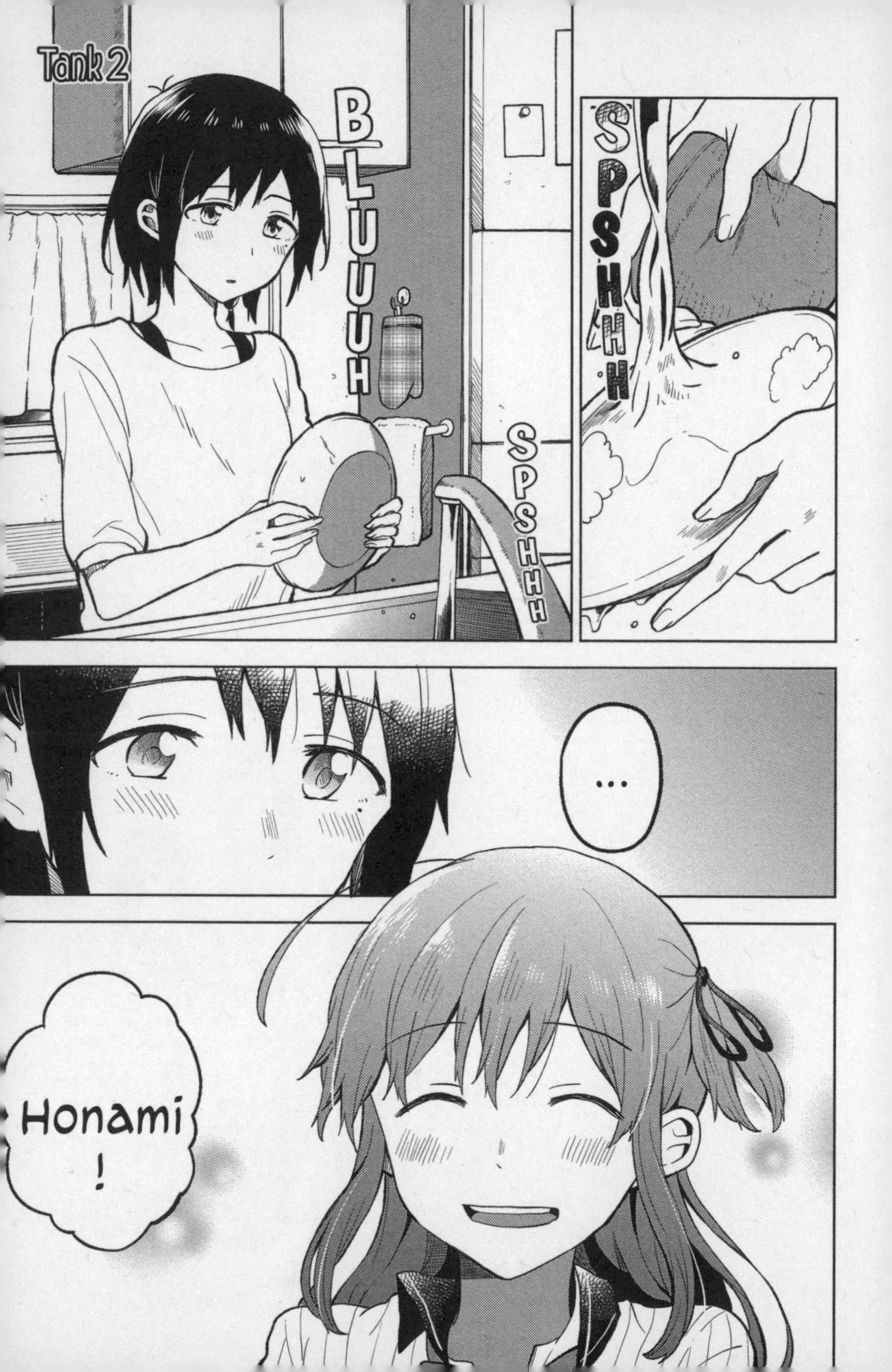
Tank 2
SPSHHH
BLUUUH
SPSHHH
...
Honami!

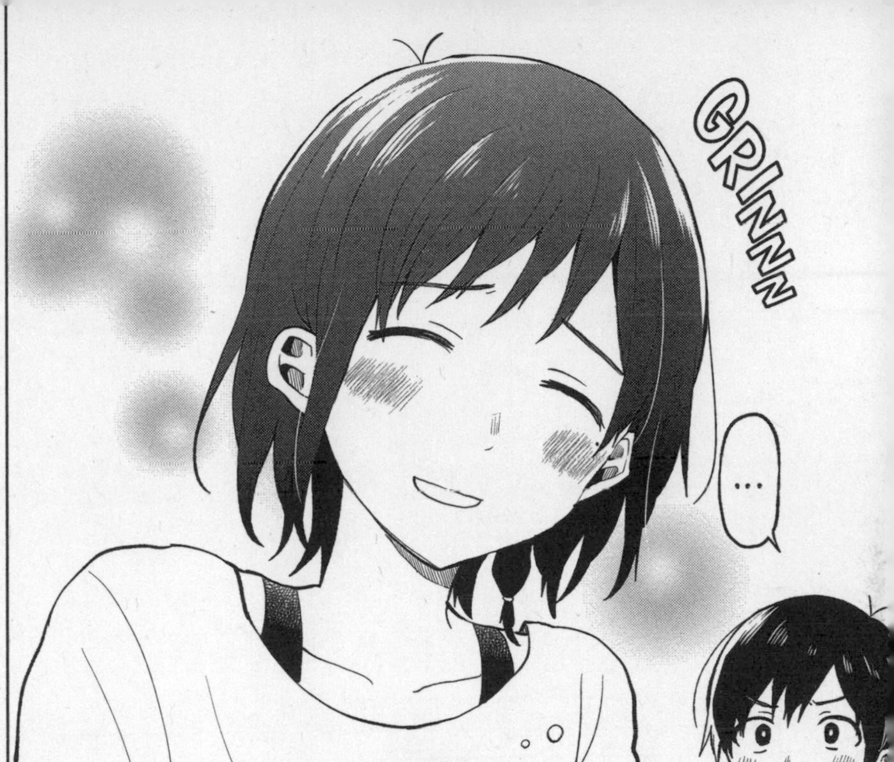
GRINNN
...
Tank 2:
Koyuki Honami Isn't Happy
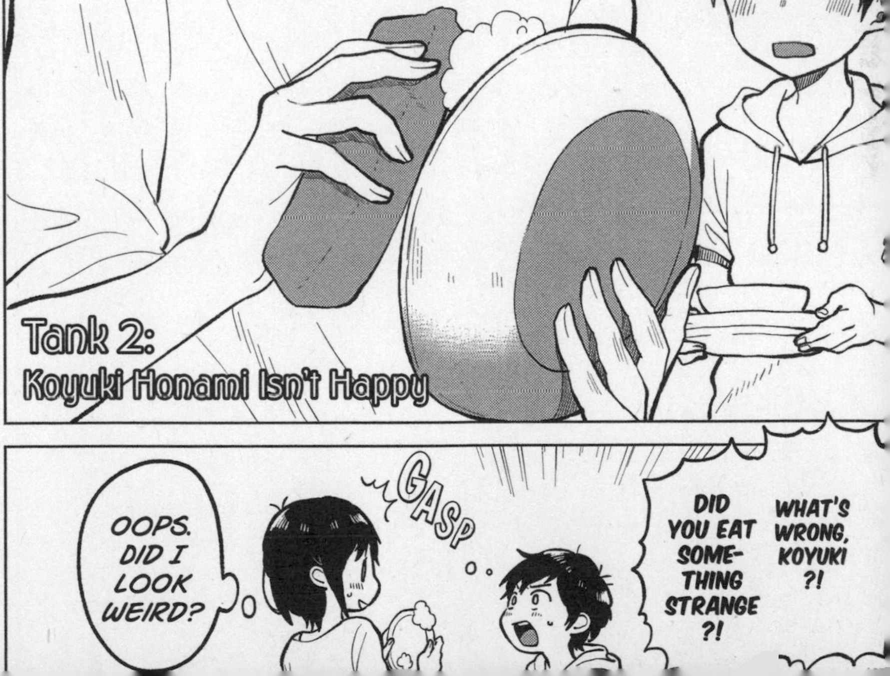
WHAT'S WRONG, KOYUKI?!
DID YOU EAT SOME-THING STRANGE?!
GASP
OOPS. DID I LOOK WEIRD?

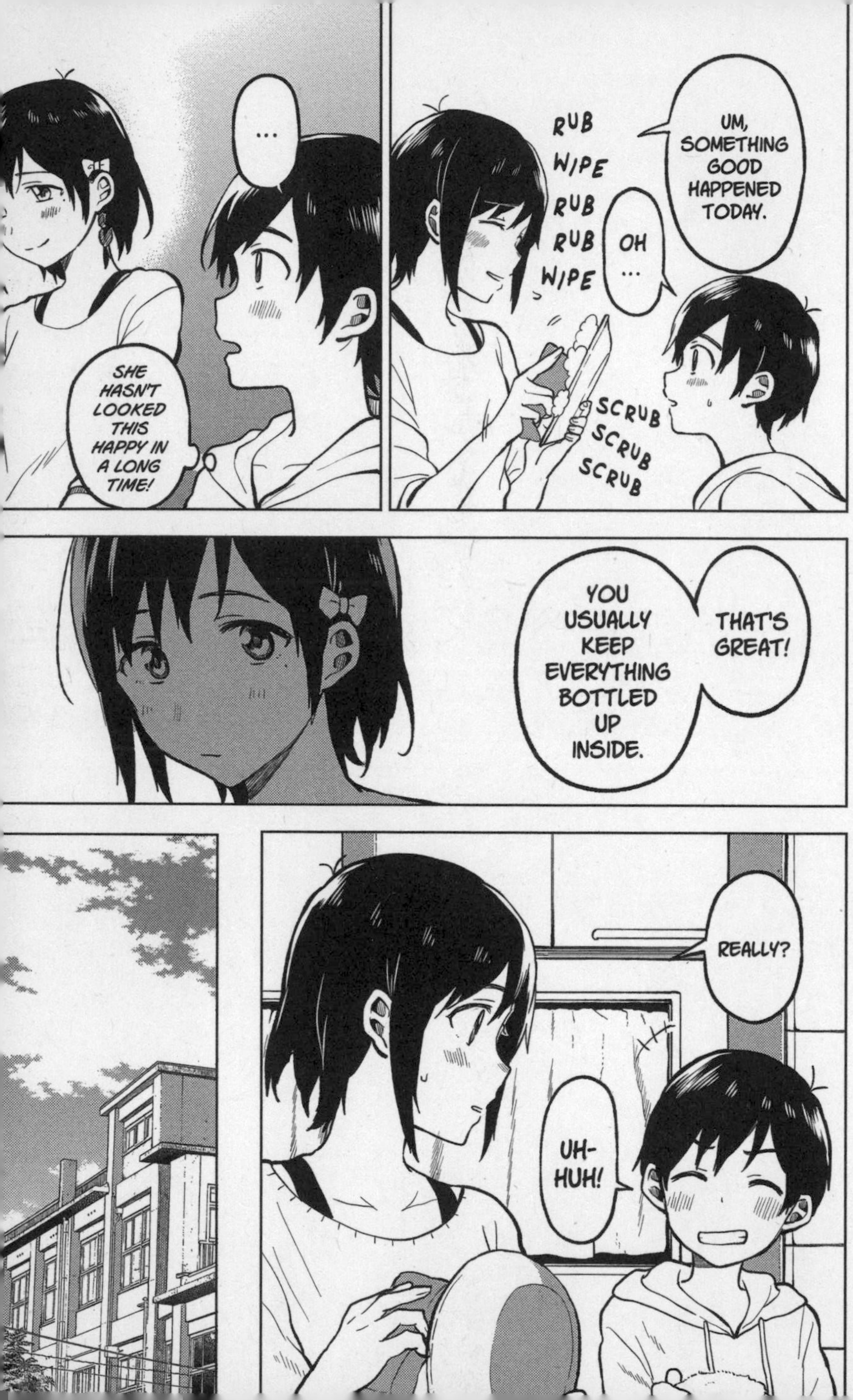
UM, SOMETHING GOOD HAPPENED TODAY.
OH ...
RUB WIPE RUB RUB WIPE
SCRUB SCRUB SCRUB
...
SHE HASN'T LOOKED THIS HAPPY IN A LONG TIME!
THAT'S GREAT!
YOU USUALLY KEEP EVERYTHING BOTTLED UP INSIDE.
REALLY?
UH-HUH!

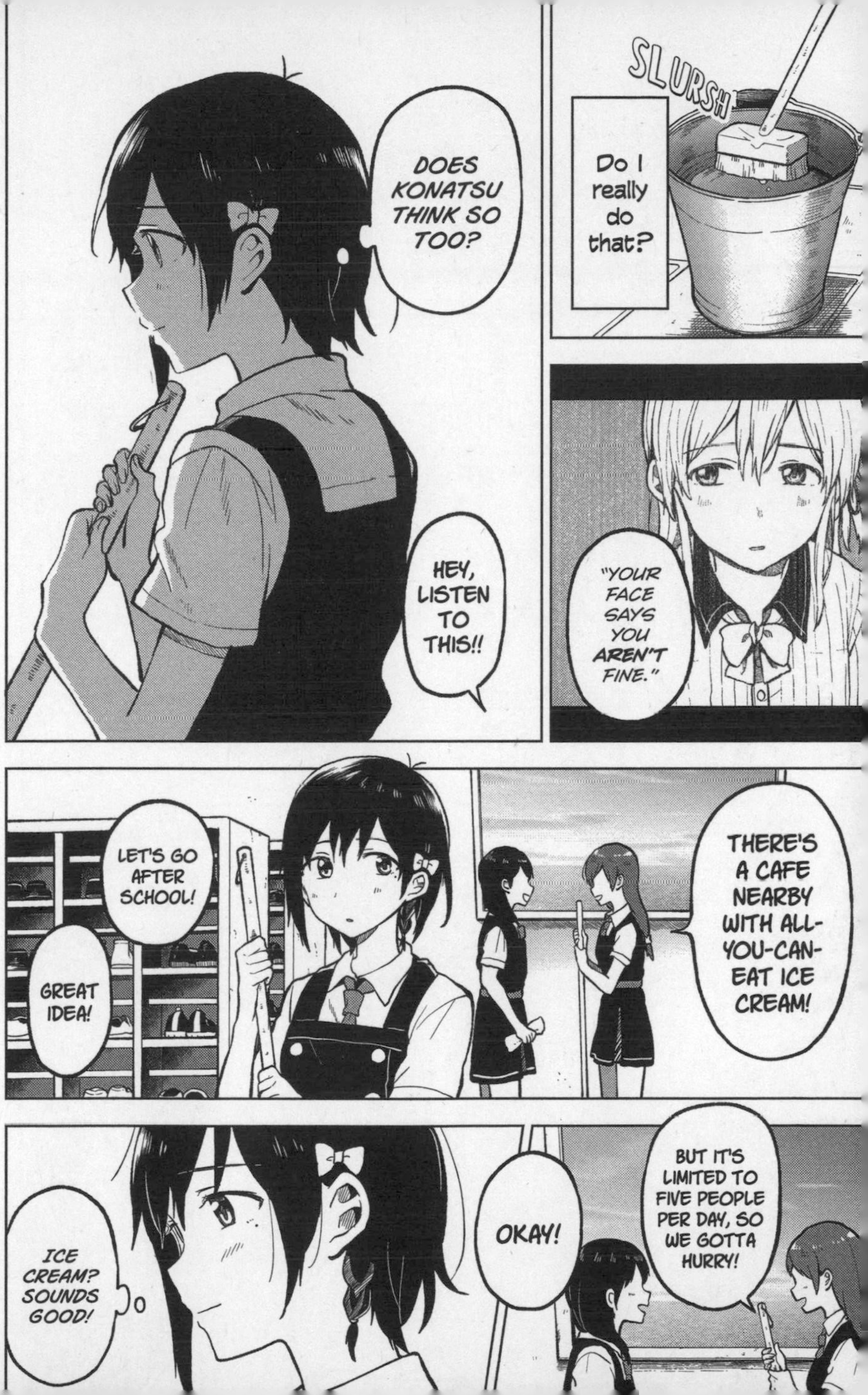
SLURSH
Do I really do that?
"YOUR FACE SAYS YOU AREN'T FINE."
DOES KONATSU THINK SO TOO?
HEY, LISTEN TO THIS!!
THERE'S A CAFE NEARBY WITH ALL-YOU-CAN-EAT ICE CREAM!
LET'S GO AFTER SCHOOL!
GREAT IDEA!
BUT IT'S LIMITED TO FIVE PEOPLE PER DAY, SO WE GOTTA HURRY!
OKAY!
ICE CREAM? SOUNDS GOOD!

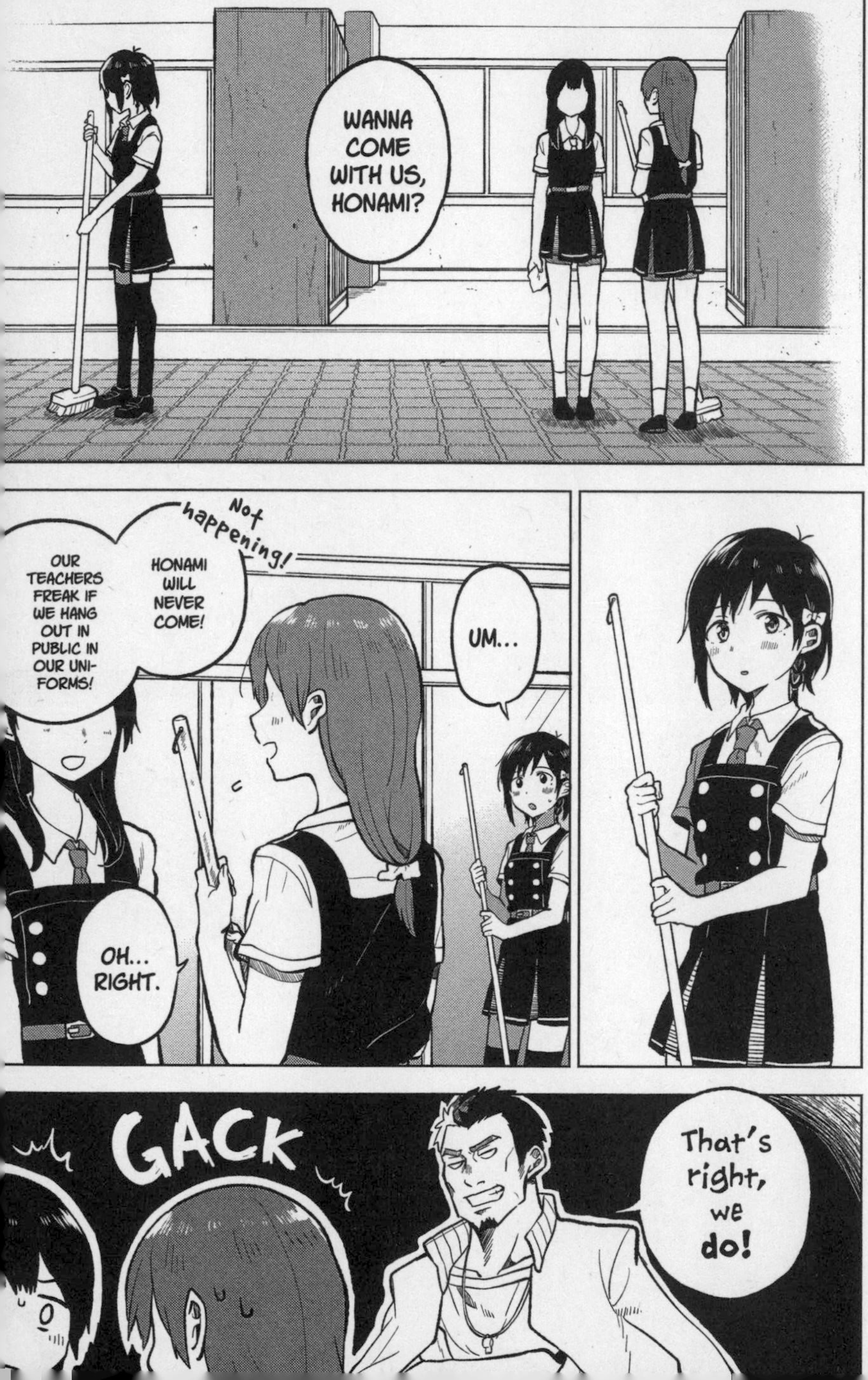
WANNA COME WITH US, HONAMI?
Not happening!
HONAMI WILL NEVER COME!
OUR TEACHERS FREAK IF WE HANG OUT IN PUBLIC IN OUR UNI-FORMS!
UM...
OH... RIGHT.
That's right, we do!
GACK

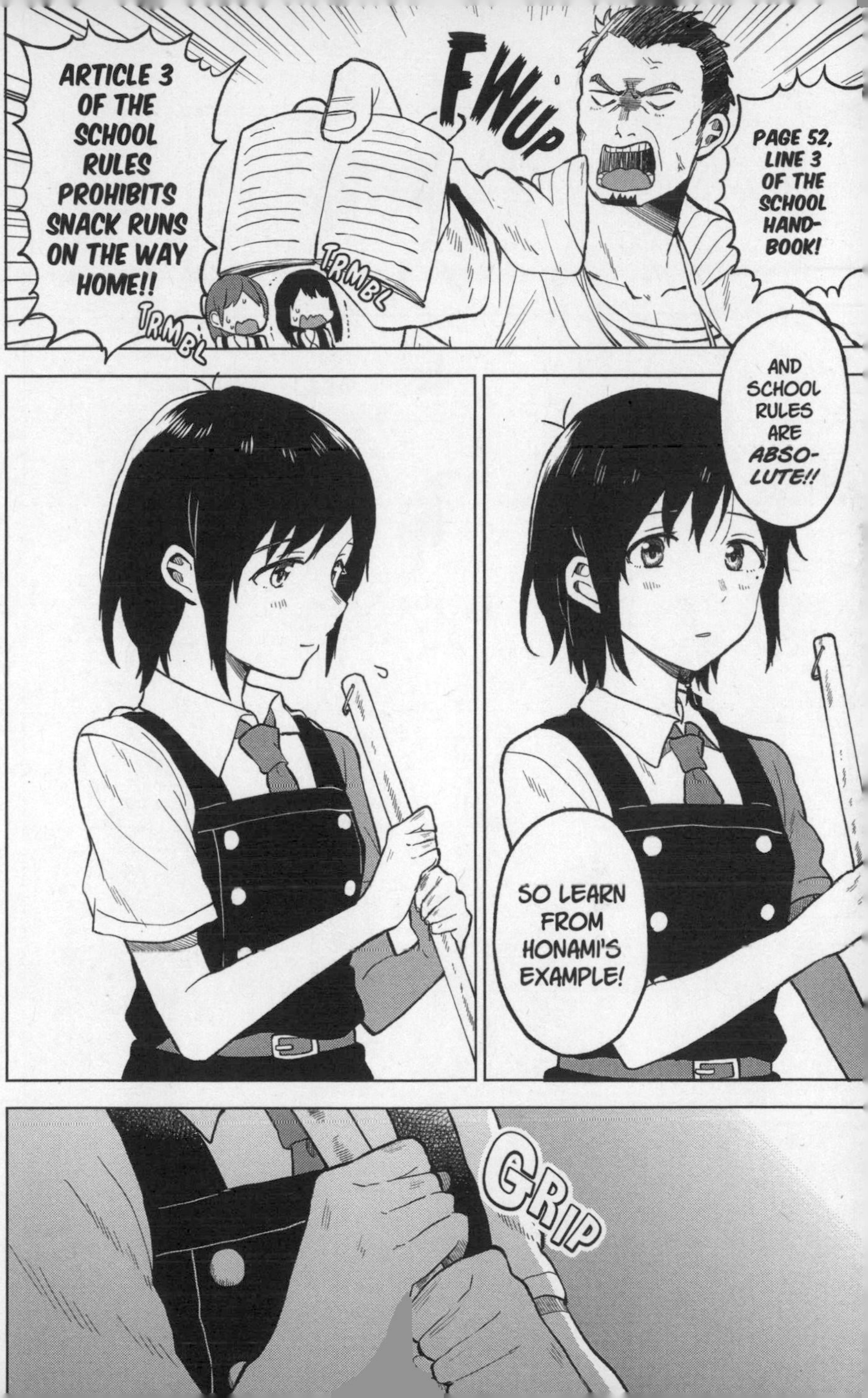
PAGE 52, LINE 3 OF THE SCHOOL HAND-BOOK!
FWUP
ARTICLE 3 OF THE SCHOOL RULES PROHIBITS SNACK RUNS ON THE WAY HOME!!
TRMBL
TRMBL
AND SCHOOL RULES ARE ABSO-LUTE!!
SO LEARN FROM HONAMI'S EXAMPLE!
GRIP

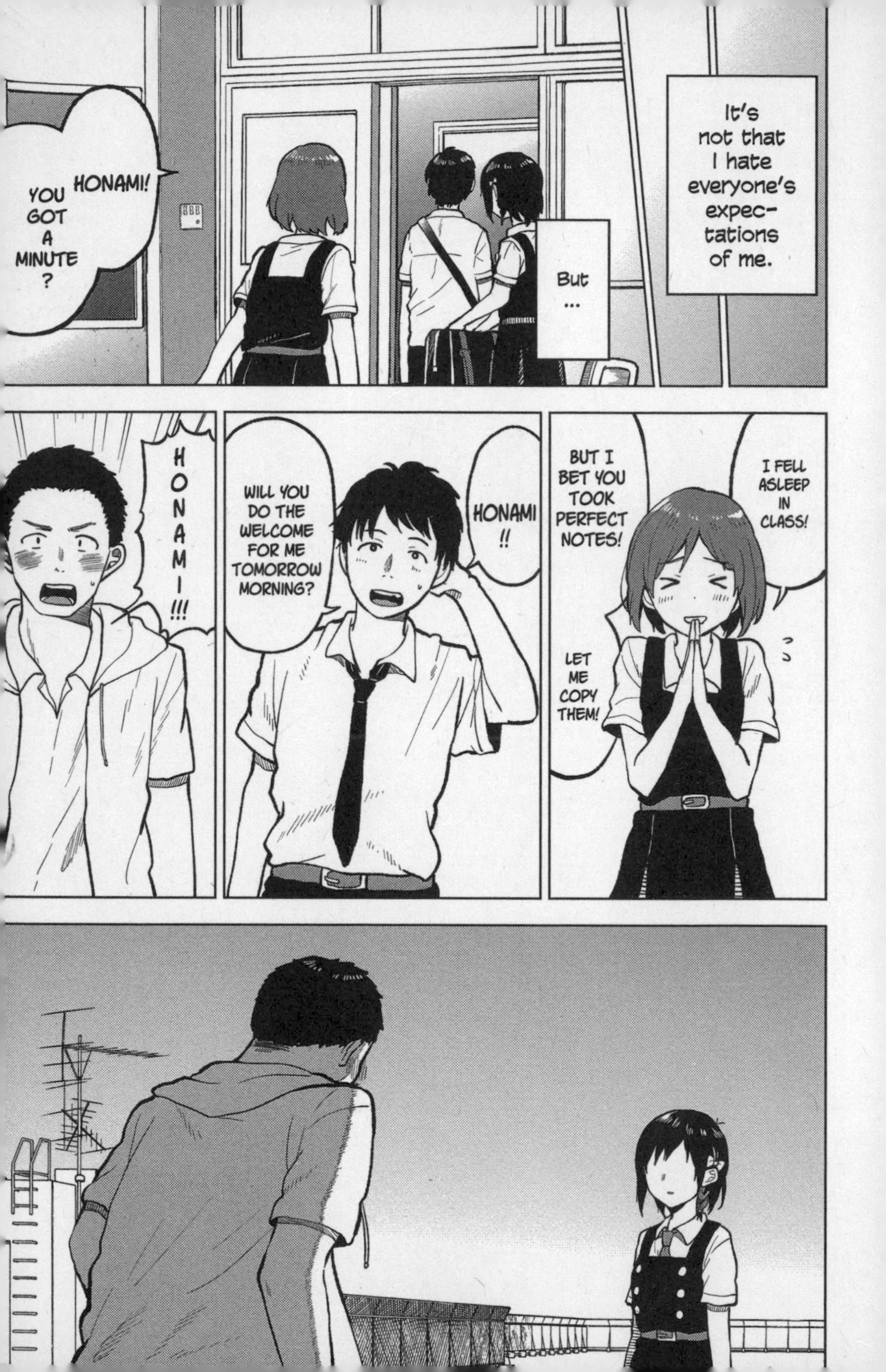
It's not that I hate everyone's expectations of me.
But ...
HONAMI!
YOU GOT A MINUTE?
I FELL ASLEEP IN CLASS!
BUT I BET YOU TOOK PERFECT NOTES!
LET ME COPY THEM!
HONAMI!!
WILL YOU DO THE WELCOME FOR ME TOMORROW MORNING?
HONAMI!!!

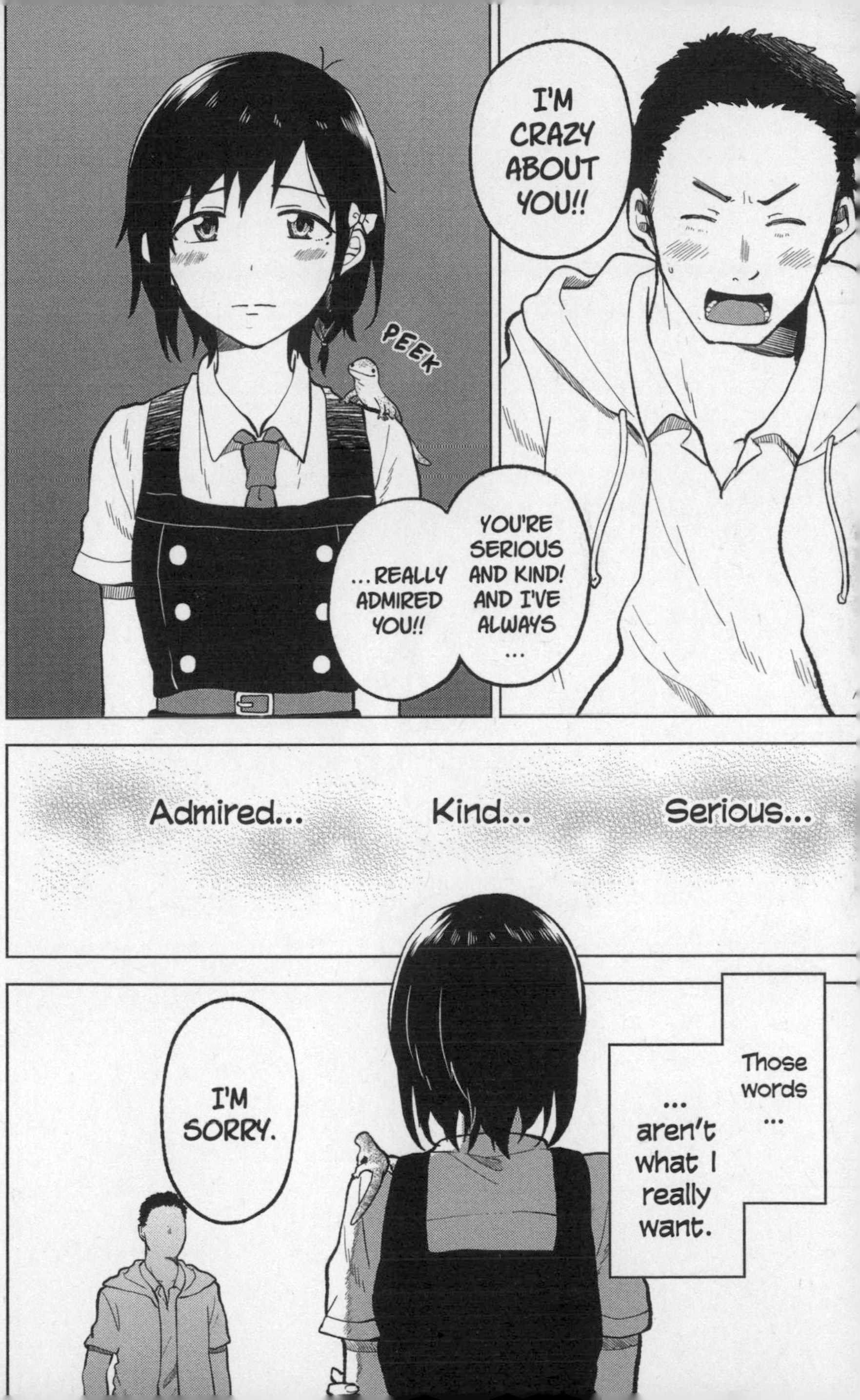
I'M CRAZY ABOUT YOU!!
PEEK
YOU'RE SERIOUS AND KIND! AND I'VE ALWAYS ...
...REALLY ADMIRED YOU!!
Serious...
Kind...
Admired...
Those words ...
... aren't what I really want.
I'M SORRY.

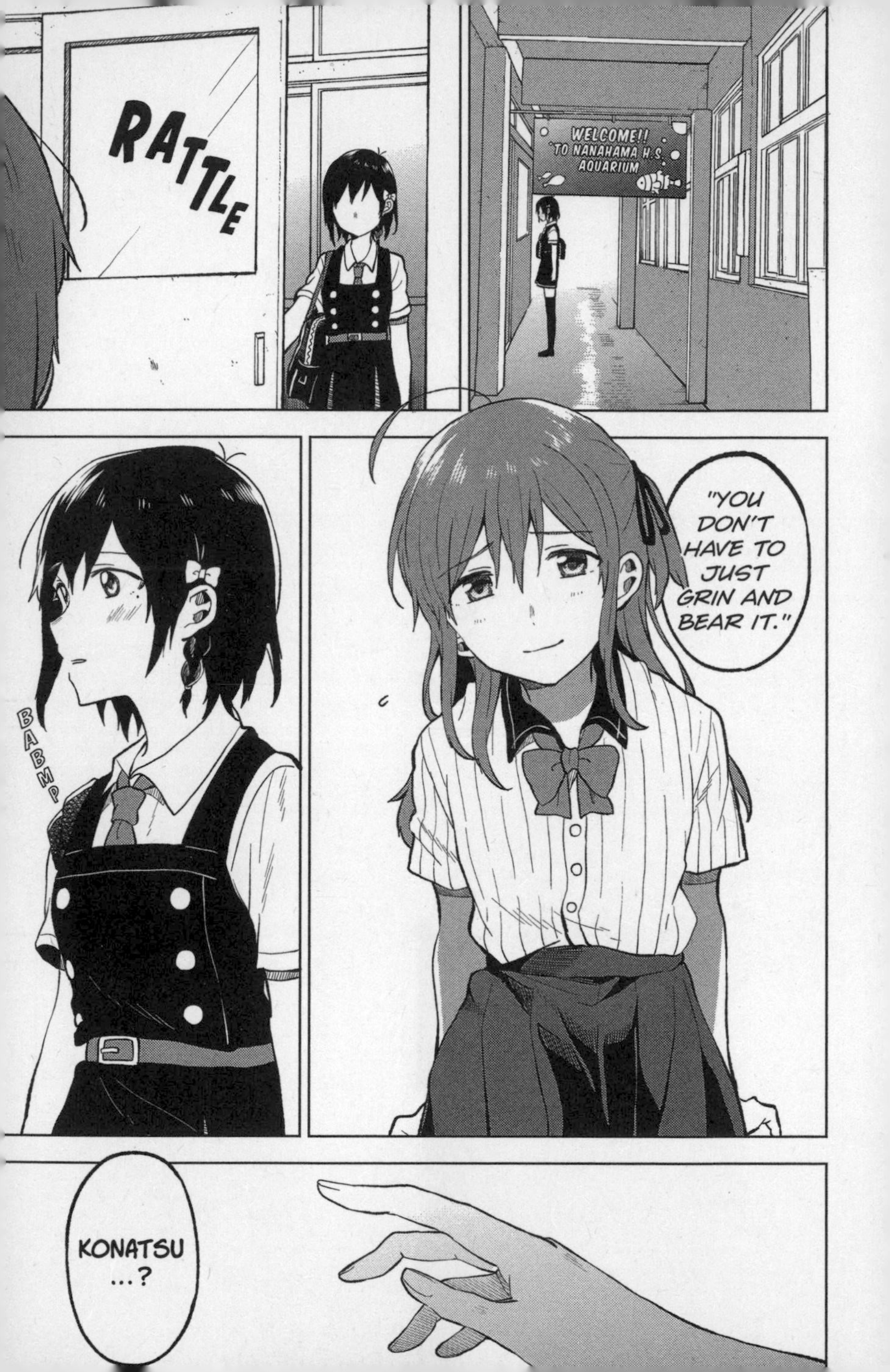
WELCOME!! TO NANAHAMA H.S. AQUARIUM
RATTLE
"YOU DON'T HAVE TO JUST GRIN AND BEAR IT."
BABMP
KONATSU ...?

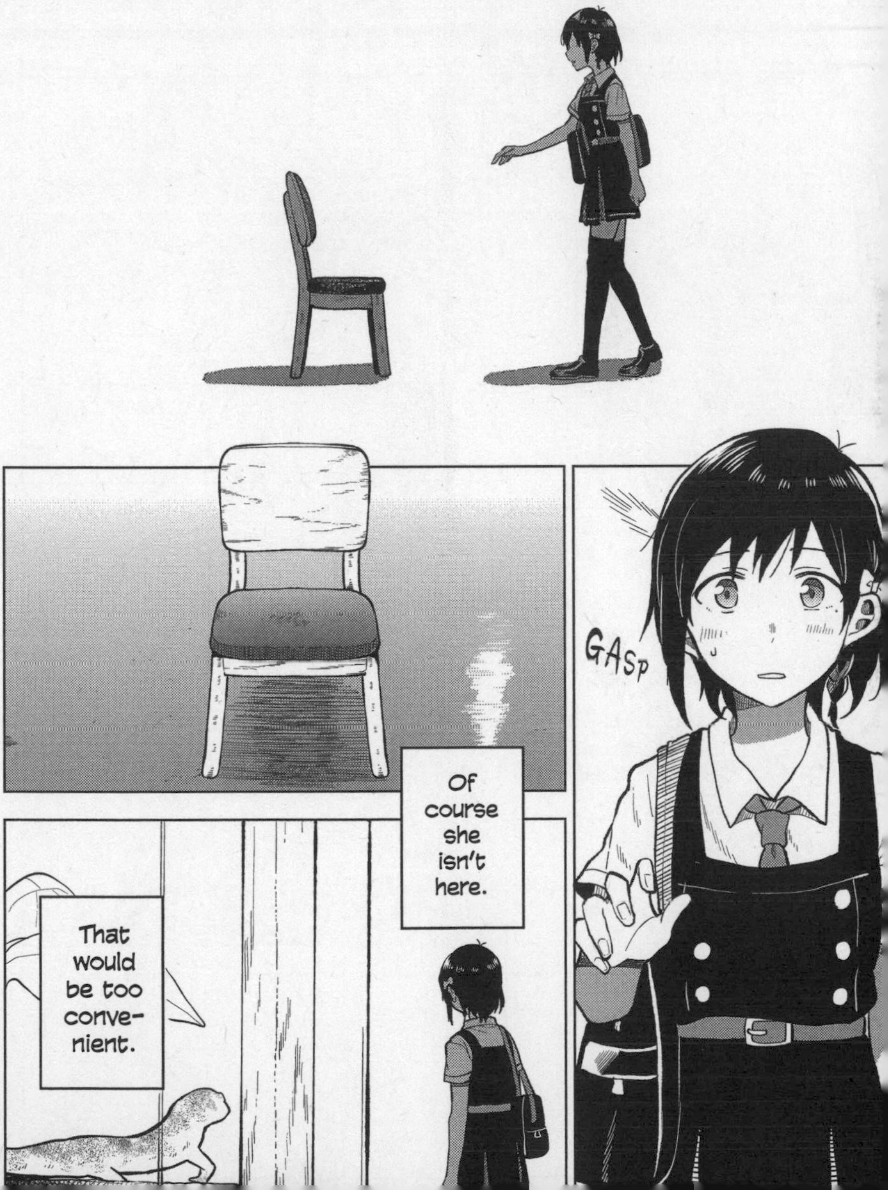
GASP
Of course she isn't here.
That would be too convenient.

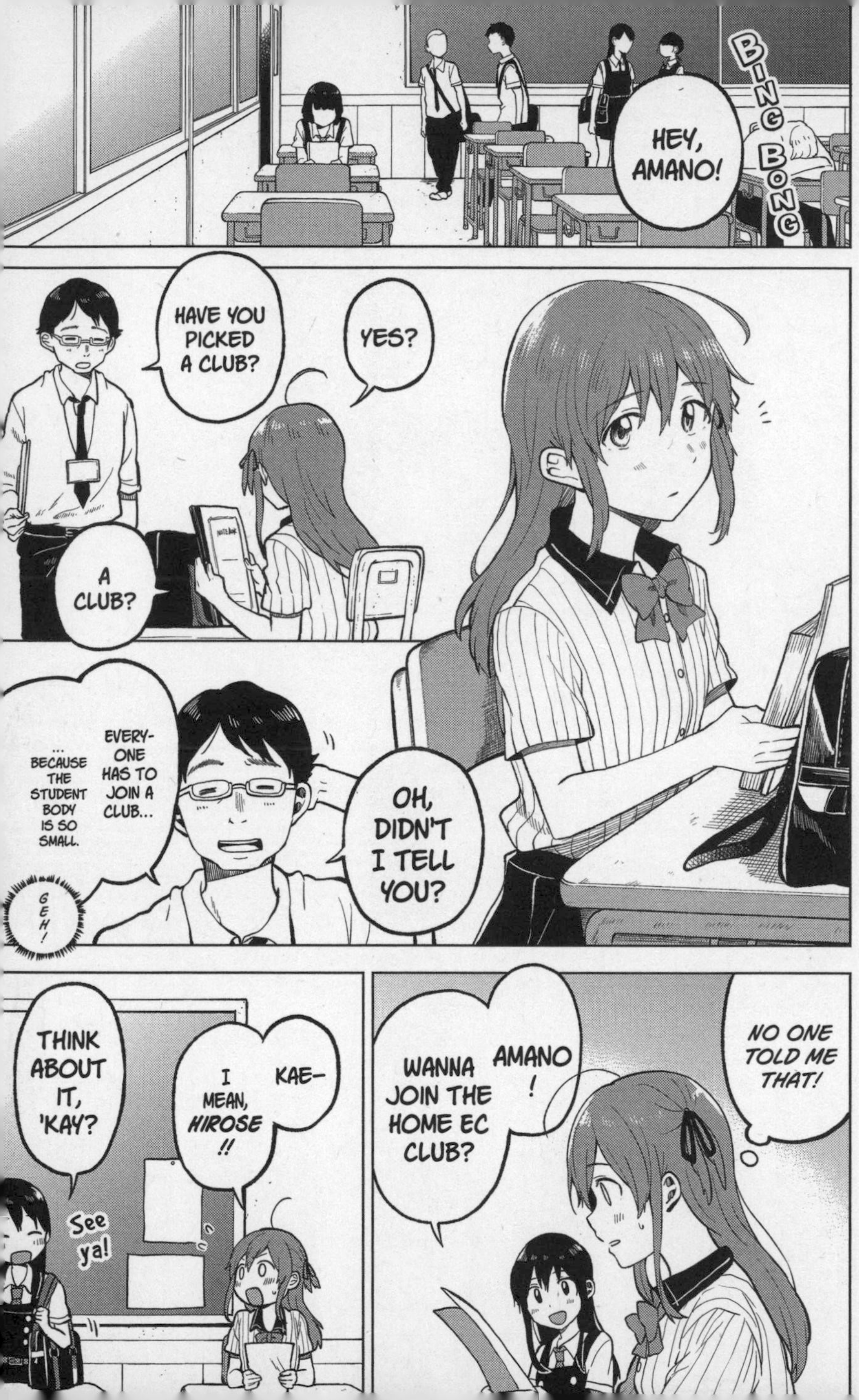
BING BONG
HEY, AMANO!
YES?
HAVE YOU PICKED A CLUB?
A CLUB?
OH, DIDN'T I TELL YOU?
EVERY-ONE HAS TO JOIN A CLUB...
...BECAUSE THE STUDENT BODY IS SO SMALL.
GEH!
NO ONE TOLD ME THAT!
AMANO!
WANNA JOIN THE HOME EC CLUB?
KAE-
I MEAN, HIROSE!!
THINK ABOUT IT, 'KAY?
See ya!

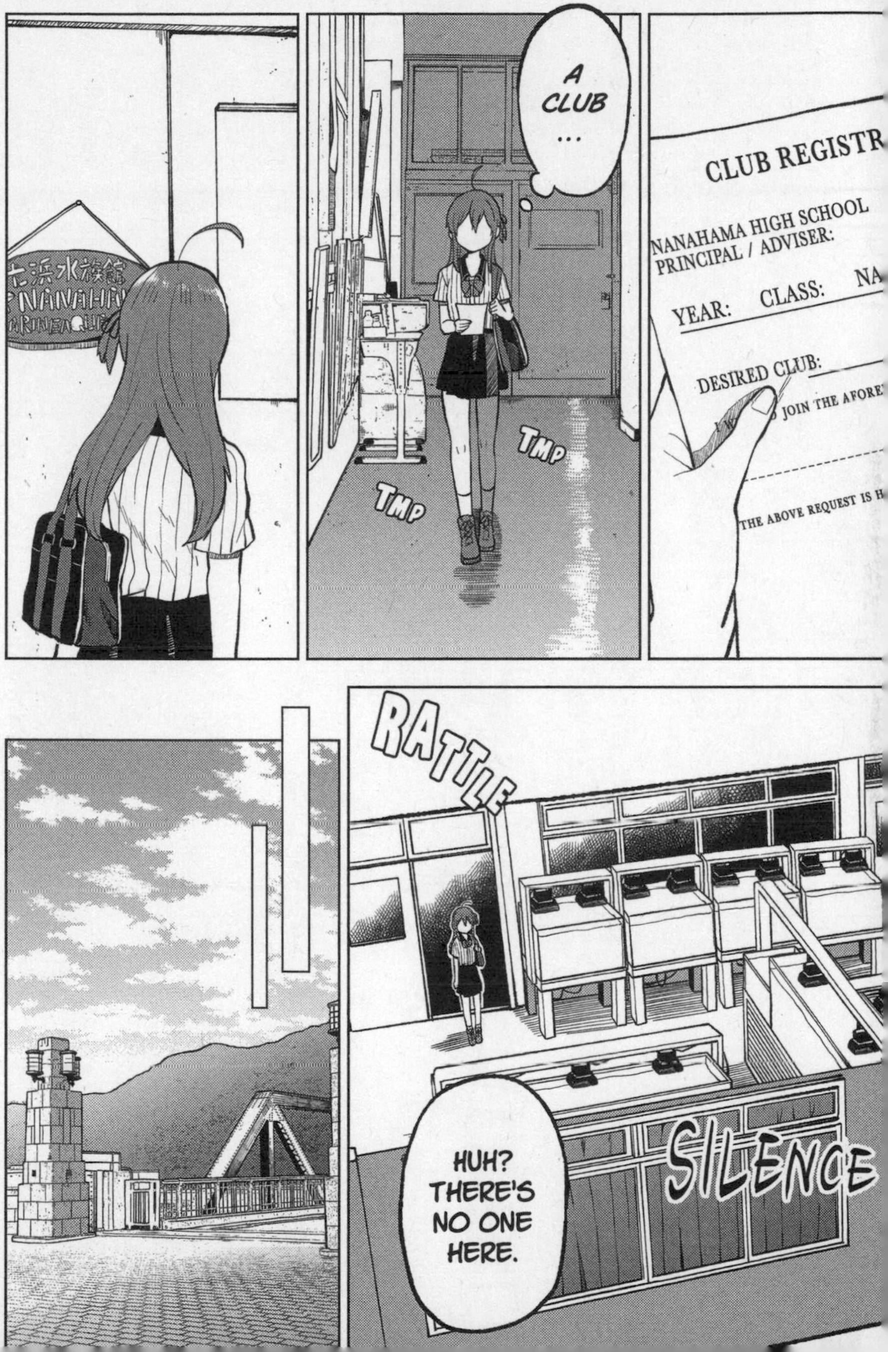
CLUB REGISTR
NANAHAMA HIGH SCHOOL
PRINCIPAL / ADVISER:
YEAR: CLASS: NA
DESIRED CLUB:
JOIN THE AFORE
THE ABOVE REQUEST IS H
A CLUB ...
TMP
TMP
RATTLE
HUH? THERE'S NO ONE HERE.
SILENCE

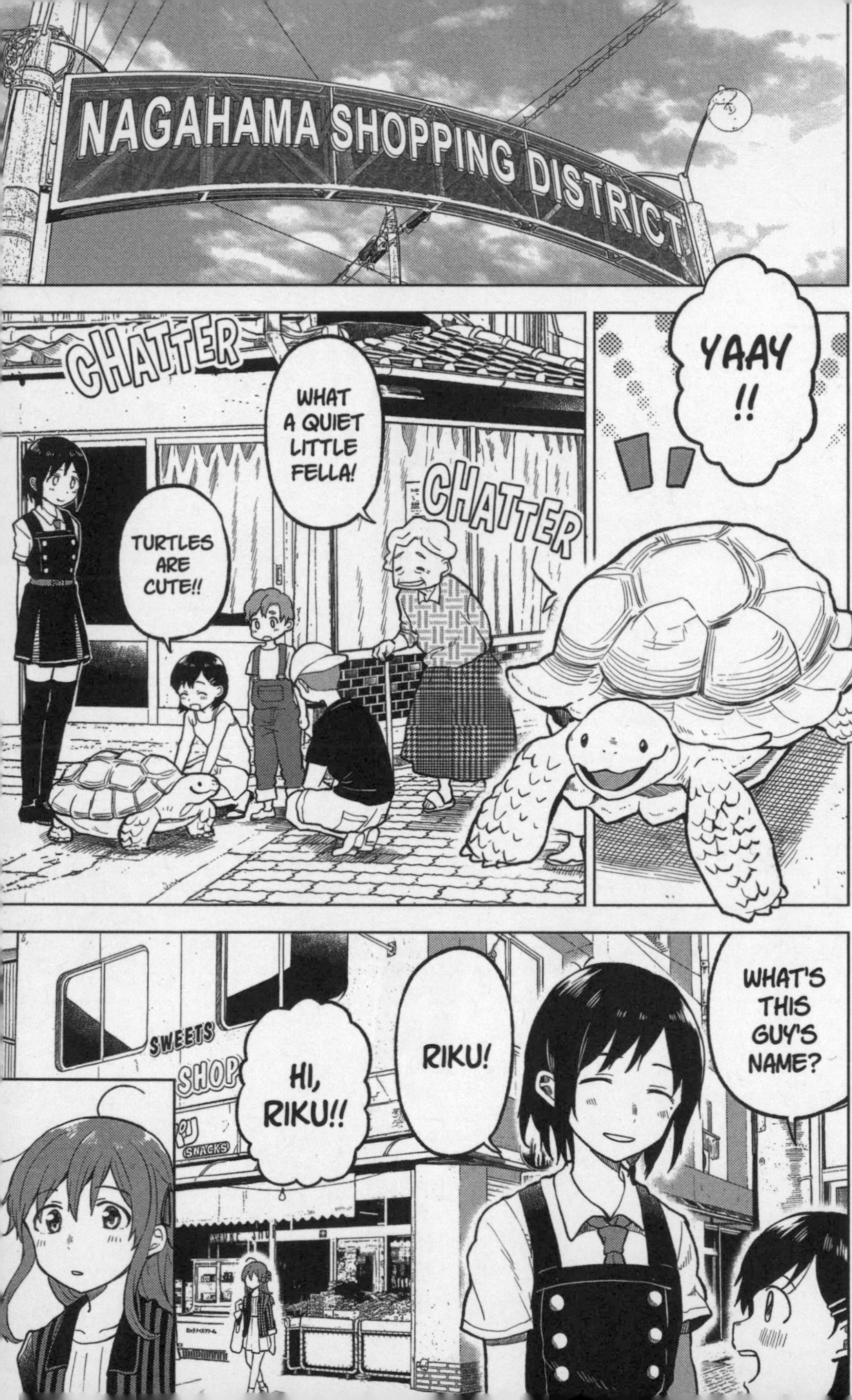
NAGAHAMA SHOPPING DISTRICT
YAAY!!
CHATTER
WHAT A QUIET LITTLE FELLA!
CHATTER
TURTLES ARE CUTE!!
WHAT'S THIS GUY'S NAME?
RIKU!
HI, RIKU!!
SWEETS SHOP
SNACKS

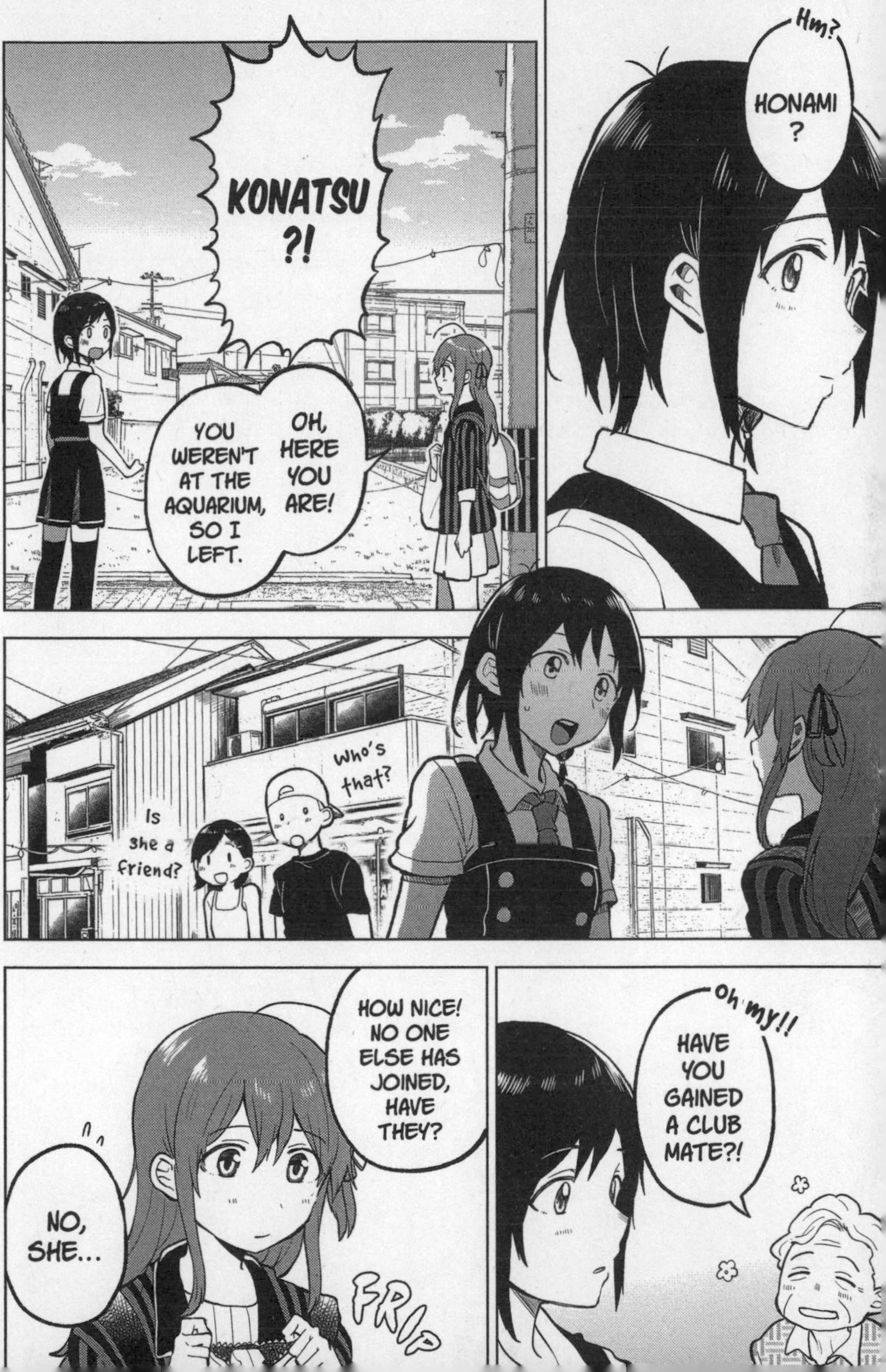
Hm?
HONAMI?
KONATSU?!
OH, HERE YOU ARE!
YOU WEREN'T AT THE AQUARIUM, SO I LEFT.
Who's that?
Is she a friend?
Oh my!!
HAVE YOU GAINED A CLUB MATE?!
HOW NICE! NO ONE ELSE HAS JOINED, HAVE THEY?
NO, SHE...
FRIP

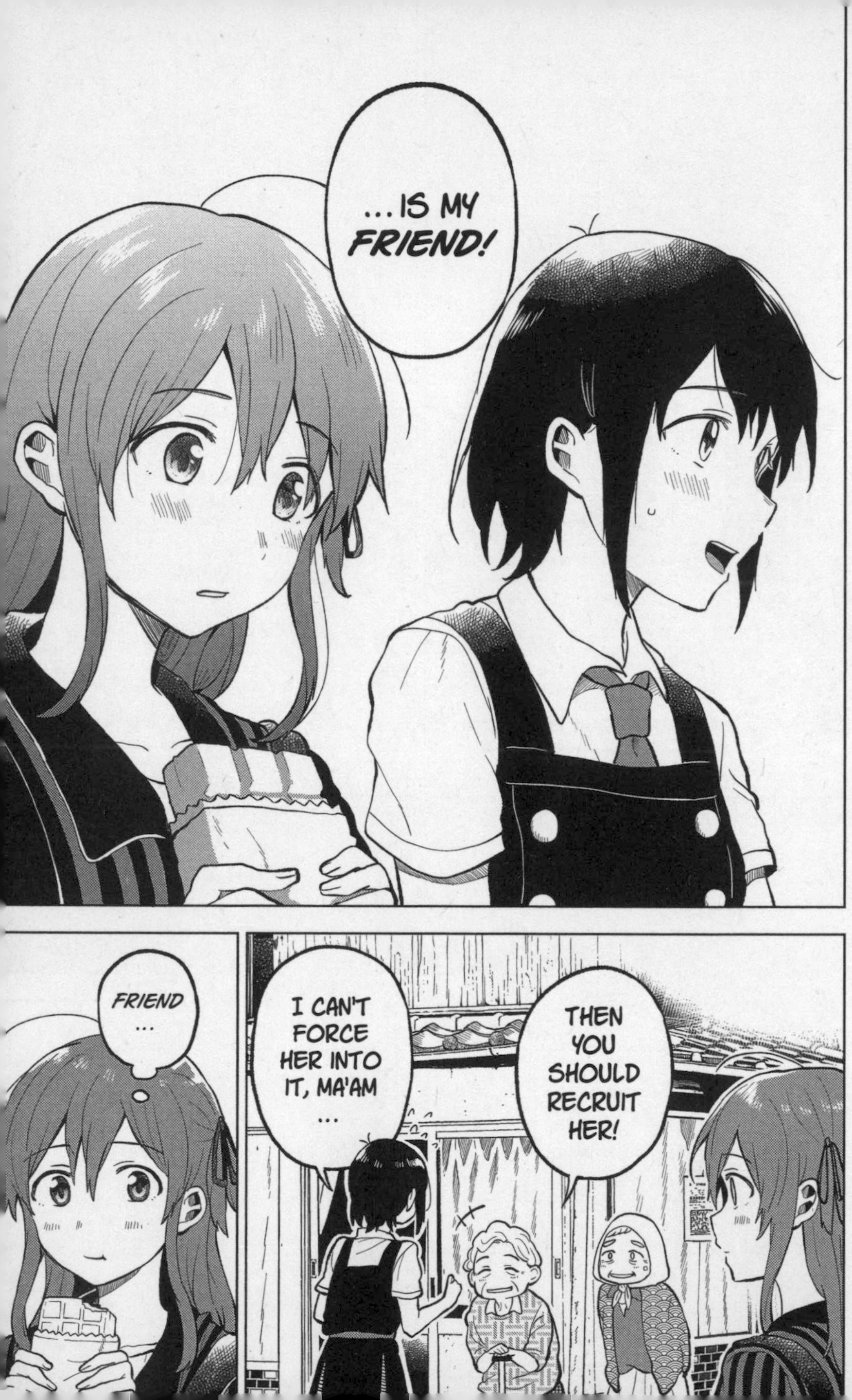
...IS MY FRIEND!
THEN YOU SHOULD RECRUIT HER!
I CAN'T FORCE HER INTO IT, MA'AM ...
FRIEND ...

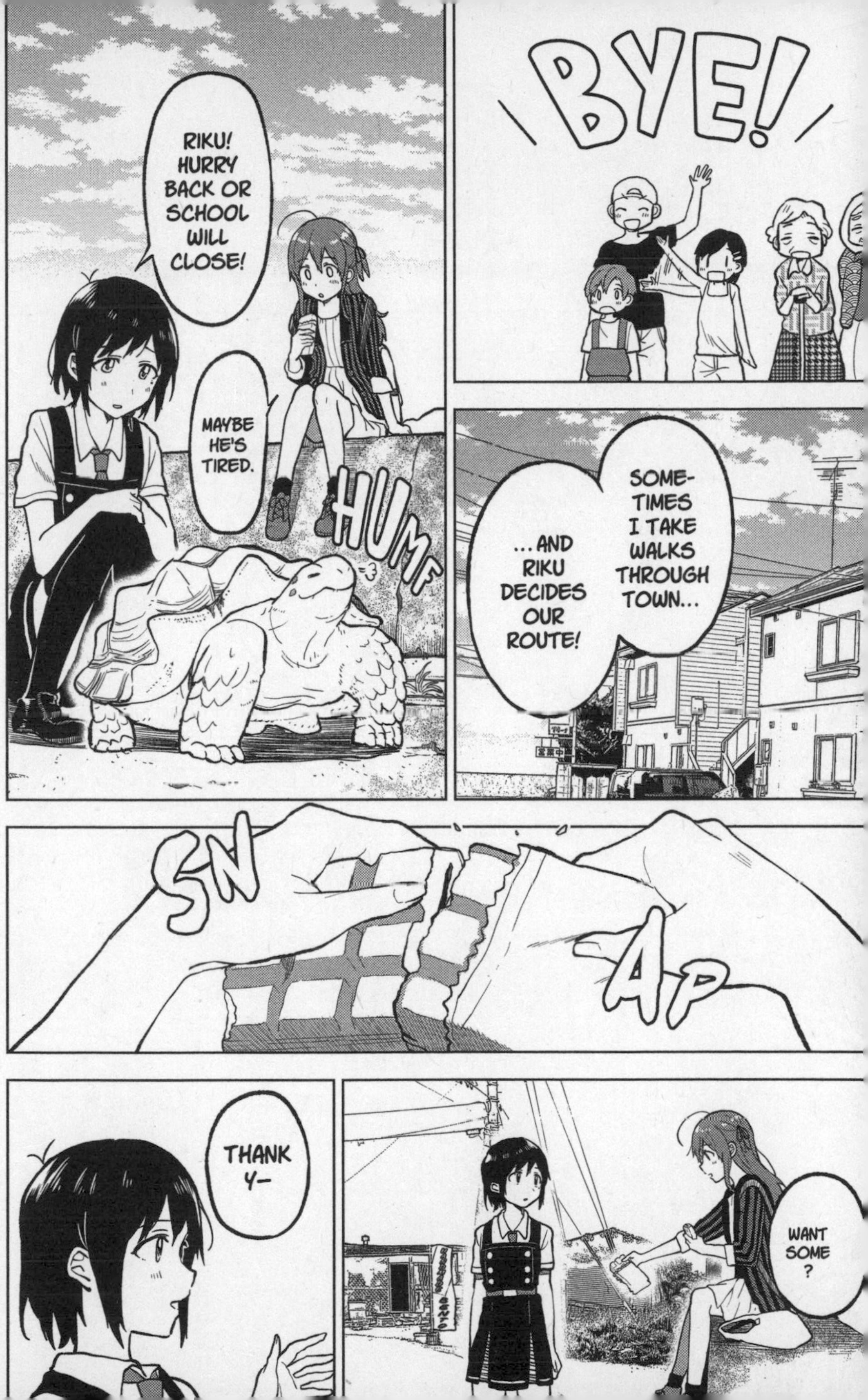
BYE!
SOME-TIMES I TAKE WALKS THROUGH TOWN...
...AND RIKU DECIDES OUR ROUTE!
RIKU! HURRY BACK OR SCHOOL WILL CLOSE!
MAYBE HE'S TIRED.
HUMF
SNAP
WANT SOME?
THANK Y-

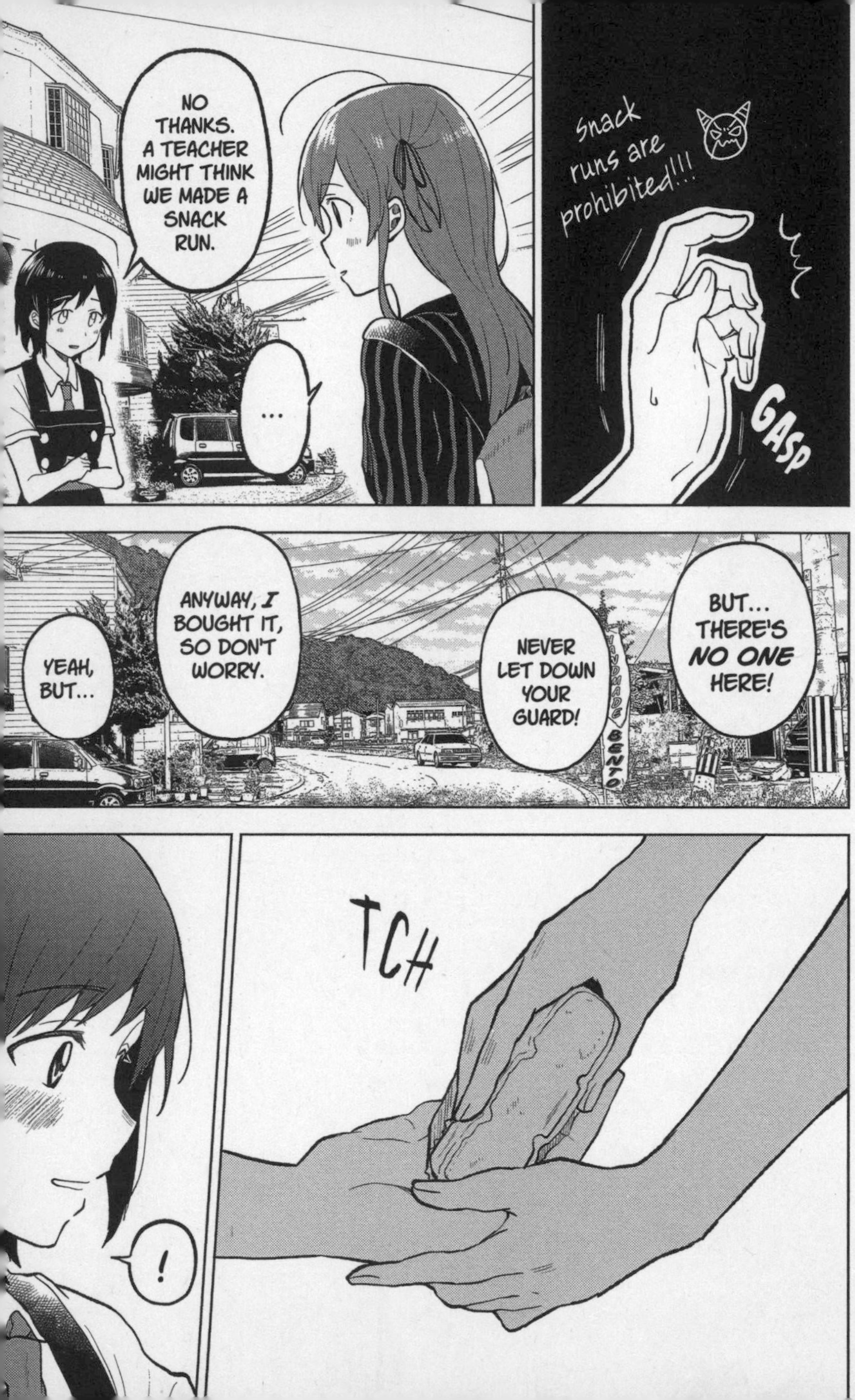

Snack runs are prohibited!!!
GASP
NO THANKS. A TEACHER MIGHT THINK WE MADE A SNACK RUN.
...
BUT... THERE'S *NO ONE* HERE!
NEVER LET DOWN YOUR GUARD!
HANDMADE BENTO
ANYWAY, *I* BOUGHT IT, SO DON'T WORRY.
YEAH, BUT...
TCH
!

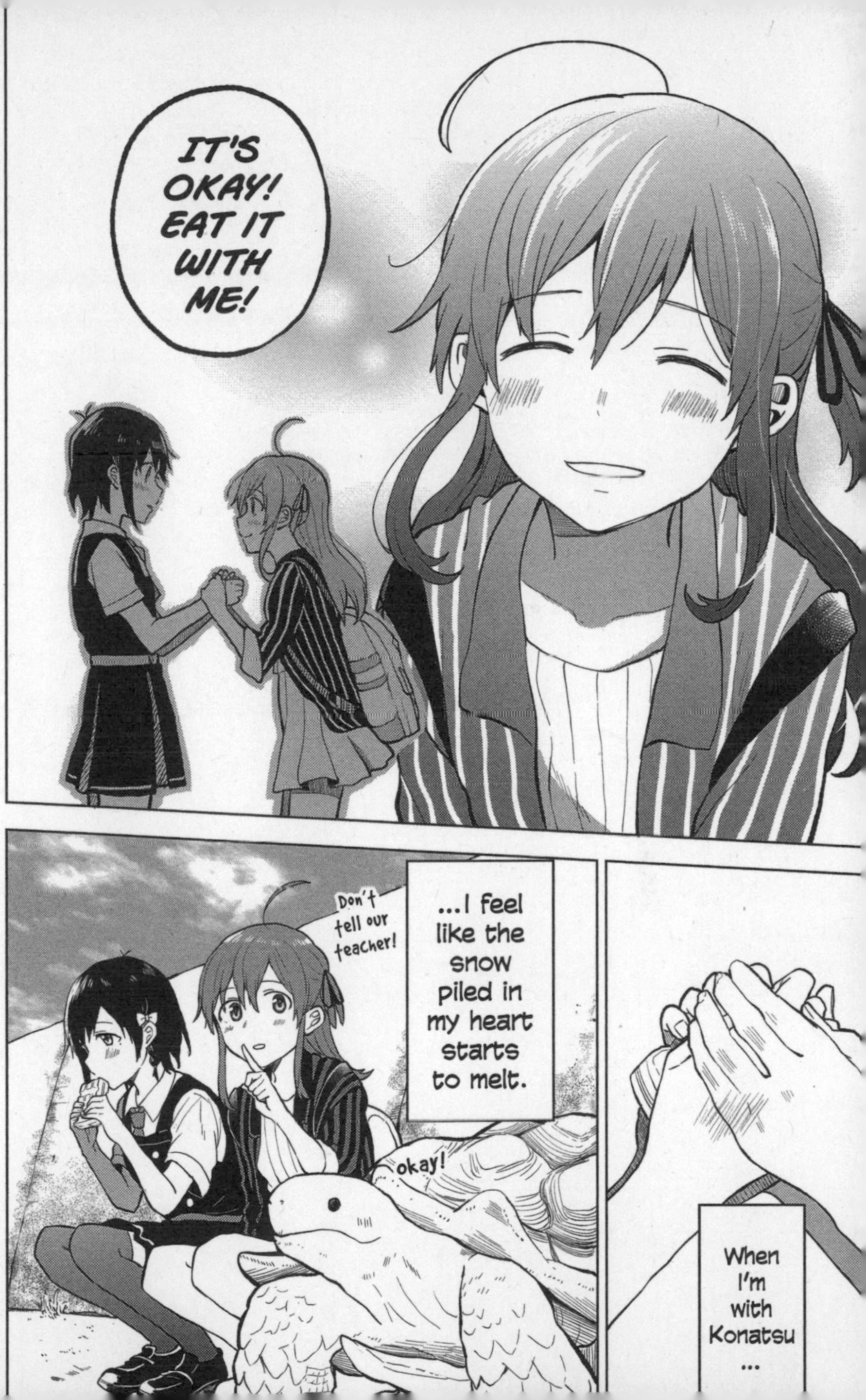
IT'S OKAY! EAT IT WITH ME!
When I'm with Konatsu ...
...I feel like the snow piled in my heart starts to melt.
Don't tell our teacher!
okay!

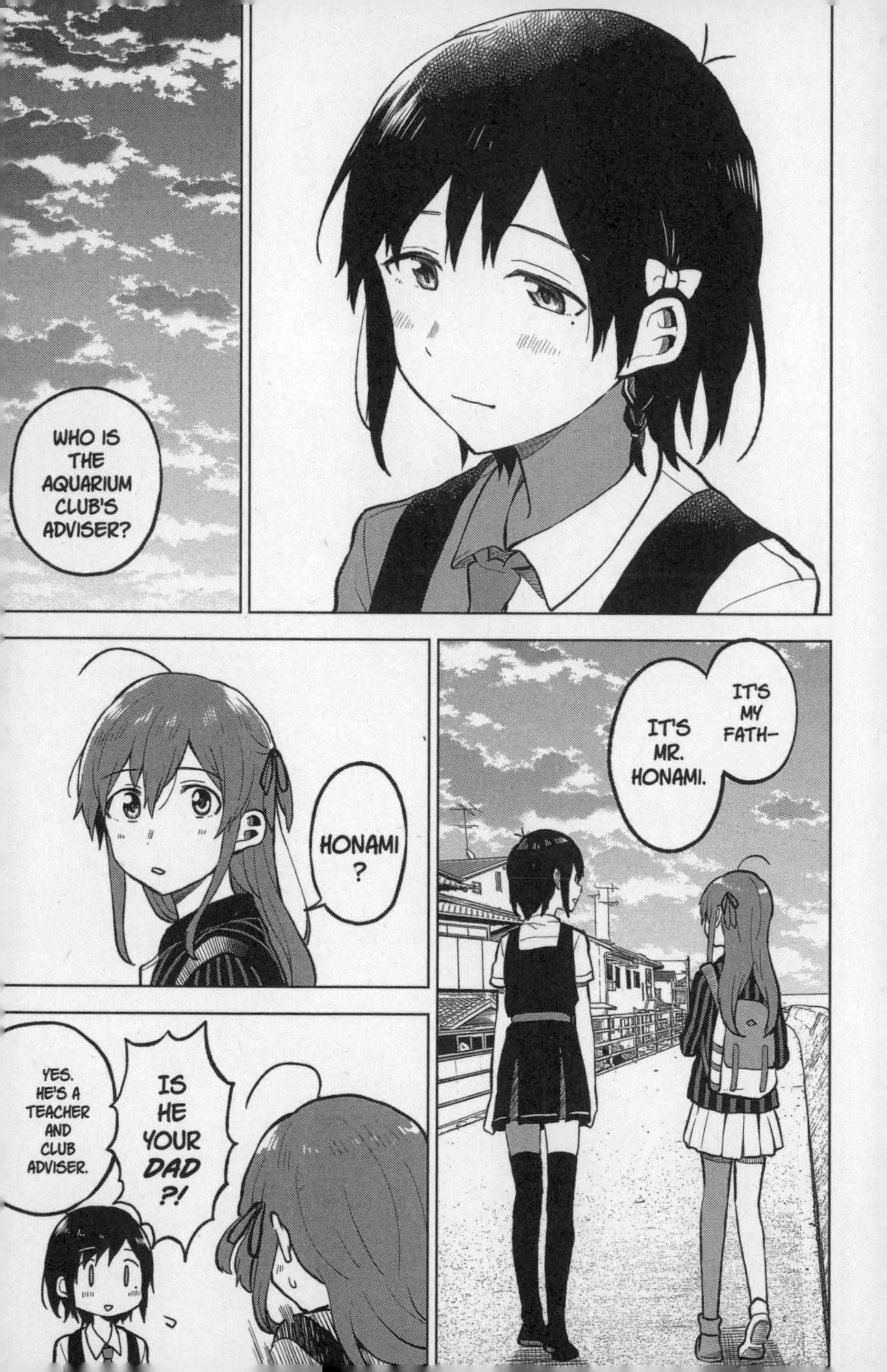
WHO IS THE AQUARIUM CLUB'S ADVISER?
IT'S MY FATH—
IT'S MR. HONAMI.
HONAMI?
IS HE YOUR *DAD*?!
YES. HE'S A TEACHER AND CLUB ADVISER.

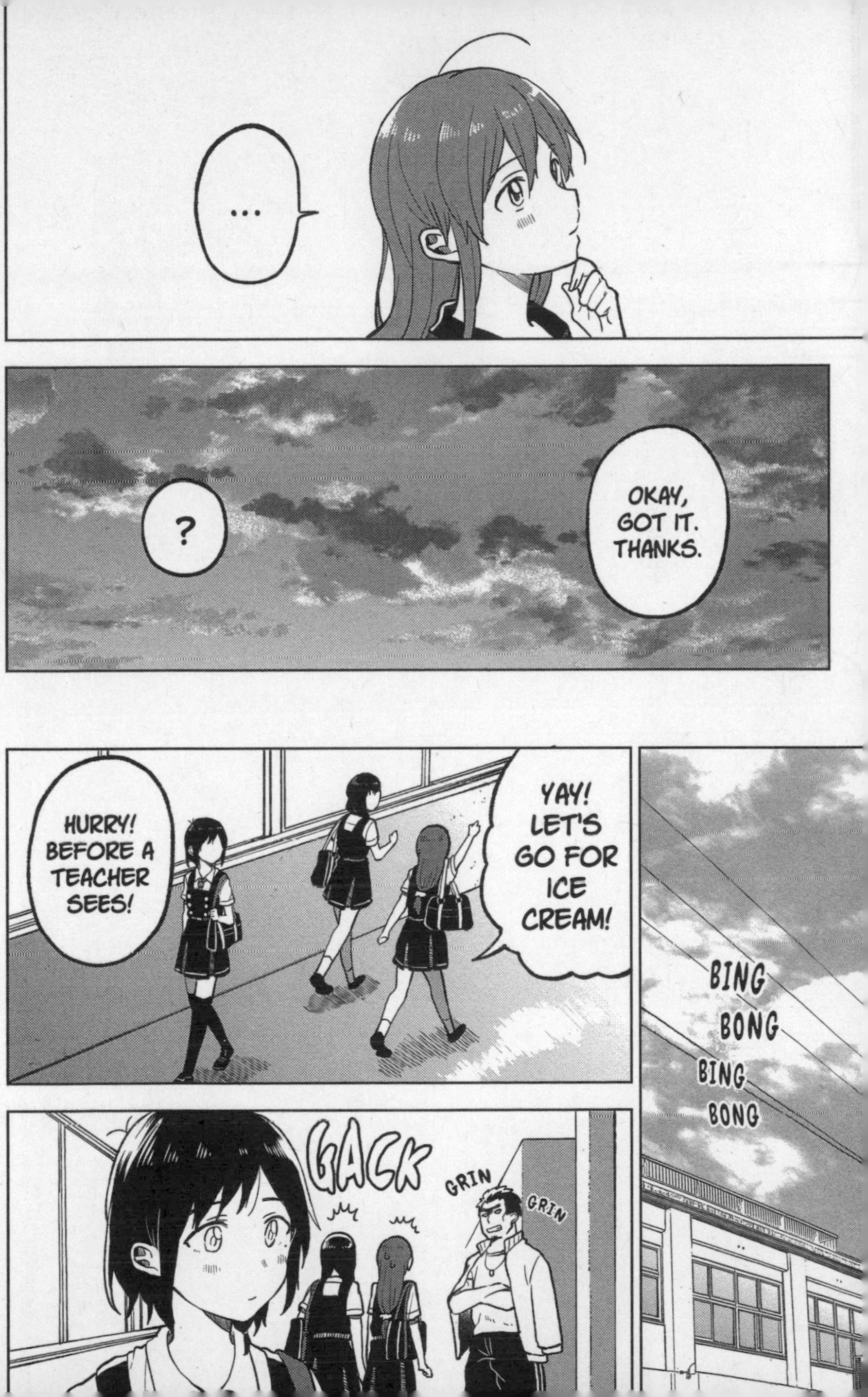
...
OKAY, GOT IT. THANKS.
?
BING
BONG
BING
BONG
YAY! LET'S GO FOR ICE CREAM!
HURRY! BEFORE A TEACHER SEES!
GRIN
GRIN
GACK

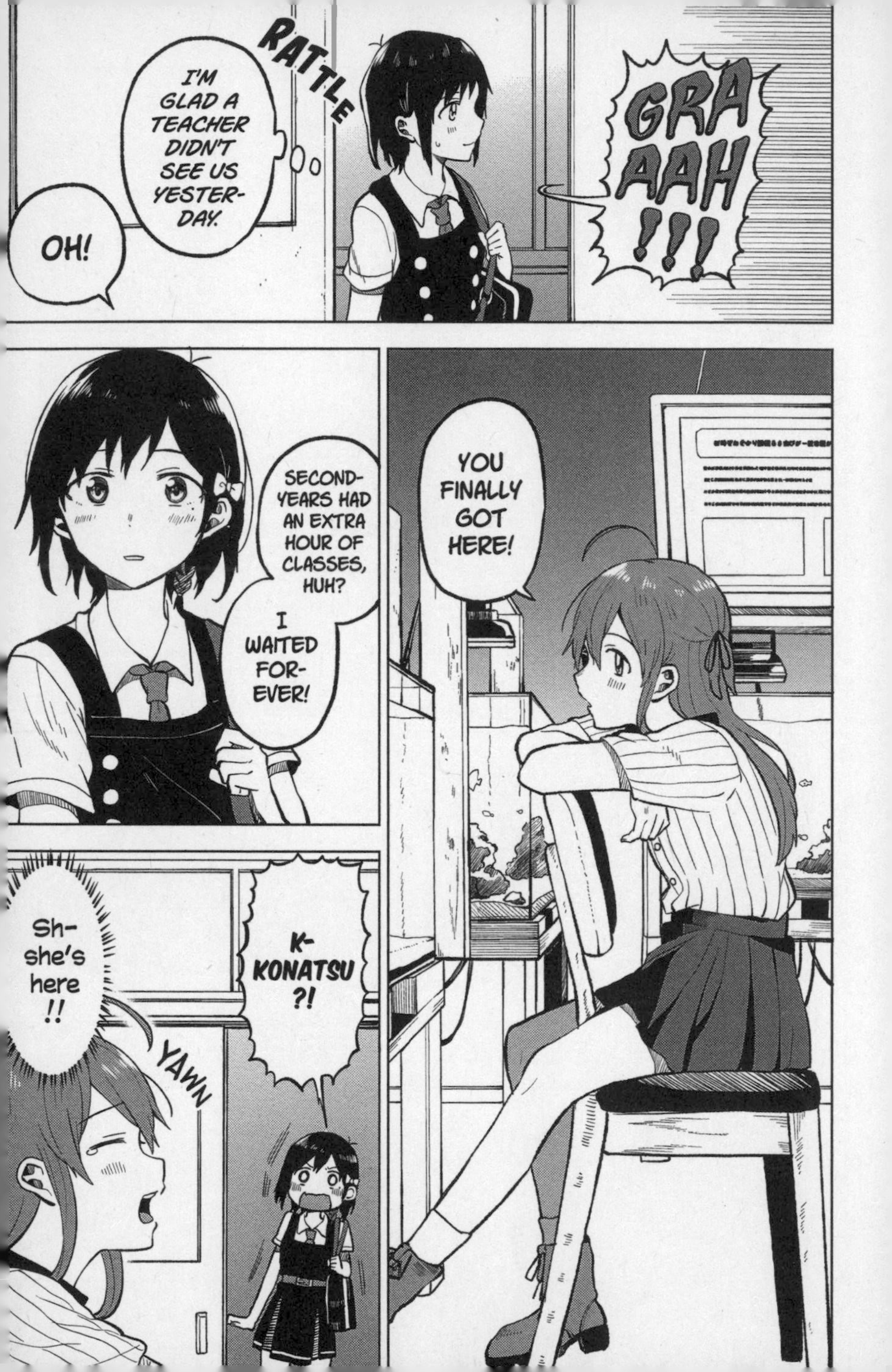
GRAAAH!!!
RATTLE
I'M GLAD A TEACHER DIDN'T SEE US YESTERDAY.
OH!
YOU FINALLY GOT HERE!
SECOND-YEARS HAD AN EXTRA HOUR OF CLASSES, HUH?
I WAITED FOREVER!
K-KONATSU?!
YAWN
Sh-she's here!!

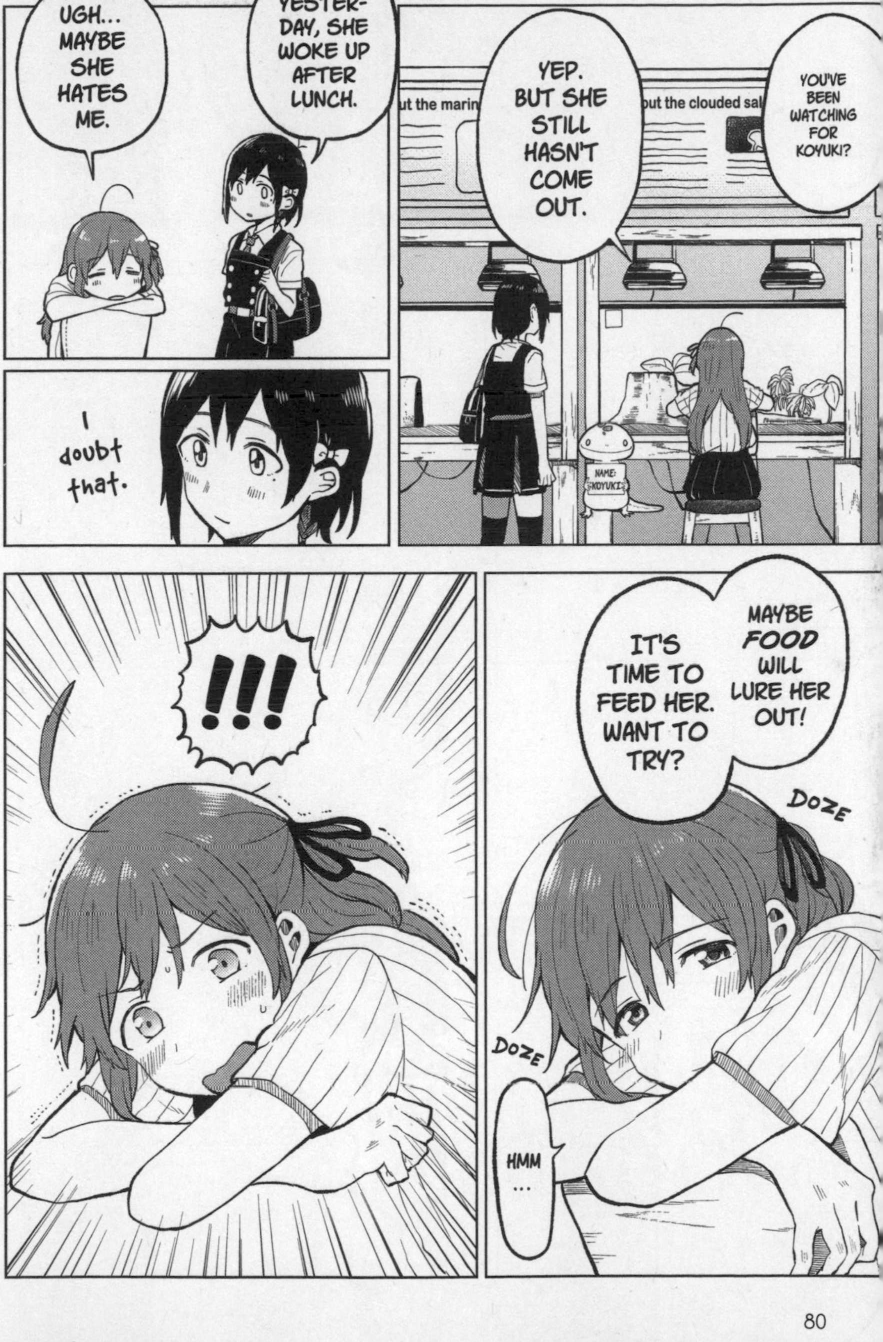
YOU'VE BEEN WATCHING FOR KOYUKI?
YEP. BUT SHE STILL HASN'T COME OUT.
ut the marin
out the clouded sal
NAME: KOYUKI
YESTER-DAY, SHE WOKE UP AFTER LUNCH.
UGH... MAYBE SHE HATES ME.
I doubt that.
MAYBE FOOD WILL LURE HER OUT!
IT'S TIME TO FEED HER. WANT TO TRY?
DOZE
DOZE
HMM ...
!!!

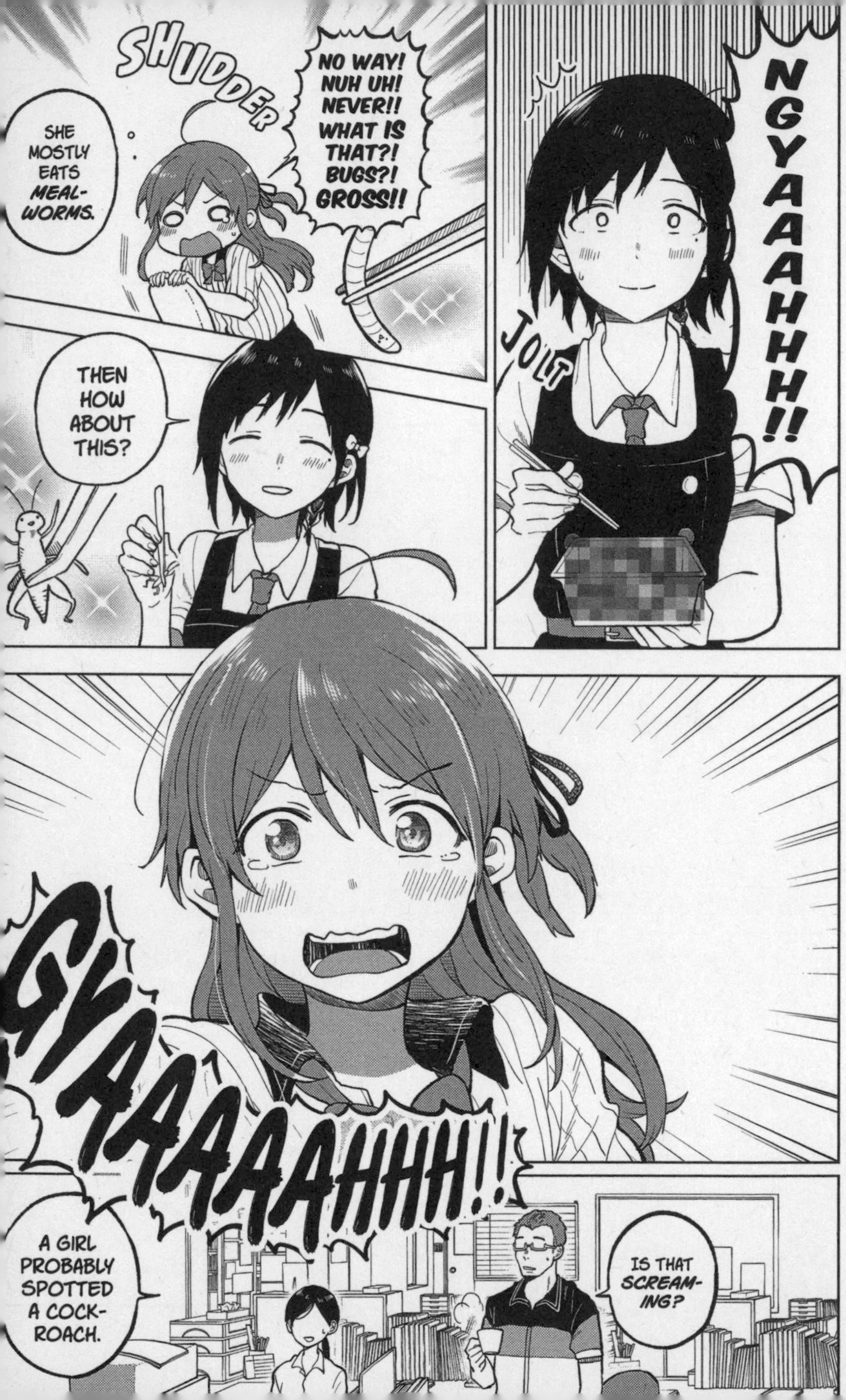
NGYAAAAHHHH!!
JOLT
SHE MOSTLY EATS MEAL-WORMS.
NO WAY! NUH UH! NEVER!! WHAT IS THAT?! BUGS?! GROSS!!
SHUDDER
THEN HOW ABOUT THIS?
GYAAAAAHHH!!
IS THAT SCREAM-ING?
A GIRL PROBABLY SPOTTED A COCK-ROACH.

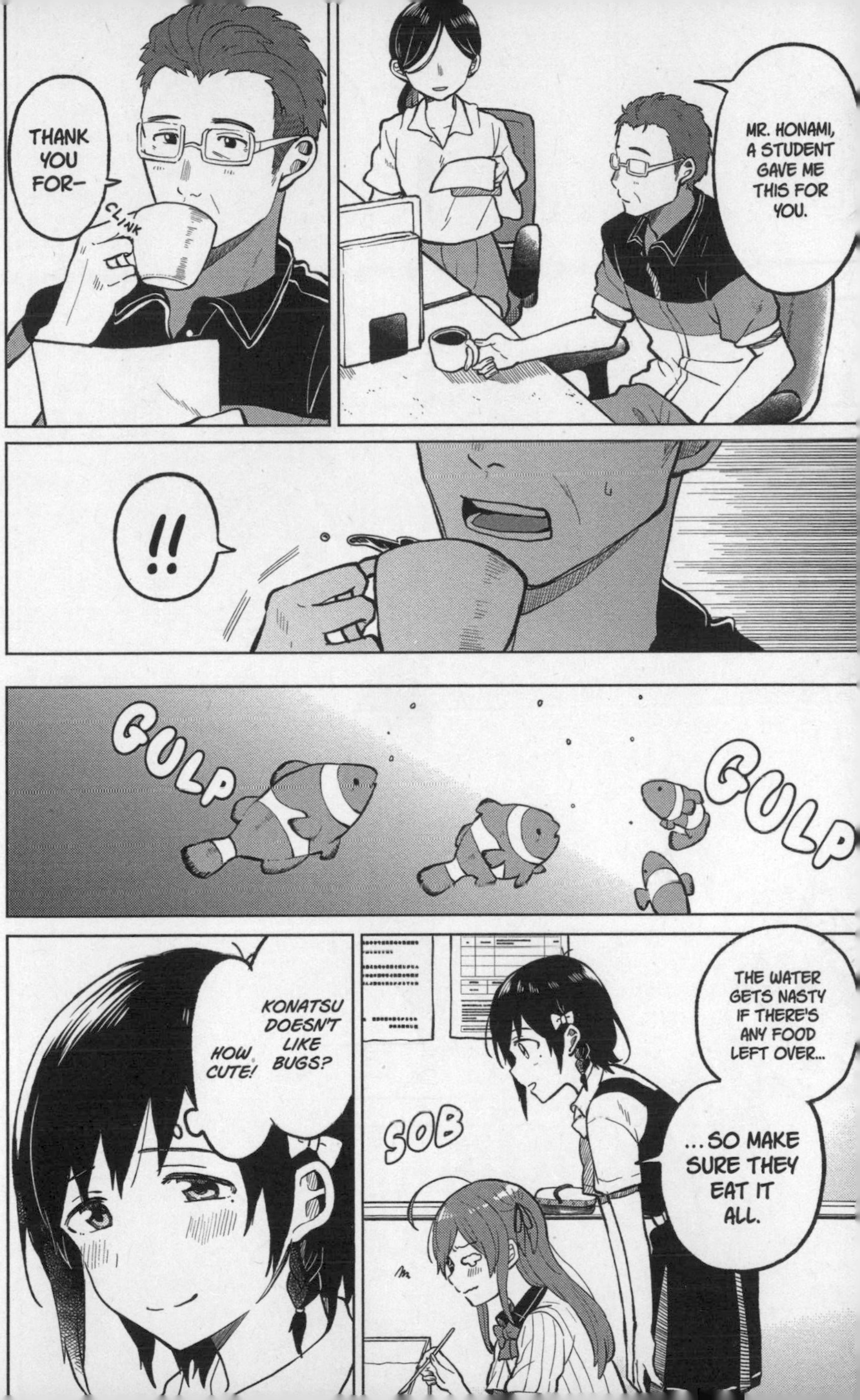
MR. HONAMI, A STUDENT GAVE ME THIS FOR YOU.
THANK YOU FOR–
CLINK
!!
GULP
GULP
THE WATER GETS NASTY IF THERE'S ANY FOOD LEFT OVER...
...SO MAKE SURE THEY EAT IT ALL.
SOB
KONATSU DOESN'T LIKE BUGS?
HOW CUTE!

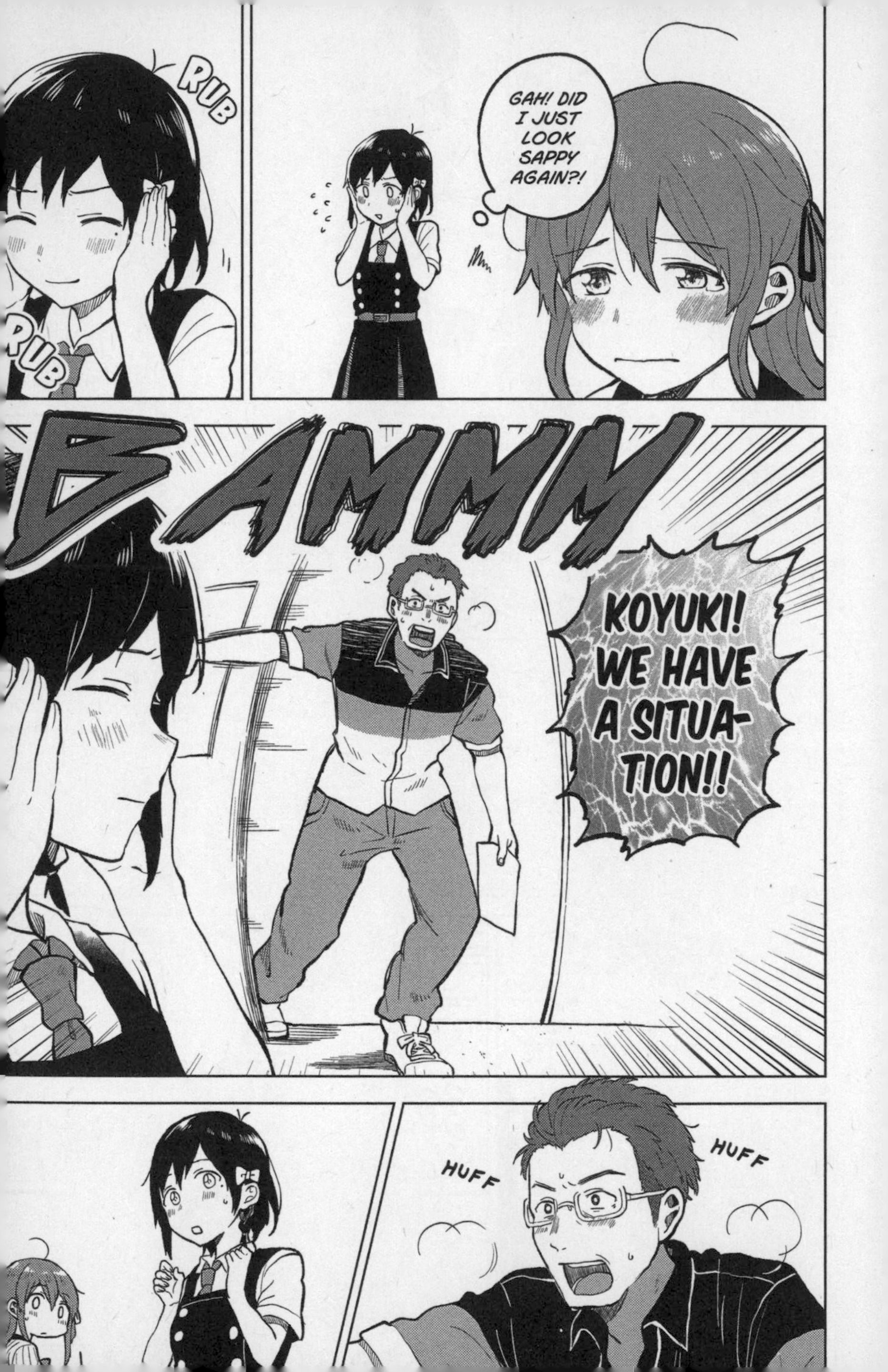
GAH! DID I JUST LOOK SAPPY AGAIN?!
RUB
RUB
BAMMM
KOYUKI! WE HAVE A SITUA-TION!!
HUFF
HUFF

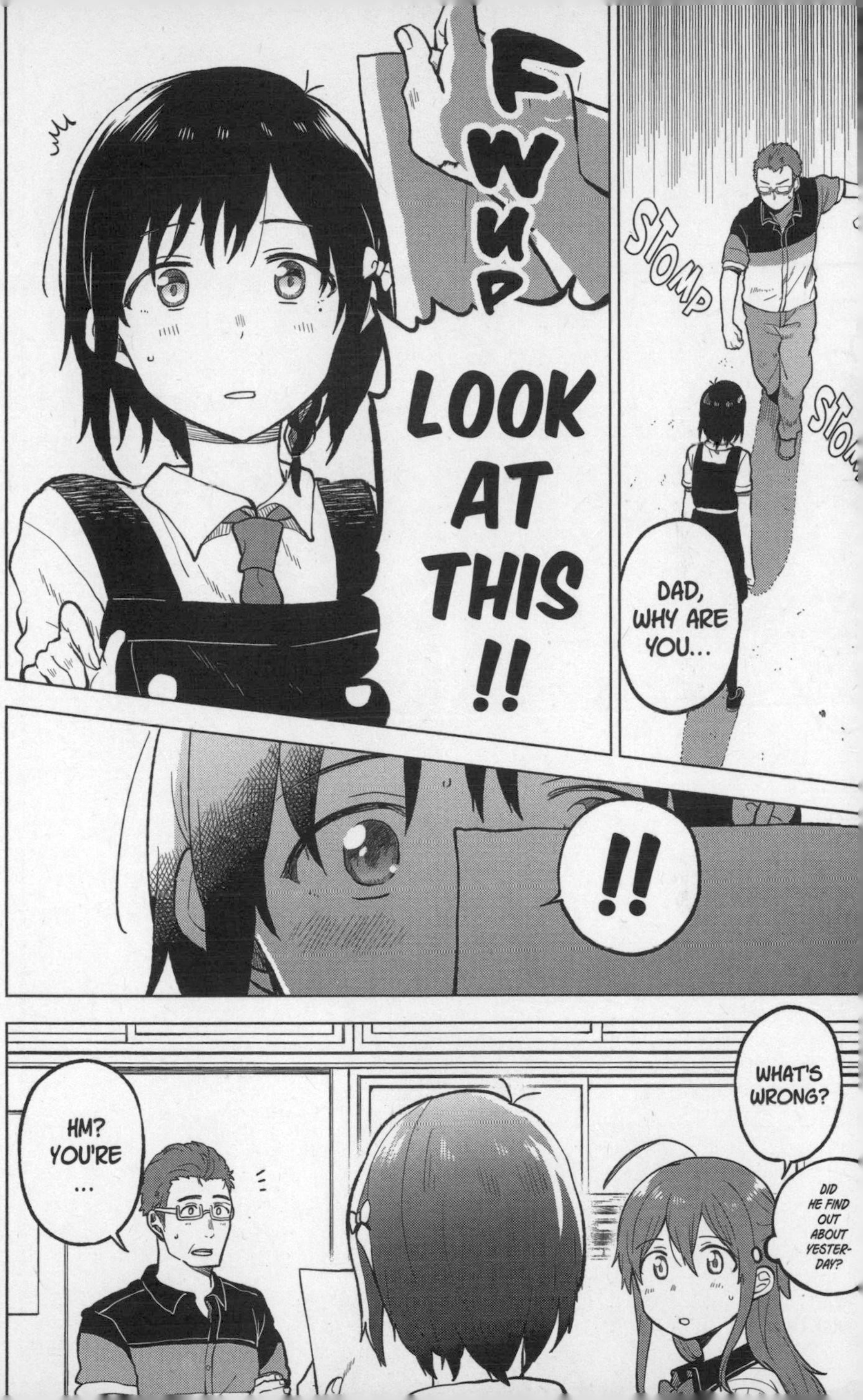
STOMP
STOMP
DAD, WHY ARE YOU...
FWUP
LOOK AT THIS!!
!!
WHAT'S WRONG?
DID HE FIND OUT ABOUT YESTERDAY?
HM? YOU'RE ...

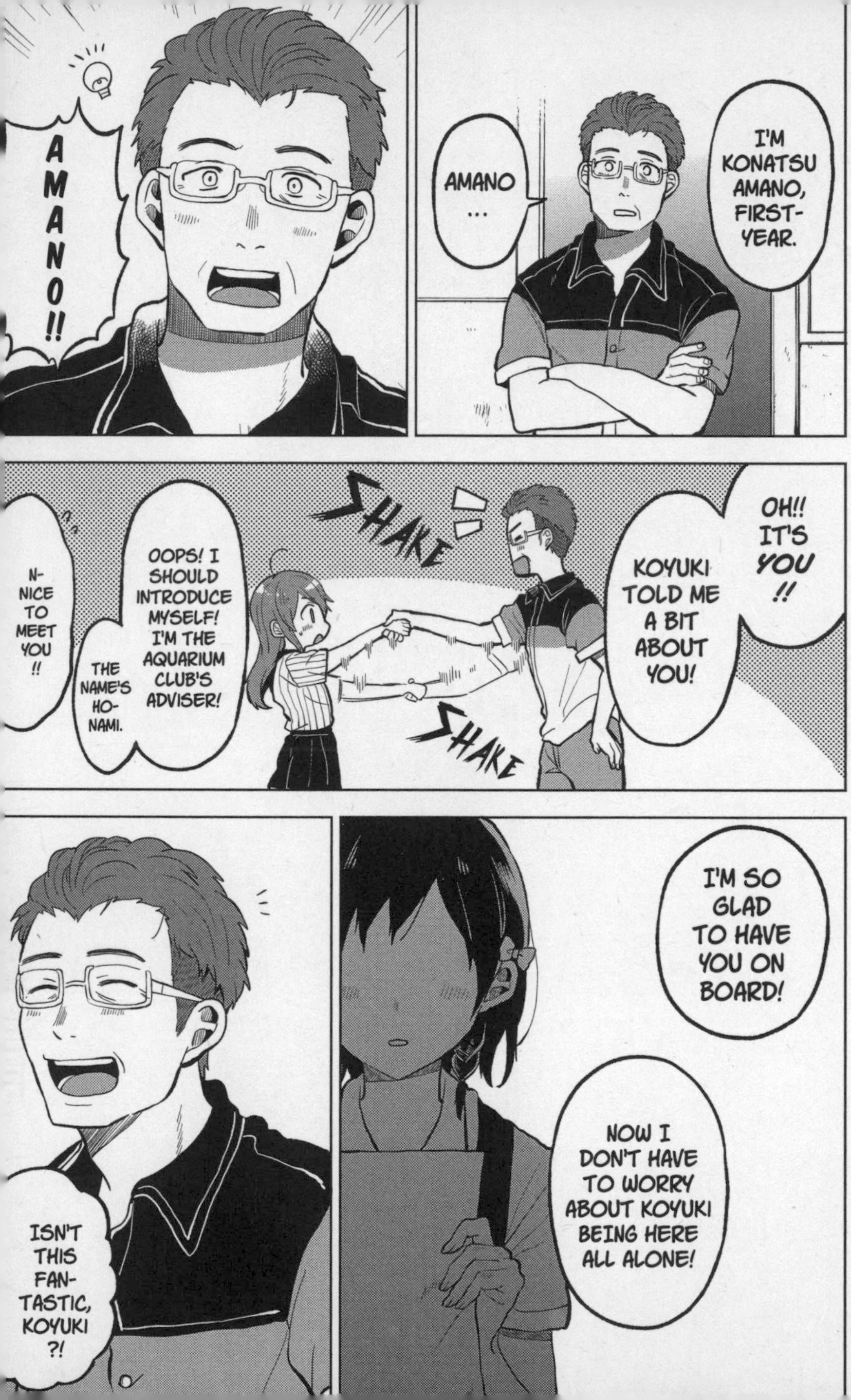
I'M KONATSU AMANO, FIRST-YEAR.
AMANO ...
AMANO!!
OH!! IT'S YOU!!
KOYUKI TOLD ME A BIT ABOUT YOU!
SHAKE
SHAKE
OOPS! I SHOULD INTRODUCE MYSELF! I'M THE AQUARIUM CLUB'S ADVISER!
THE NAME'S HO-NAMI.
N-NICE TO MEET YOU!!
I'M SO GLAD TO HAVE YOU ON BOARD!
NOW I DON'T HAVE TO WORRY ABOUT KOYUKI BEING HERE ALL ALONE!
ISN'T THIS FAN-TASTIC, KOYUKI?!

B REGISTRA
HOOL
NAME: KONATSU AMANO
AQUARIUM CLUB
NTIONED CLUB, SO
DATE:
SEAL:
SEAL:
SEAL:
SEAL:

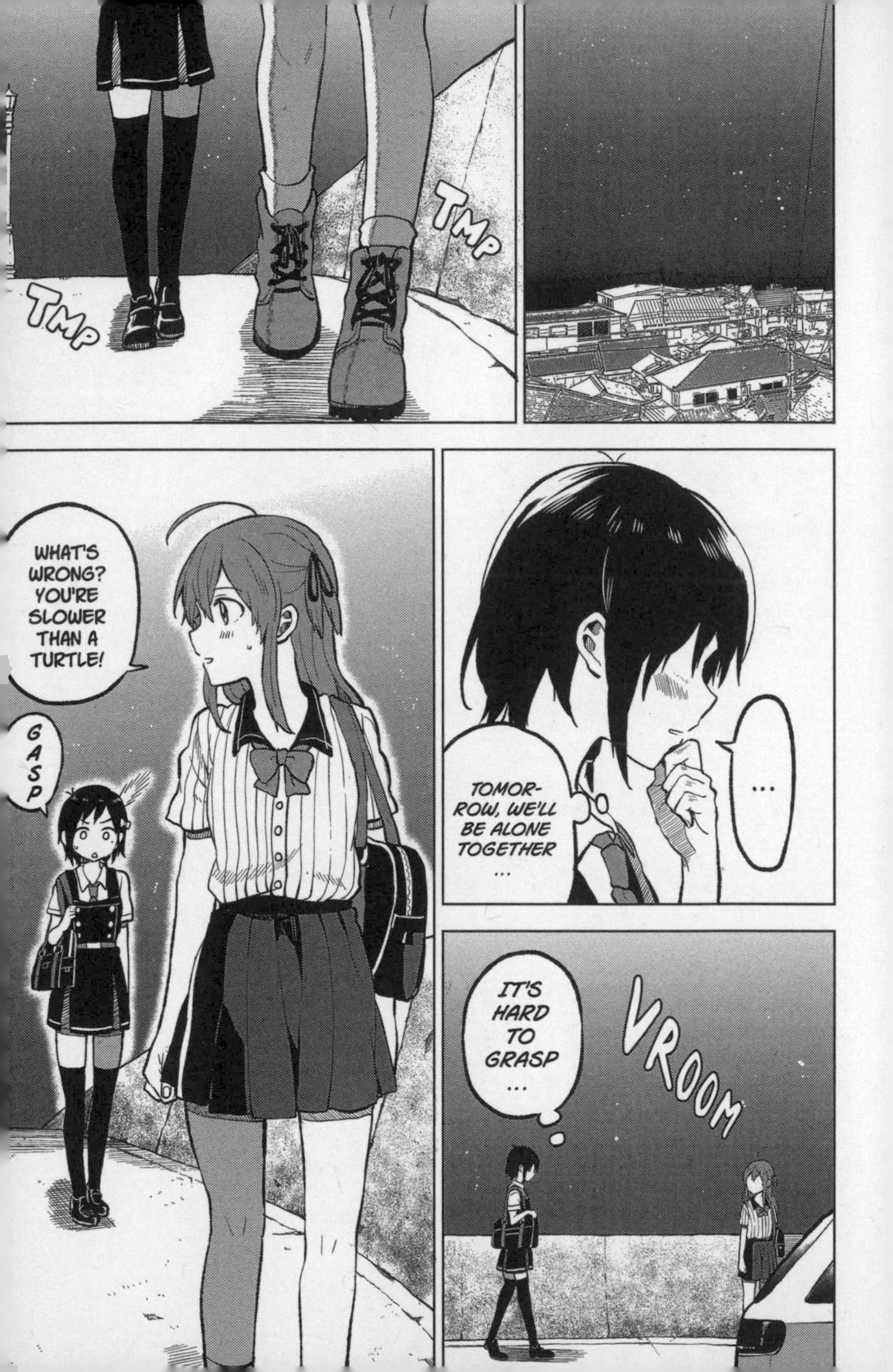
TMP
TMP
...
TOMORROW, WE'LL BE ALONE TOGETHER ...
IT'S HARD TO GRASP ...
VROOM
WHAT'S WRONG? YOU'RE SLOWER THAN A TURTLE!
GASP

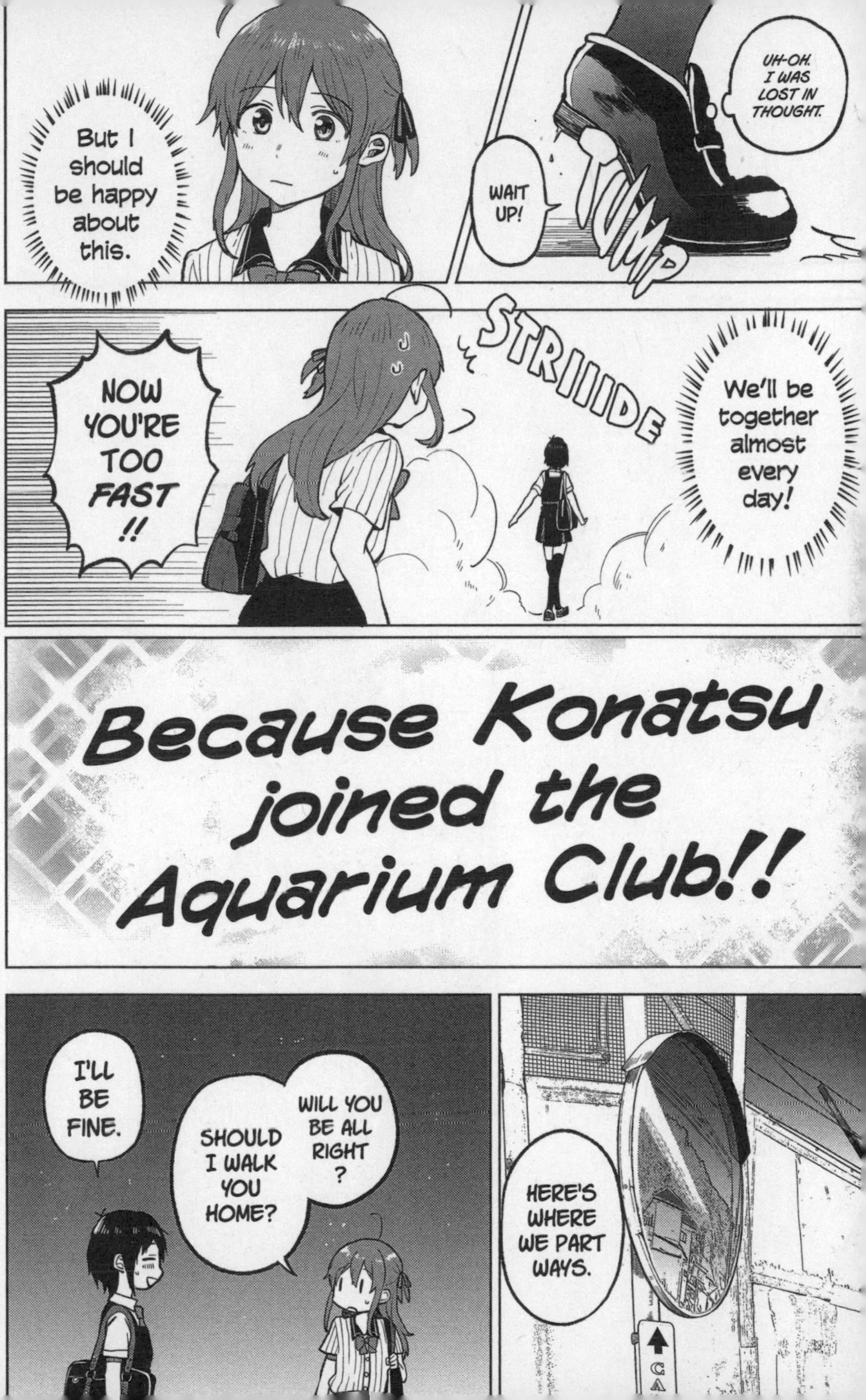
UH-OH. I WAS LOST IN THOUGHT.
WAIT UP!
JUMP
But I should be happy about this.
We'll be together almost every day!
STRIIIDE
NOW YOU'RE TOO FAST!!
Because Konatsu joined the Aquarium Club!!
HERE'S WHERE WE PART WAYS.
WILL YOU BE ALL RIGHT?
SHOULD I WALK YOU HOME?
I'LL BE FINE.

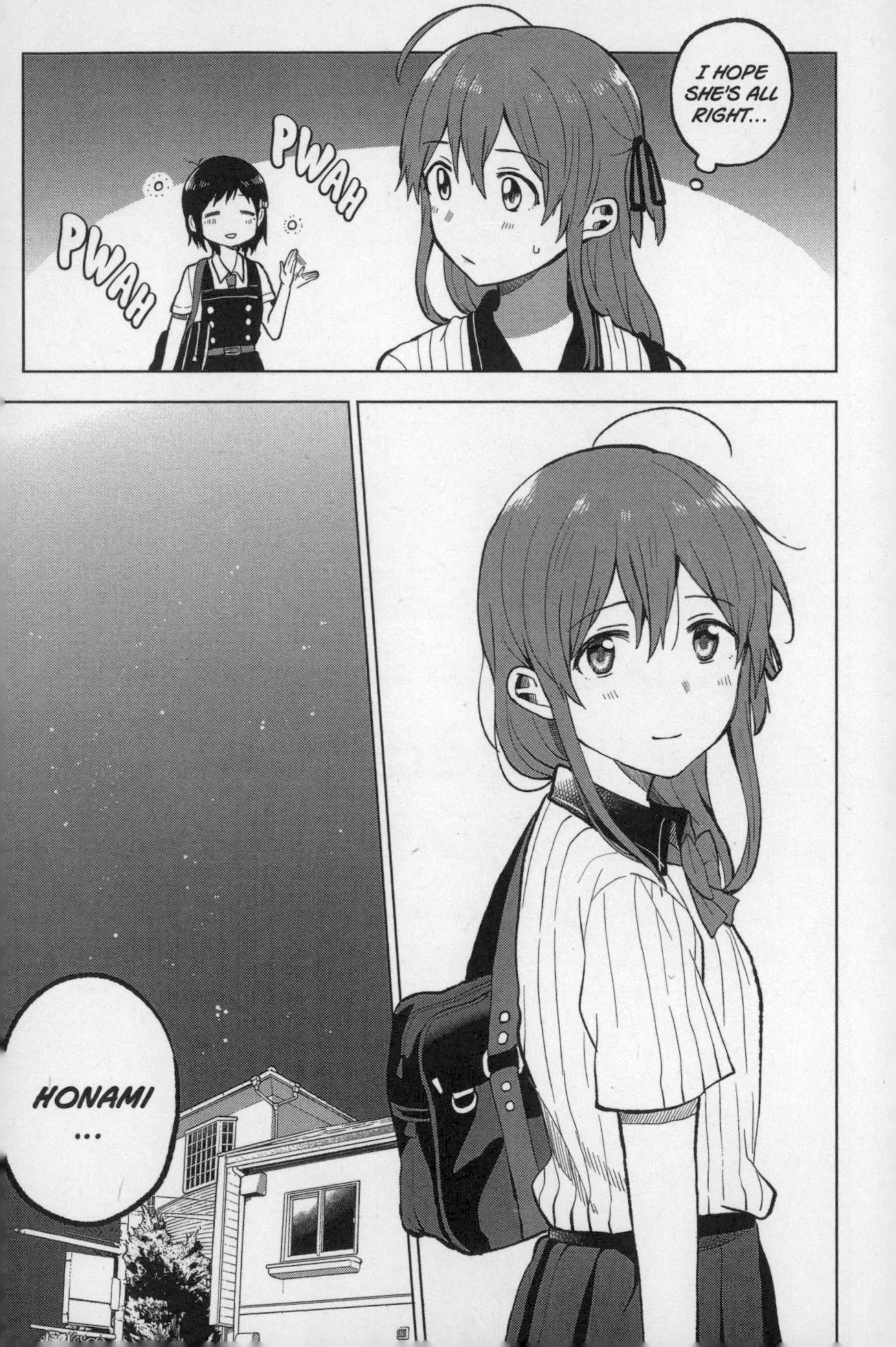
I HOPE SHE'S ALL RIGHT...
PWAH
PWAH
HONAMI ...

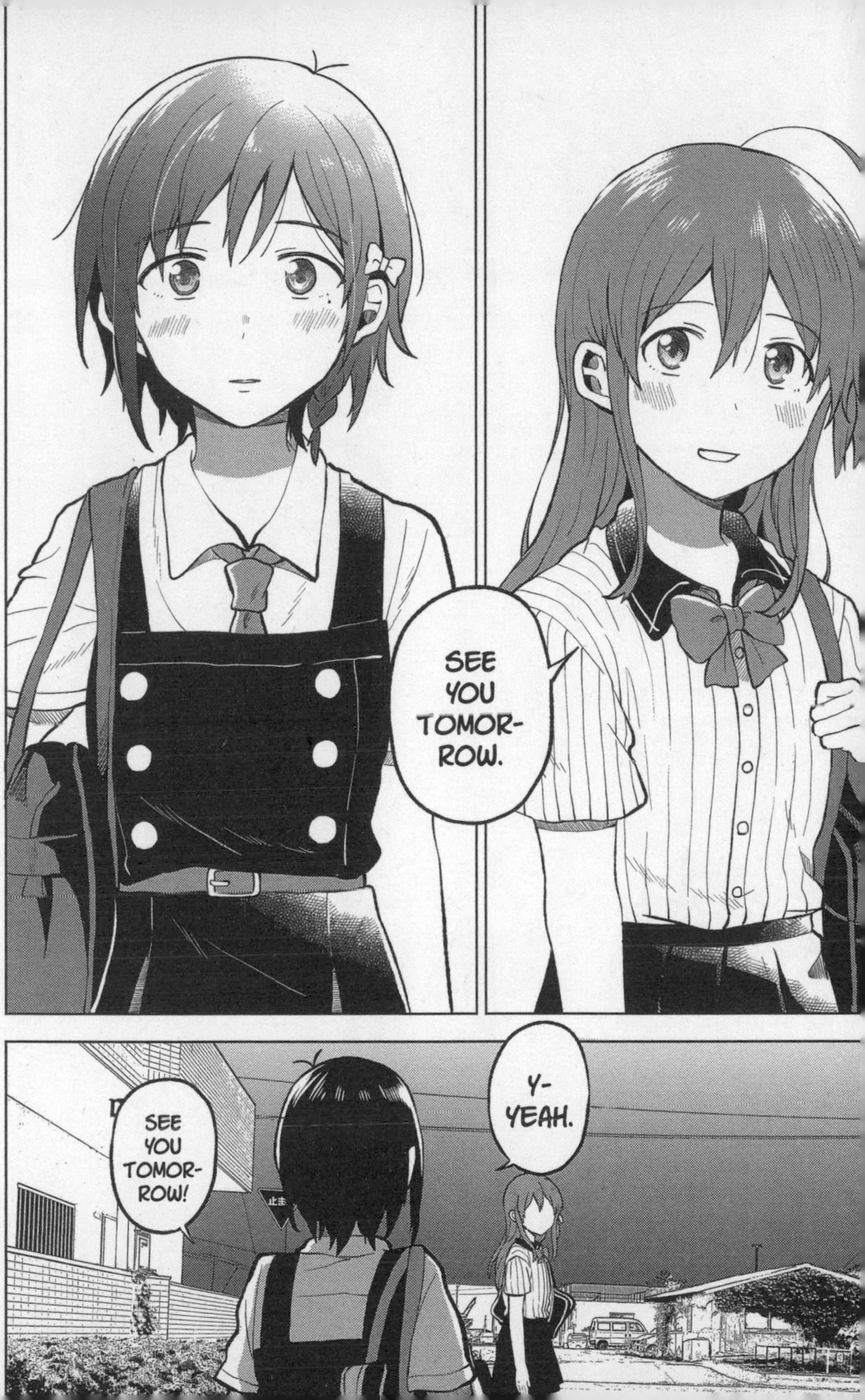
SEE YOU TOMOR-ROW.
Y-YEAH.
SEE YOU TOMOR-ROW!

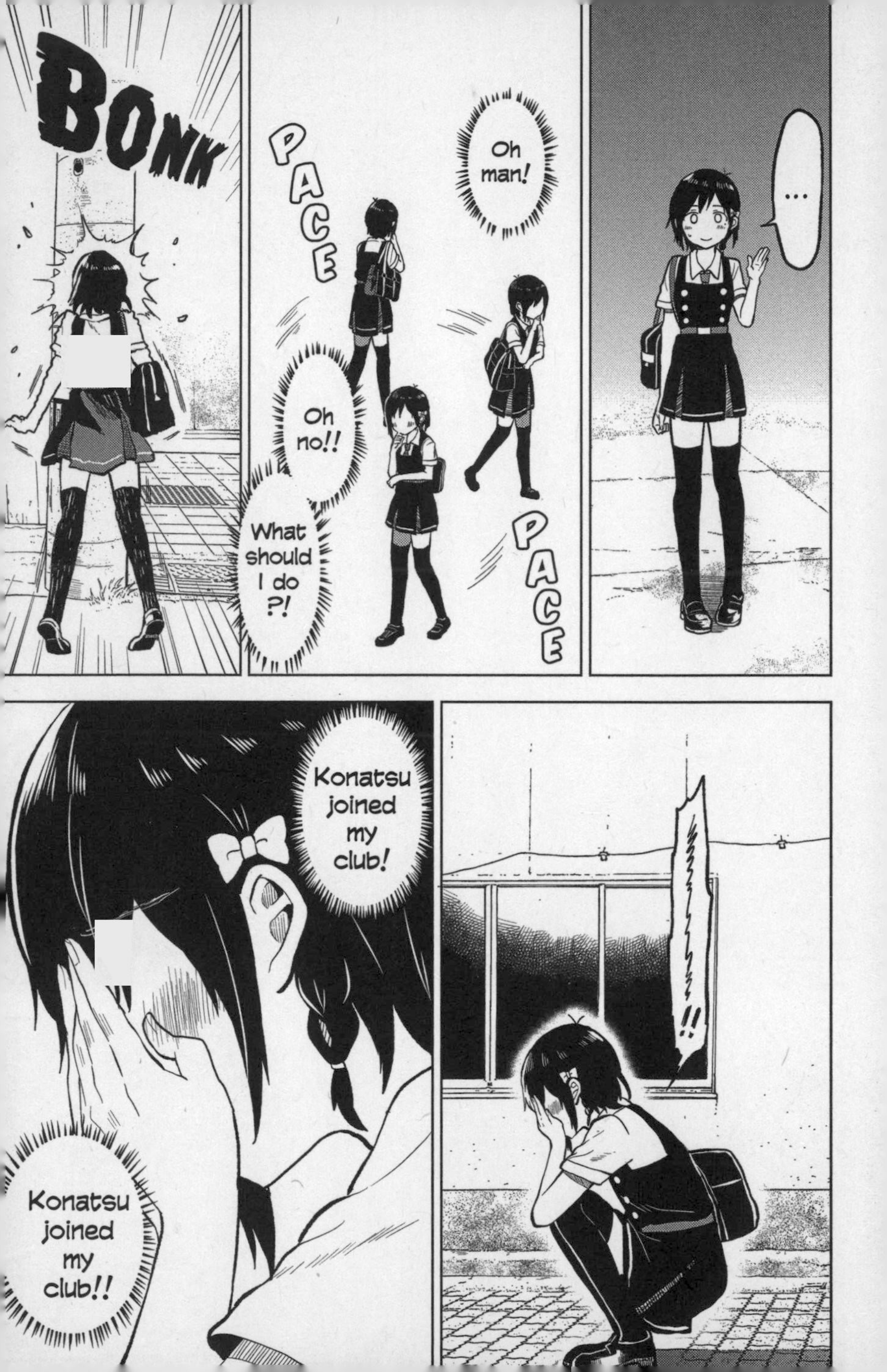
...
Oh man!
PACE
Oh no!!
PACE
What should I do?!
BONK
!!
Konatsu joined my club!
Konatsu joined my club!!

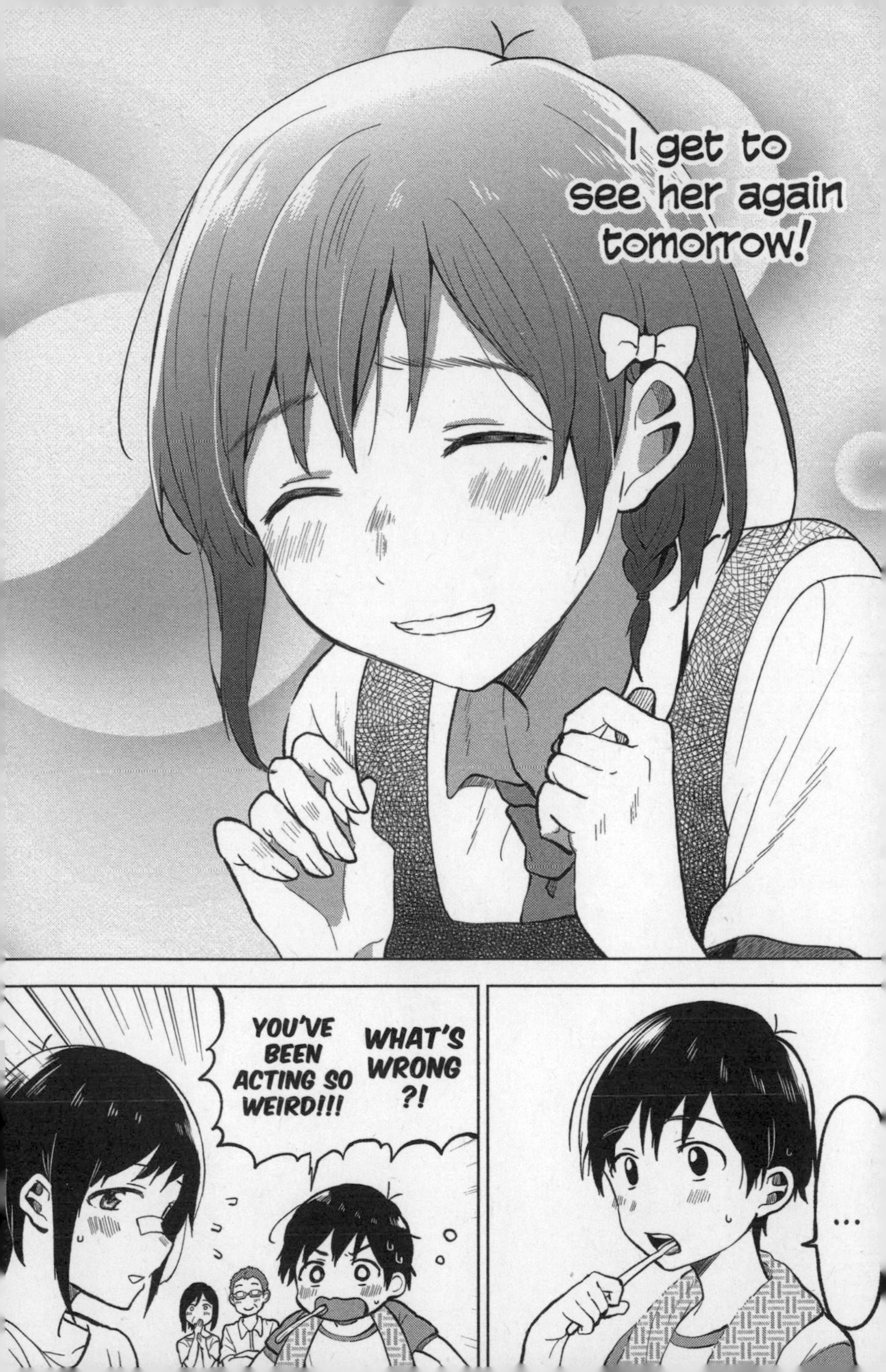
I get to see her again tomorrow!
...
WHAT'S WRONG ?!
YOU'VE BEEN ACTING SO WEIRD!!!

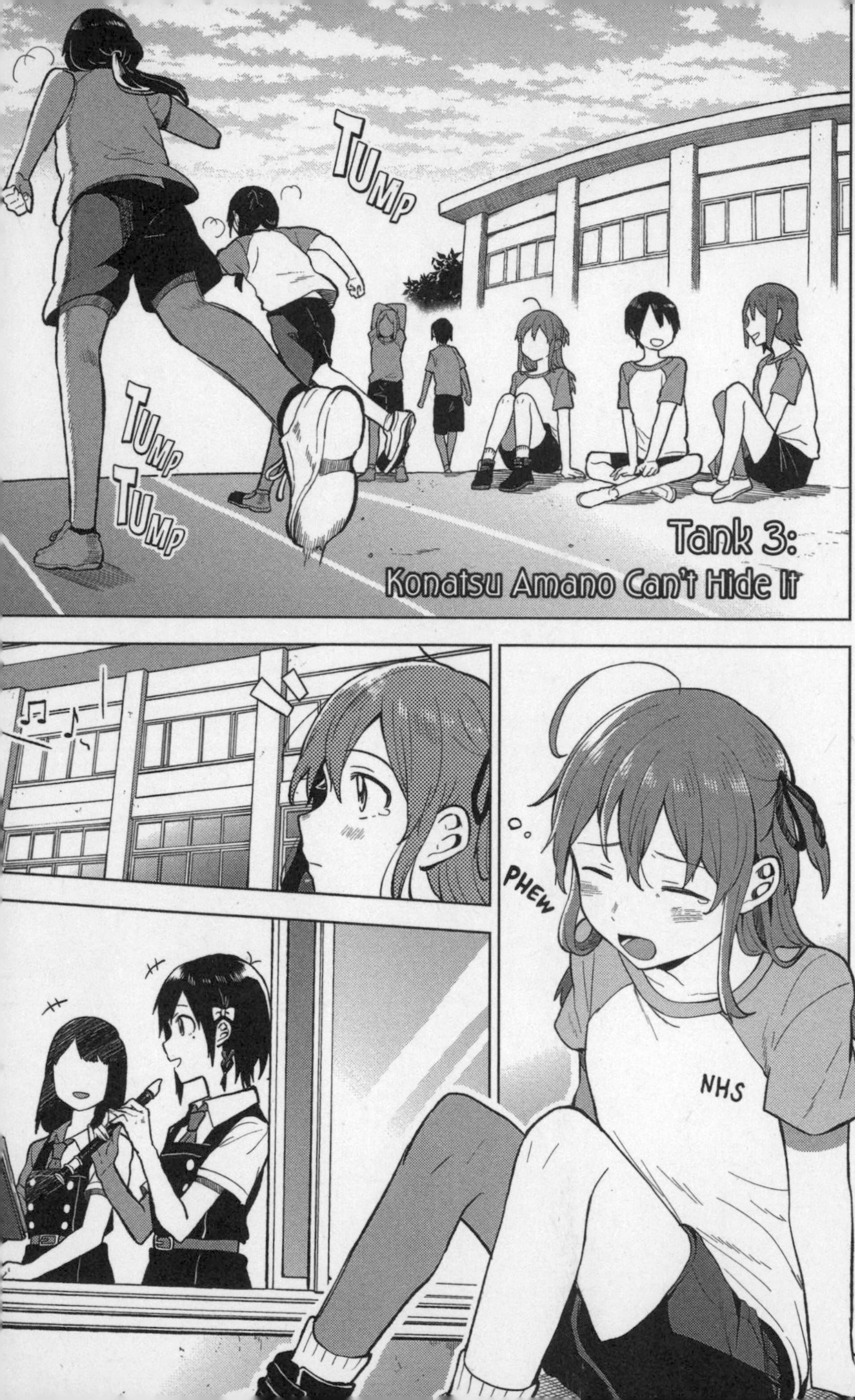
TUMP
TUMP
TUMP
Tank 3:
Konatsu Amano Can't Hide It
PHEW
NHS

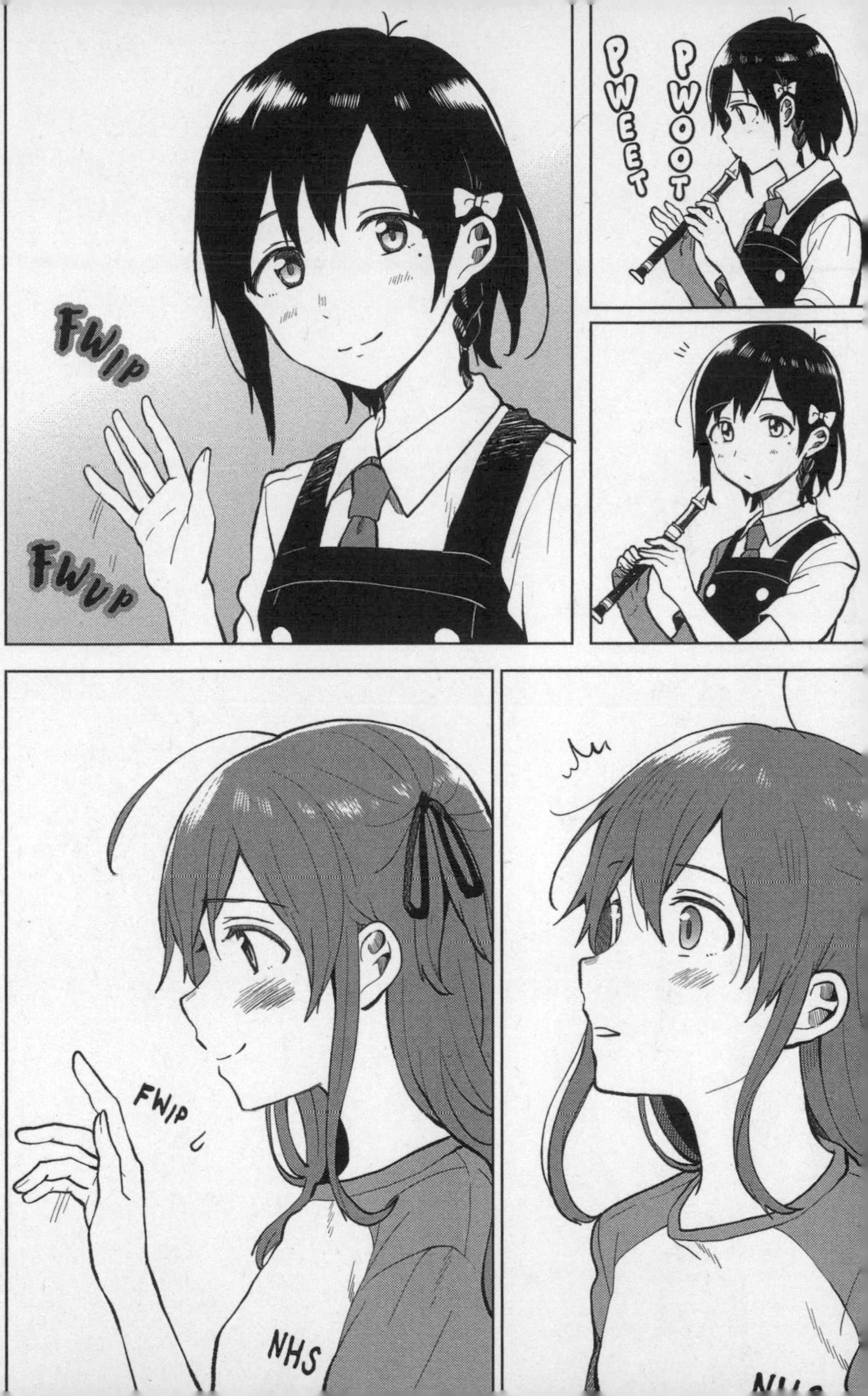
PWOOT
PWEET
FWIP
FWUP
FWIP
NHS

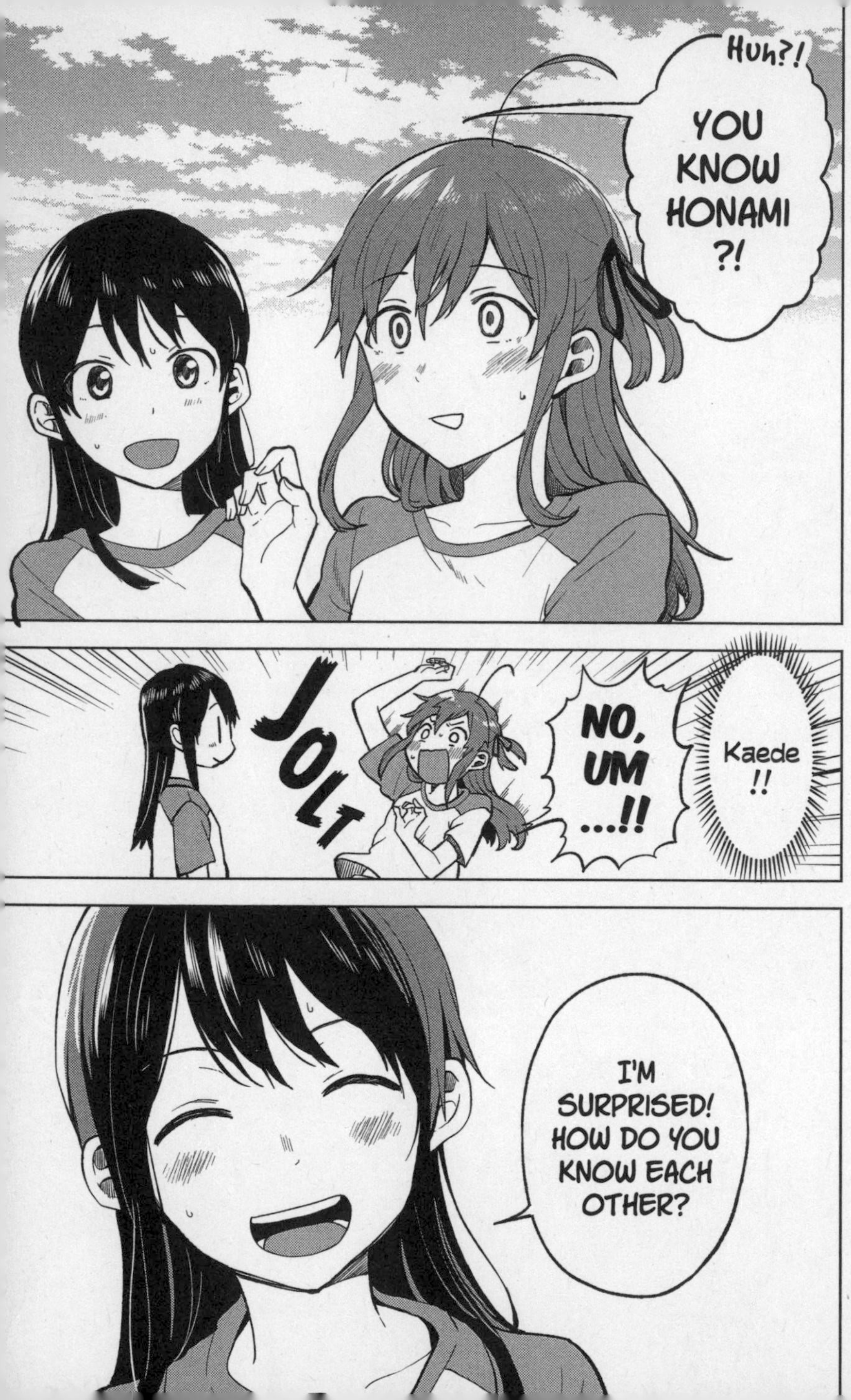
Huh?!
YOU KNOW HONAMI?!
Kaede!!
NO, UM ...!!
JOLT
I'M SURPRISED! HOW DO YOU KNOW EACH OTHER?

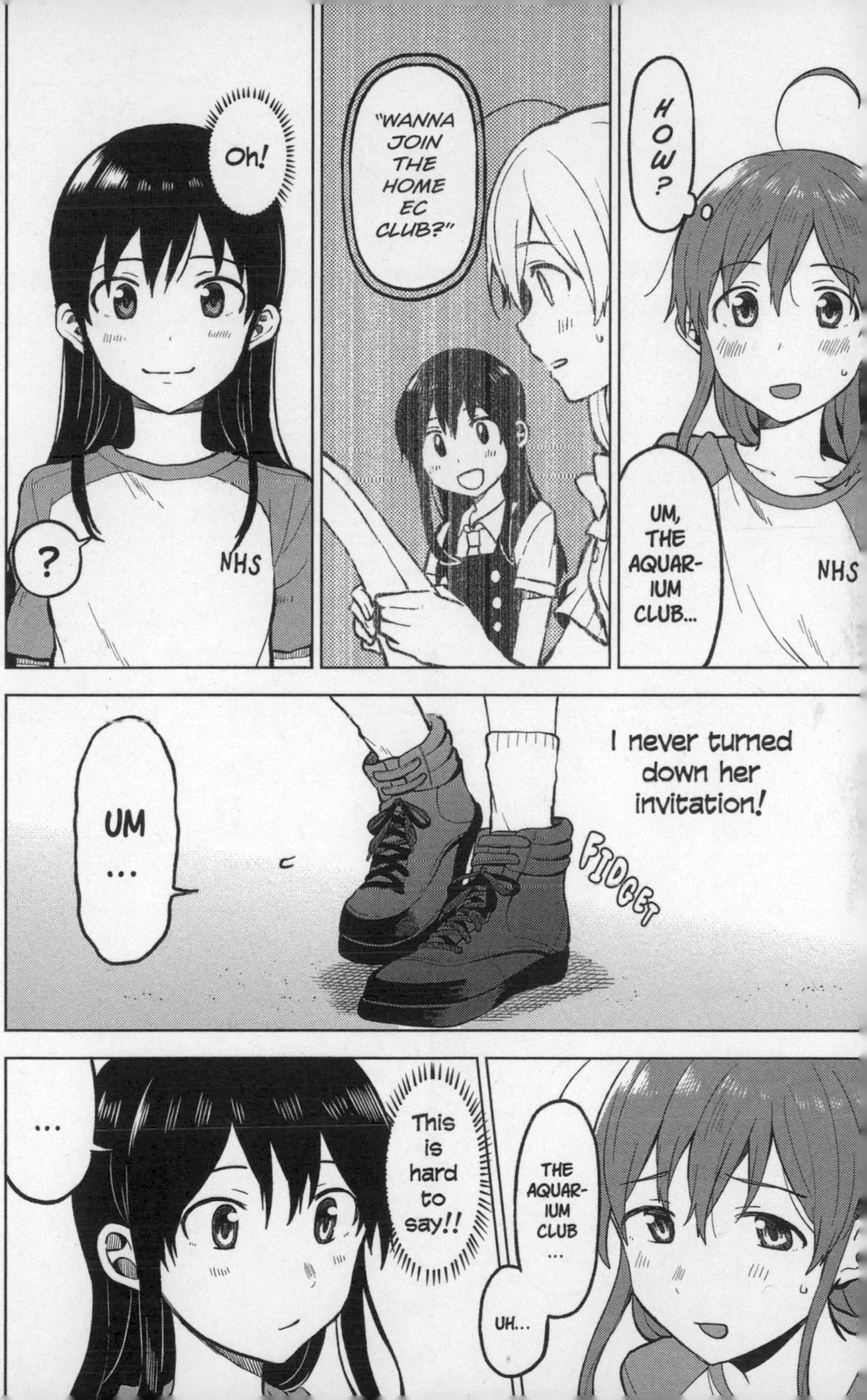
HOW?
UM, THE AQUAR-IUM CLUB...
"WANNA JOIN THE HOME EC CLUB?"
Oh!
?
NHS
NHS
I never turned down her invitation!
FIDGET
UM ...
THE AQUAR-IUM CLUB ...
UH...
This is hard to say!!
...

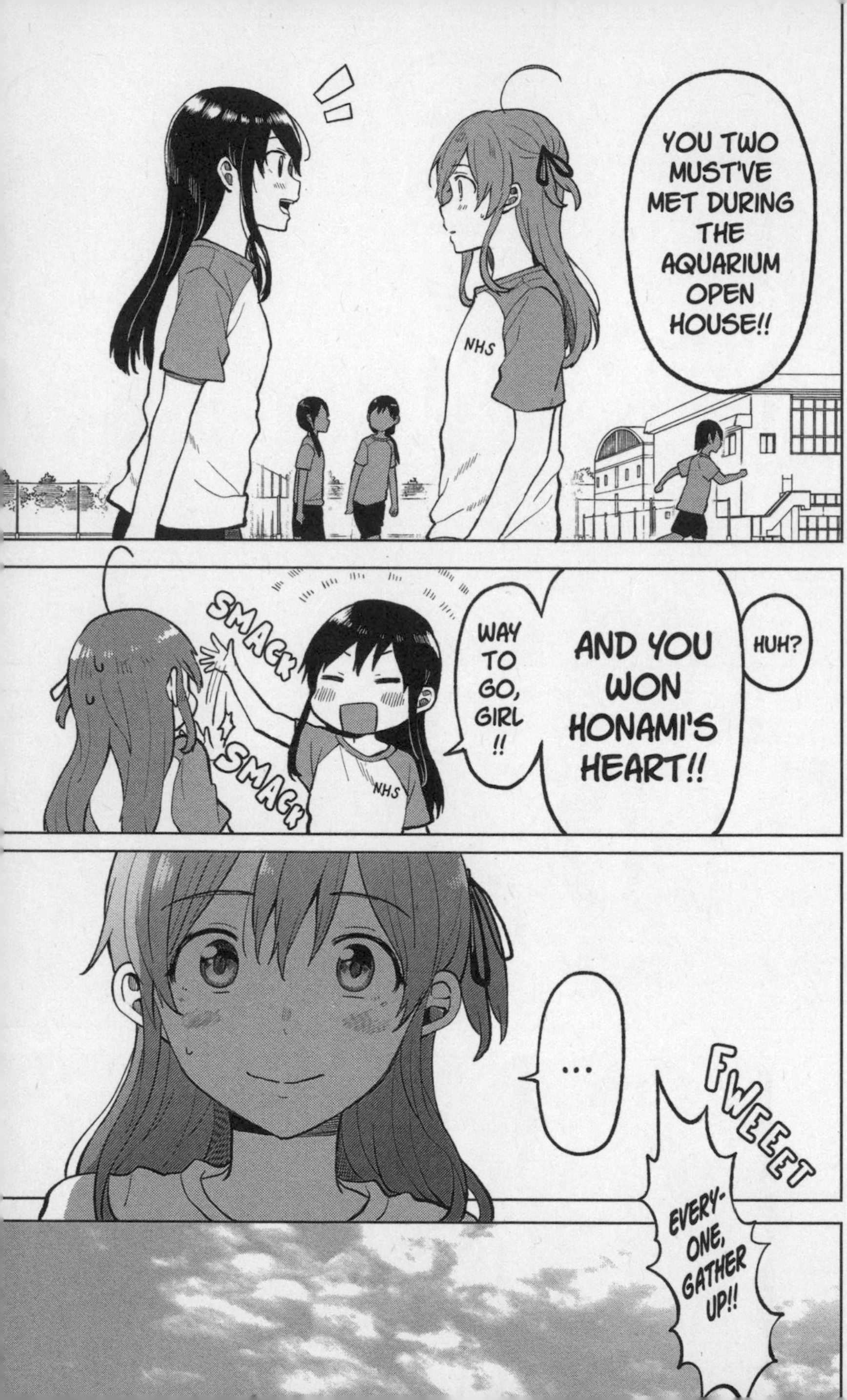
!!
YOU TWO MUST'VE MET DURING THE AQUARIUM OPEN HOUSE!!
NHS
HUH?
AND YOU WON HONAMI'S HEART!!
WAY TO GO, GIRL!!
SMACK
SMACK
NHS
...
FWEEET
EVERY-ONE, GATHER UP!!

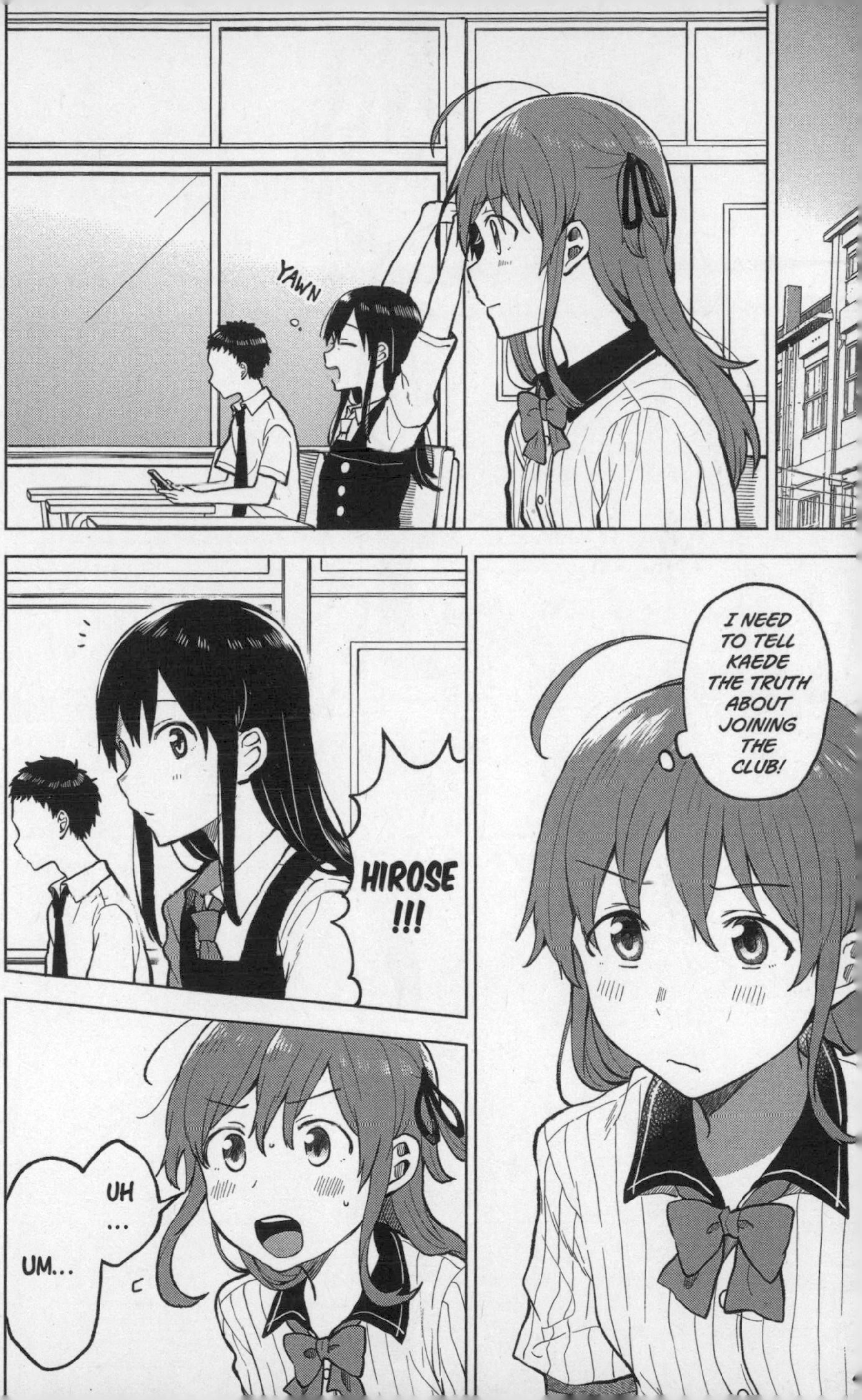
YAWN
I NEED TO TELL KAEDE THE TRUTH ABOUT JOINING THE CLUB!
HIROSE !!!
UH ...
UM...

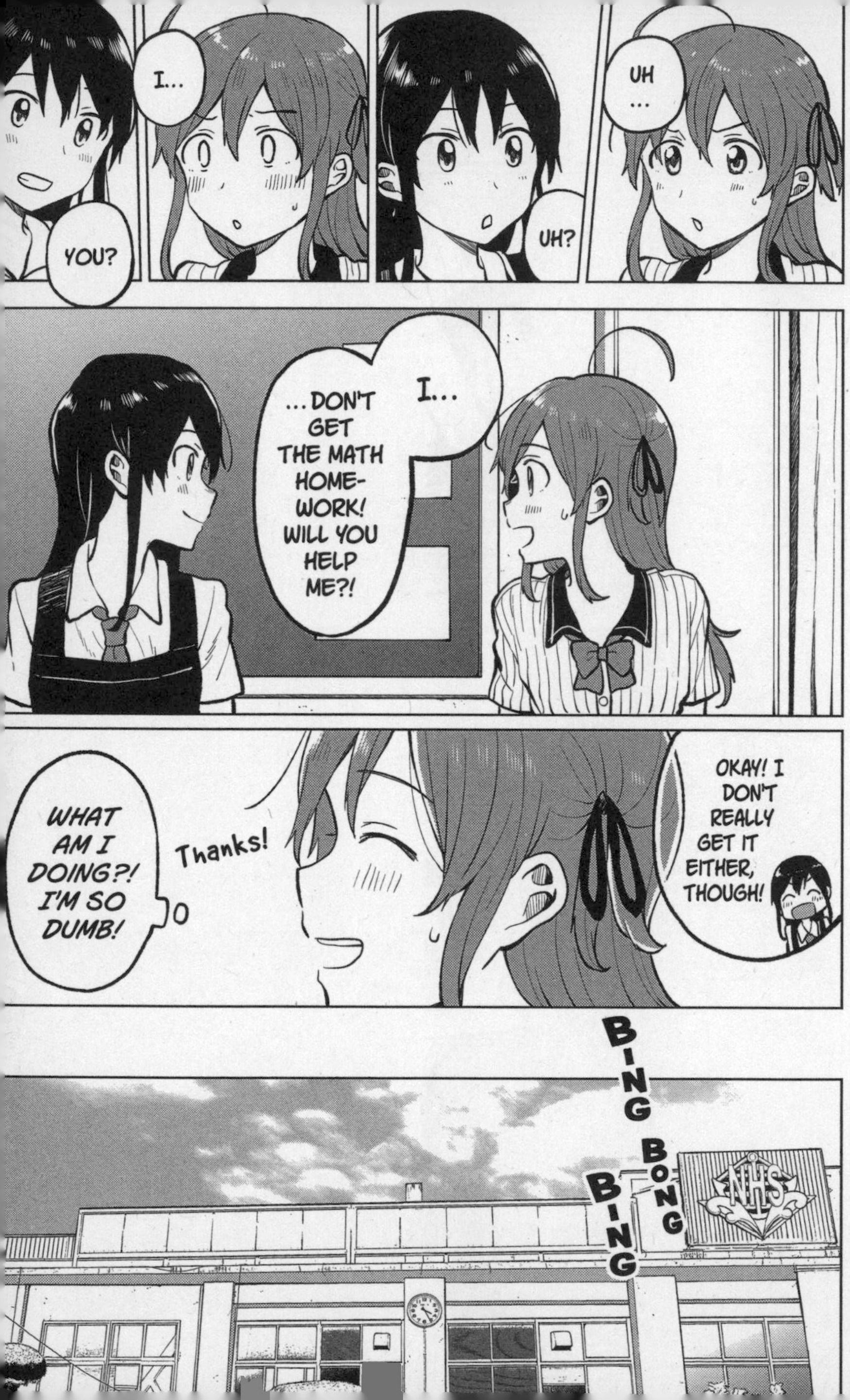
UH ...
UH?
I...
YOU?
I... ...DON'T GET THE MATH HOMEWORK! WILL YOU HELP ME?!
OKAY! I DON'T REALLY GET IT EITHER, THOUGH!
Thanks!
WHAT AM I DOING?! I'M SO DUMB!
BING BONG BING
NHS

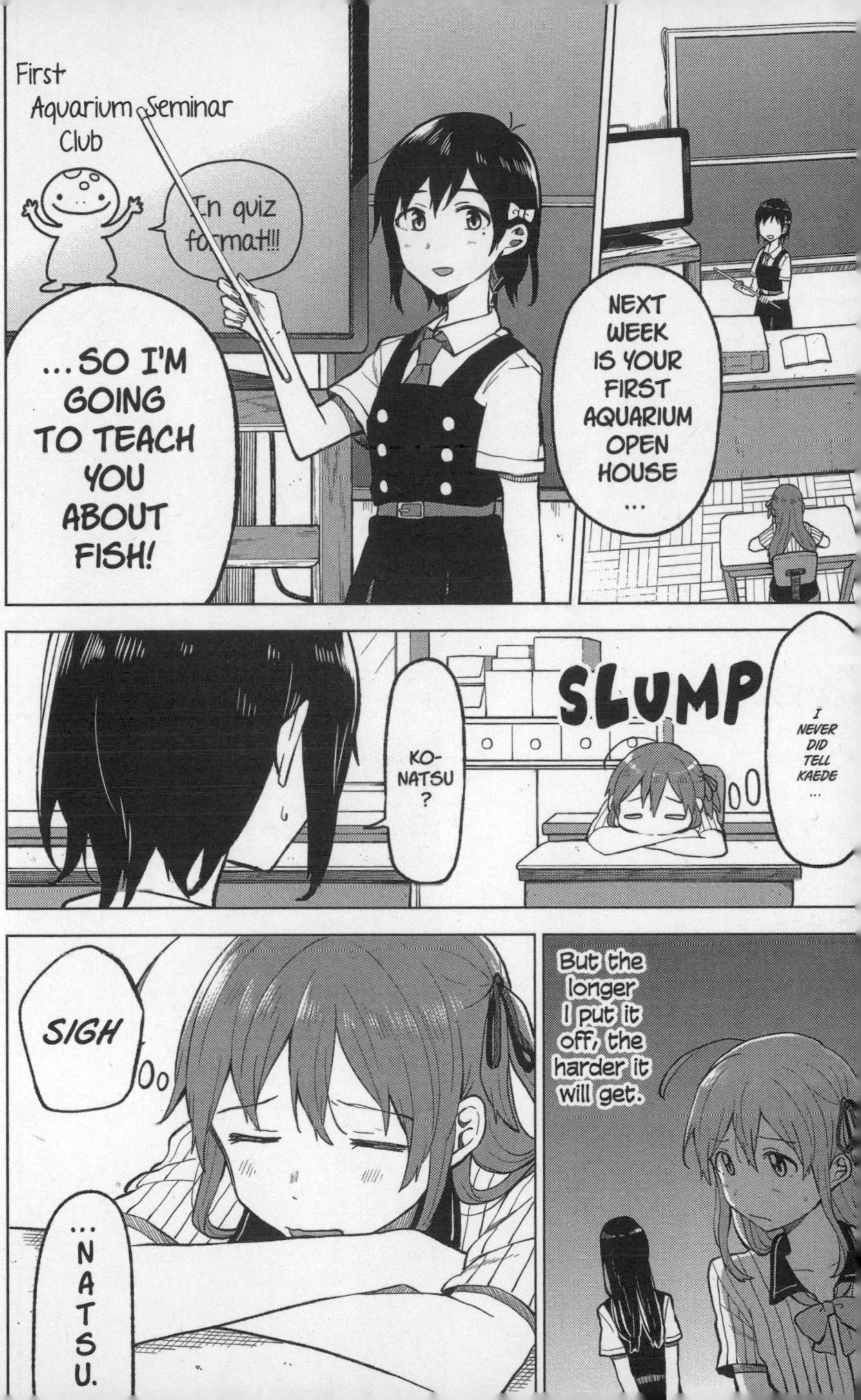
NEXT WEEK IS YOUR FIRST AQUARIUM OPEN HOUSE ...
...SO I'M GOING TO TEACH YOU ABOUT FISH!
First Aquarium Seminar Club
In quiz format!!
I NEVER DID TELL KAEDE ...
SLUMP
KO-NATSU?
But the longer I put it off, the harder it will get.
SIGH
...NATSU.

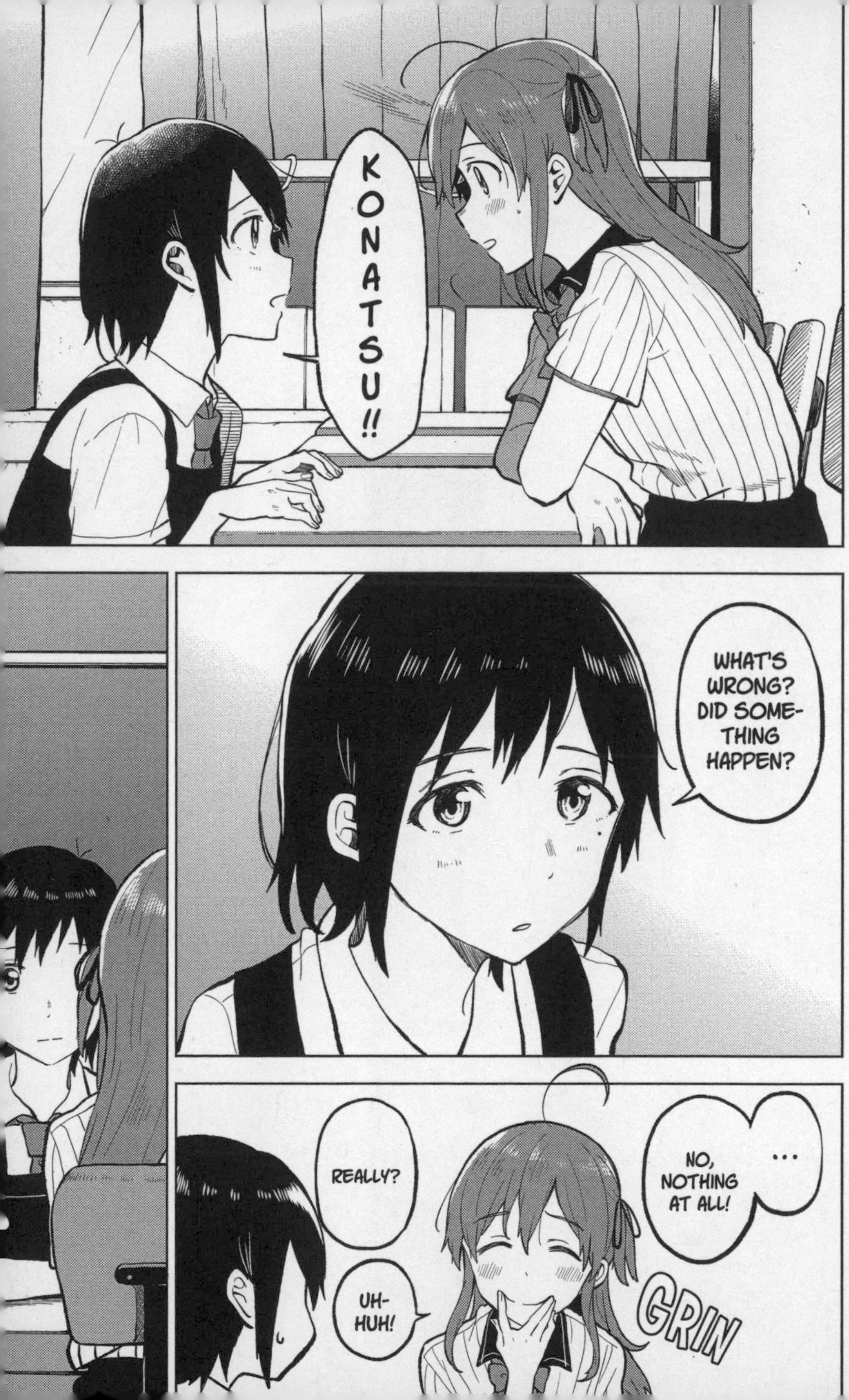
KONATSU!!
WHAT'S WRONG? DID SOME-THING HAPPEN?
...
NO, NOTHING AT ALL!
REALLY?
GRIN
UH-HUH!

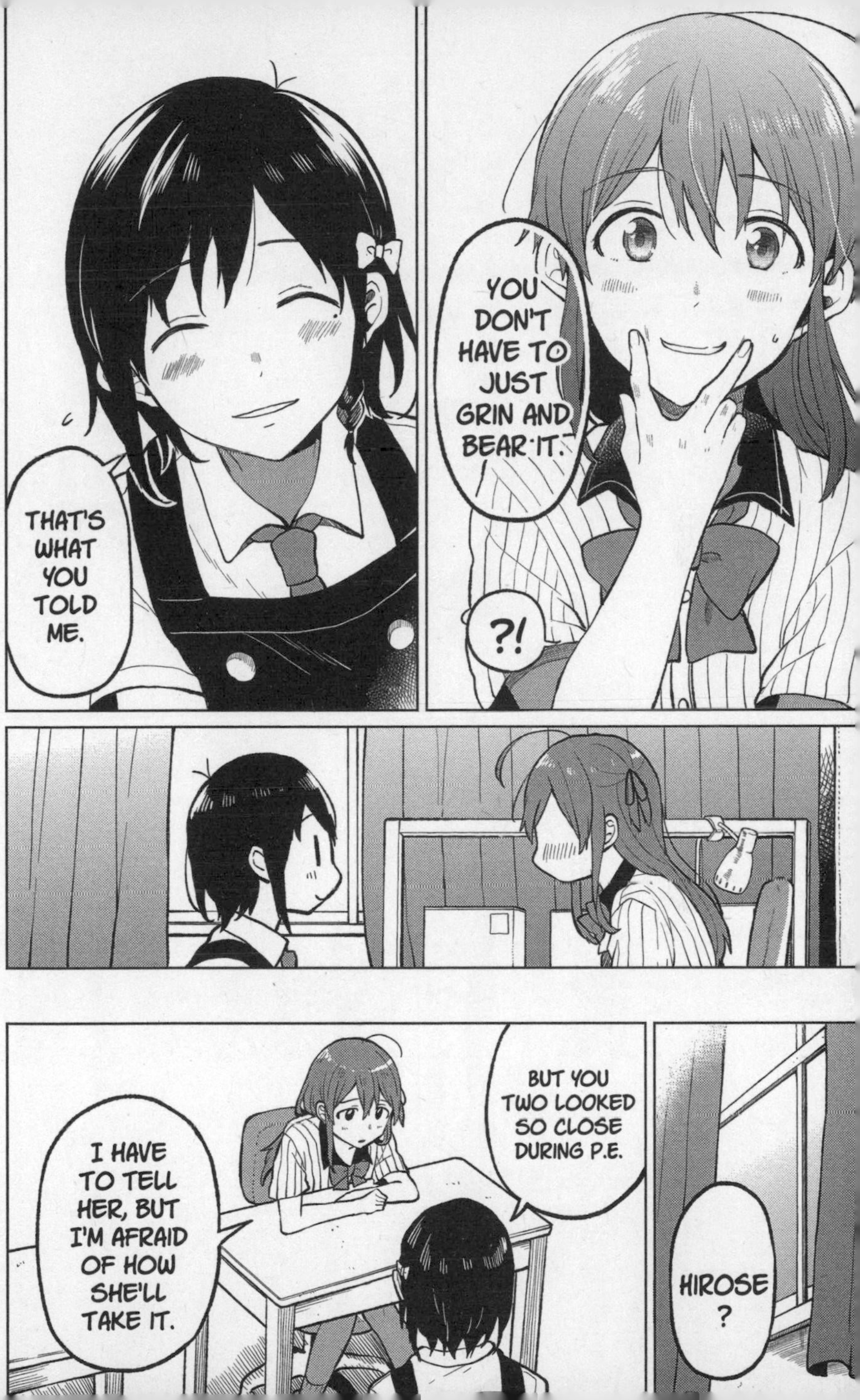
YOU DON'T HAVE TO JUST GRIN AND BEAR IT.
?!
THAT'S WHAT YOU TOLD ME.
HIROSE?
BUT YOU TWO LOOKED SO CLOSE DURING P.E.
I HAVE TO TELL HER, BUT I'M AFRAID OF HOW SHE'LL TAKE IT.

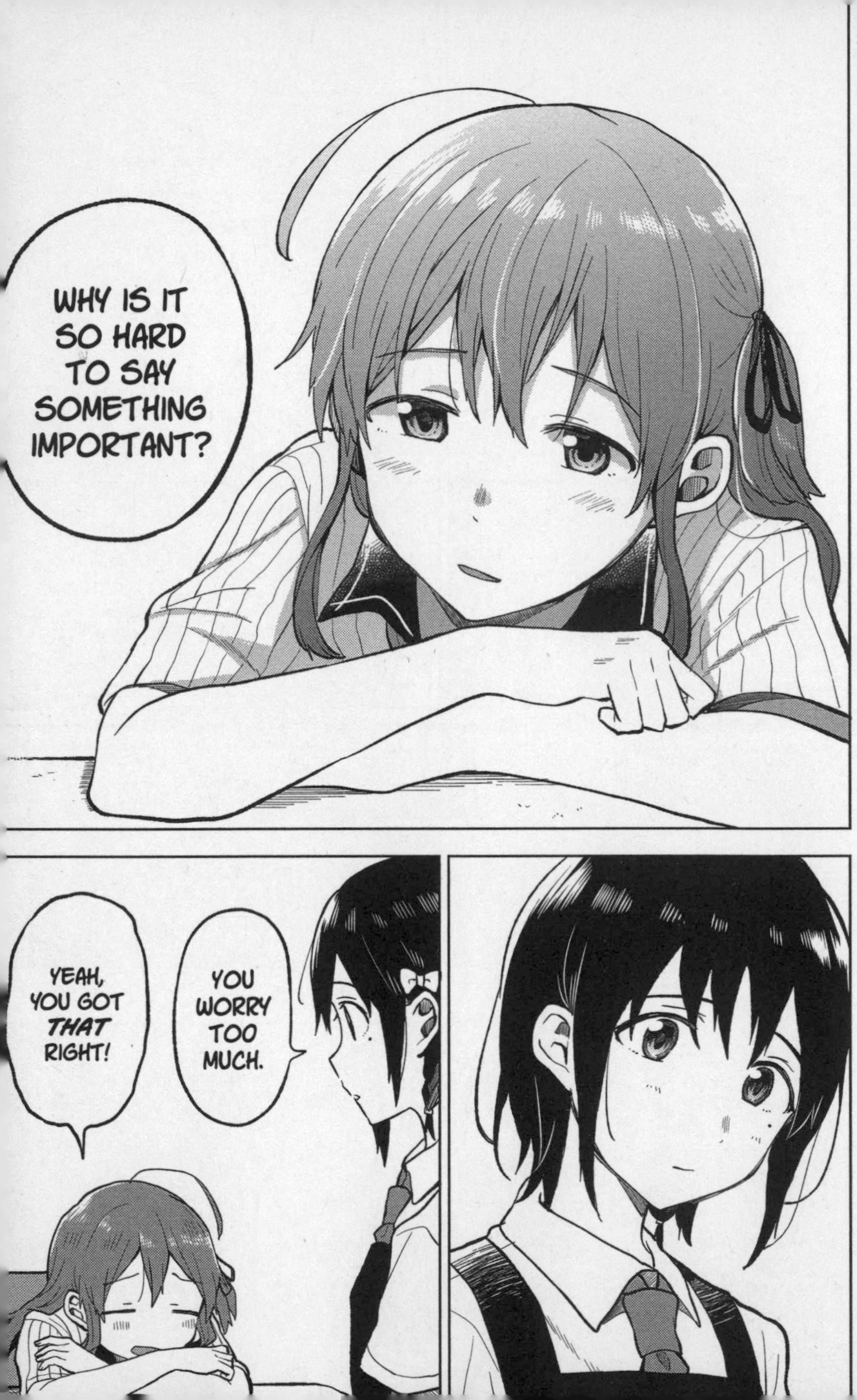
WHY IS IT SO HARD TO SAY SOMETHING IMPORTANT?
YOU WORRY TOO MUCH.
YEAH, YOU GOT *THAT* RIGHT!

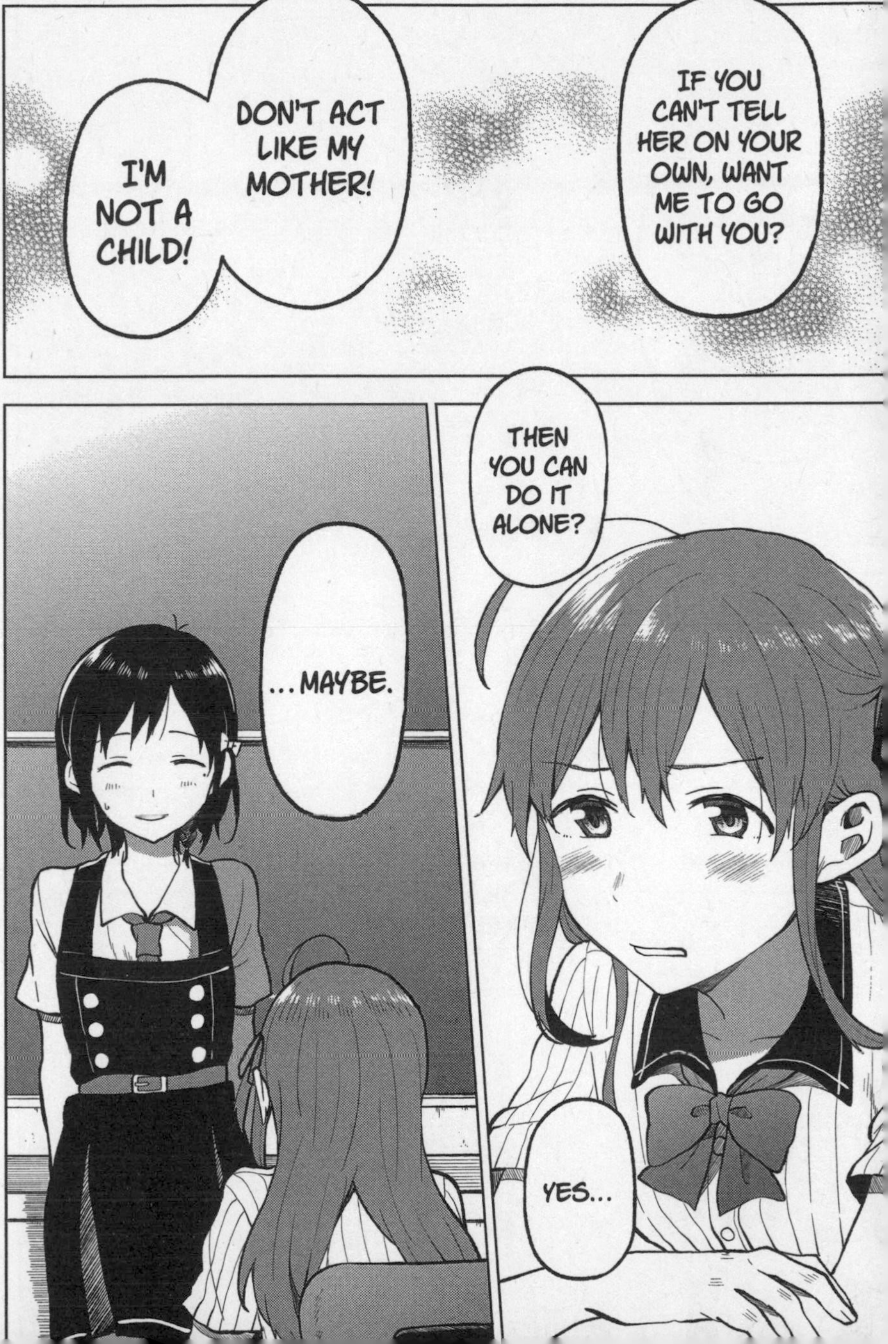
IF YOU CAN'T TELL HER ON YOUR OWN, WANT ME TO GO WITH YOU?
DON'T ACT LIKE MY MOTHER!
I'M NOT A CHILD!
THEN YOU CAN DO IT ALONE?
YES...
...MAYBE.

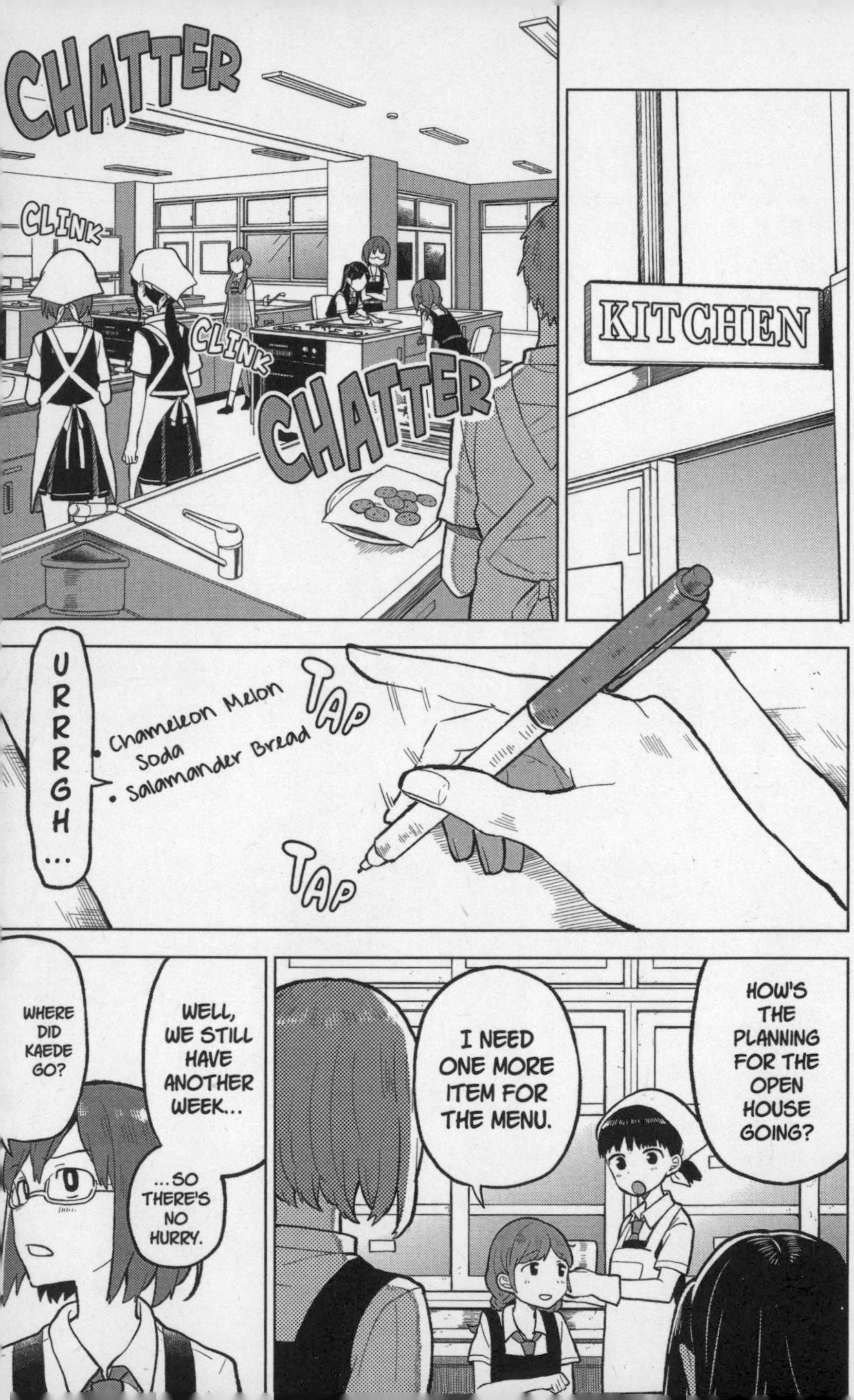
KITCHEN
CHATTER
CLINK
CLINK
CHATTER
TAP
• Chameleon Melon Soda
• Salamander Bread
URRRGH...
TAP
HOW'S THE PLANNING FOR THE OPEN HOUSE GOING?
I NEED ONE MORE ITEM FOR THE MENU.
WELL, WE STILL HAVE ANOTHER WEEK...
...SO THERE'S NO HURRY.
WHERE DID KAEDE GO?

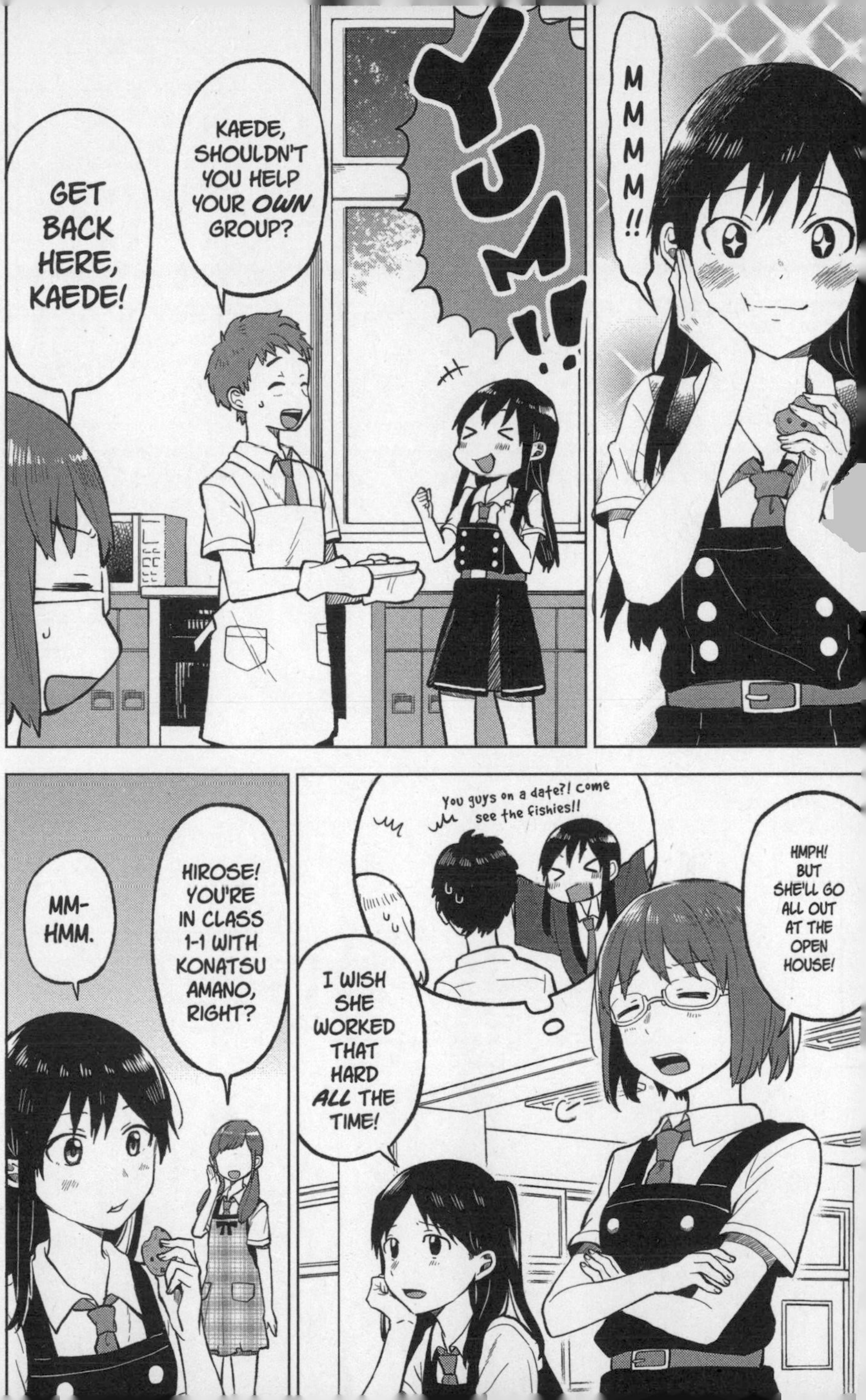
MMMMM!!
YUM!!
KAEDE, SHOULDN'T YOU HELP YOUR OWN GROUP?
GET BACK HERE, KAEDE!
HMPH! BUT SHE'LL GO ALL OUT AT THE OPEN HOUSE!
You guys on a date?! come see the fishies!!
I WISH SHE WORKED THAT HARD ALL THE TIME!
HIROSE! YOU'RE IN CLASS 1-1 WITH KONATSU AMANO, RIGHT?
MM-HMM.

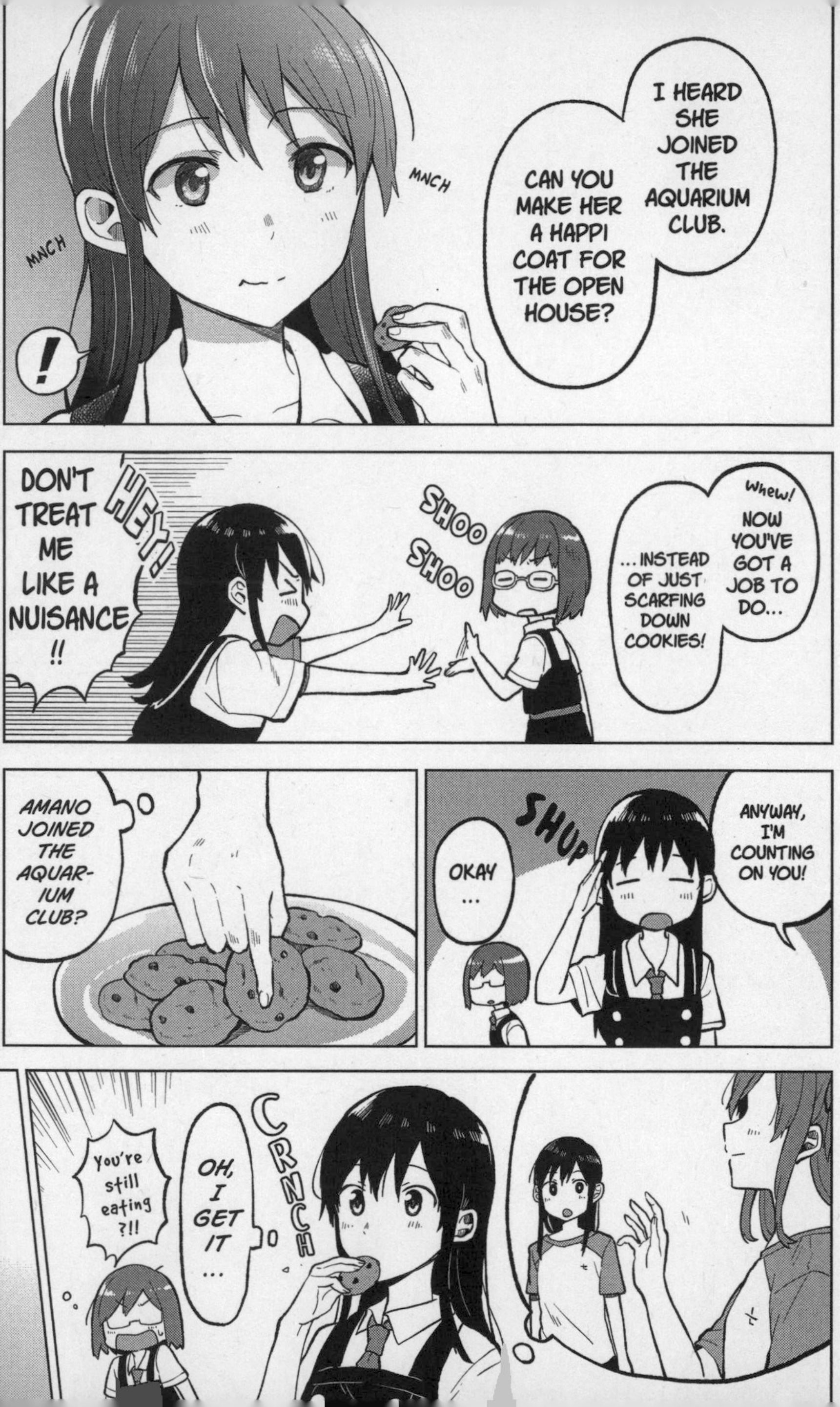
I HEARD SHE JOINED THE AQUARIUM CLUB.
CAN YOU MAKE HER A HAPPI COAT FOR THE OPEN HOUSE?
MNCH
MNCH
!
Whew!
NOW YOU'VE GOT A JOB TO DO...
...INSTEAD OF JUST SCARFING DOWN COOKIES!
SHOO
SHOO
HEY!
DON'T TREAT ME LIKE A NUISANCE !!
ANYWAY, I'M COUNTING ON YOU!
SHUP
OKAY ...
AMANO JOINED THE AQUARIUM CLUB?
CRNCH
OH, I GET IT ...
You're still eating ?!!

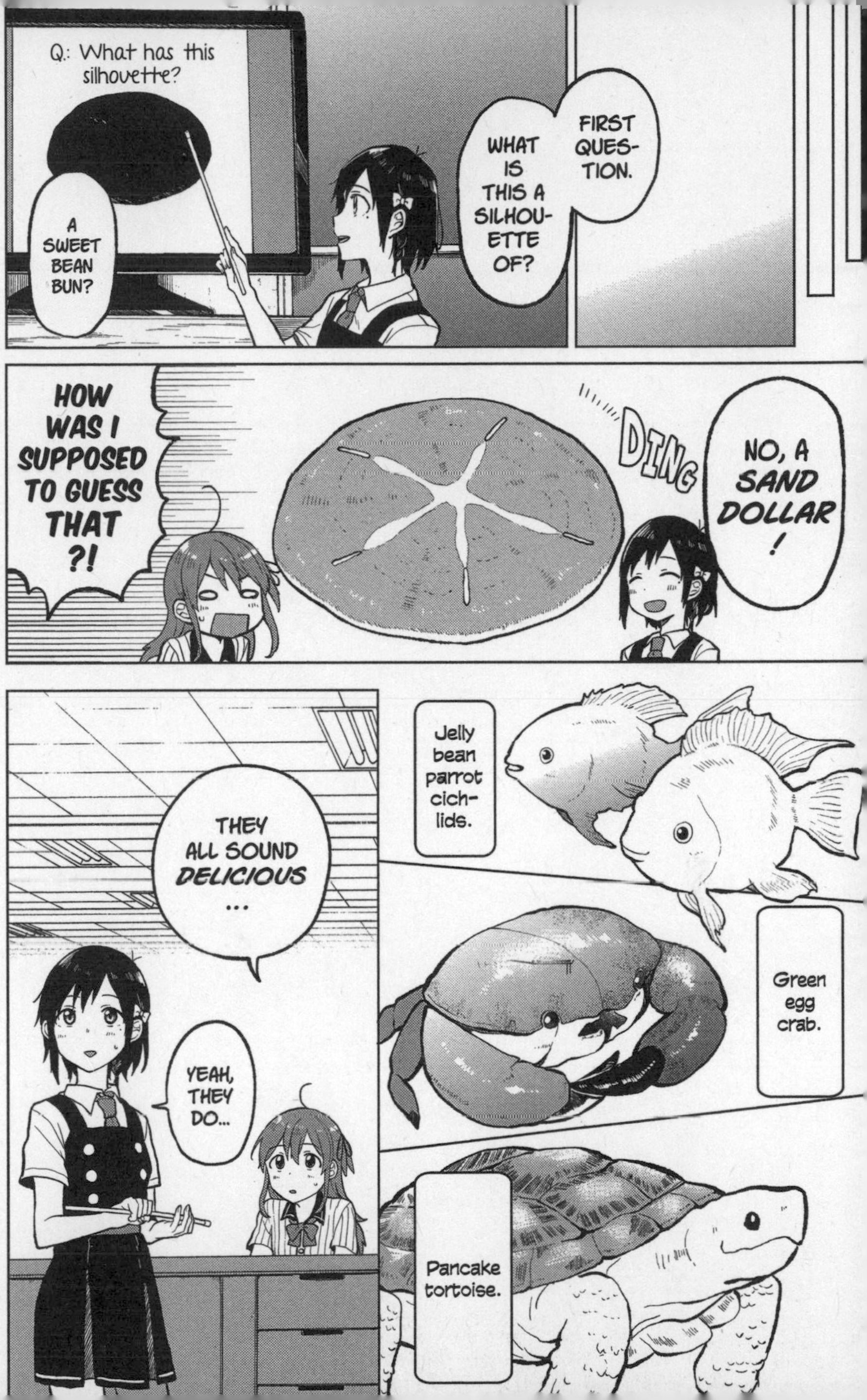
FIRST QUESTION. WHAT IS THIS A SILHOUETTE OF?
Q.: What has this silhouette?
A SWEET BEAN BUN?
NO, A SAND DOLLAR!
DING
HOW WAS I SUPPOSED TO GUESS THAT?!
Jelly bean parrot cichlids.
Green egg crab.
Pancake tortoise.
THEY ALL SOUND DELICIOUS...
YEAH, THEY DO...

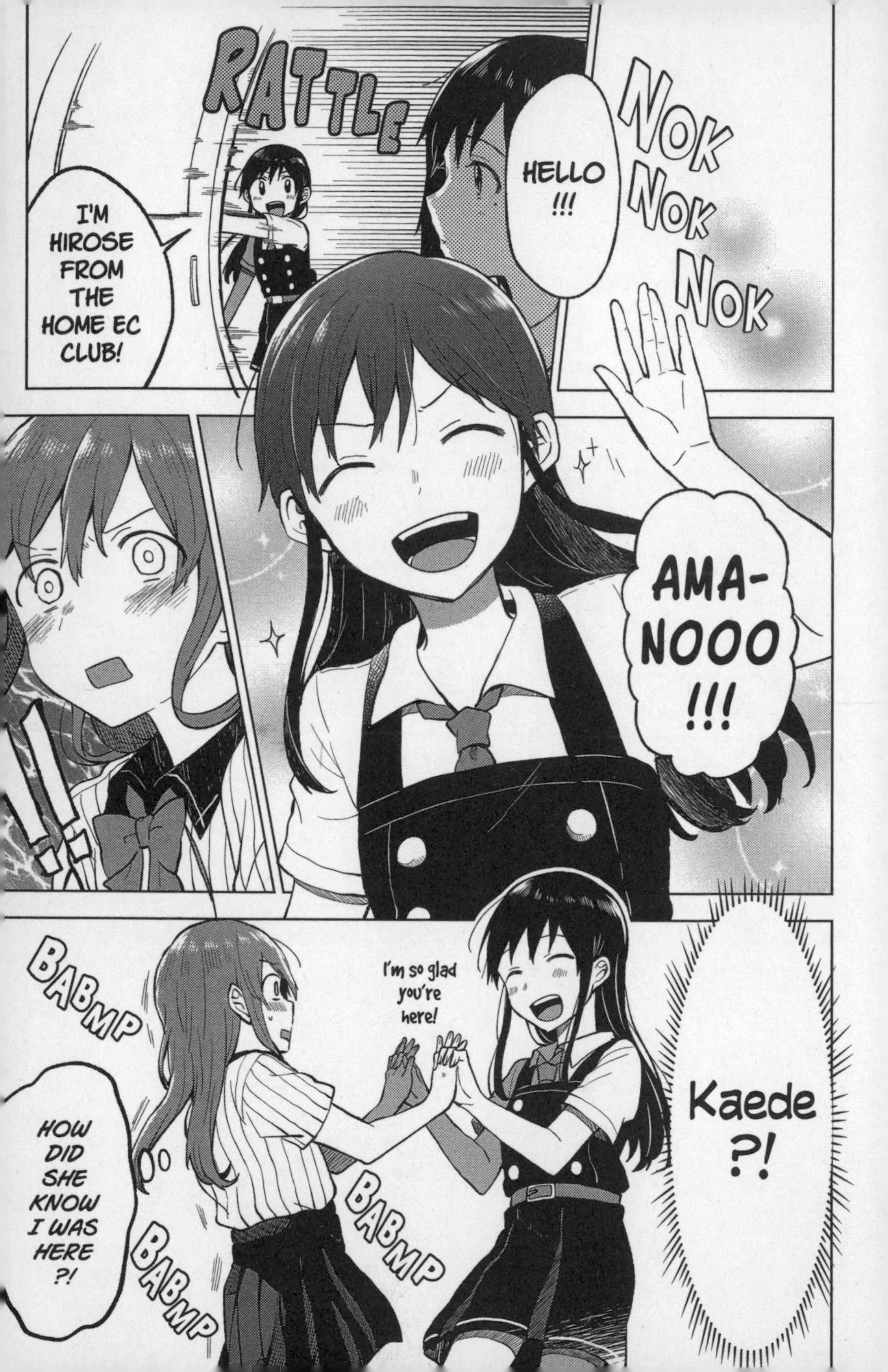
NOK NOK NOK
HELLO !!!
RATTLE
I'M HIROSE FROM THE HOME EC CLUB!
AMA-NOOO !!!
!!
Kaede ?!
I'm so glad you're here!
BABMP
BABMP
BABMP
HOW DID SHE KNOW I WAS HERE ?!

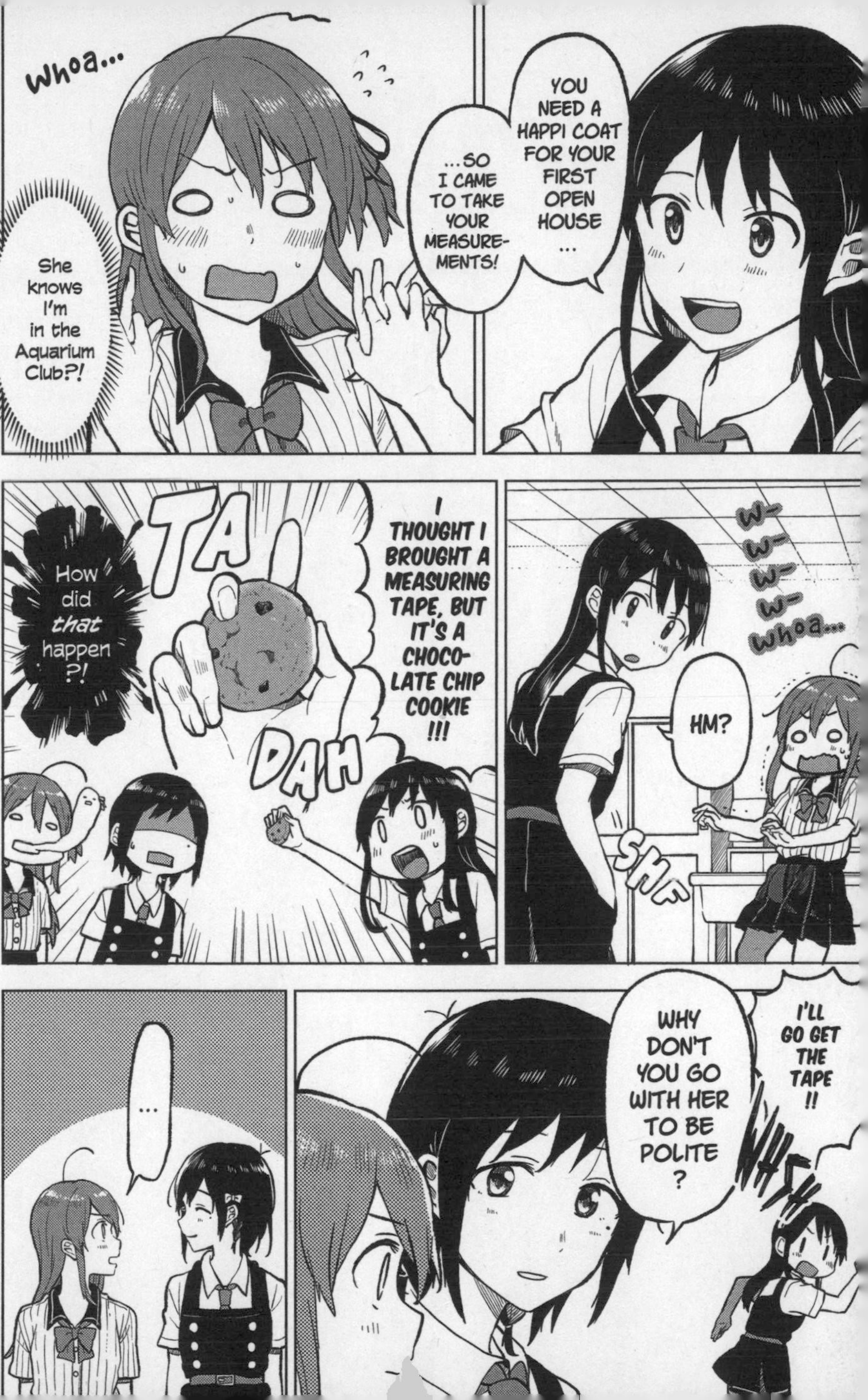
YOU NEED A HAPPI COAT FOR YOUR FIRST OPEN HOUSE ...
...SO I CAME TO TAKE YOUR MEASUREMENTS!
Whoa...
She knows I'm in the Aquarium Club?!
W-W-W-W-Whoa...
HM?
SHF
I THOUGHT I BROUGHT A MEASURING TAPE, BUT IT'S A CHOCOLATE CHIP COOKIE!!!
TA
DAH
How did that happen?!
I'LL GO GET THE TAPE!!
WHY DON'T YOU GO WITH HER TO BE POLITE?
...

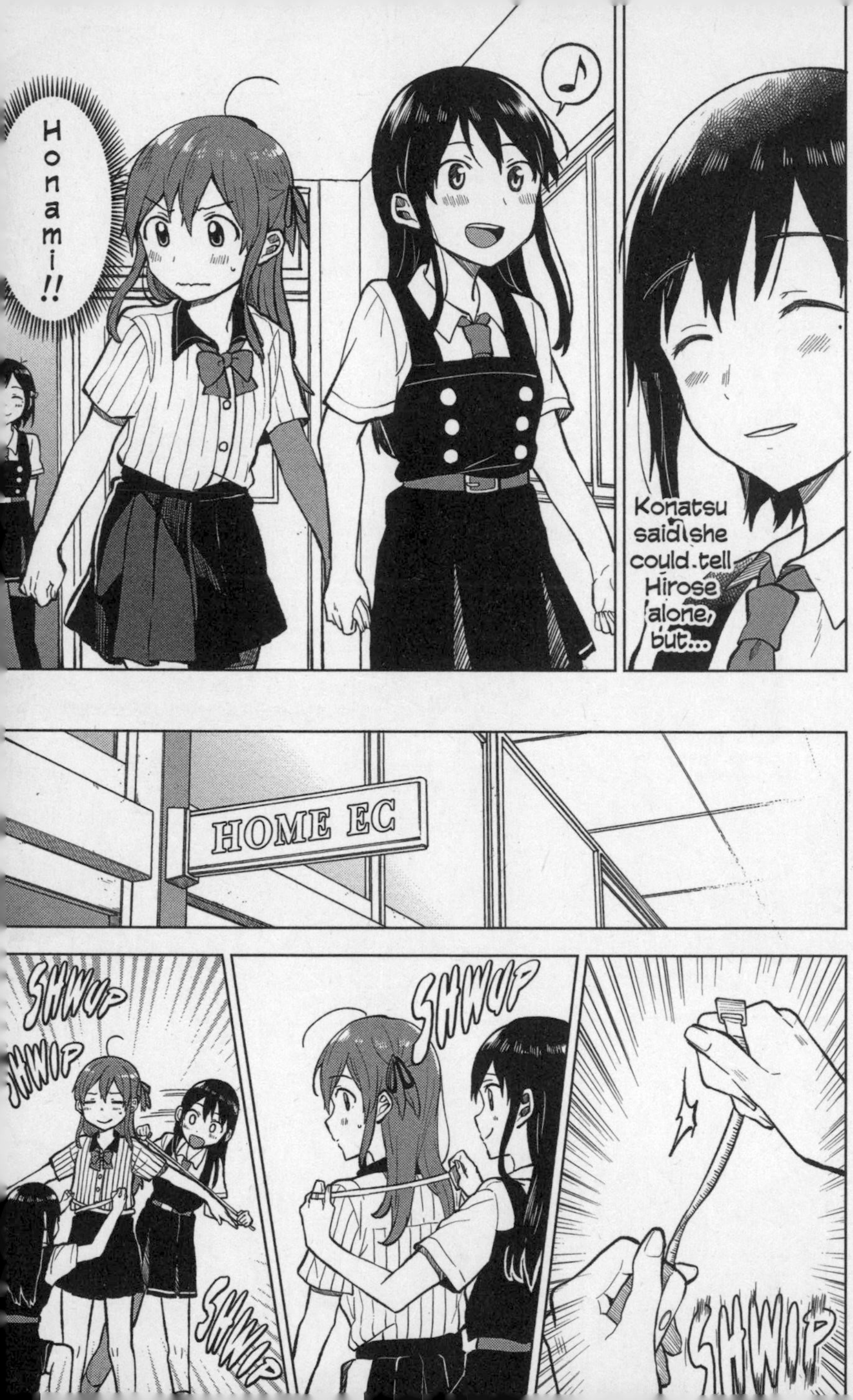
Konatsu said she could tell Hirose alone, but...
♪
Honami!!
HOME EC
SHWIP
SHWUP
SHWUP
SHWIP
SHWUP

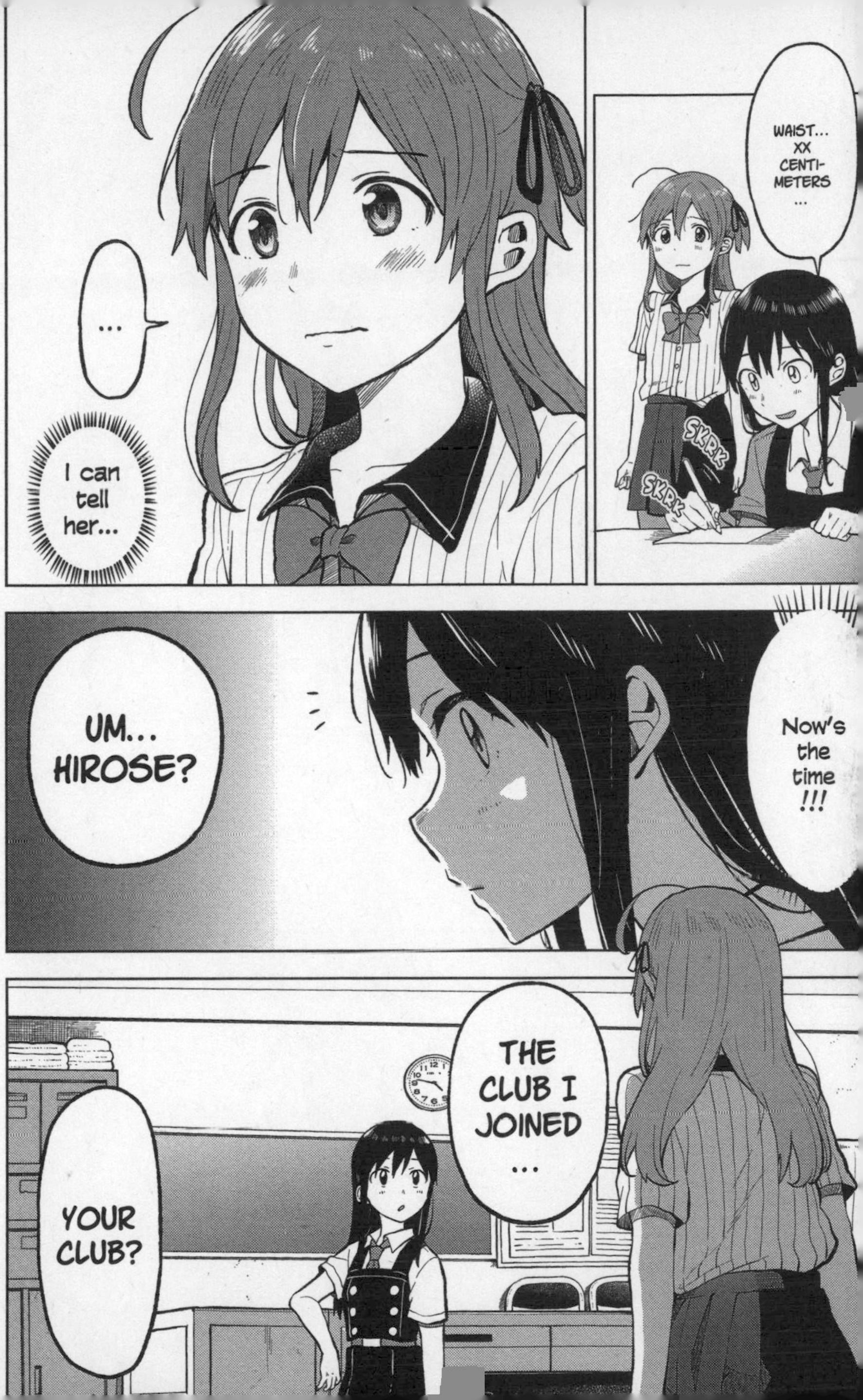
WAIST... XX CENTI-METERS ...
SKRK
SKRK
...
I can tell her...
Now's the time !!!
UM... HIROSE?
THE CLUB I JOINED ...
YOUR CLUB?

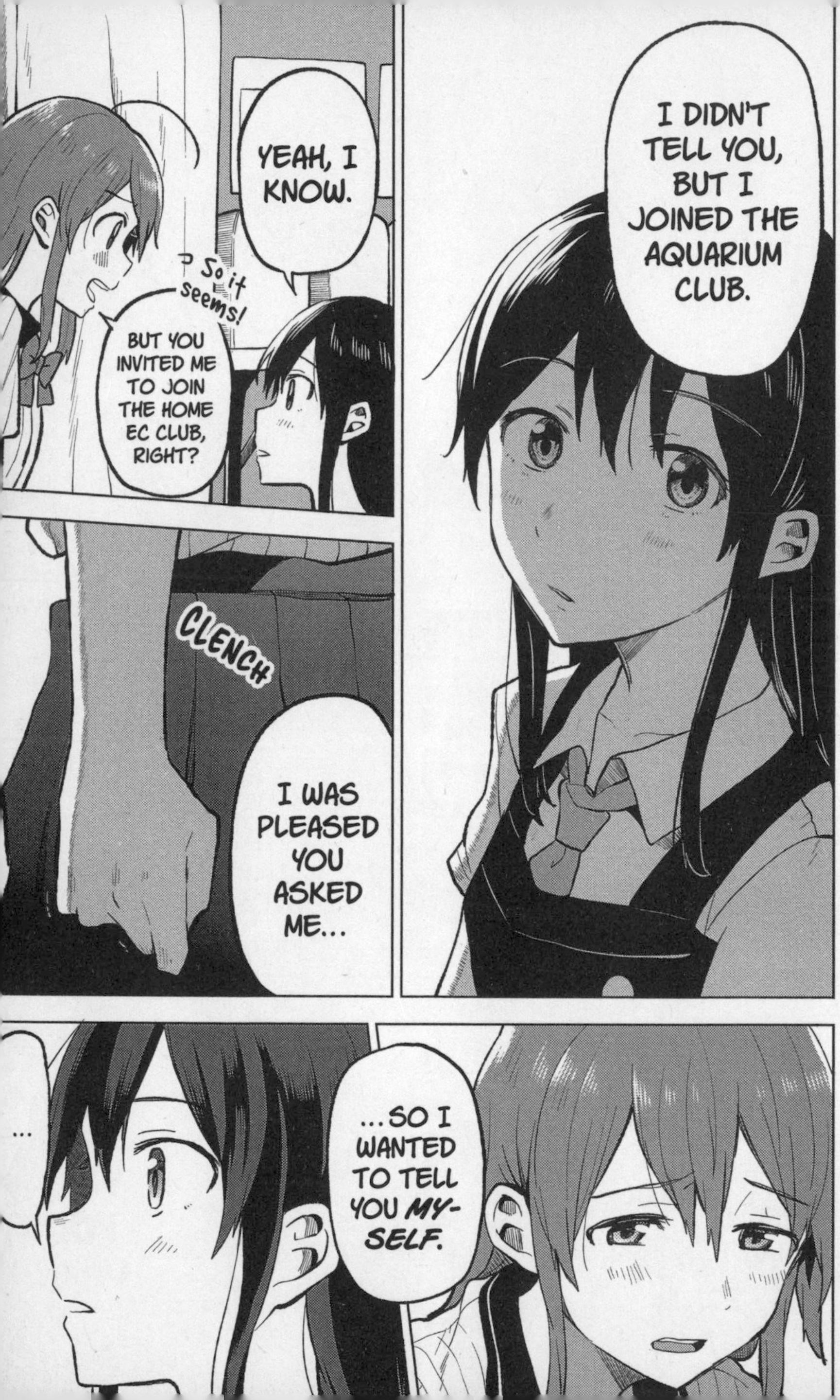
I DIDN'T TELL YOU, BUT I JOINED THE AQUARIUM CLUB.
YEAH, I KNOW.
So it seems!
BUT YOU INVITED ME TO JOIN THE HOME EC CLUB, RIGHT?
CLENCH
I WAS PLEASED YOU ASKED ME...
...SO I WANTED TO TELL YOU *MY-SELF*.
...

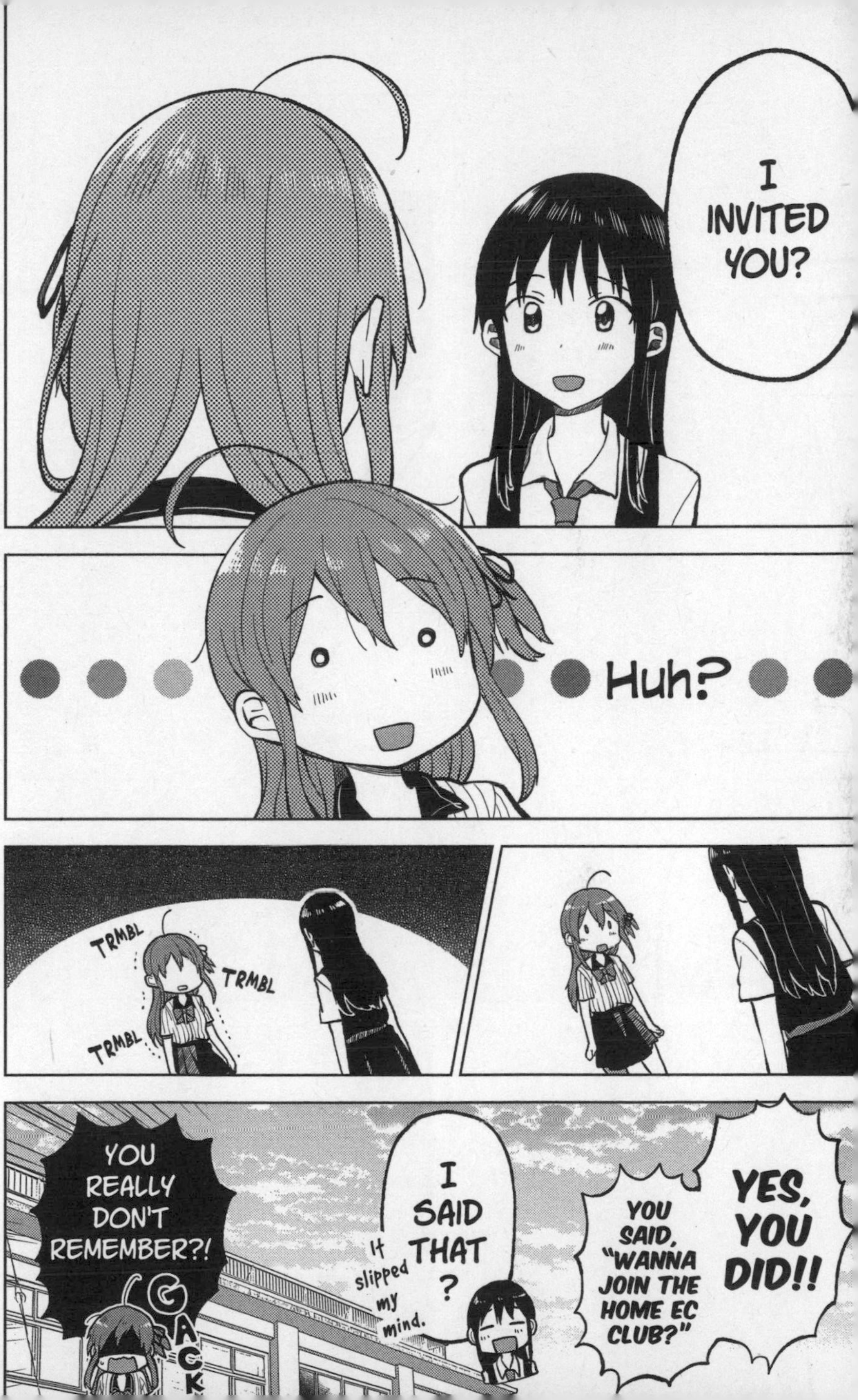
I INVITED YOU?
Huh?
TRMBL
TRMBL
TRMBL
YES, YOU DID!!
YOU SAID, "WANNA JOIN THE HOME EC CLUB?"
I SAID THAT?
It slipped my mind.
YOU REALLY DON'T REMEMBER?!
GACK

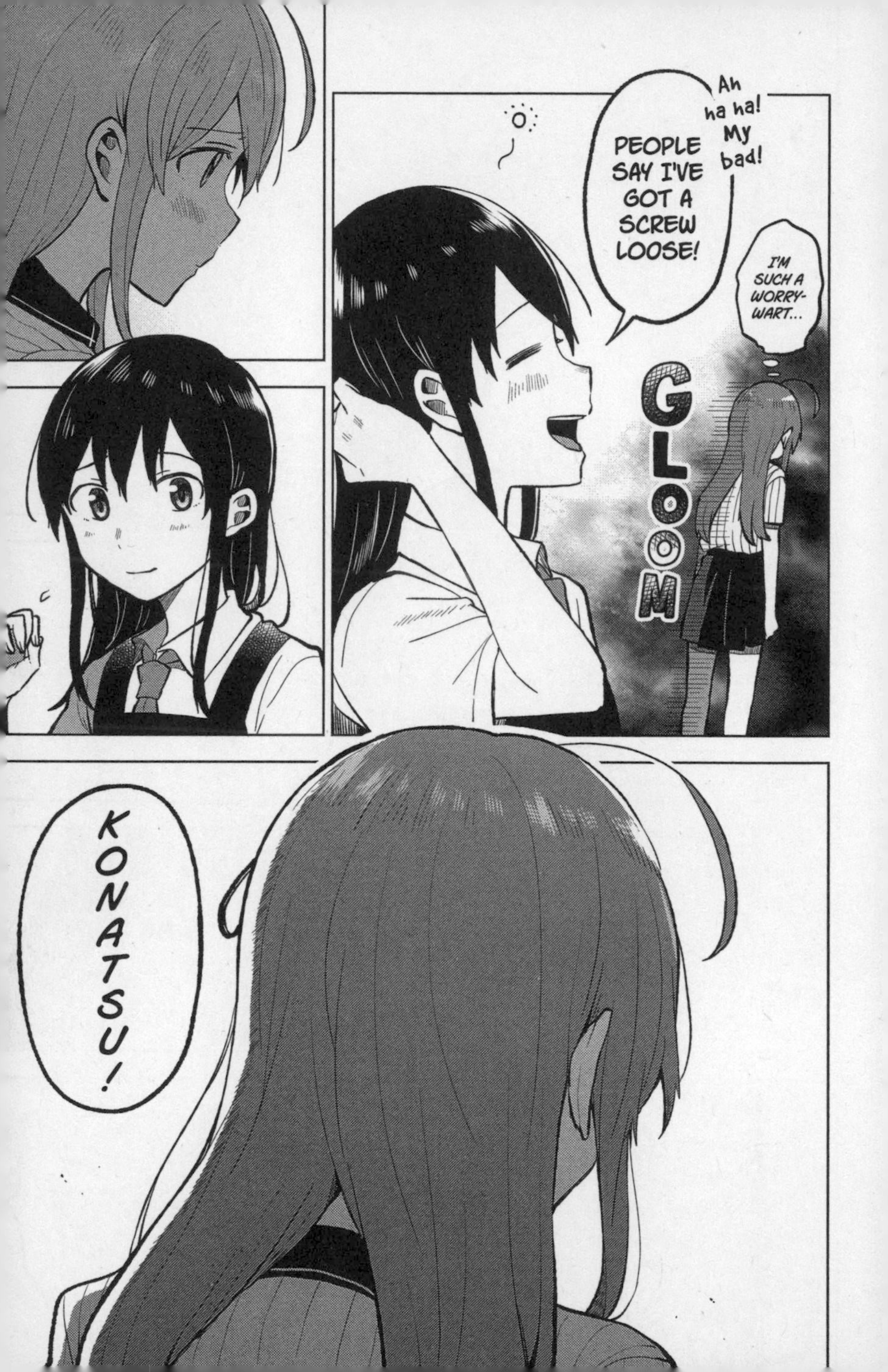

Ah ha ha! My bad!
PEOPLE SAY I'VE GOT A SCREW LOOSE!
I'M SUCH A WORRY-WART...
GLOOM
KONATSU!

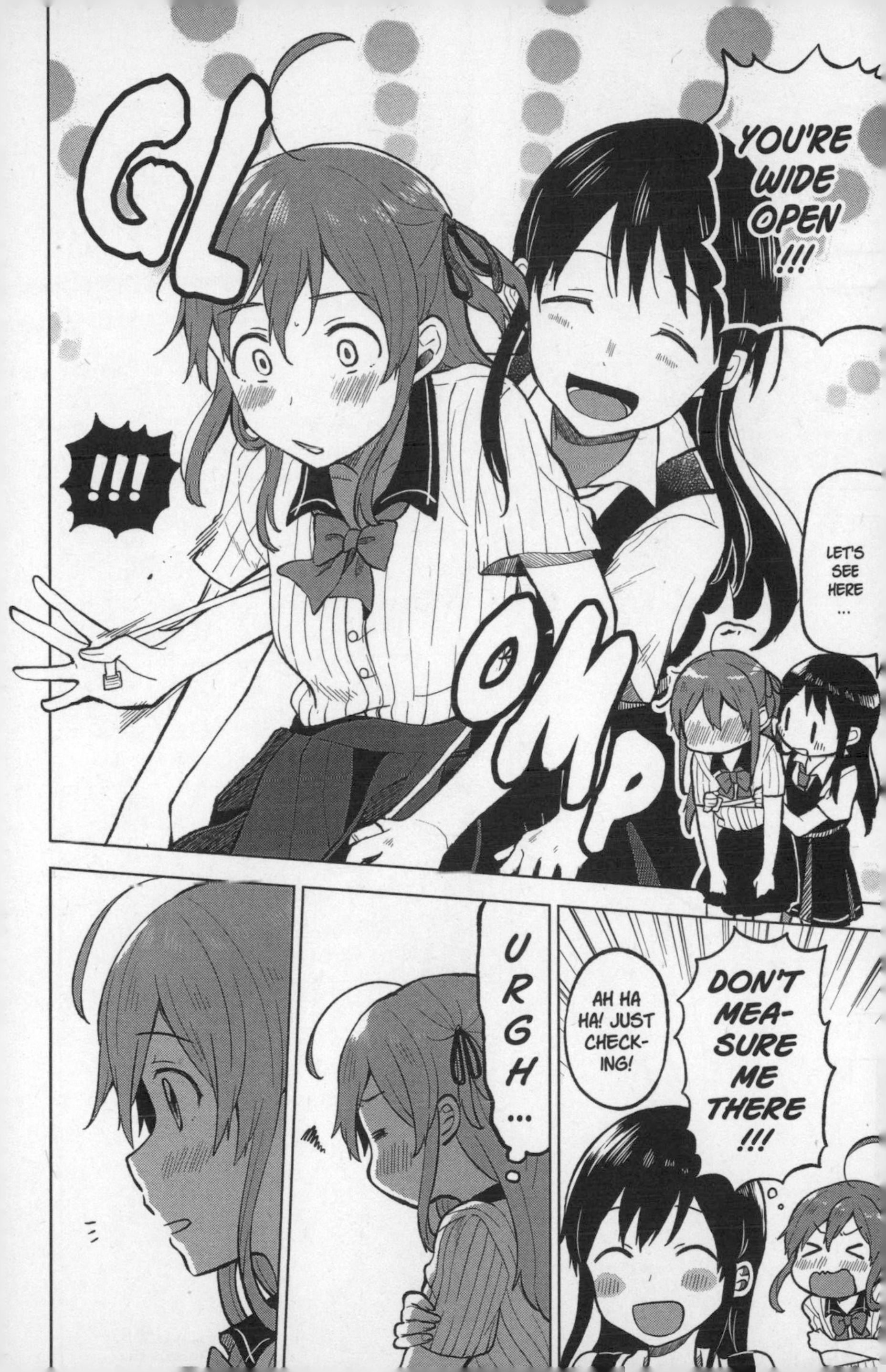
YOU'RE WIDE OPEN!!!
GL
OMP
!!!
LET'S SEE HERE...
DON'T MEA-SURE ME THERE!!!
AH HA HA! JUST CHECK-ING!
URGH...

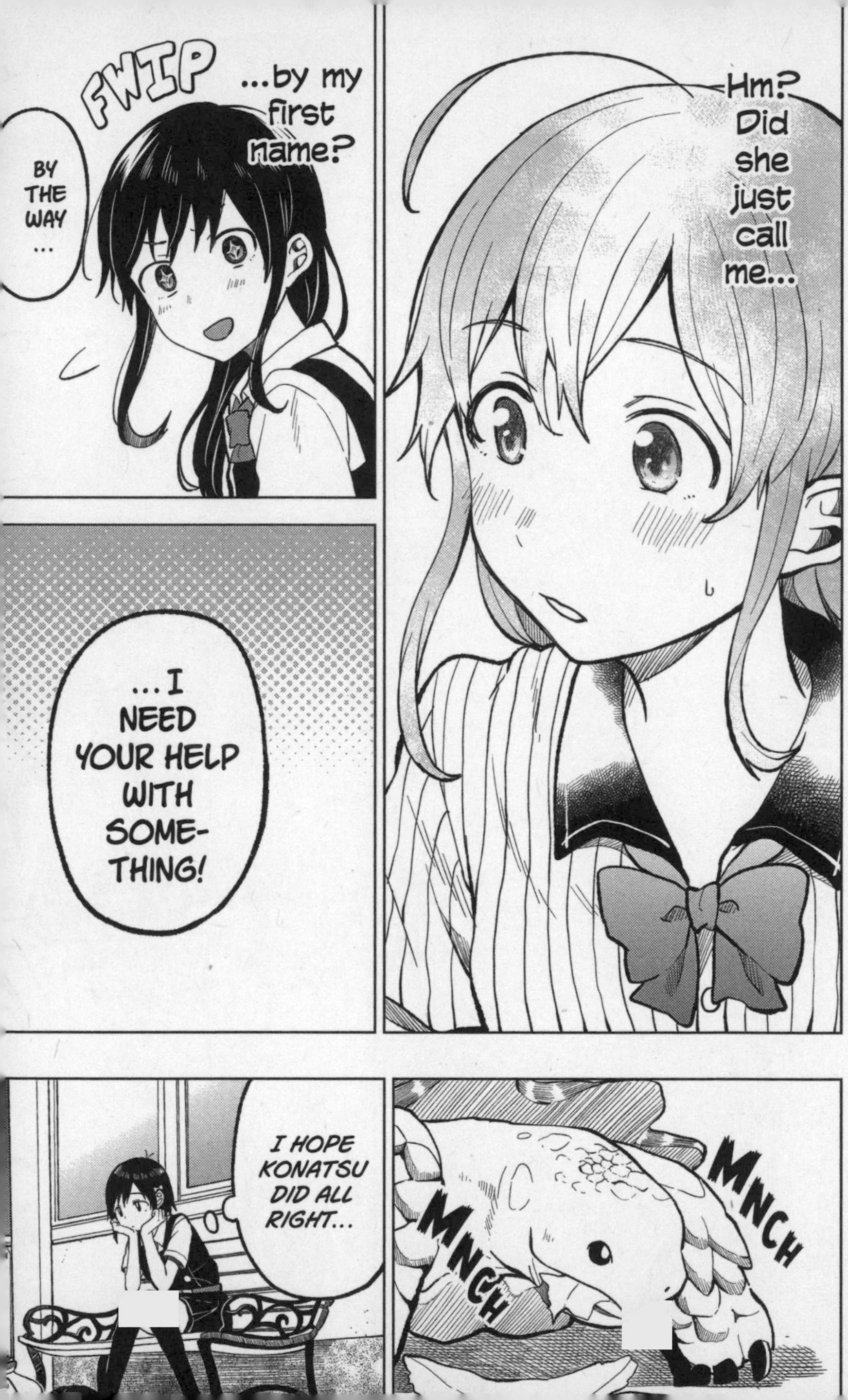
Hm? Did she just call me...
...by my first name?
FWIP
BY THE WAY...
...I NEED YOUR HELP WITH SOME-THING!
MNCH
MNCH
I HOPE KONATSU DID ALL RIGHT...

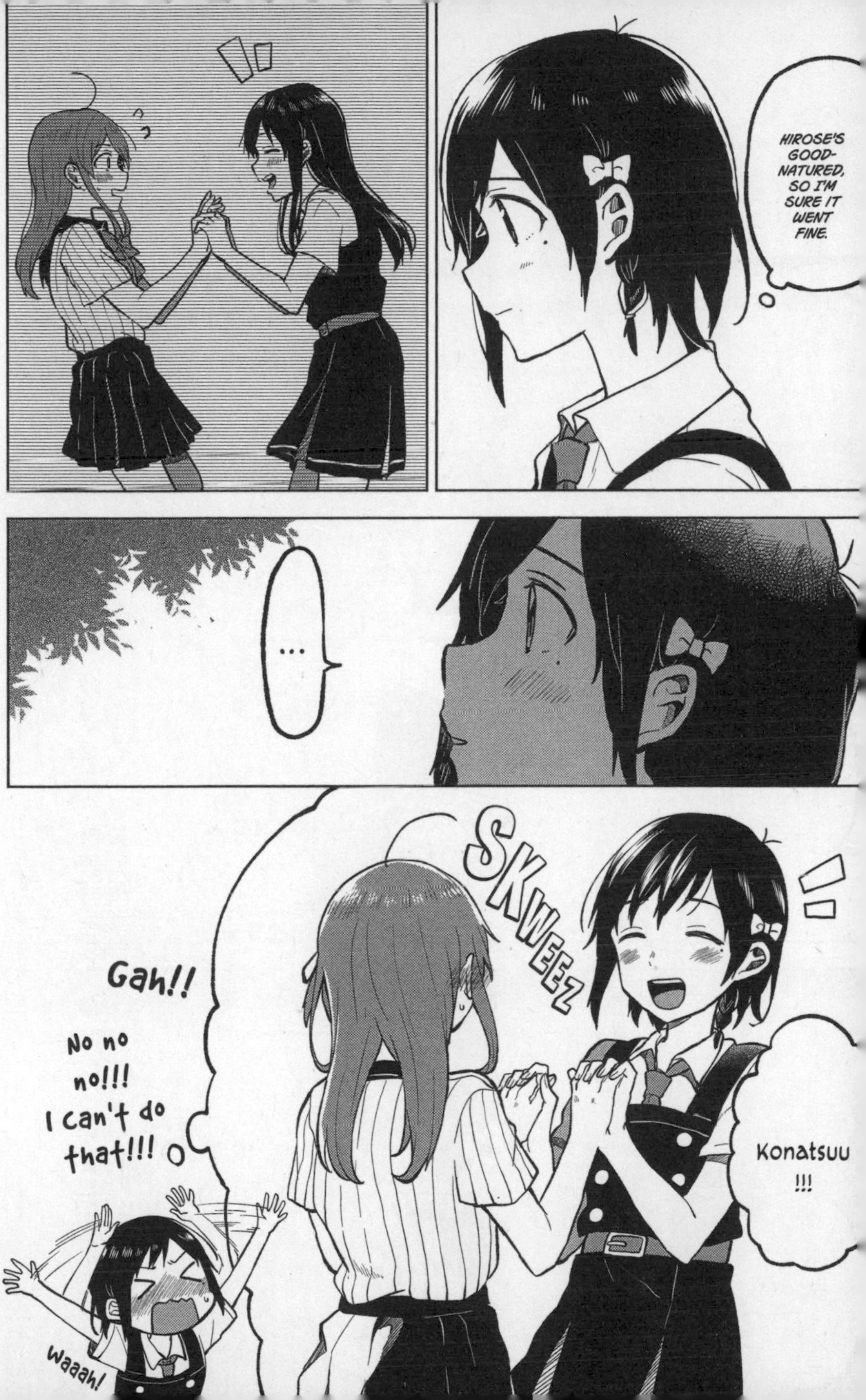
HIROSE'S GOOD-NATURED, SO I'M SURE IT WENT FINE.
...
SKWEEZ
Konatsuu!!!
Gah!!
No no no!!! I can't do that!!!
Waaah!

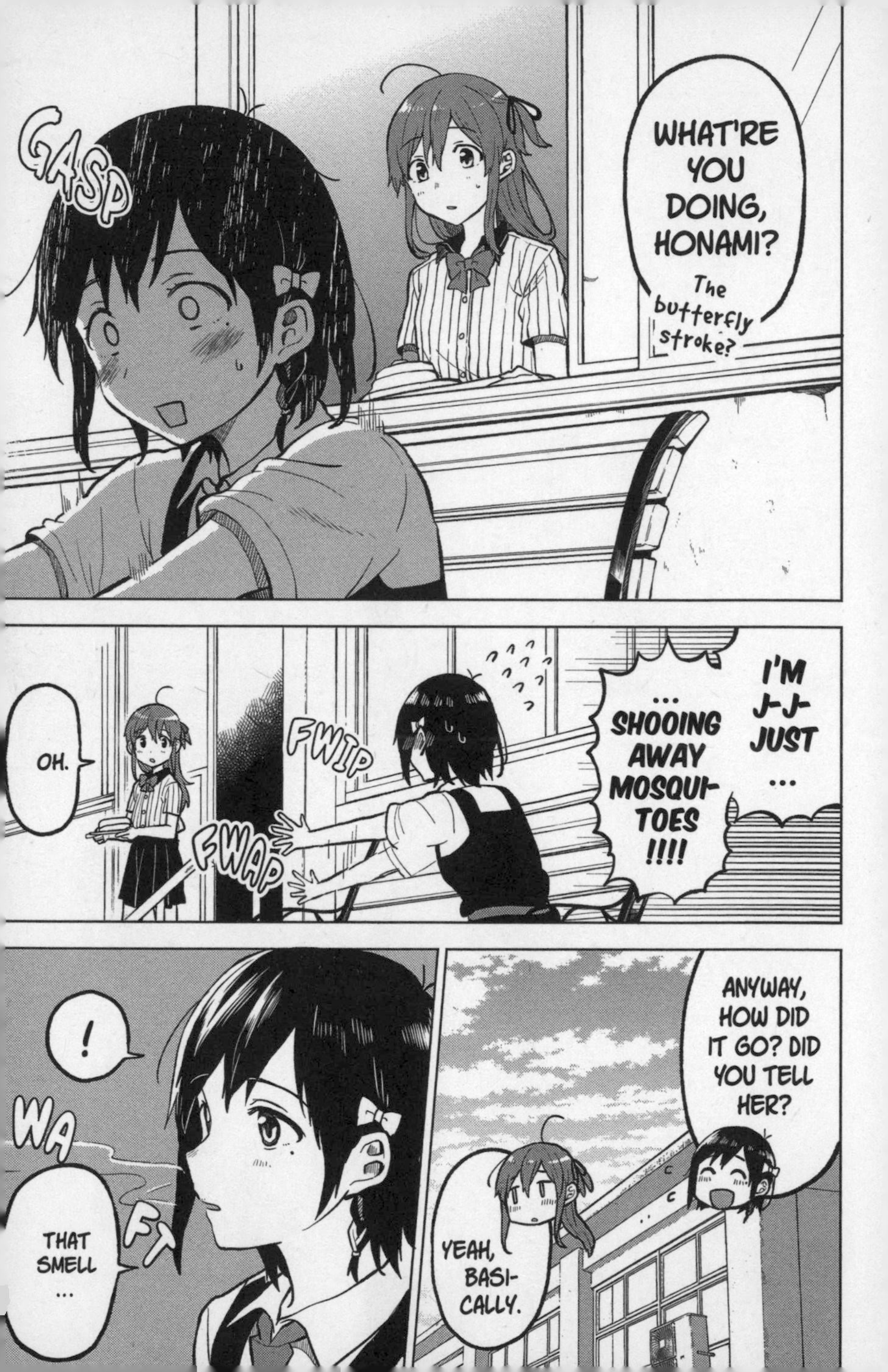
WHAT'RE YOU DOING, HONAMI?
The butterfly stroke?
GASP
I'M J-J-JUST ...
... SHOOING AWAY MOSQUI-TOES !!!!
FWIP
FWAP
OH.
ANYWAY, HOW DID IT GO? DID YOU TELL HER?
YEAH, BASI-CALLY.
!
WAFT
THAT SMELL ...

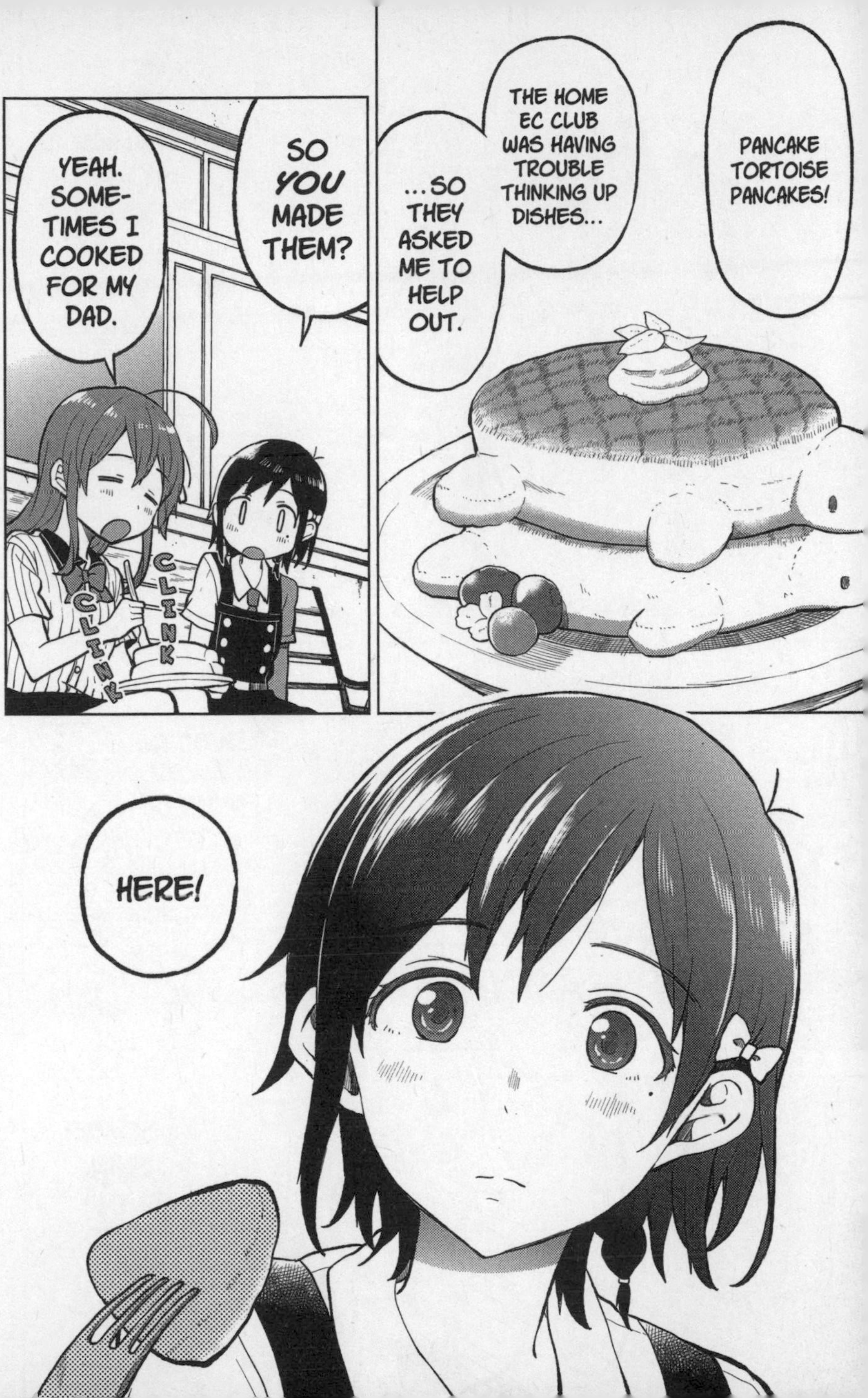
PANCAKE TORTOISE PANCAKES!
THE HOME EC CLUB WAS HAVING TROUBLE THINKING UP DISHES...
...SO THEY ASKED ME TO HELP OUT.
SO *YOU* MADE THEM?
YEAH. SOME-TIMES I COOKED FOR MY DAD.
CLINK
CLINK
HERE!

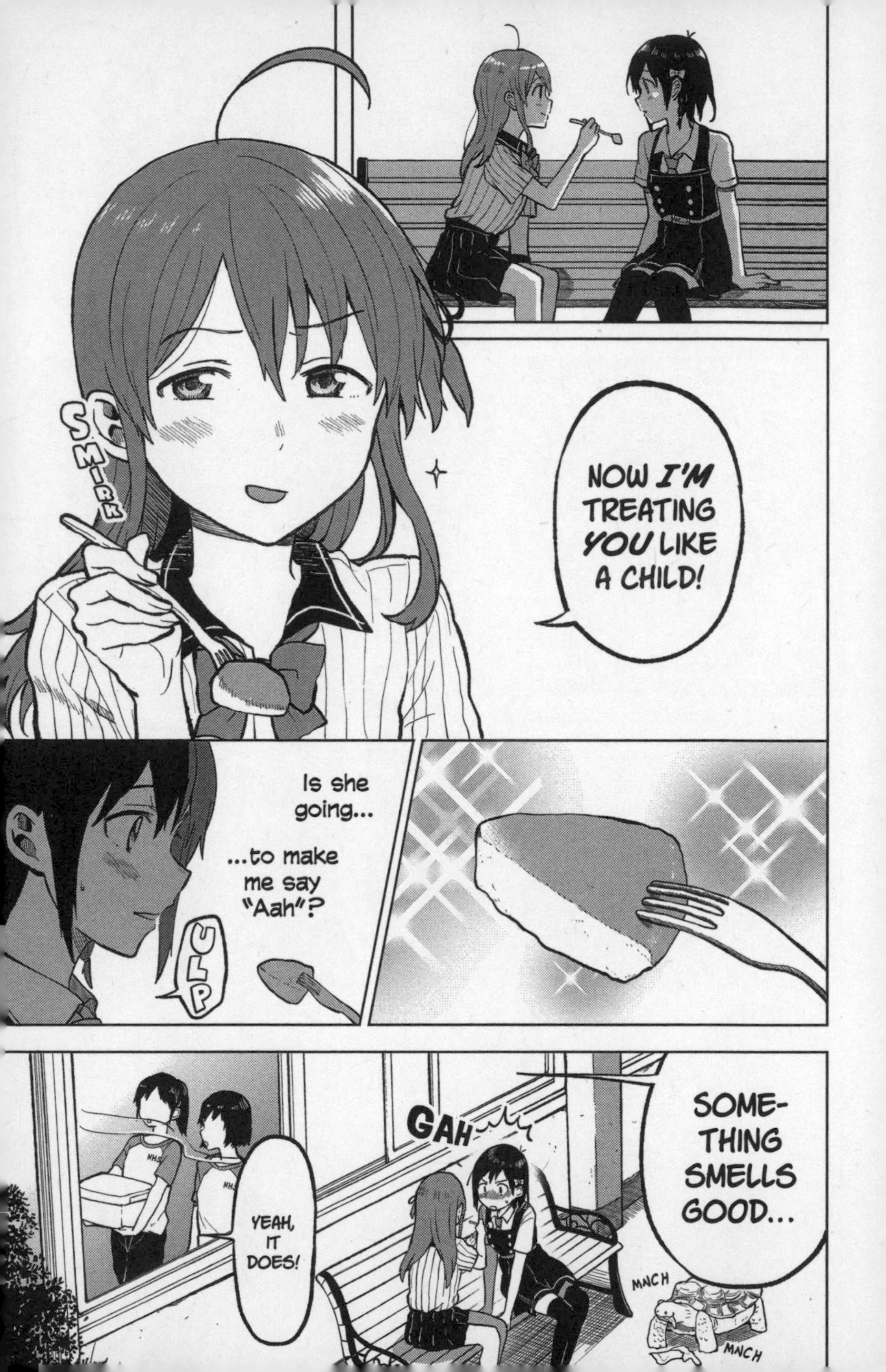
NOW I'M TREATING YOU LIKE A CHILD!
SMIRK
Is she going...
...to make me say "Aah"?
ULP
SOME-THING SMELLS GOOD...
GAH
YEAH, IT DOES!
MNCH
MNCH

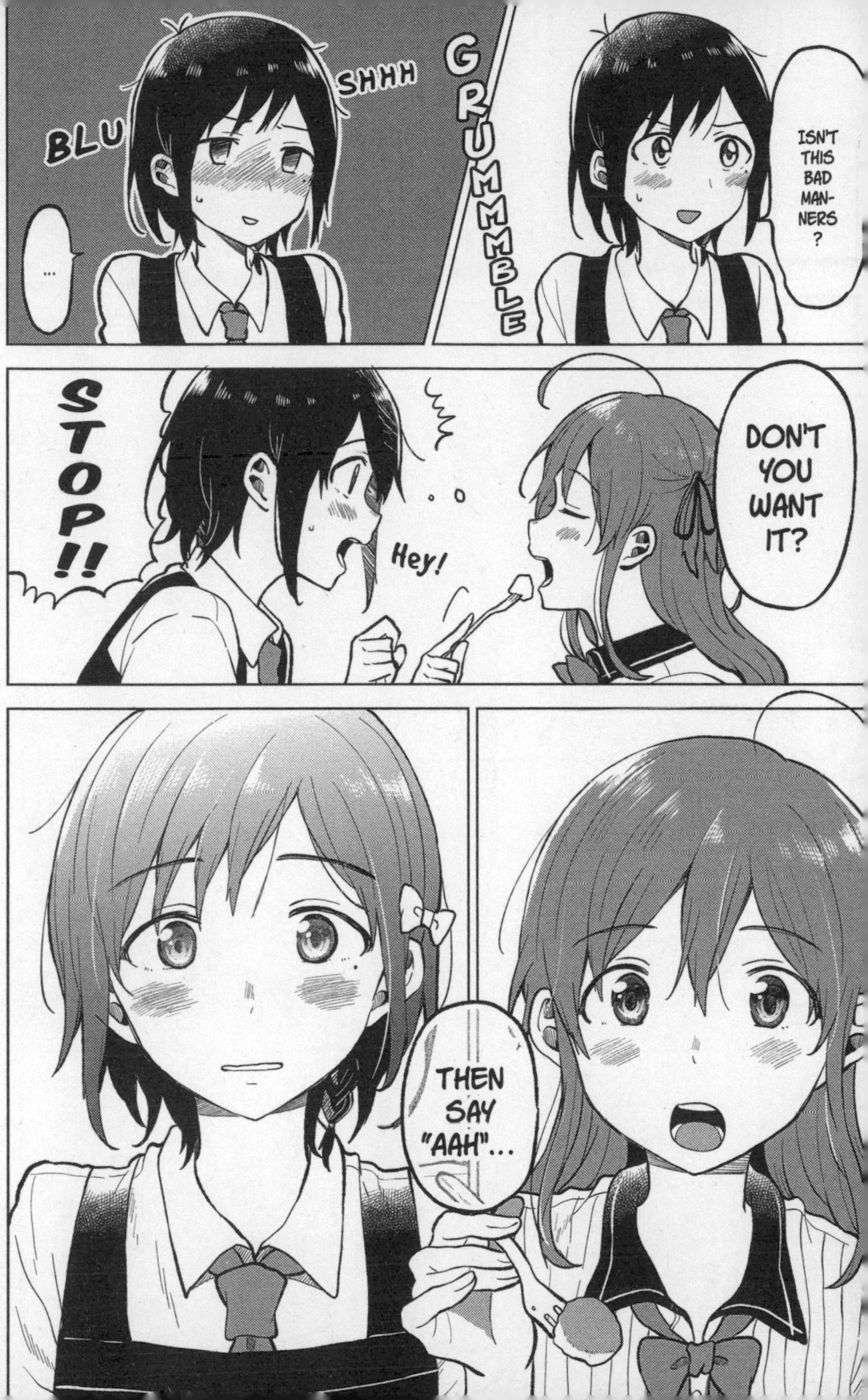
ISN'T THIS BAD MAN-NERS?
GRUMMBLE
BLU SHHH
...
DON'T YOU WANT IT?
Hey!
STOP!!
THEN SAY "AAH"...

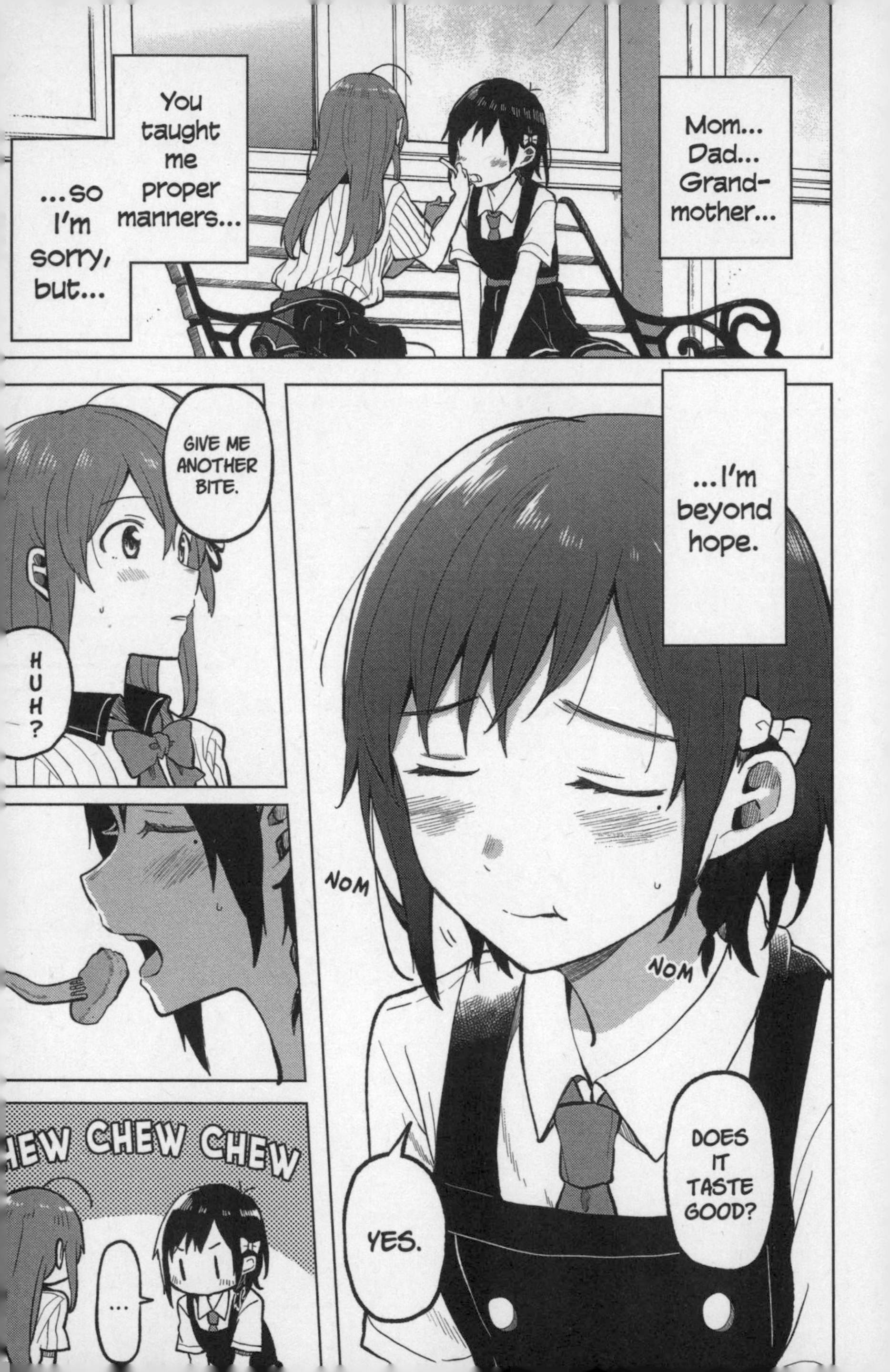
Mom... Dad... Grand-mother...
You taught me proper manners...
...so I'm sorry, but...
...I'm beyond hope.
NOM
NOM
DOES IT TASTE GOOD?
YES.
GIVE ME ANOTHER BITE.
HUH?
HEW CHEW CHEW
...

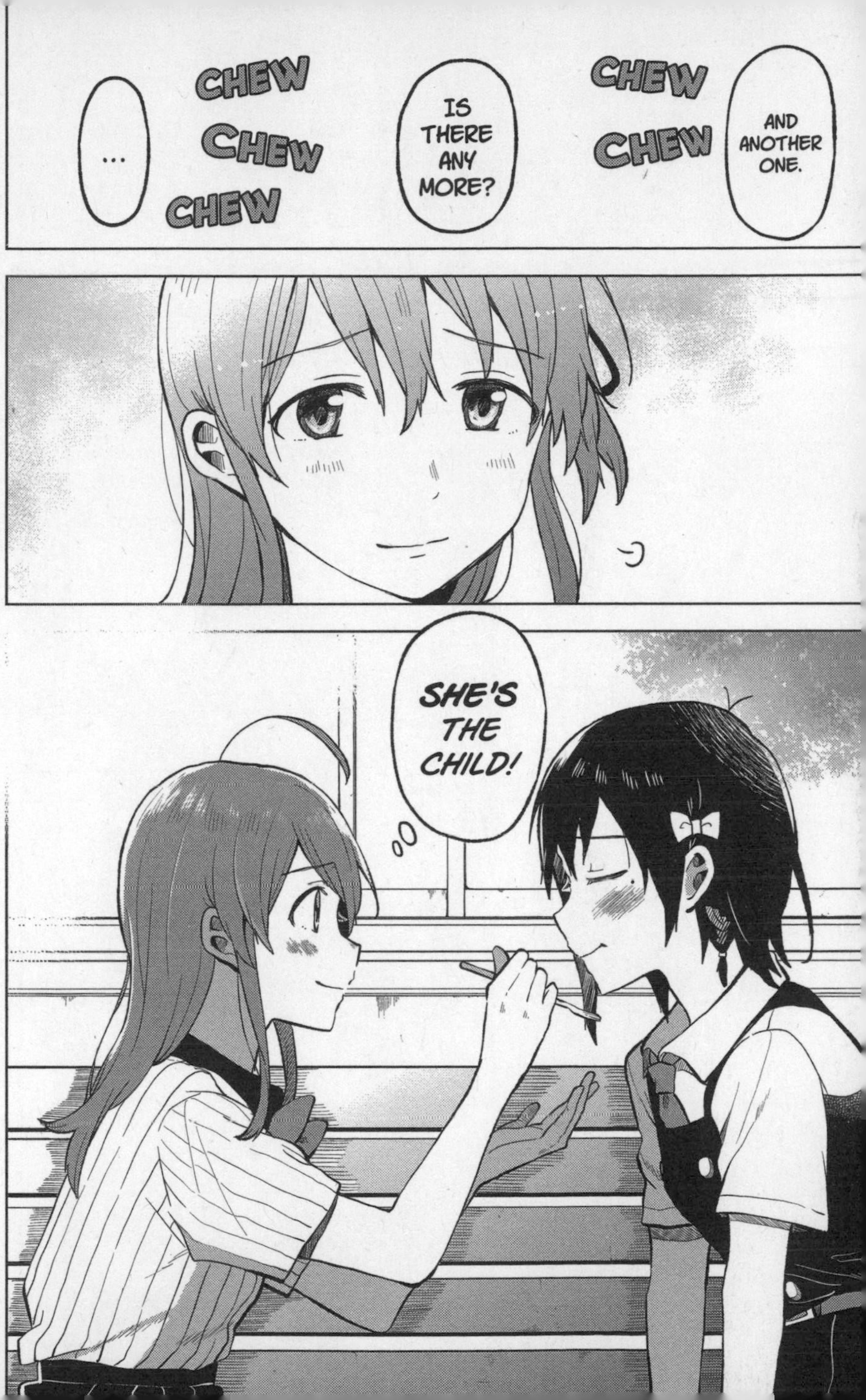
AND ANOTHER ONE.
CHEW
CHEW
IS THERE ANY MORE?
CHEW
CHEW
CHEW
...
SHE'S THE CHILD!

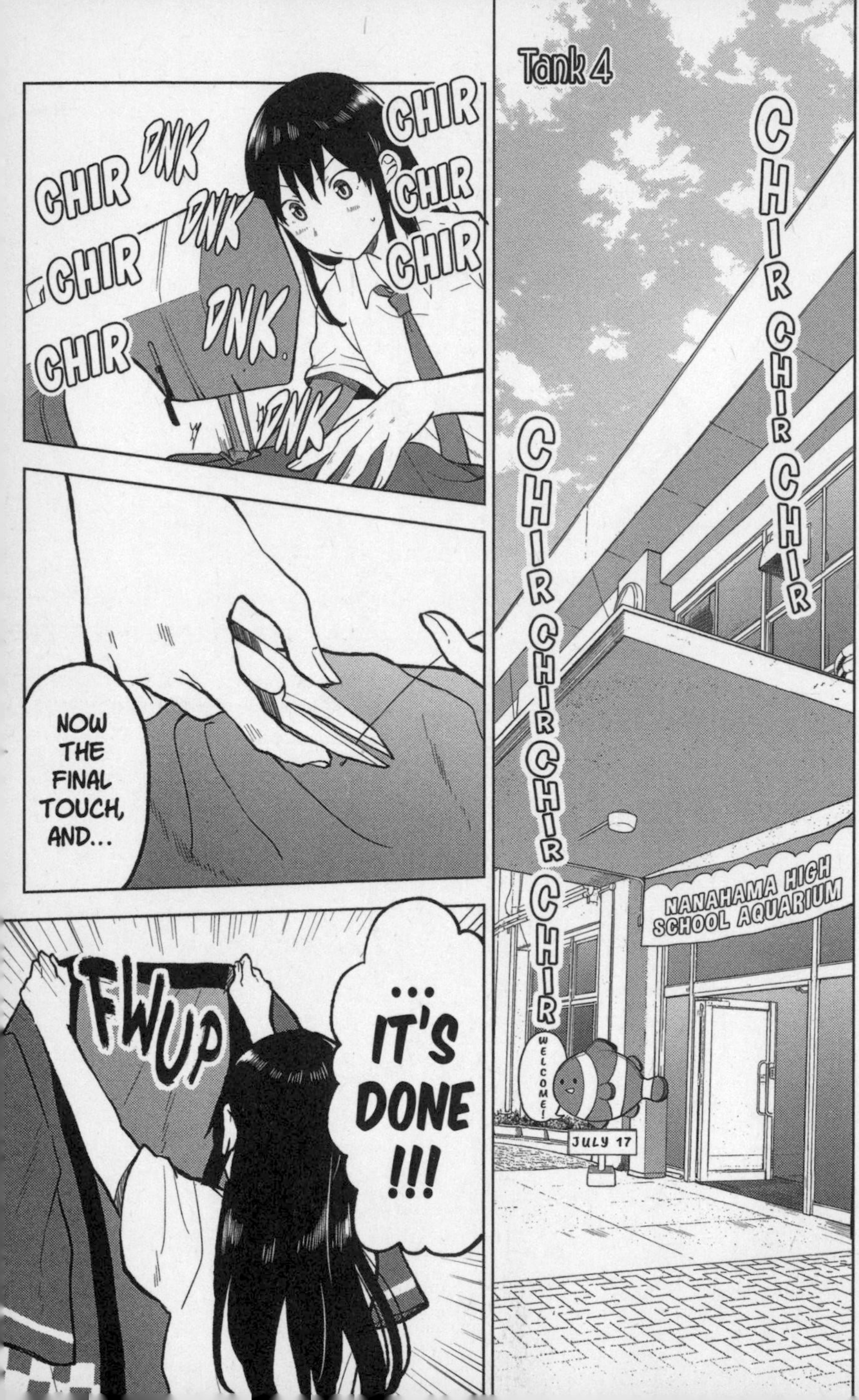
Tank 4
CHIR CHIR CHIR CHIR
CHIR CHIR CHIR CHIR
NANAHAMA HIGH SCHOOL AQUARIUM
WELCOME!
JULY 17
CHIR
CHIR
CHIR
DNK
CHIR
DNK
CHIR
DNK
CHIR
DNK
NOW THE FINAL TOUCH, AND...
... IT'S DONE !!!
TFWUP

Tank 4:
Koyuki Honami Can't Bear It

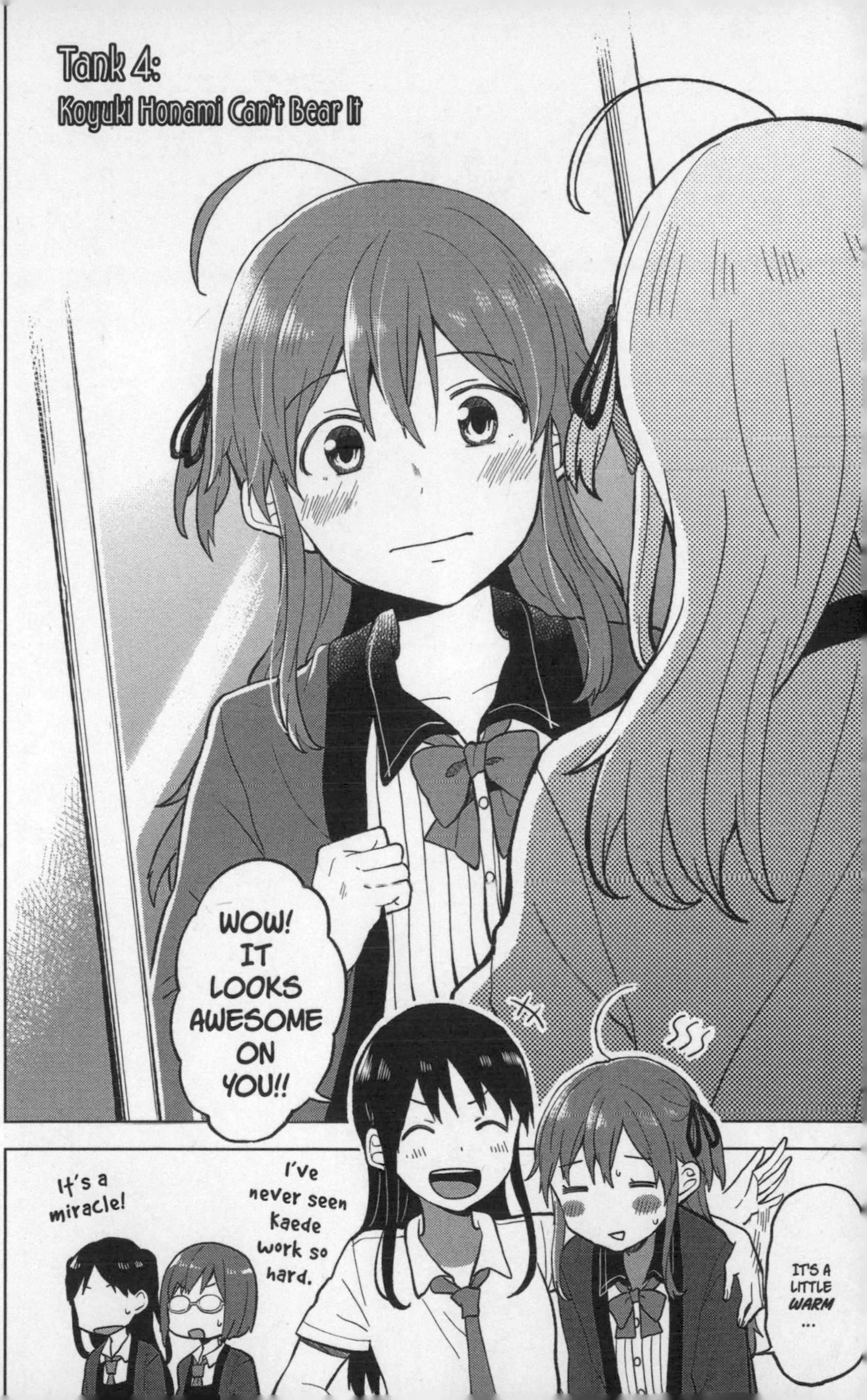
WOW! IT LOOKS AWESOME ON YOU!!
IT'S A LITTLE WARM...
I've never seen Kaede work so hard.
It's a miracle!

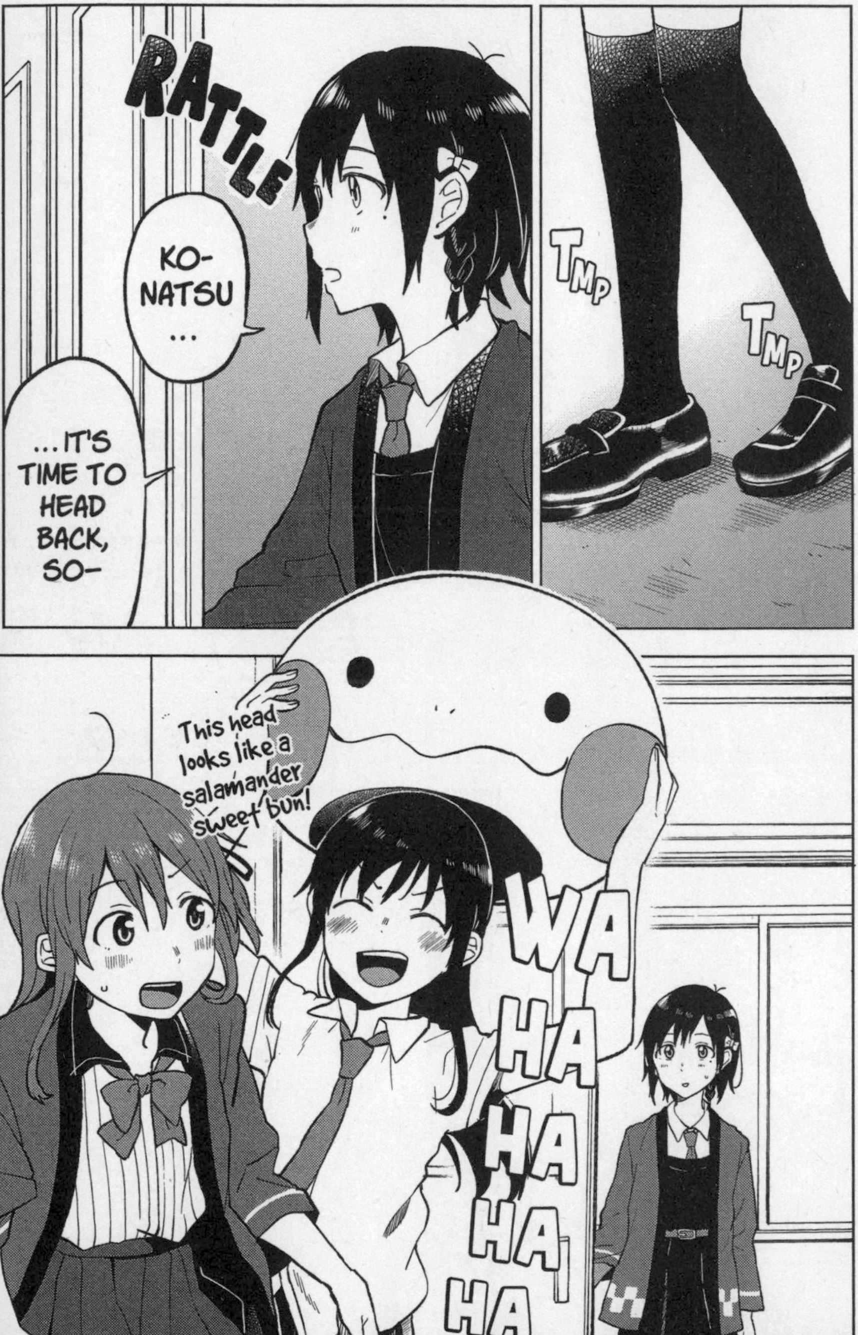
TMP
TMP
RATTLE
KO-NATSU ...
... IT'S TIME TO HEAD BACK, SO-
WA HA HA HA HA HA
This head looks like a salamander sweet bun!

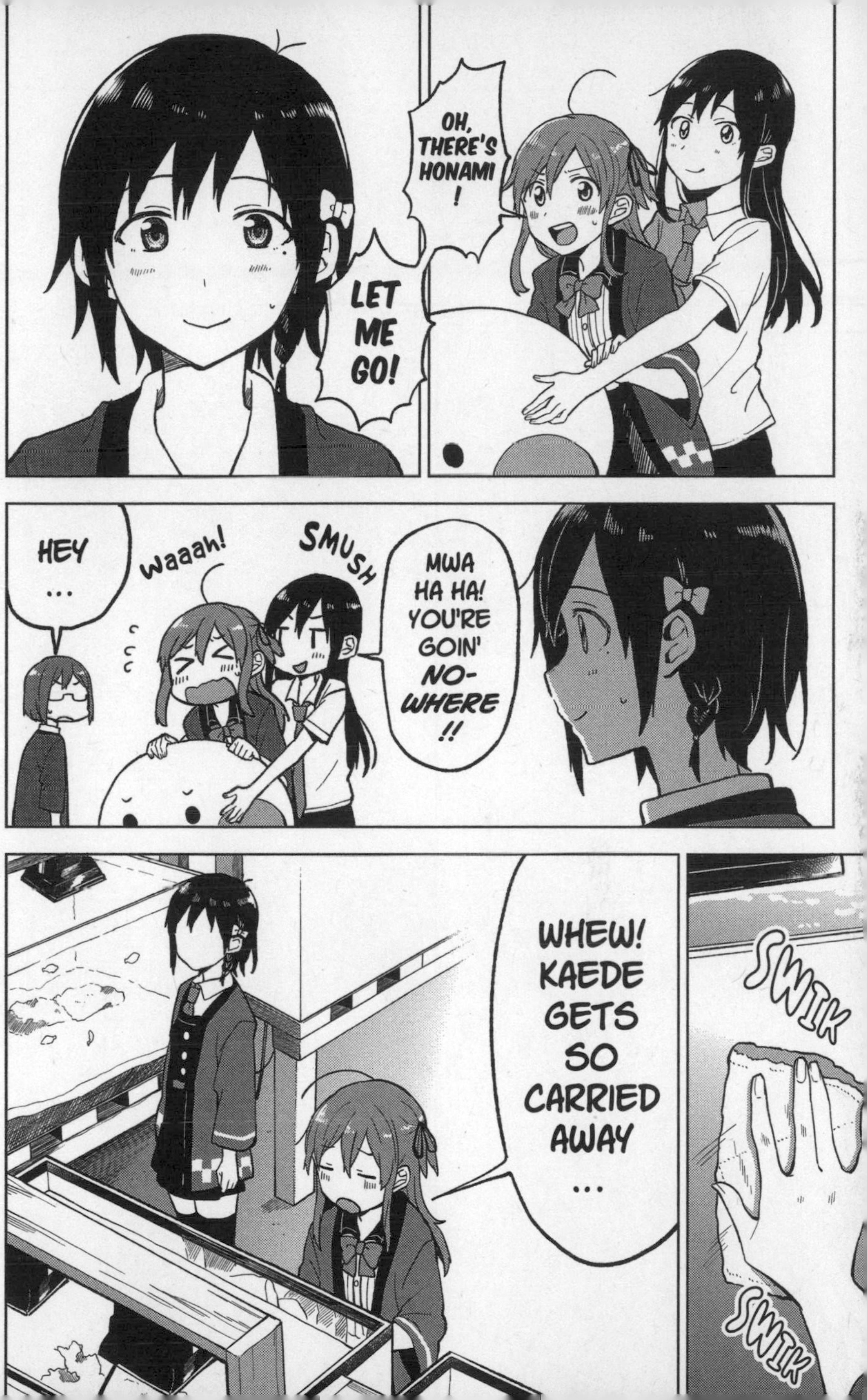
OH, THERE'S HONAMI !
LET ME GO!
MWA HA HA! YOU'RE GOIN' NO-WHERE !!
SMUSH
Waaah!
HEY ...
SWIK
SWIK
WHEW! KAEDE GETS SO CARRIED AWAY ...

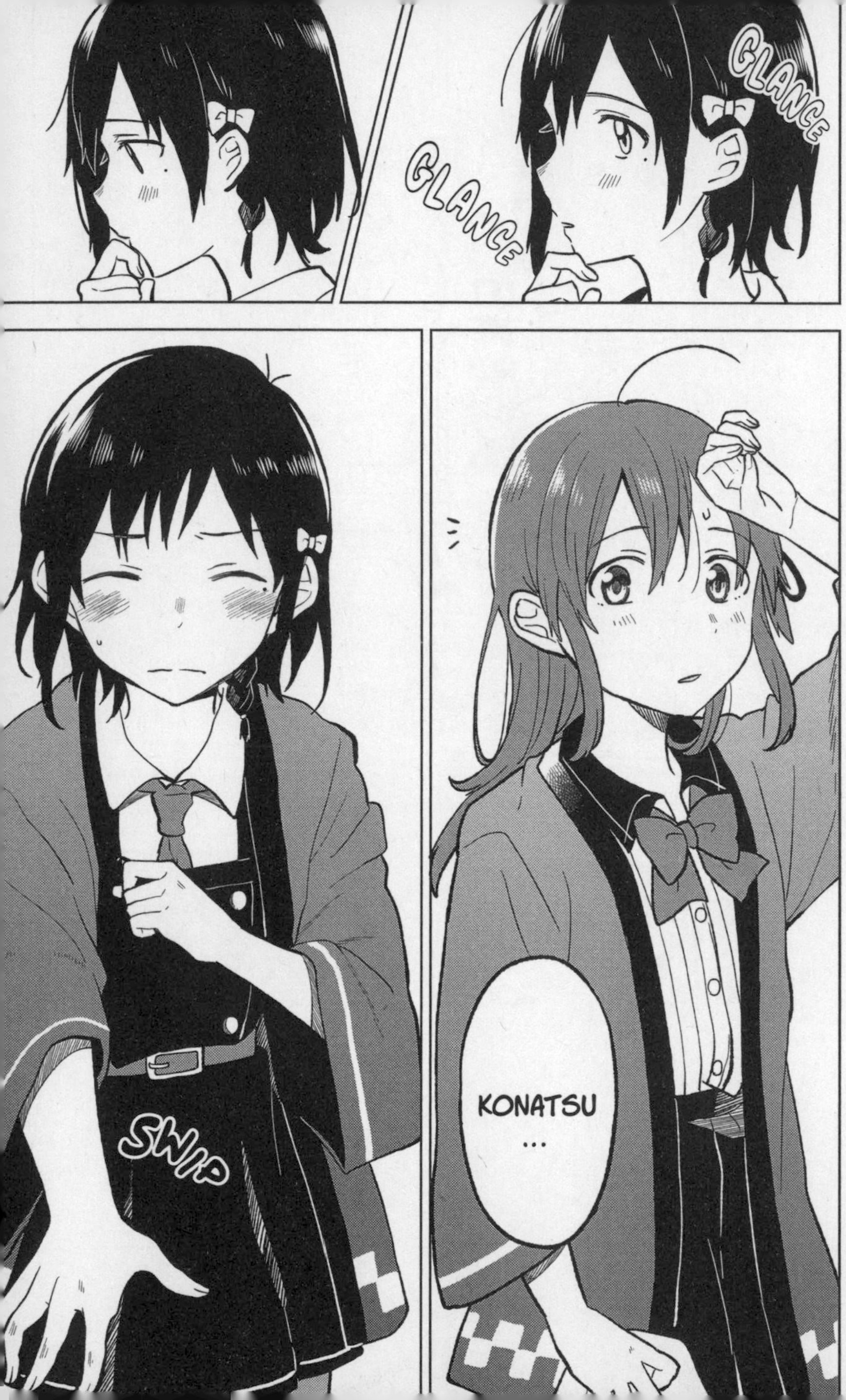
GLANCE
GLANCE
KONATSU ...
SWIP

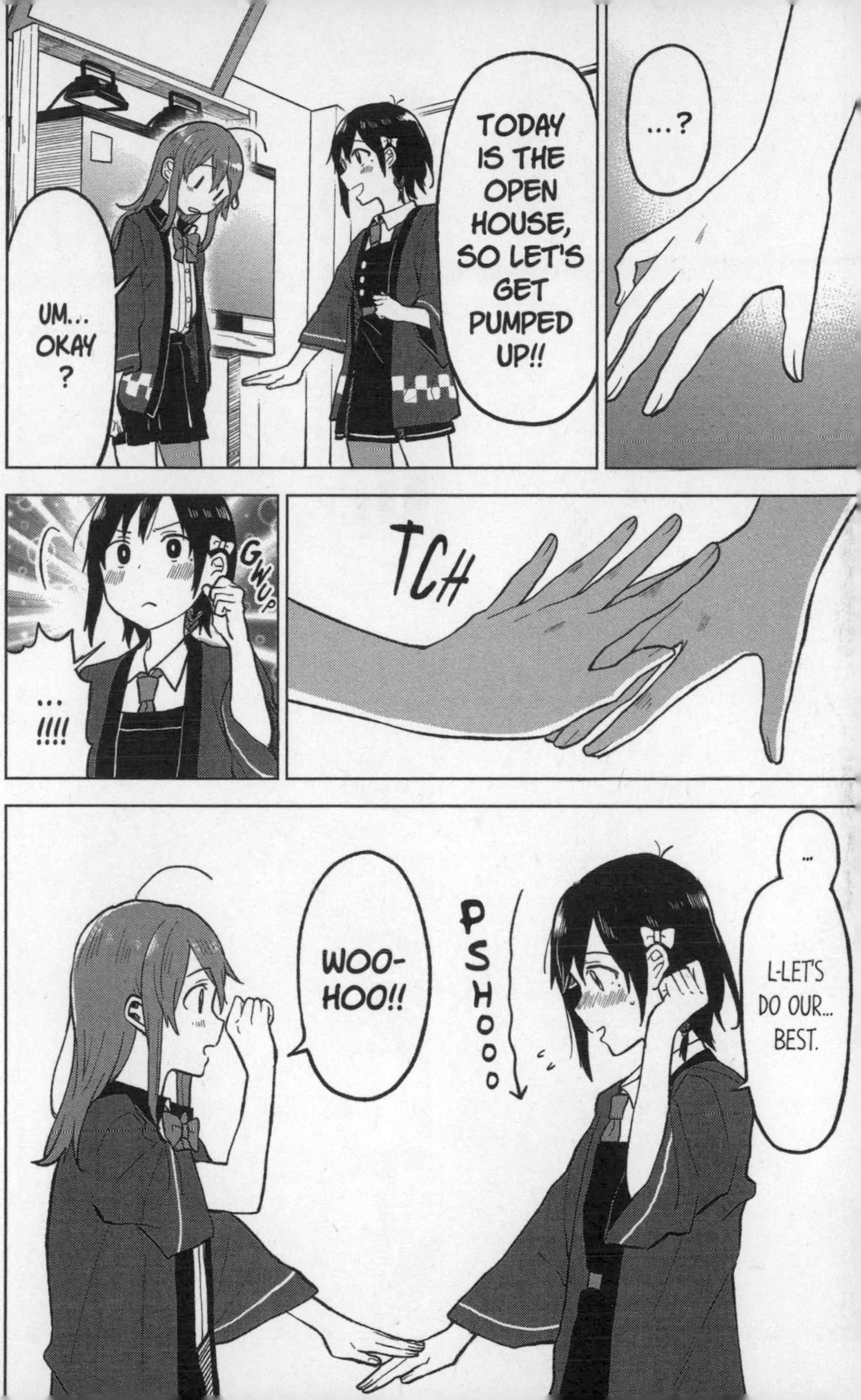
...?
TODAY IS THE OPEN HOUSE, SO LET'S GET PUMPED UP!!
UM... OKAY?
TCH
GWUP
... !!!!
...
L-LET'S DO OUR... BEST.
PSHOOO
WOO-HOO!!

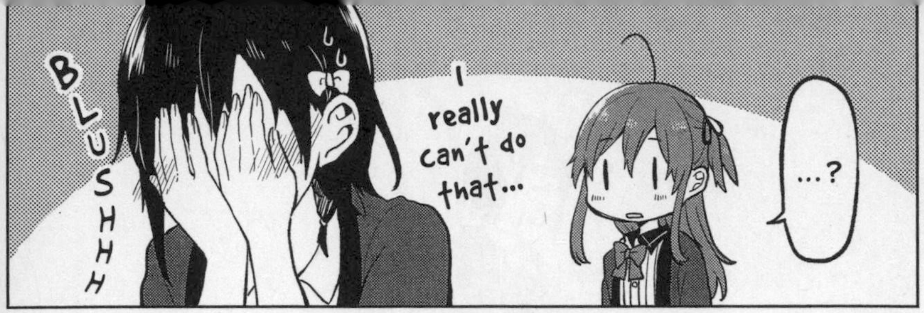
...?
I really can't do that...
BLUSHHH

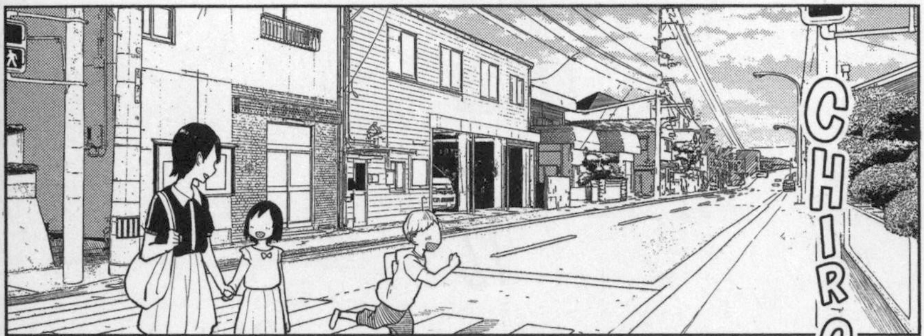
CHIR CHIR CHIR

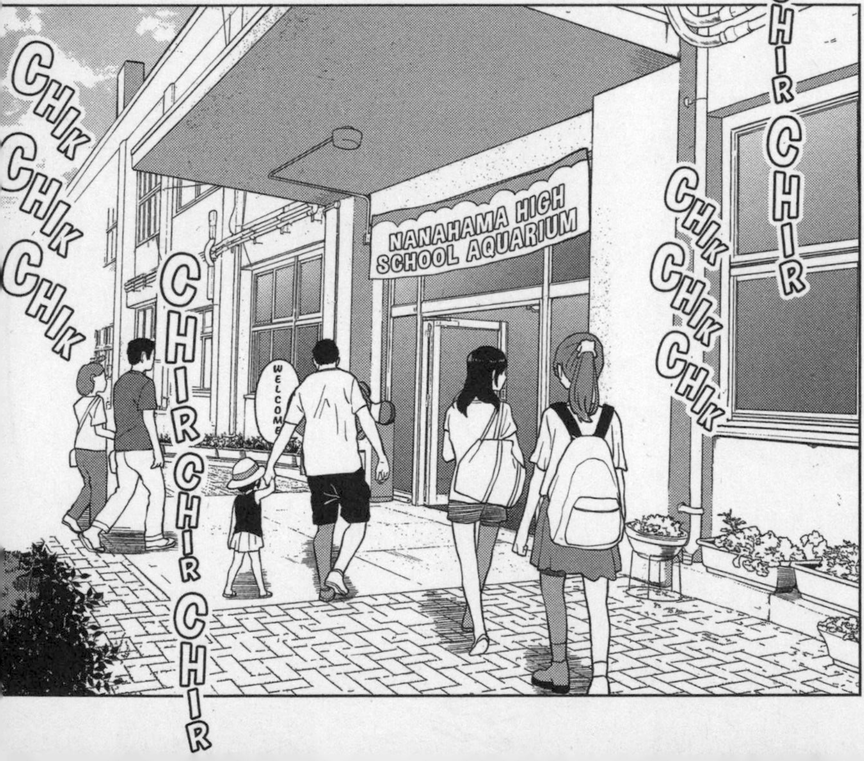
CHIK CHIK CHIK
NANAHAMA HIGH SCHOOL AQUARIUM
WELCOME
CHIR CHIR CHIR
CHIK CHIK CHIK

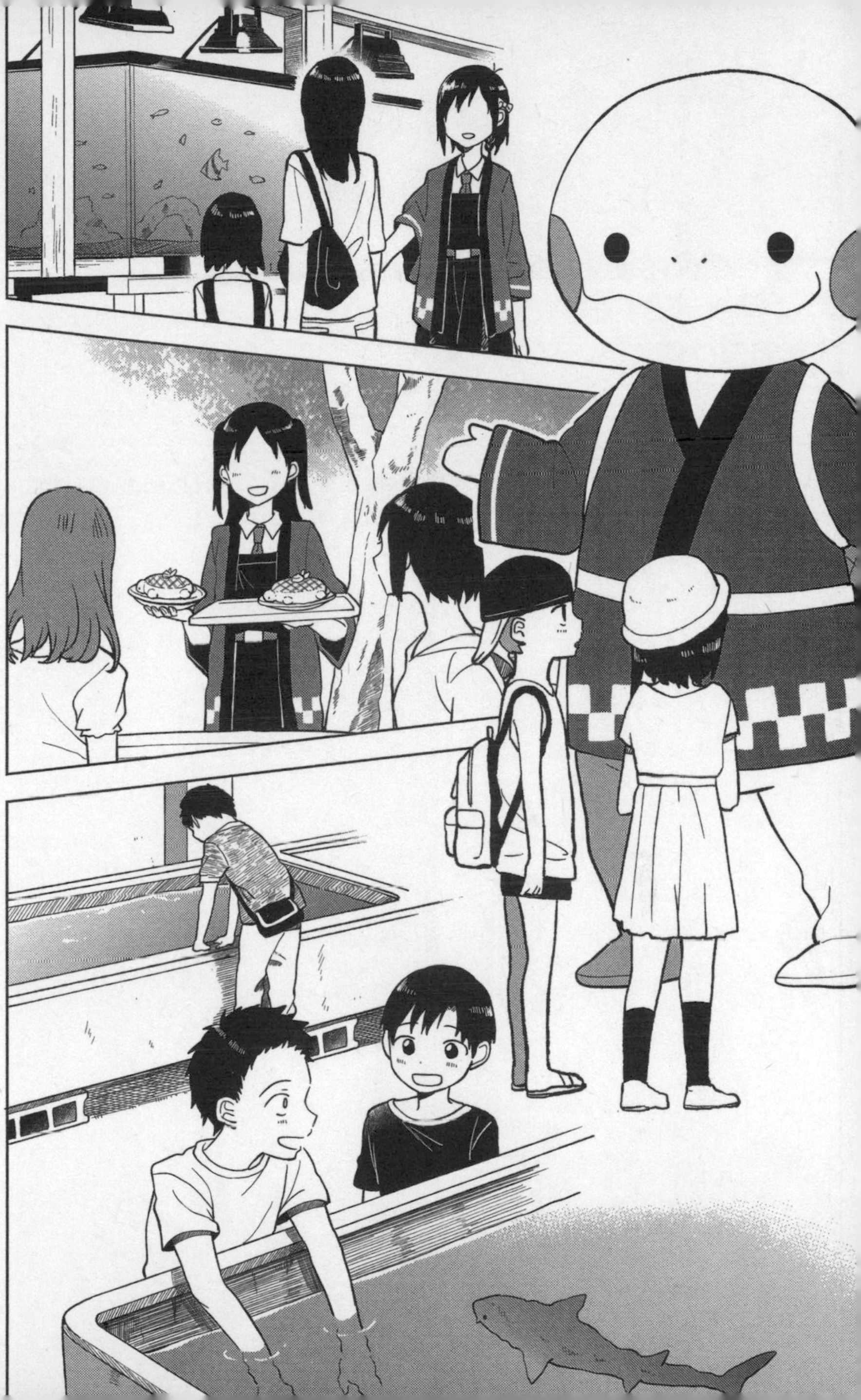

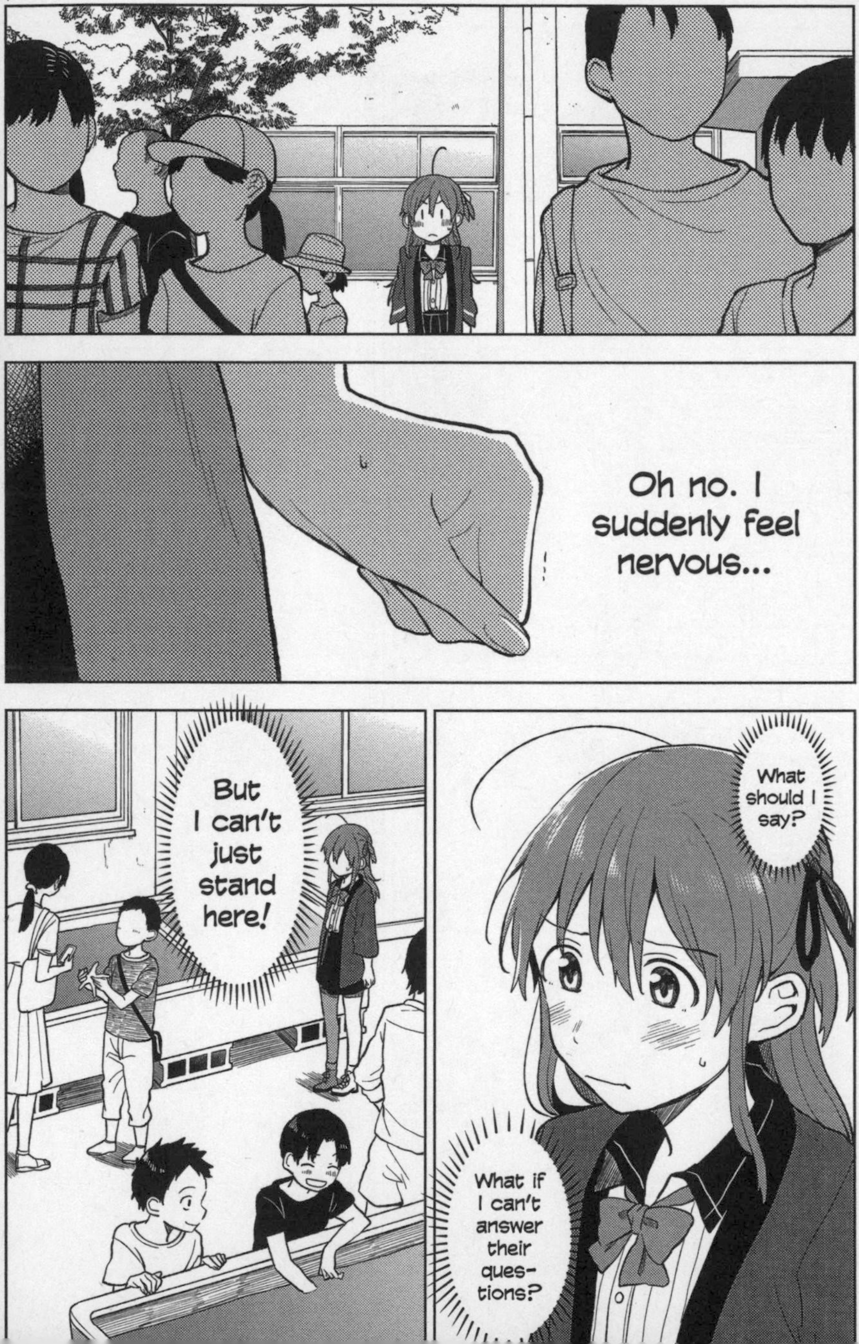
Oh no. I suddenly feel nervous...
What should I say?
What if I can't answer their ques-tions?
But I can't just stand here!

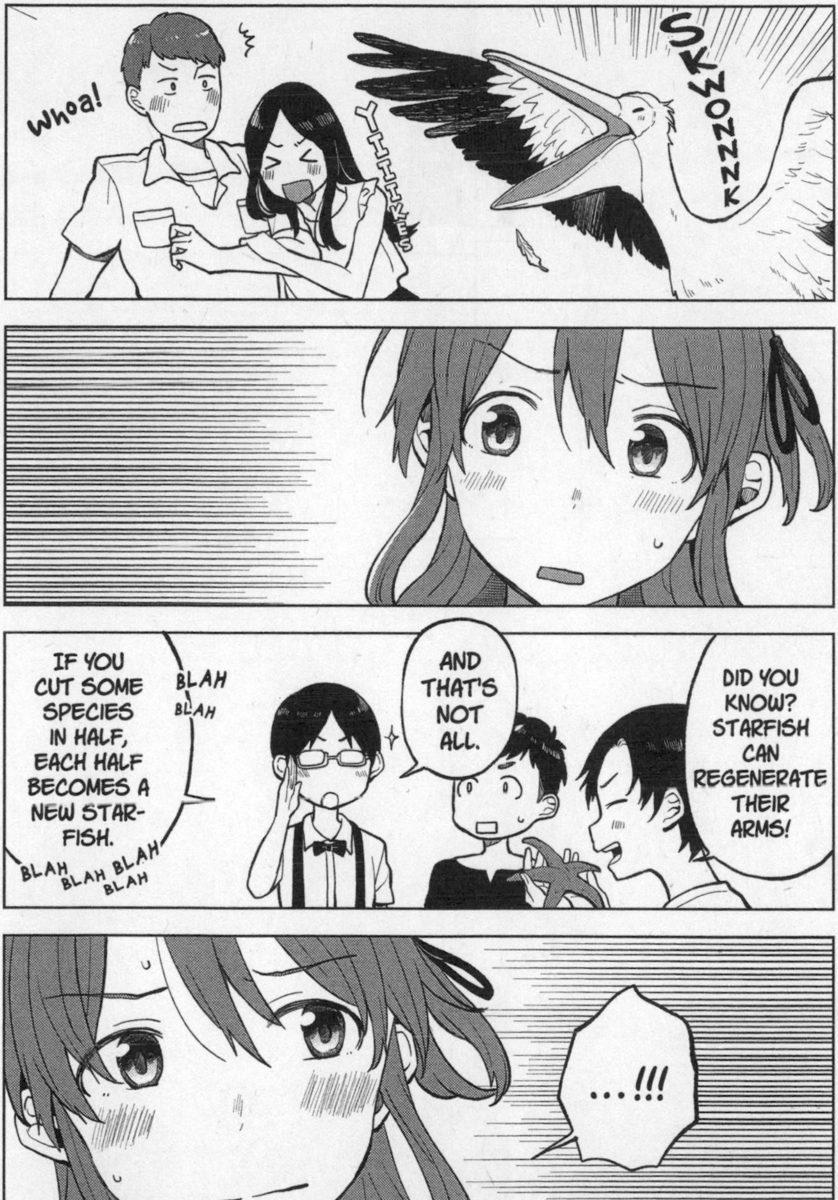
SKWONNK
YIIIIKES
Whoa!
DID YOU KNOW? STARFISH CAN REGENERATE THEIR ARMS!
AND THAT'S NOT ALL.
BLAH BLAH
IF YOU CUT SOME SPECIES IN HALF, EACH HALF BECOMES A NEW STARFISH.
BLAH BLAH BLAH BLAH
...!!!

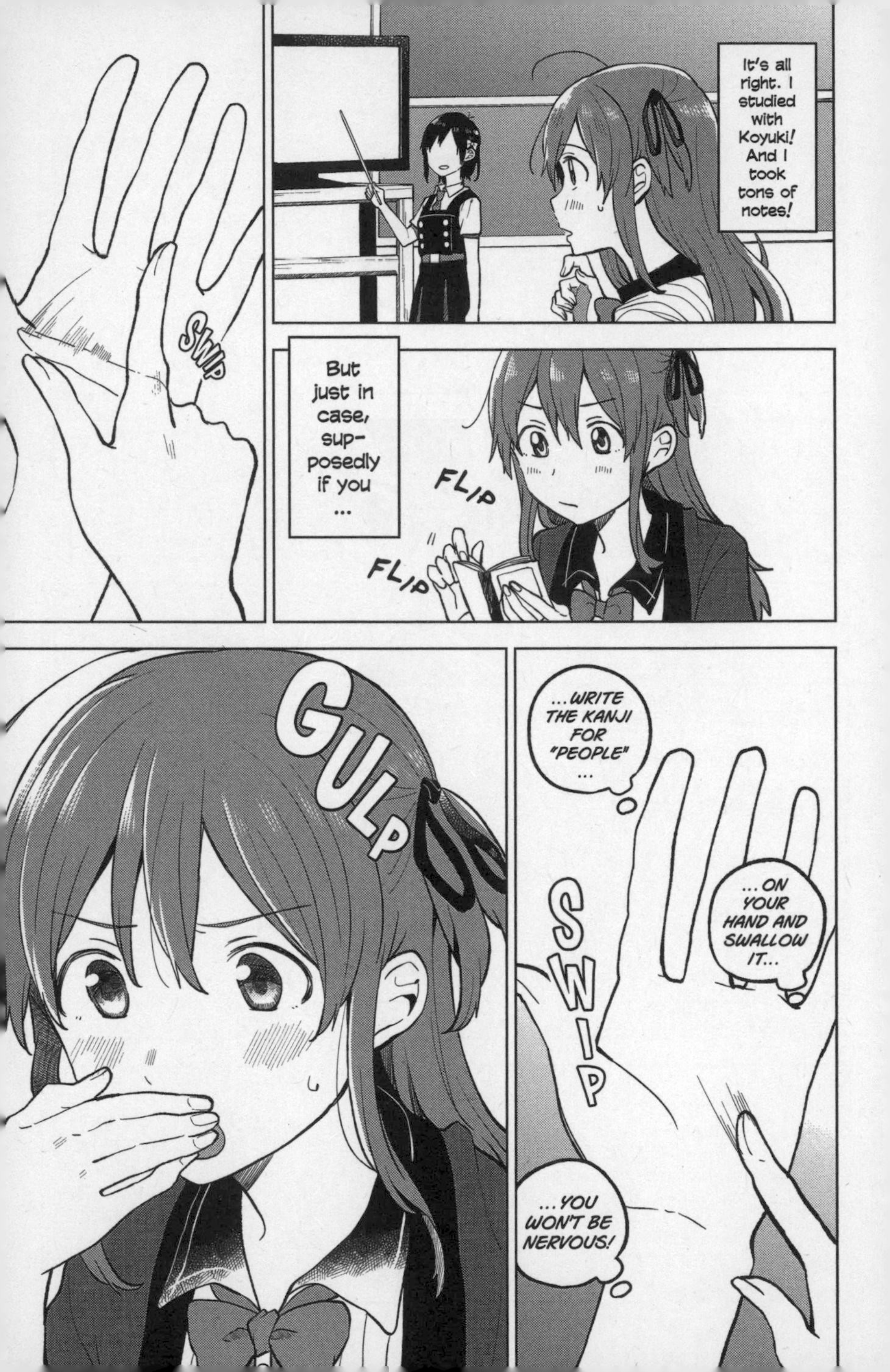
It's all right. I studied with Koyuki! And I took tons of notes!
But just in case, sup-posedly if you ...
FLip
FLip
SWIP
...WRITE THE KANJI FOR "PEOPLE" ...
SWIP
...ON YOUR HAND AND SWALLOW IT...
...YOU WON'T BE NERVOUS!
GULP

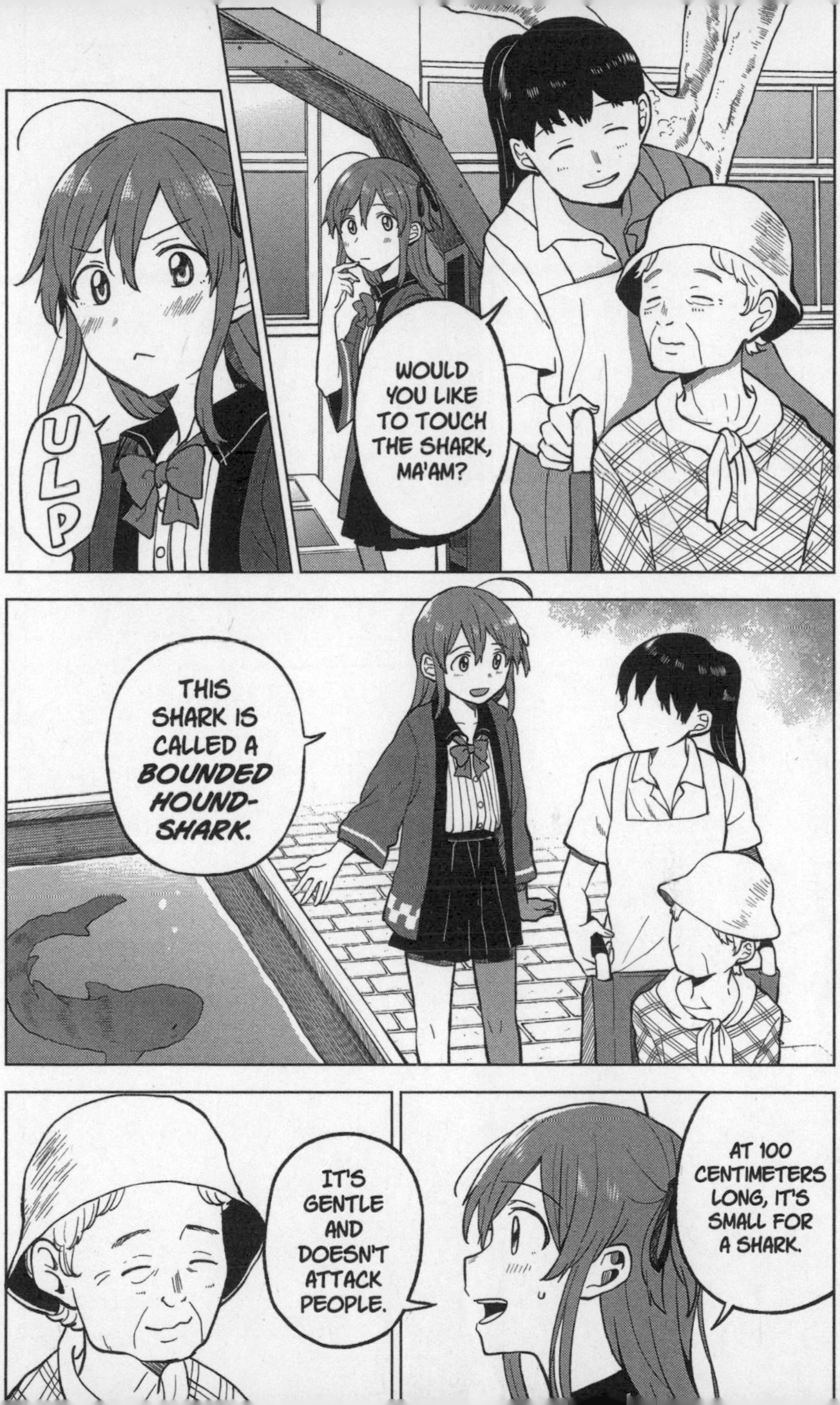
WOULD YOU LIKE TO TOUCH THE SHARK, MA'AM?
ULP
THIS SHARK IS CALLED A BOUNDED HOUND-SHARK.
AT 100 CENTIMETERS LONG, IT'S SMALL FOR A SHARK.
IT'S GENTLE AND DOESN'T ATTACK PEOPLE.

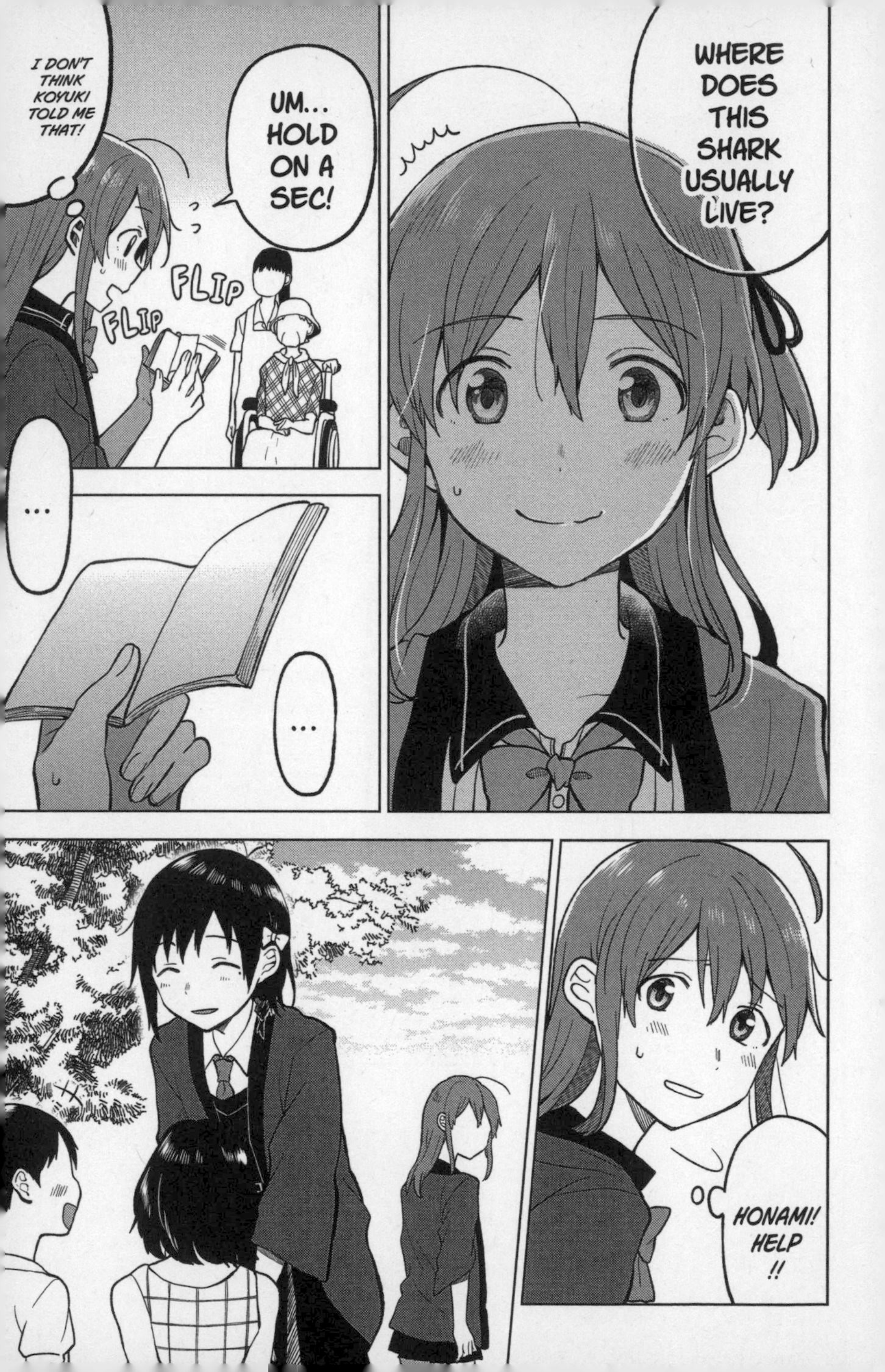
WHERE DOES THIS SHARK USUALLY LIVE?
UM... HOLD ON A SEC!
I DON'T THINK KOYUKI TOLD ME THAT!
FLIP
FLIP
...
...
HONAMI! HELP!!

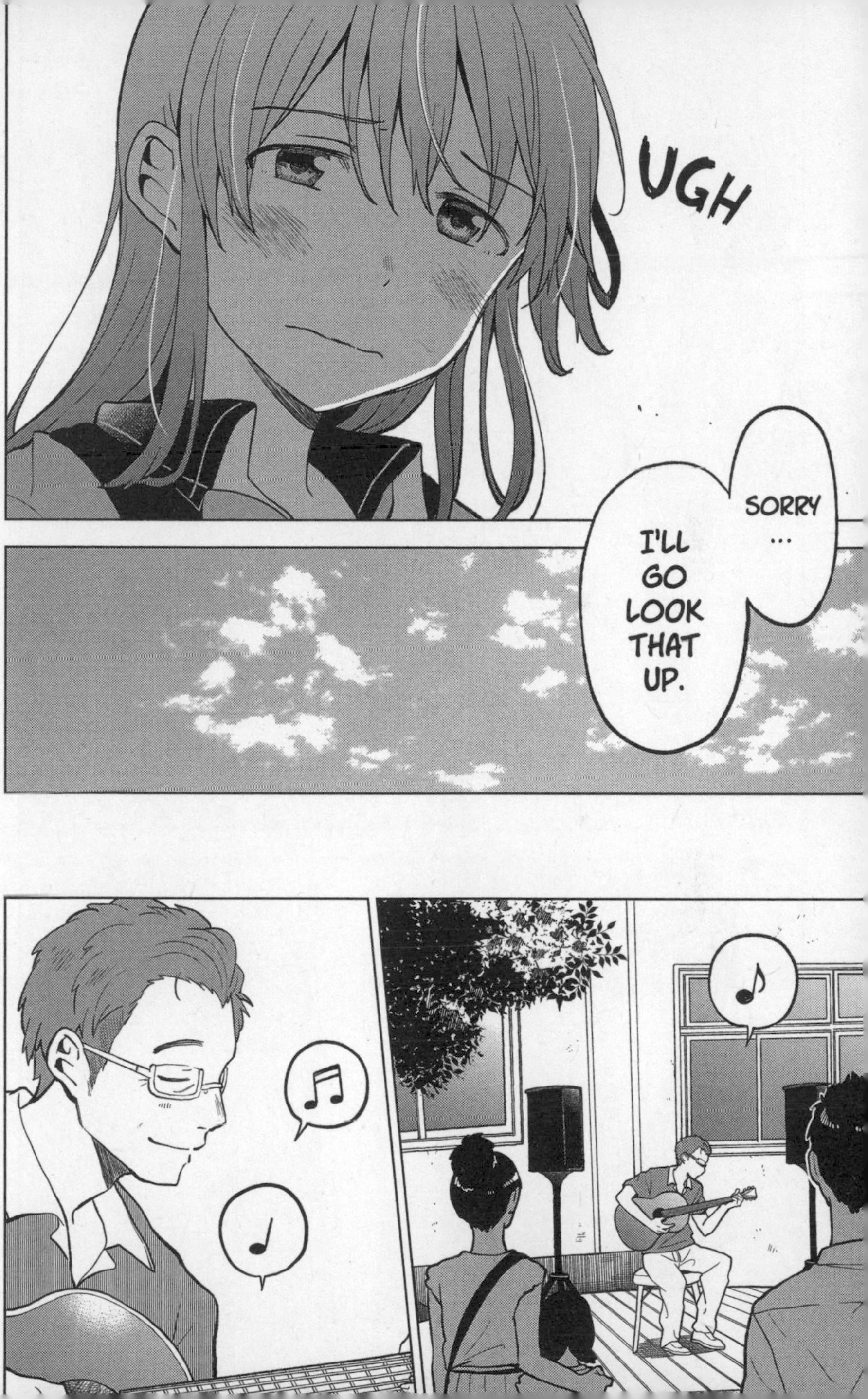
UGH
SORRY ...
I'LL GO LOOK THAT UP.

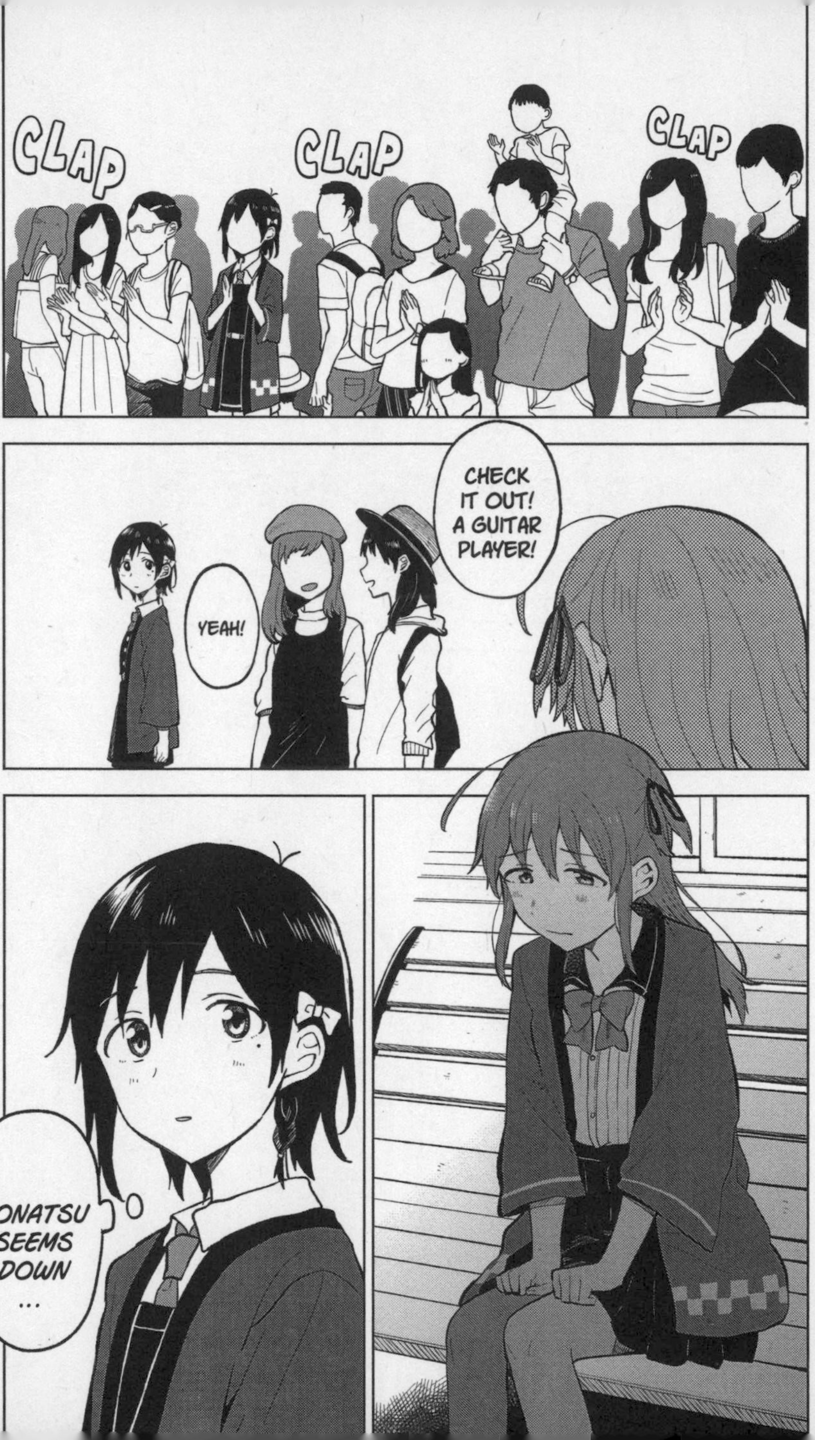
CLAP
CLAP
CLAP
CHECK IT OUT! A GUITAR PLAYER!
YEAH!
KONATSU SEEMS DOWN ...

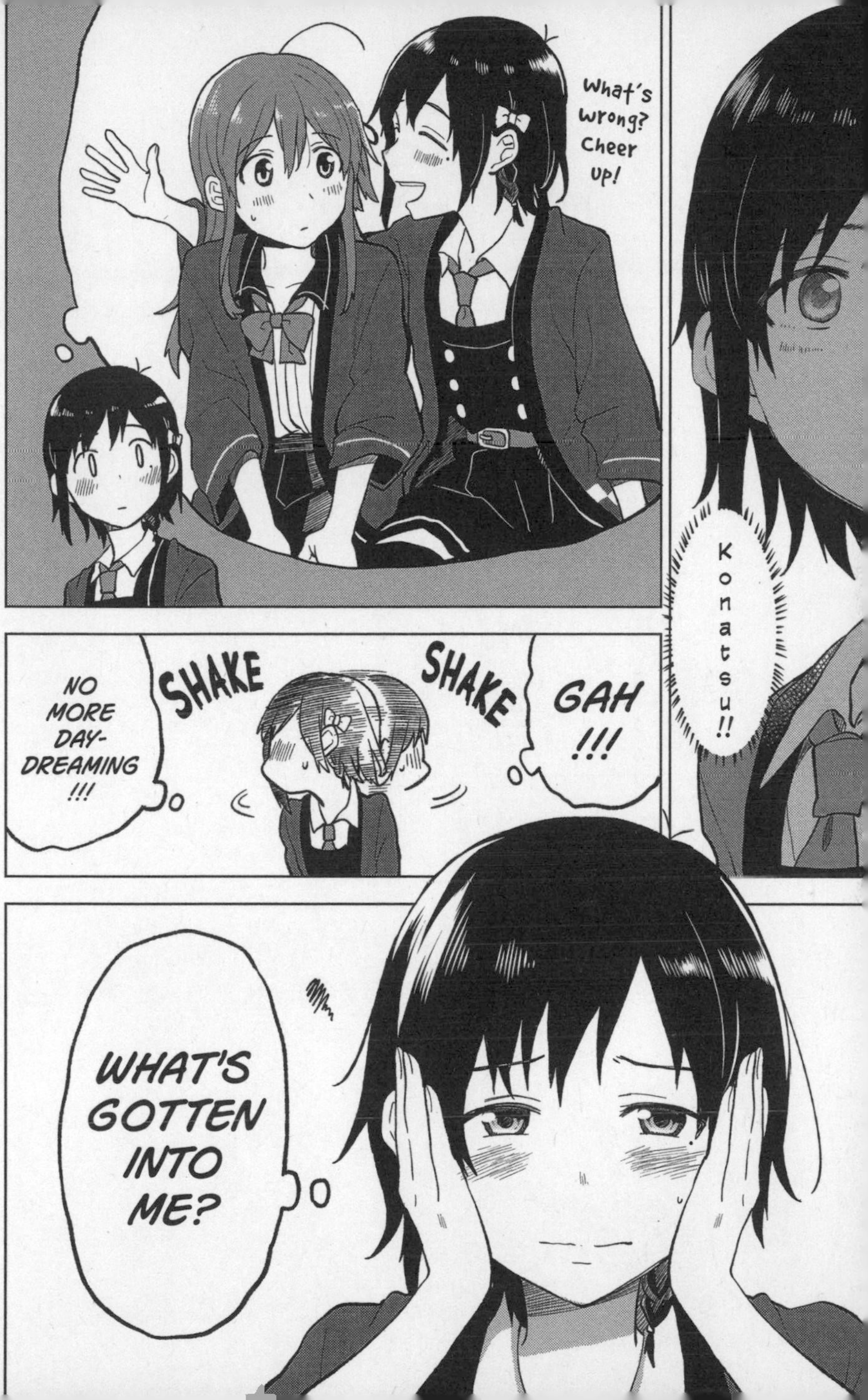
Konatsu!!
What's wrong? Cheer up!
GAH !!!
SHAKE
SHAKE
NO MORE DAY-DREAMING !!!
WHAT'S GOTTEN INTO ME?

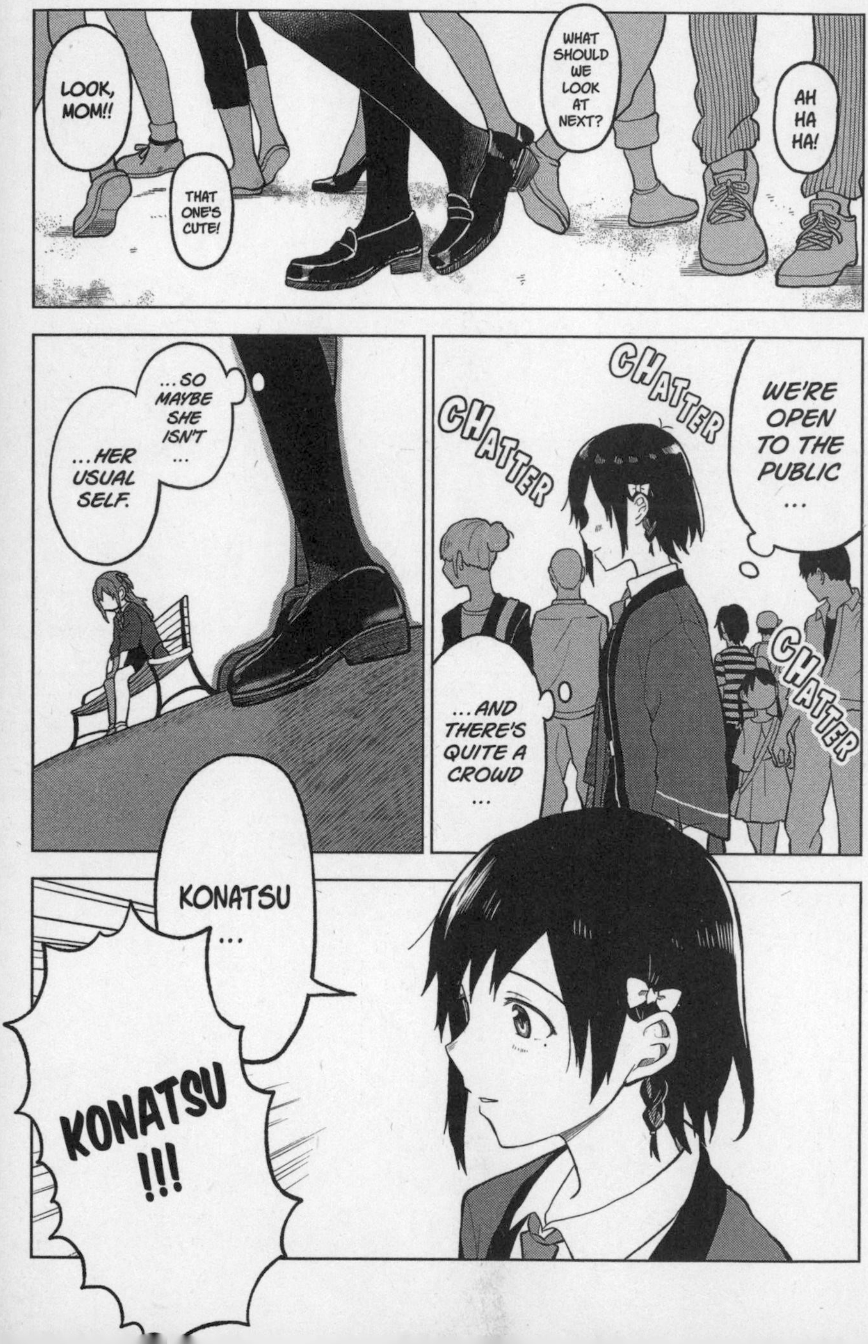
AH HA HA!
WHAT SHOULD WE LOOK AT NEXT?
LOOK, MOM!!
THAT ONE'S CUTE!
CHATTER
WE'RE OPEN TO THE PUBLIC ...
CHATTER
CHATTER
...AND THERE'S QUITE A CROWD ...
...SO MAYBE SHE ISN'T ...
...HER USUAL SELF.
KONATSU ...
KONATSU !!!

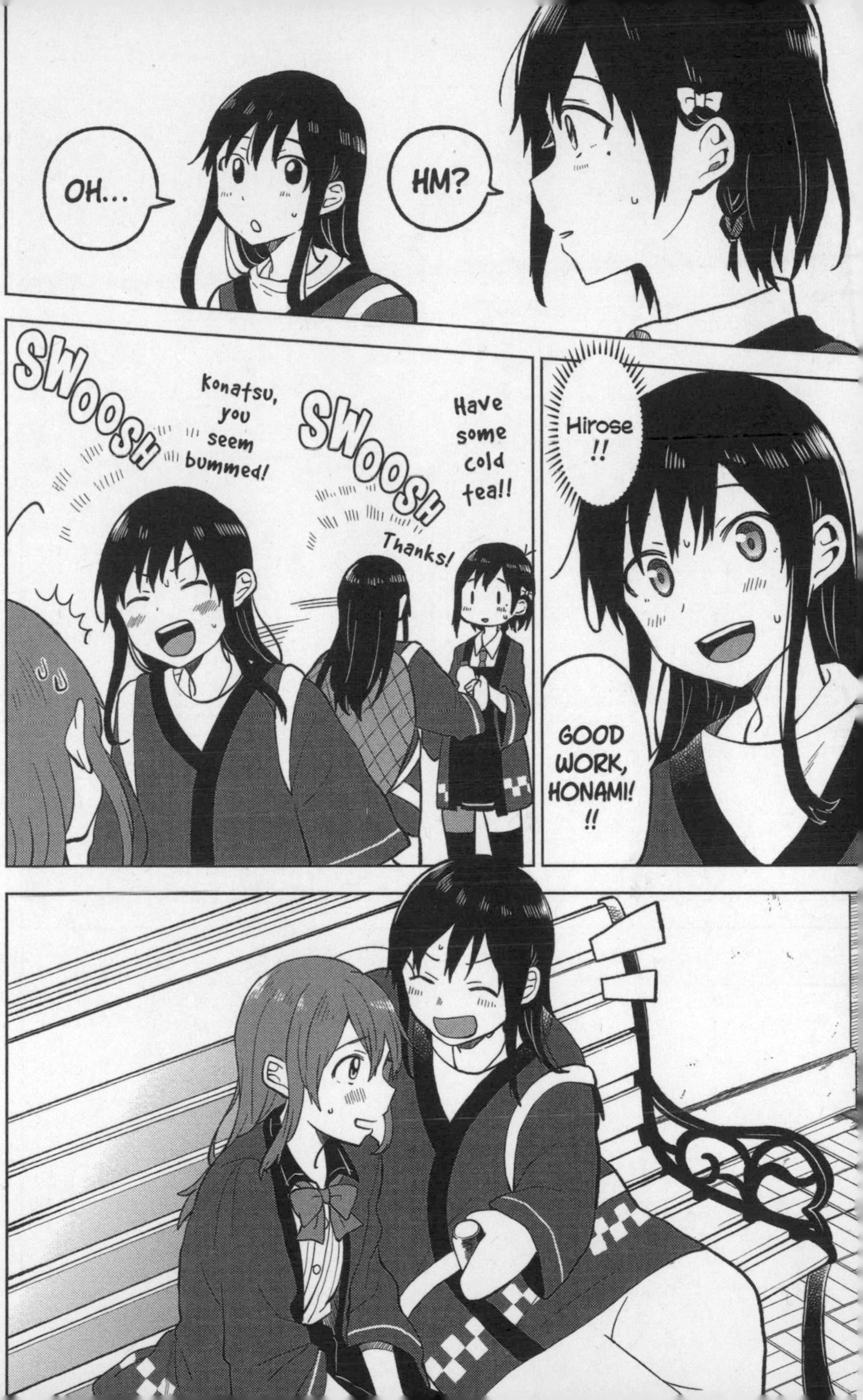
HM?
OH...
Hirose !!
GOOD WORK, HONAMI! !!
Have some cold tea!!
SWOOSH
Thanks!
Konatsu, you seem bummed!
SWOOSH

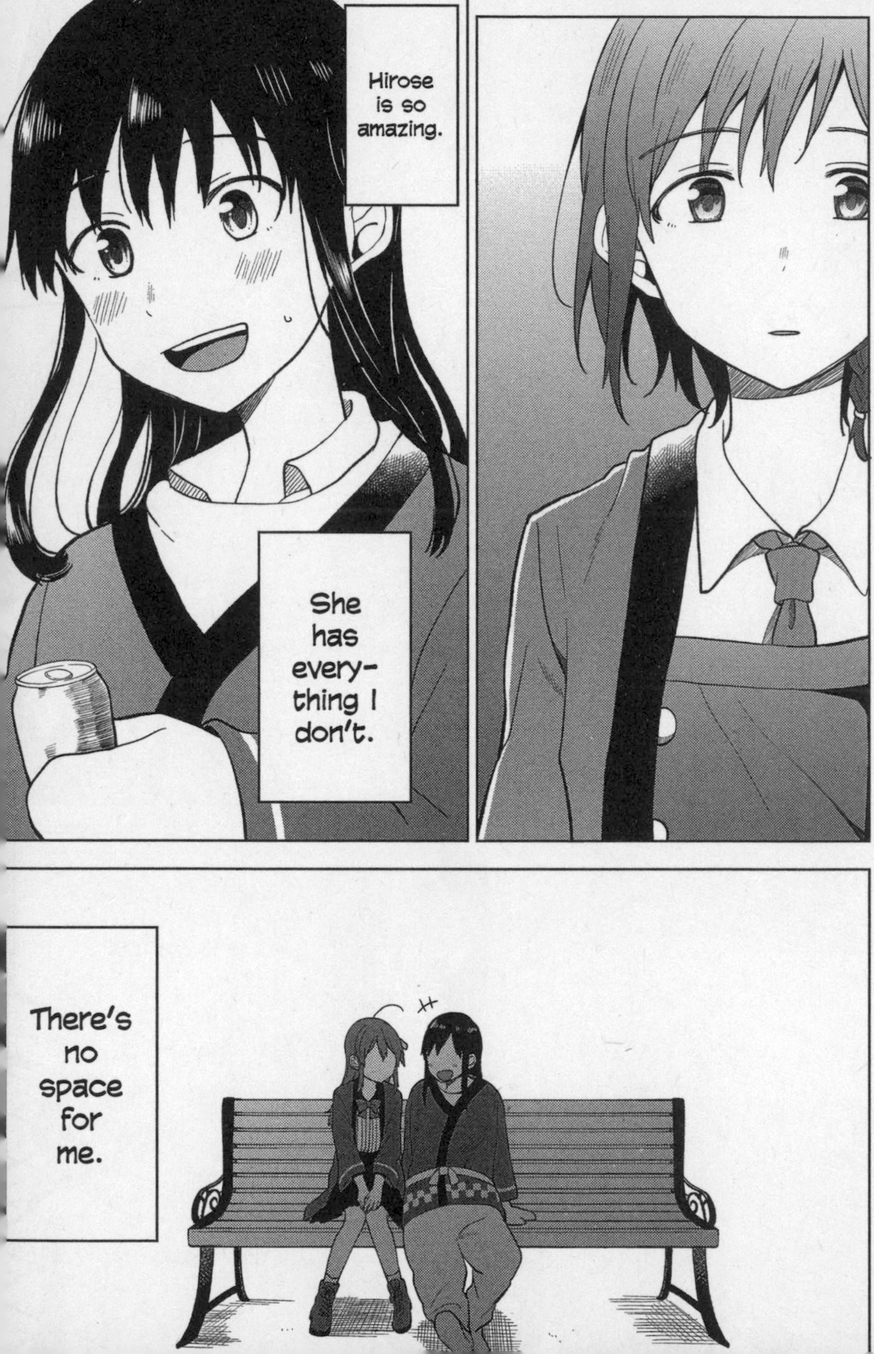
Hirose is so amazing.
She has everything I don't.
There's no space for me.

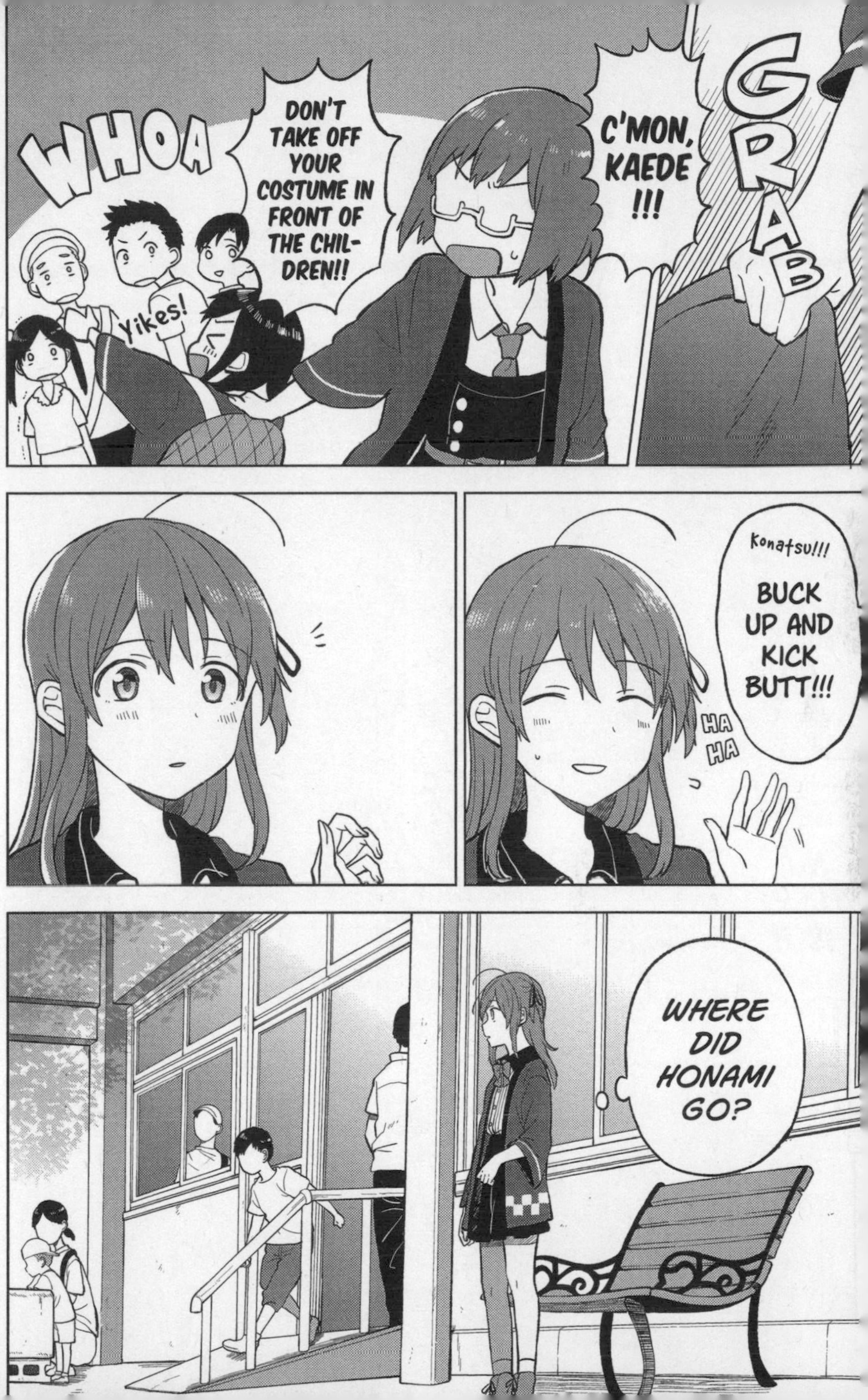
GRAB
C'MON, KAEDE!!!
DON'T TAKE OFF YOUR COSTUME IN FRONT OF THE CHILDREN!!
WHOA
Yikes!
Konatsu!!!
BUCK UP AND KICK BUTT!!!
HA HA
WHERE DID HONAMI GO?

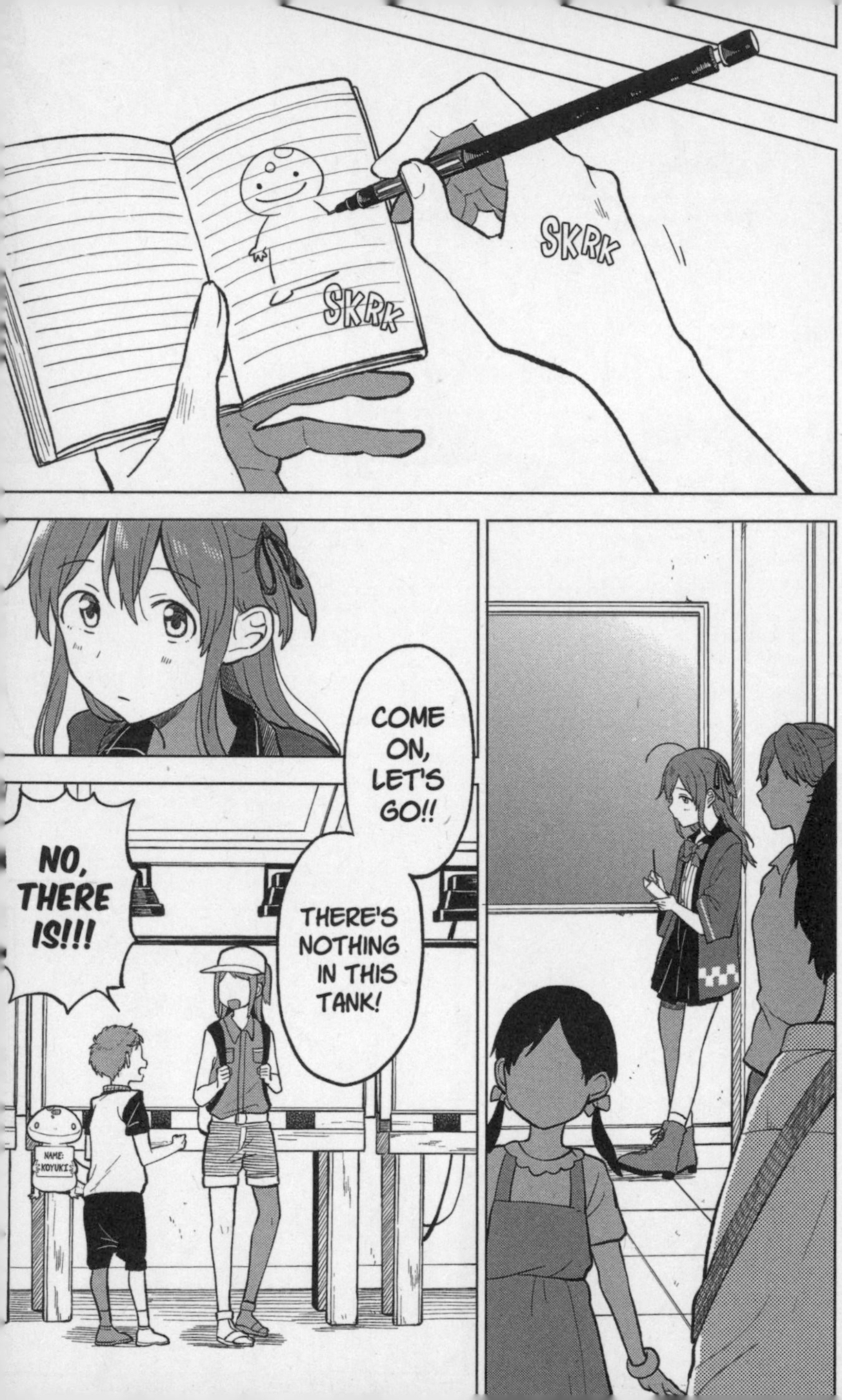
SKRK
SKRK
COME ON, LET'S GO!!
THERE'S NOTHING IN THIS TANK!
NO, THERE IS!!!
NAME: KOYUKI

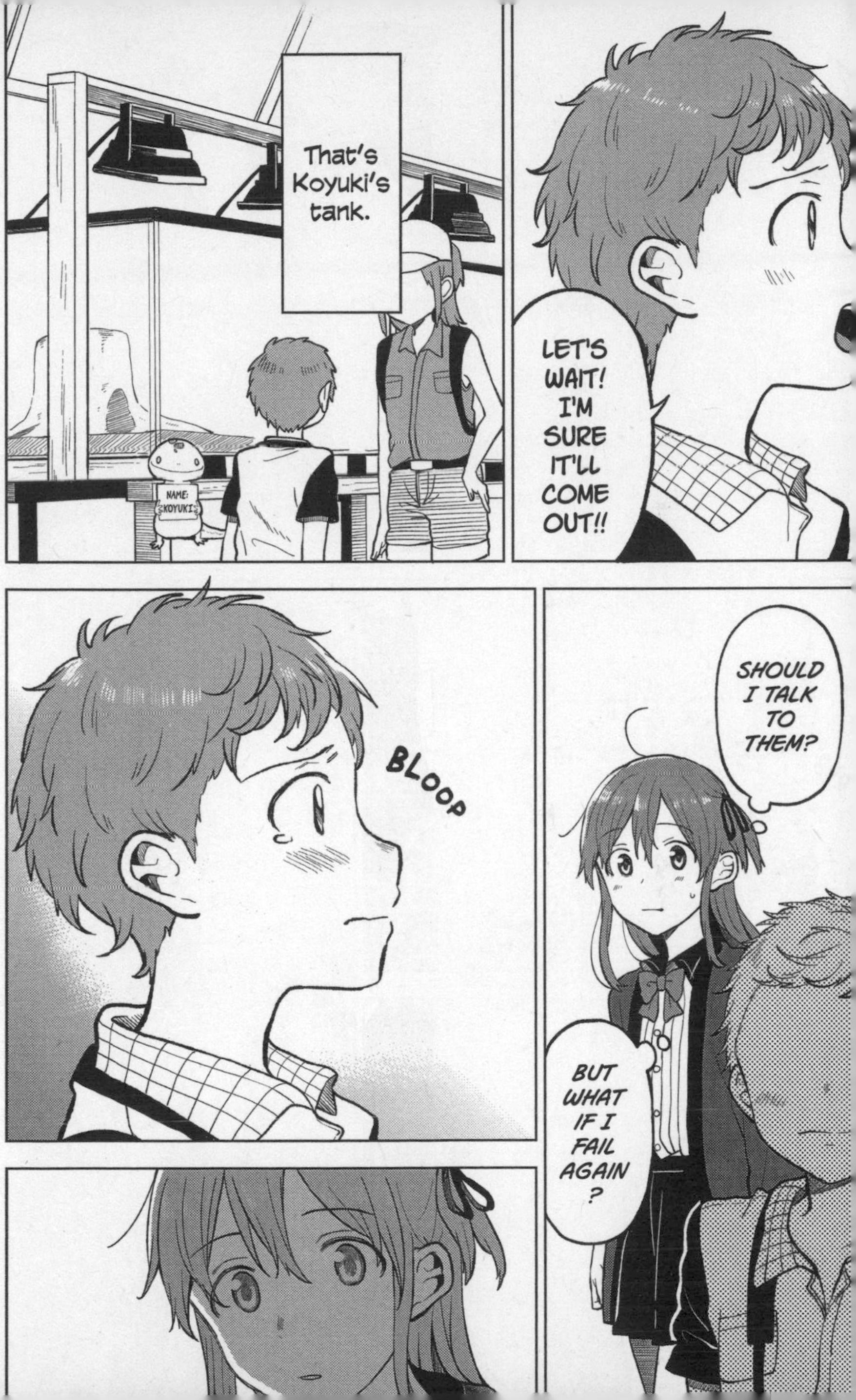
LET'S WAIT! I'M SURE IT'LL COME OUT!!
That's Koyuki's tank.
NAME: KOYUKI
SHOULD I TALK TO THEM?
BUT WHAT IF I FAIL AGAIN?
BLOOP

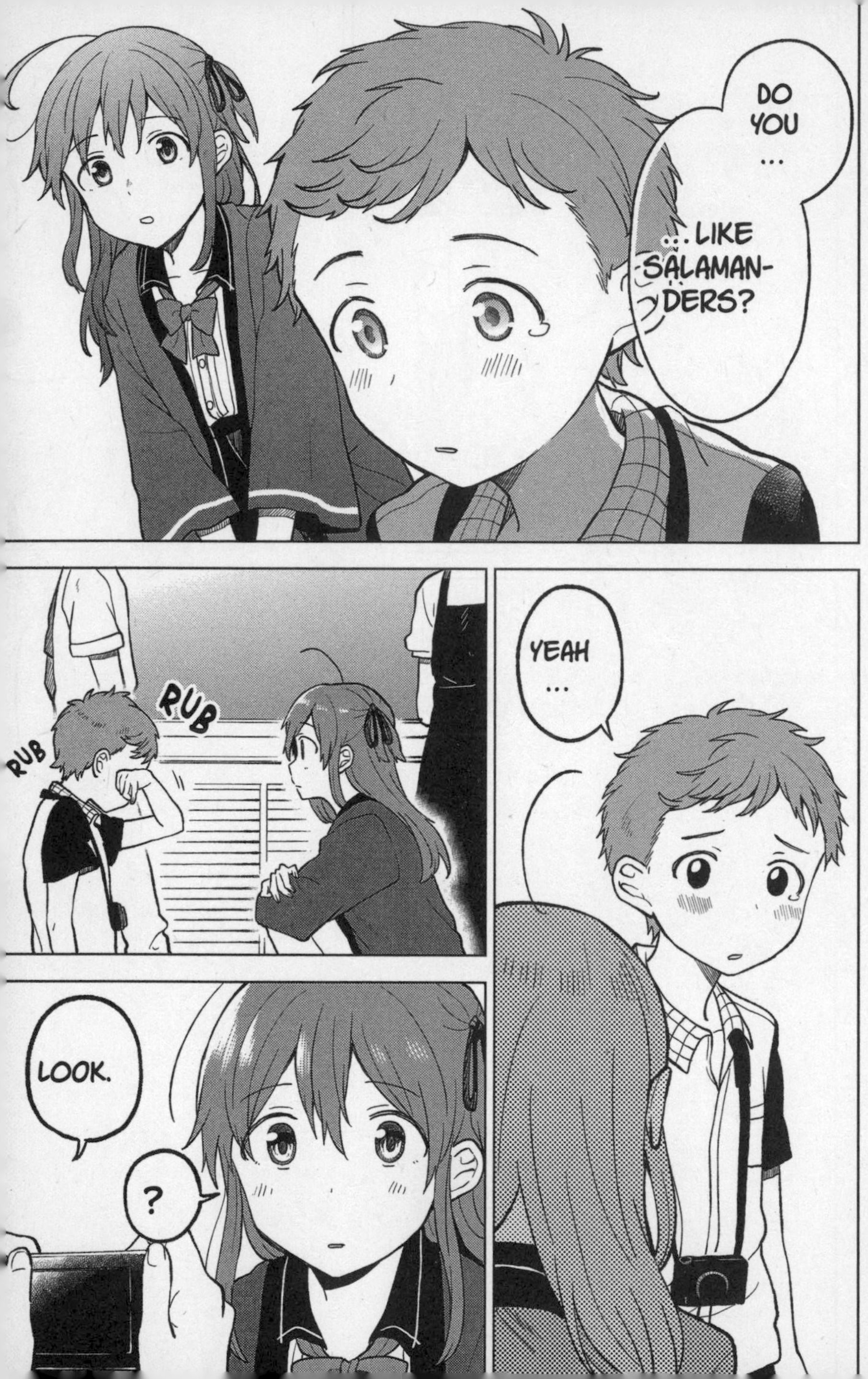
DO YOU ...
...LIKE SALAMAN-DERS?
YEAH ...
RUB
RUB
LOOK.
?

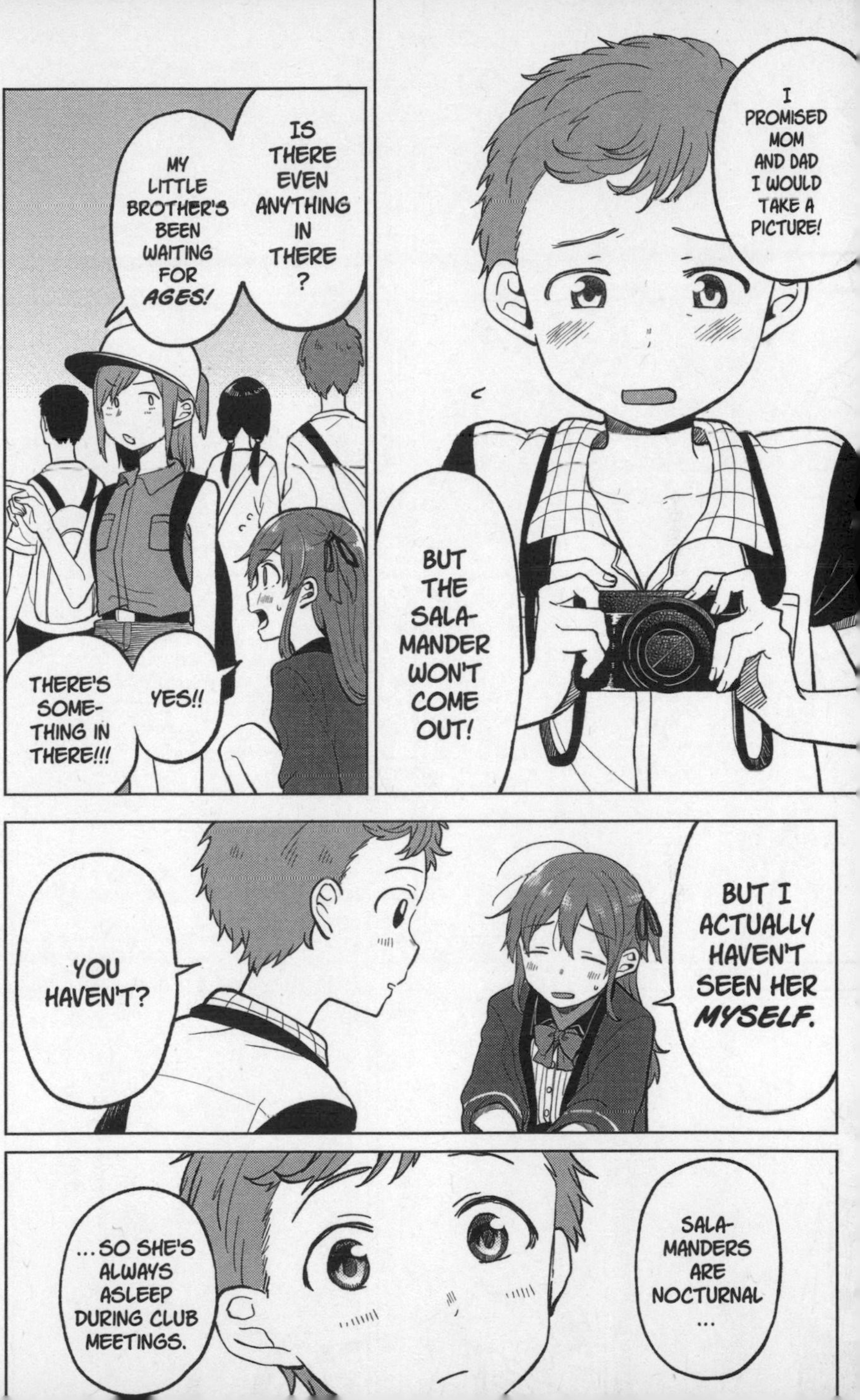
I PROMISED MOM AND DAD I WOULD TAKE A PICTURE!
BUT THE SALA-MANDER WON'T COME OUT!
IS THERE EVEN ANYTHING IN THERE?
MY LITTLE BROTHER'S BEEN WAITING FOR *AGES!*
YES!!
THERE'S SOME-THING IN THERE!!!
BUT I ACTUALLY HAVEN'T SEEN HER *MYSELF.*
YOU HAVEN'T?
SALA-MANDERS ARE NOCTURNAL...
...SO SHE'S ALWAYS ASLEEP DURING CLUB MEETINGS.

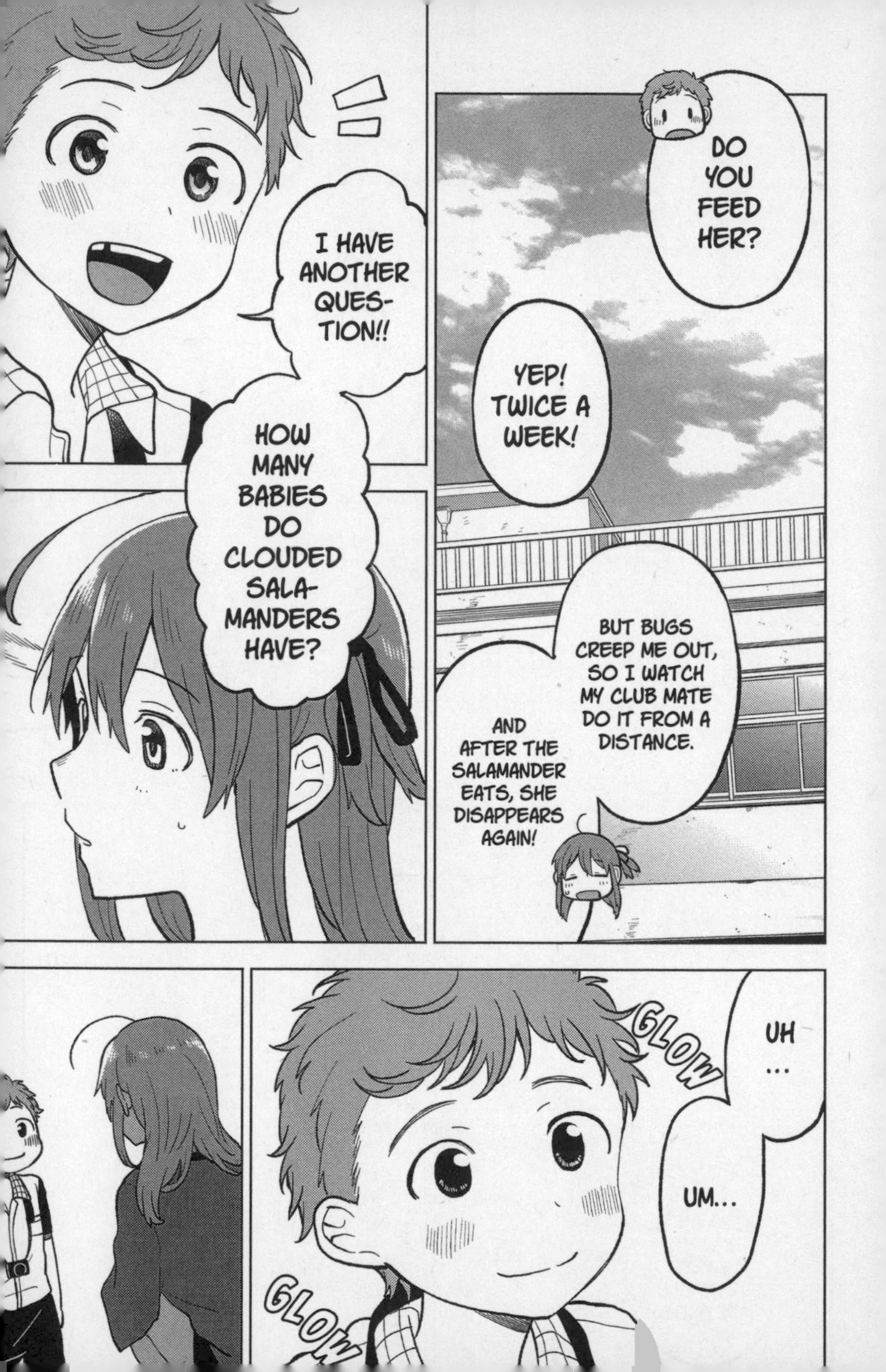
DO YOU FEED HER?
YEP! TWICE A WEEK!
BUT BUGS CREEP ME OUT, SO I WATCH MY CLUB MATE DO IT FROM A DISTANCE.
AND AFTER THE SALAMANDER EATS, SHE DISAPPEARS AGAIN!
I HAVE ANOTHER QUES-TION!!
HOW MANY BABIES DO CLOUDED SALA-MANDERS HAVE?
UH ...
UM...
GLOW
GLOW

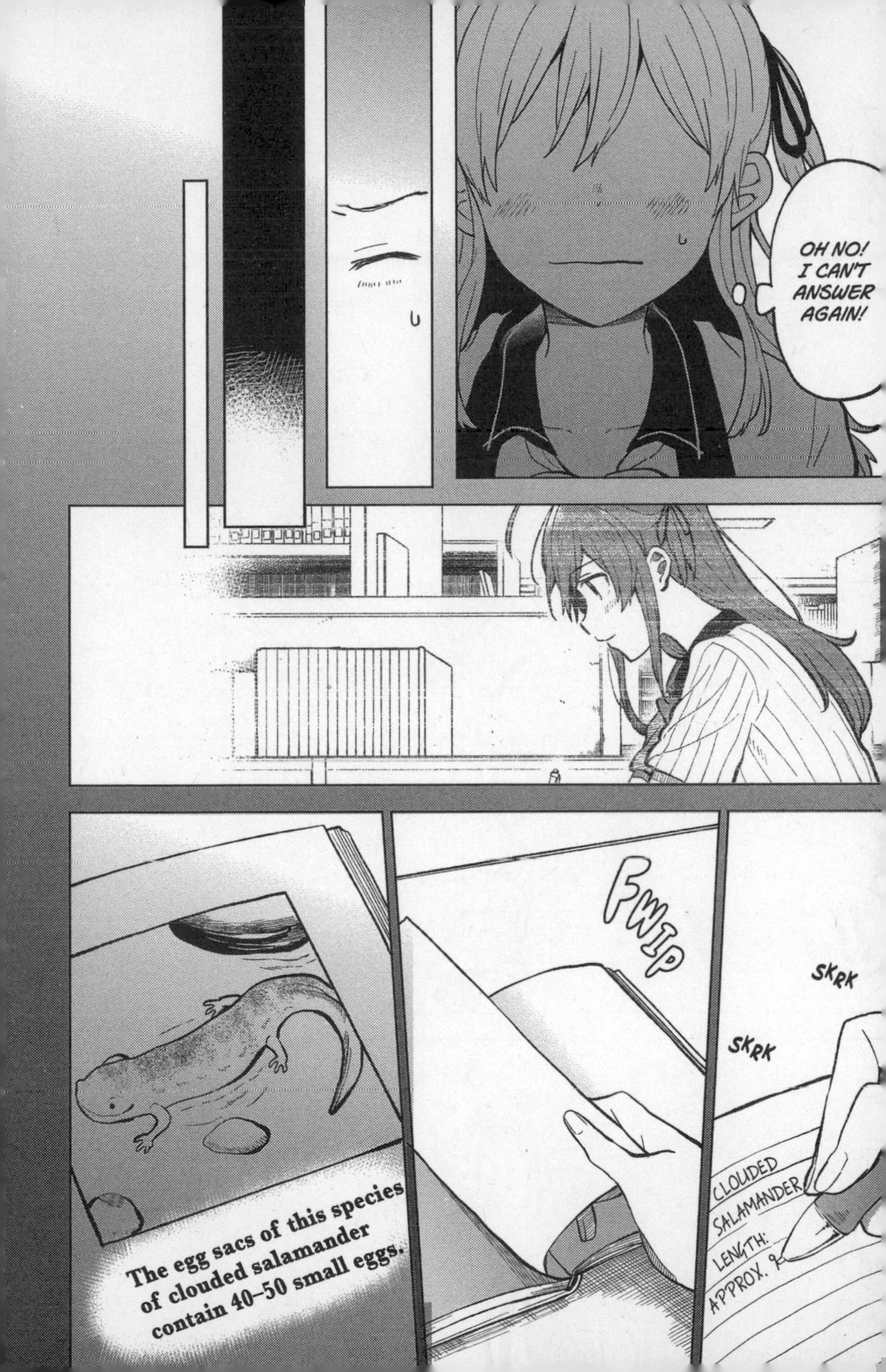
OH NO! I CAN'T ANSWER AGAIN!
SKRK
SKRK
CLOUDED SALAMANDER LENGTH: APPROX. 9
FWIP
The egg sacs of this species of clouded salamander contain 40–50 small eggs.

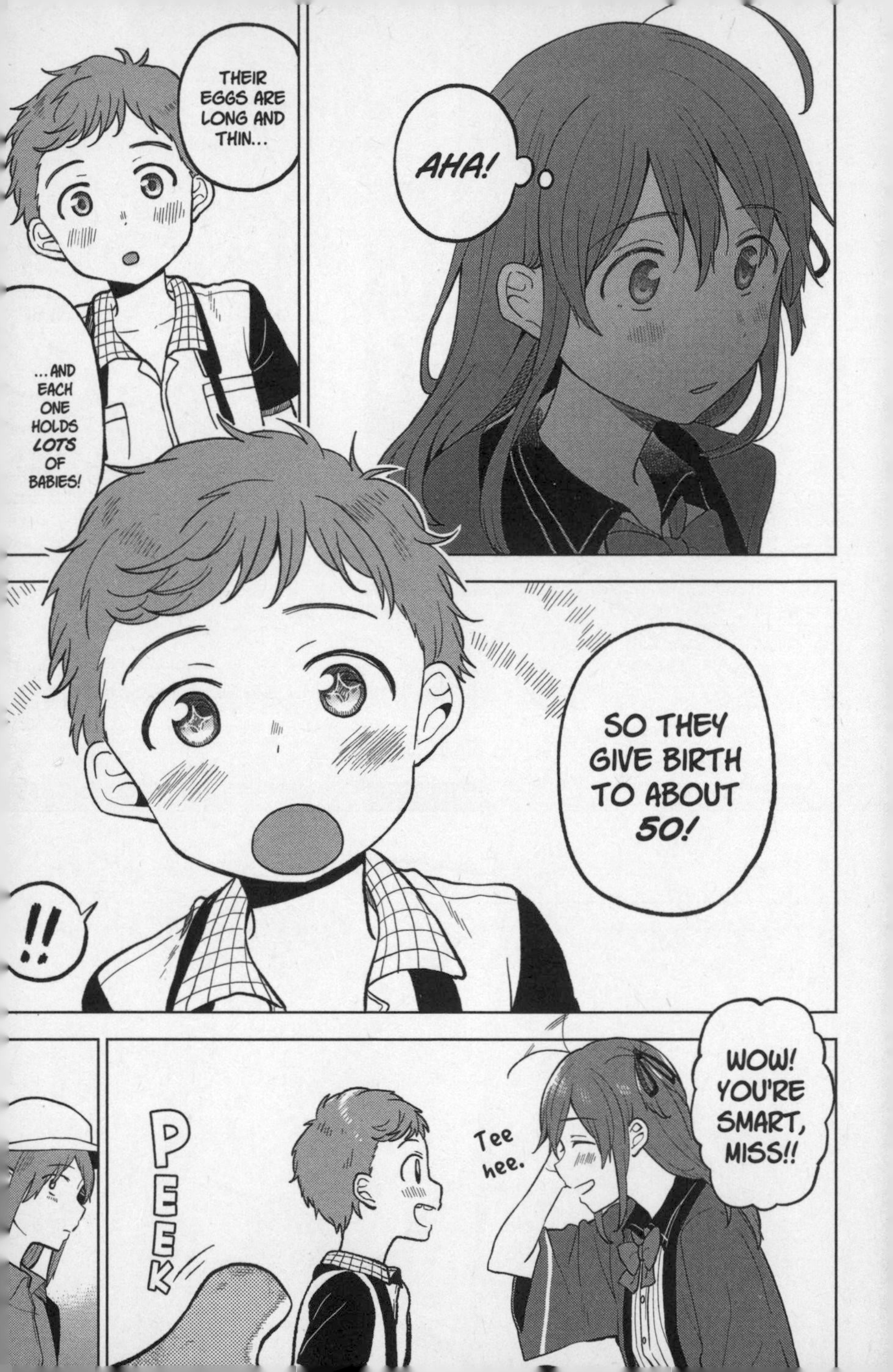
AHA!
THEIR EGGS ARE LONG AND THIN...
...AND EACH ONE HOLDS LOTS OF BABIES!
SO THEY GIVE BIRTH TO ABOUT 50!
!!
WOW! YOU'RE SMART, MISS!!
Tee hee.
PEEK

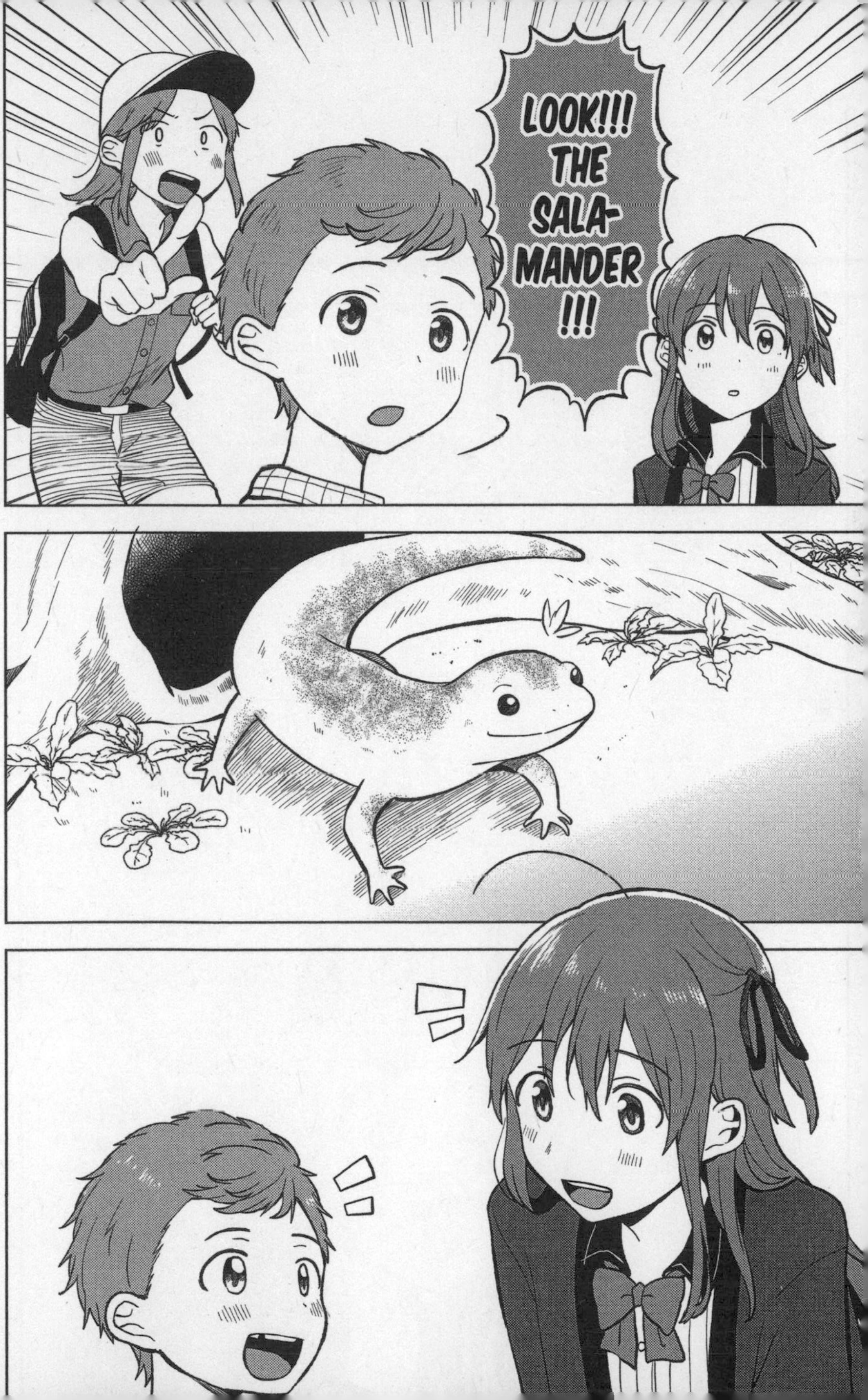
LOOK!!! THE SALA- MANDER !!!

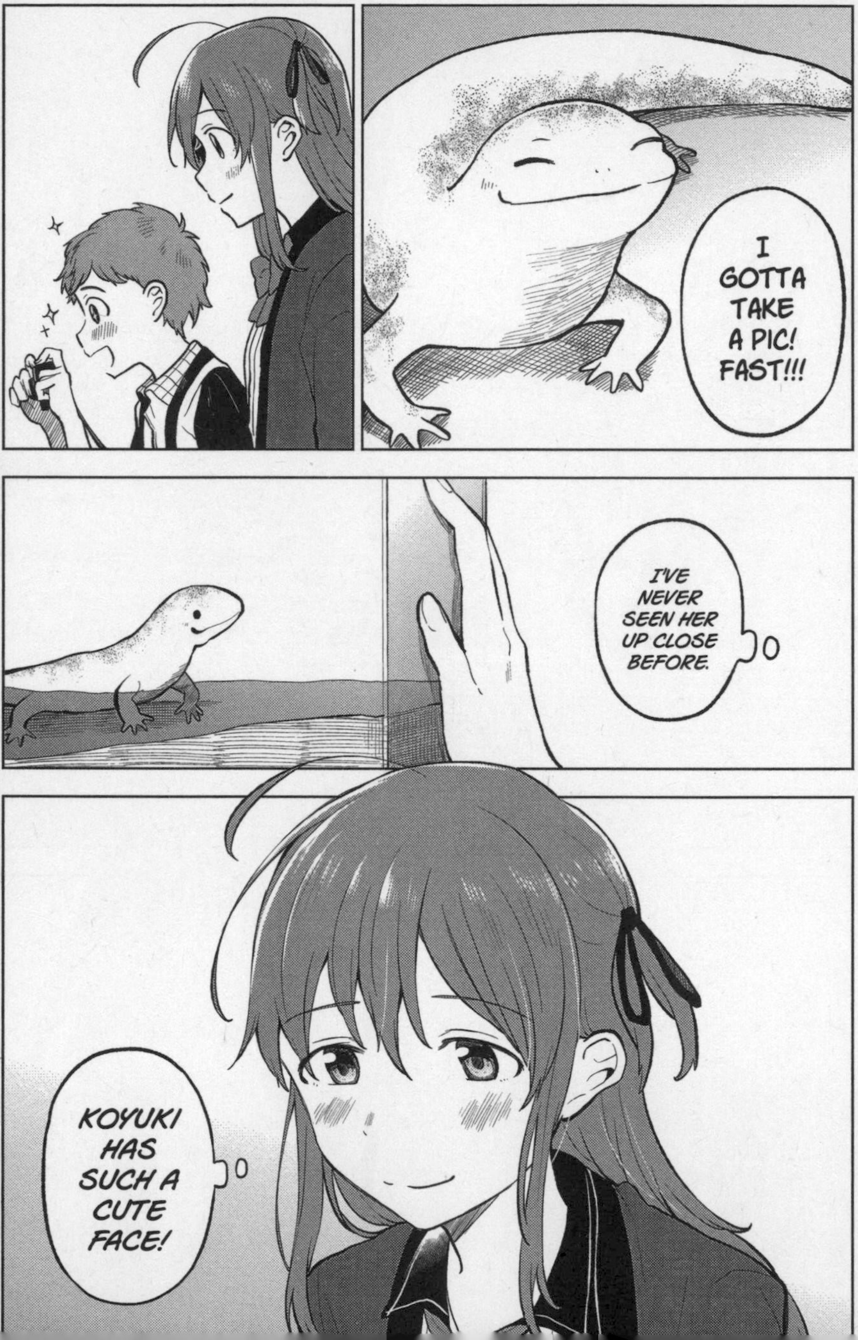
I GOTTA TAKE A PIC! FAST!!!
I'VE NEVER SEEN HER UP CLOSE BEFORE.
KOYUKI HAS SUCH A CUTE FACE!

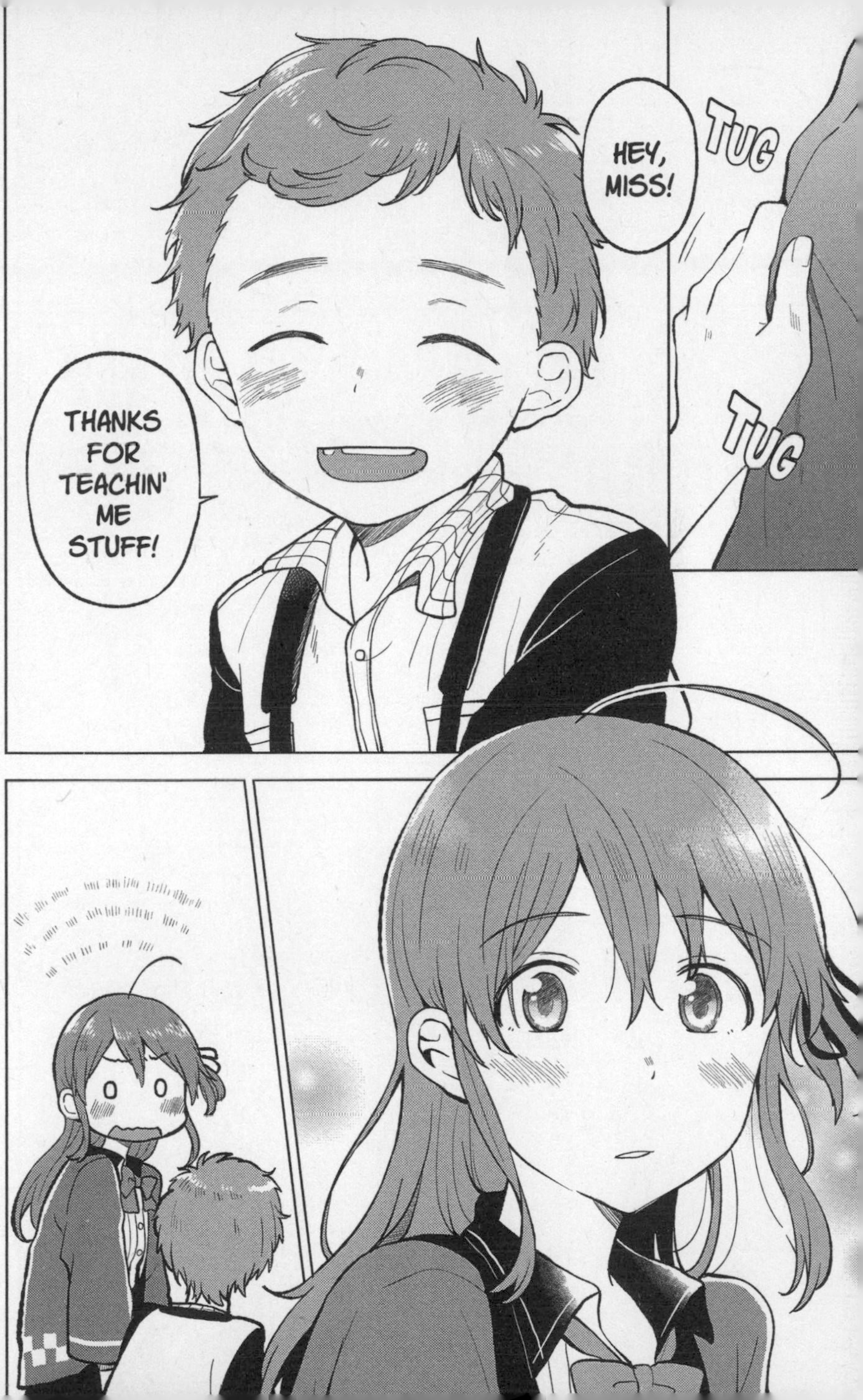
TUG
TUG
HEY, MISS!
THANKS FOR TEACHIN' ME STUFF!

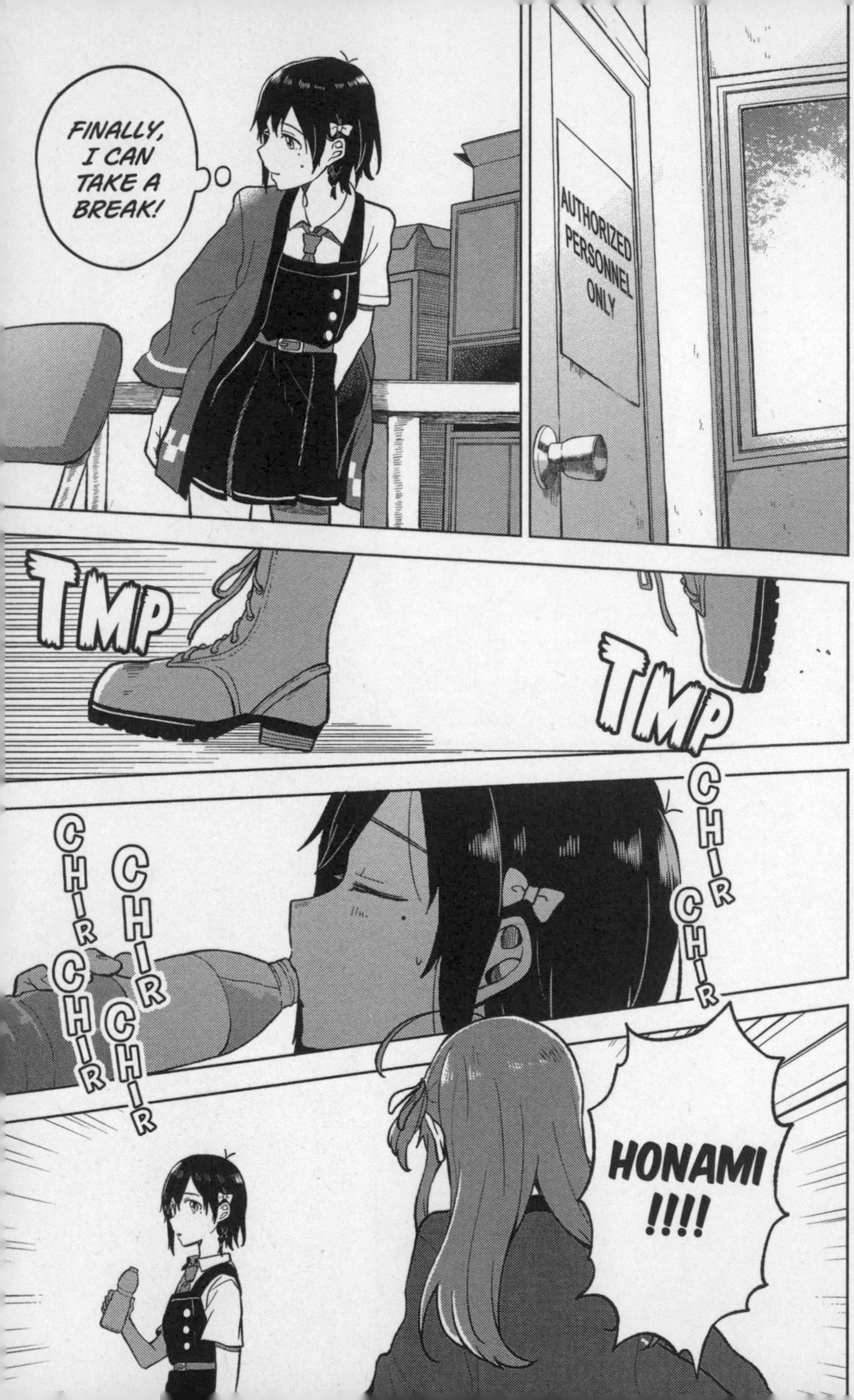
AUTHORIZED PERSONNEL ONLY
FINALLY, I CAN TAKE A BREAK!
TMP
TMP
CHIR CHIR
CHIR CHIR
CHIR CHIR
HONAMI!!!!

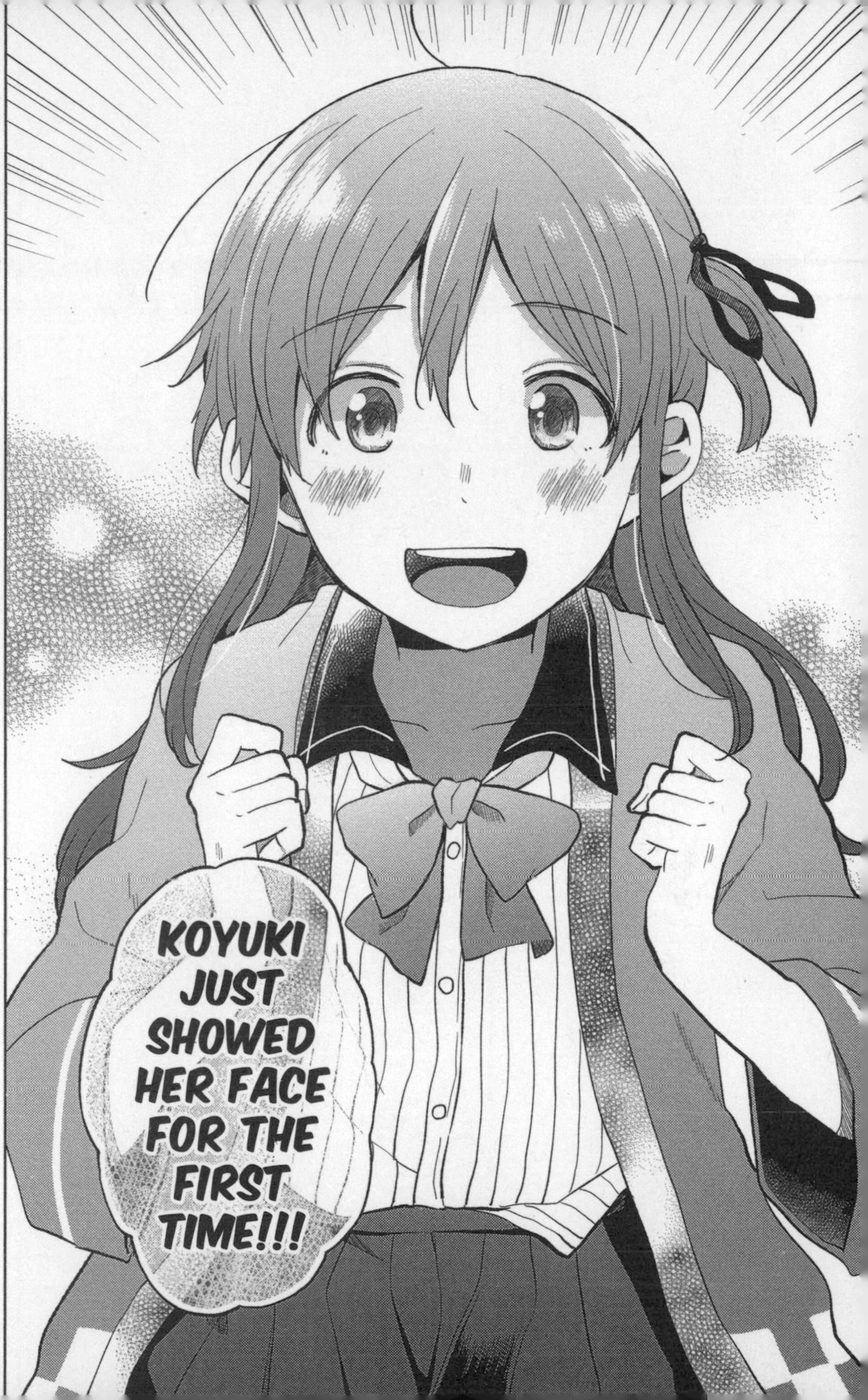
KOYUKI JUST SHOWED HER FACE FOR THE FIRST TIME!!!

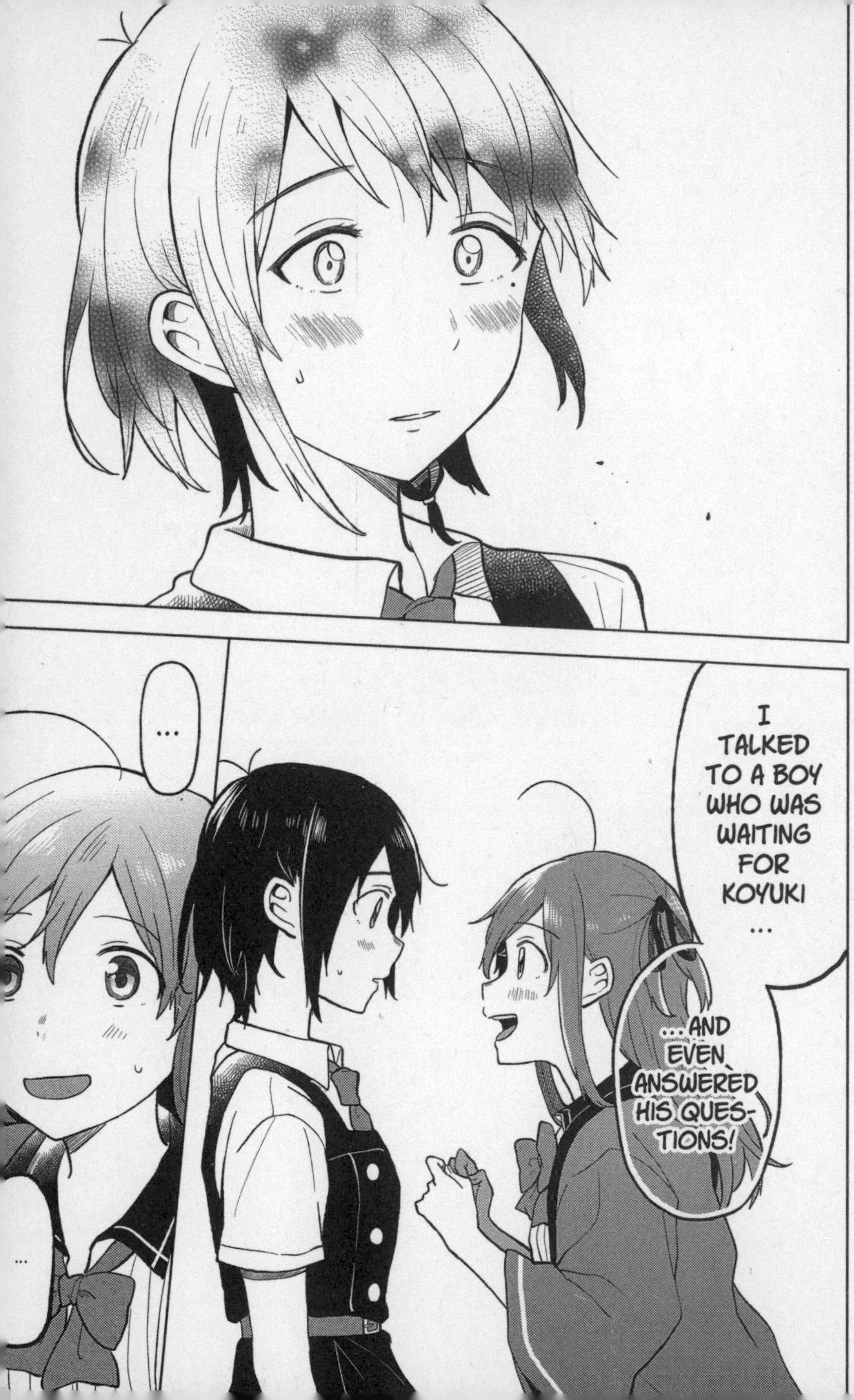
I TALKED TO A BOY WHO WAS WAITING FOR KOYUKI ...
... AND EVEN ANSWERED HIS QUES-TIONS!
...
...

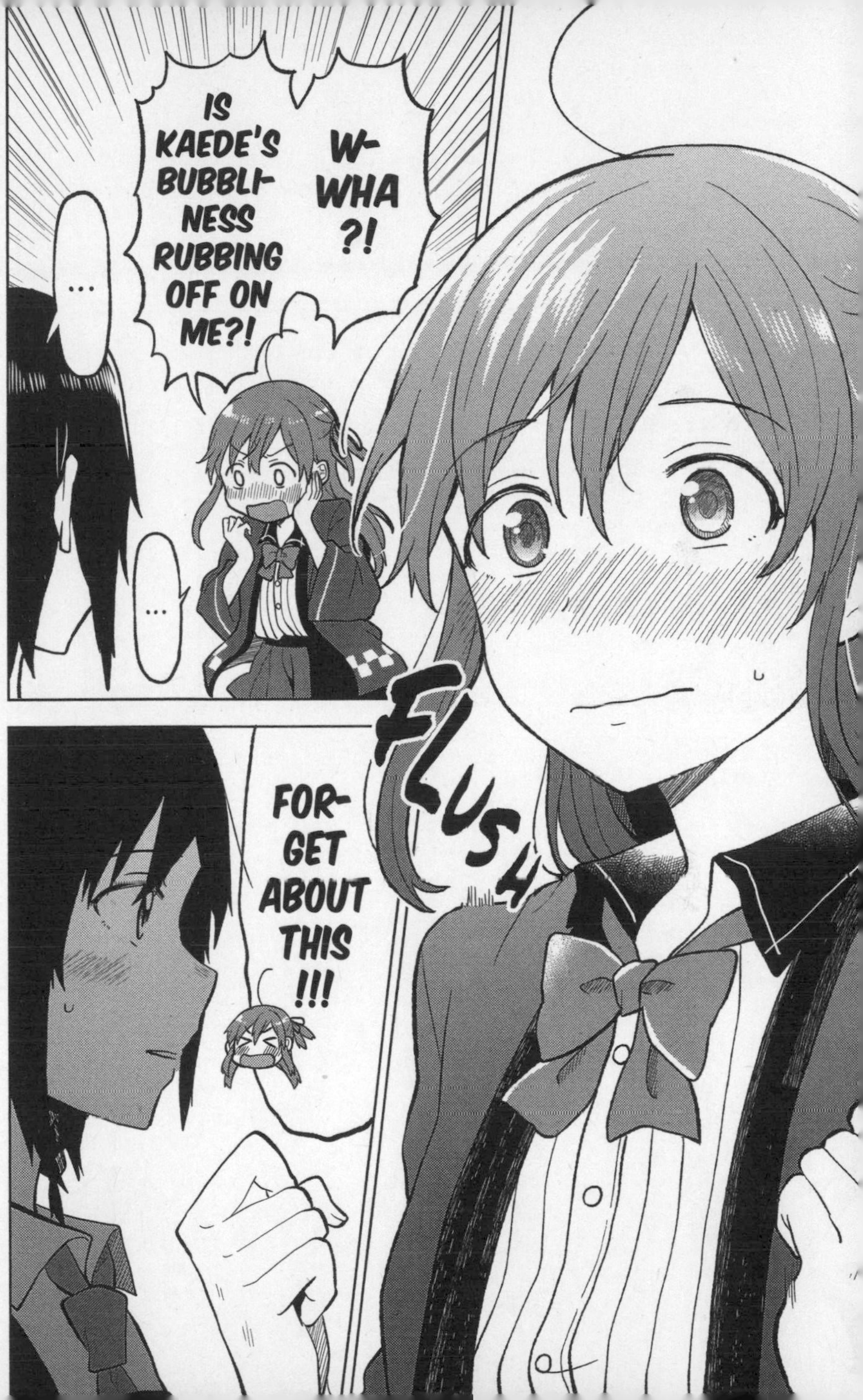
FLUSH
W-WHA?!
IS KAEDE'S BUBBLINESS RUBBING OFF ON ME?!
...
...
FORGET ABOUT THIS!!!

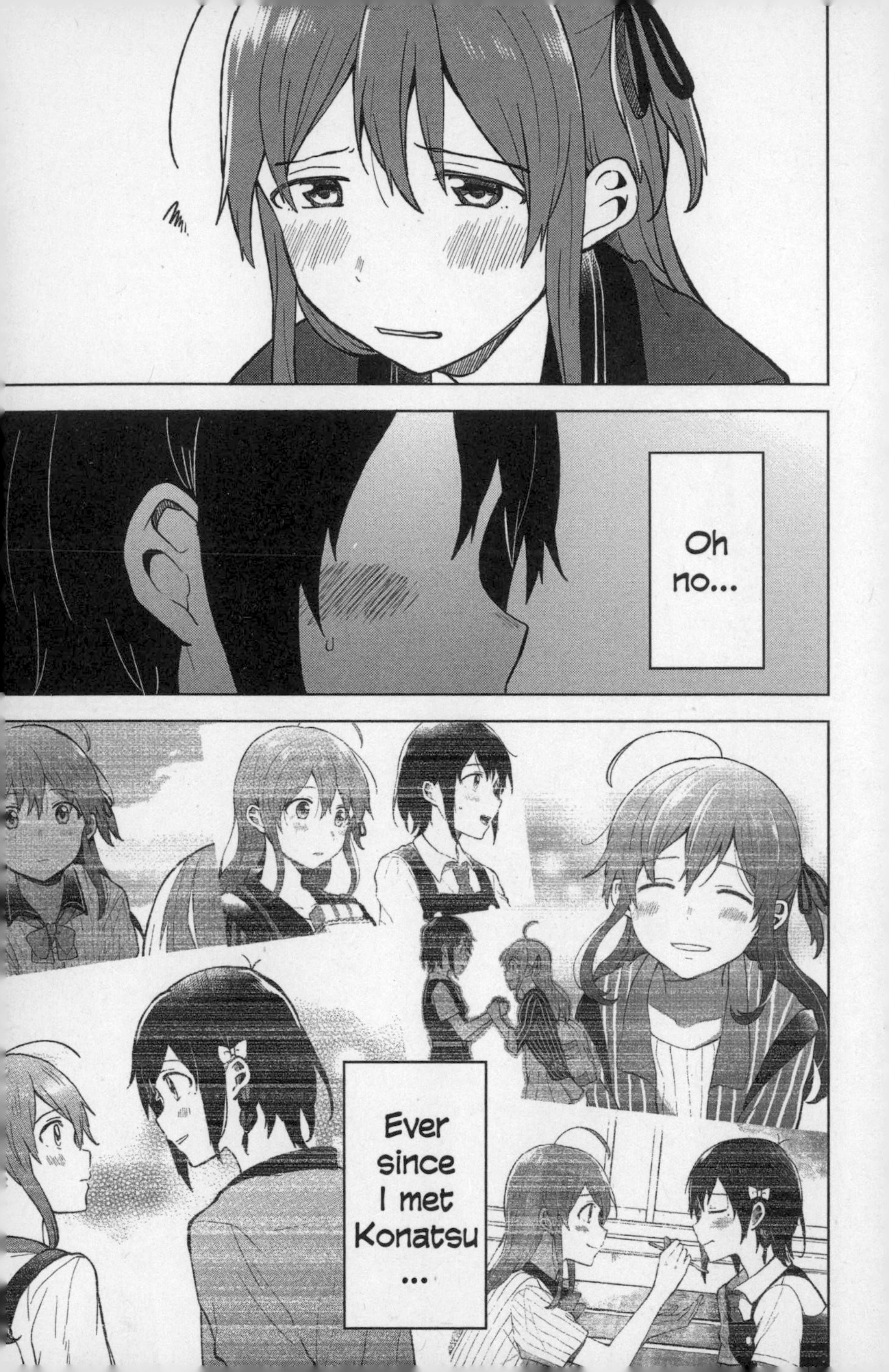
Oh no...
Ever since I met Konatsu ...

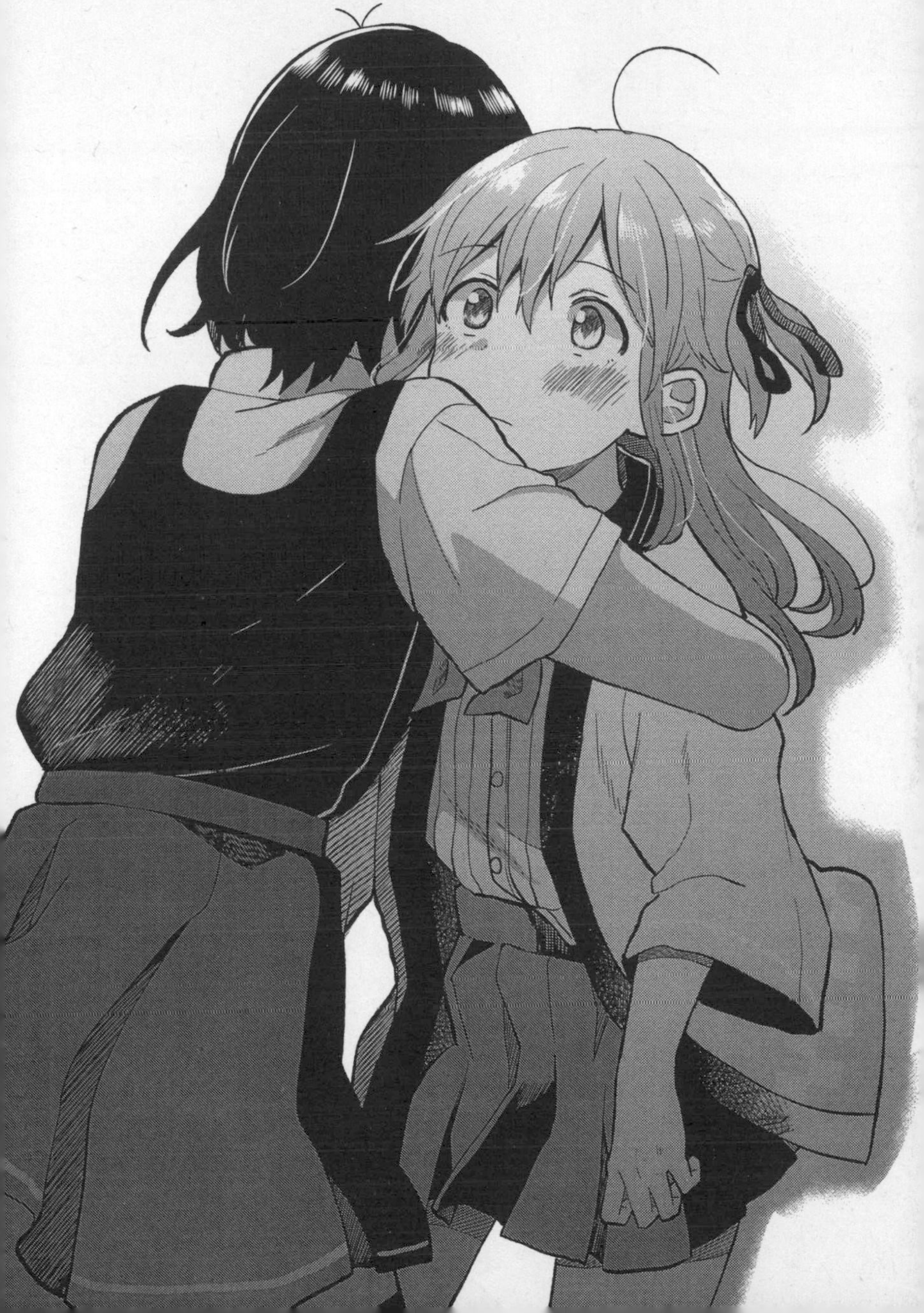

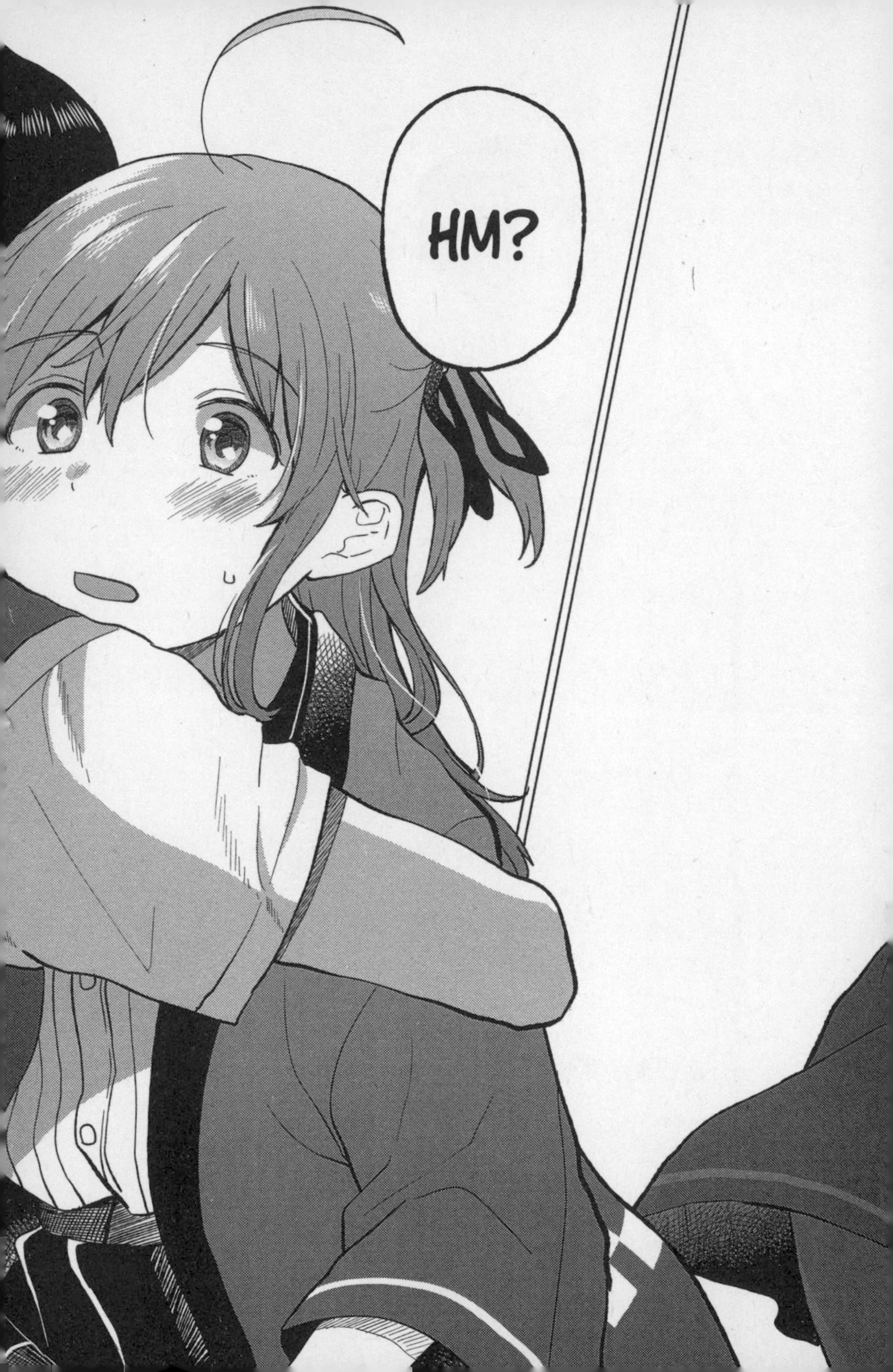
HM?

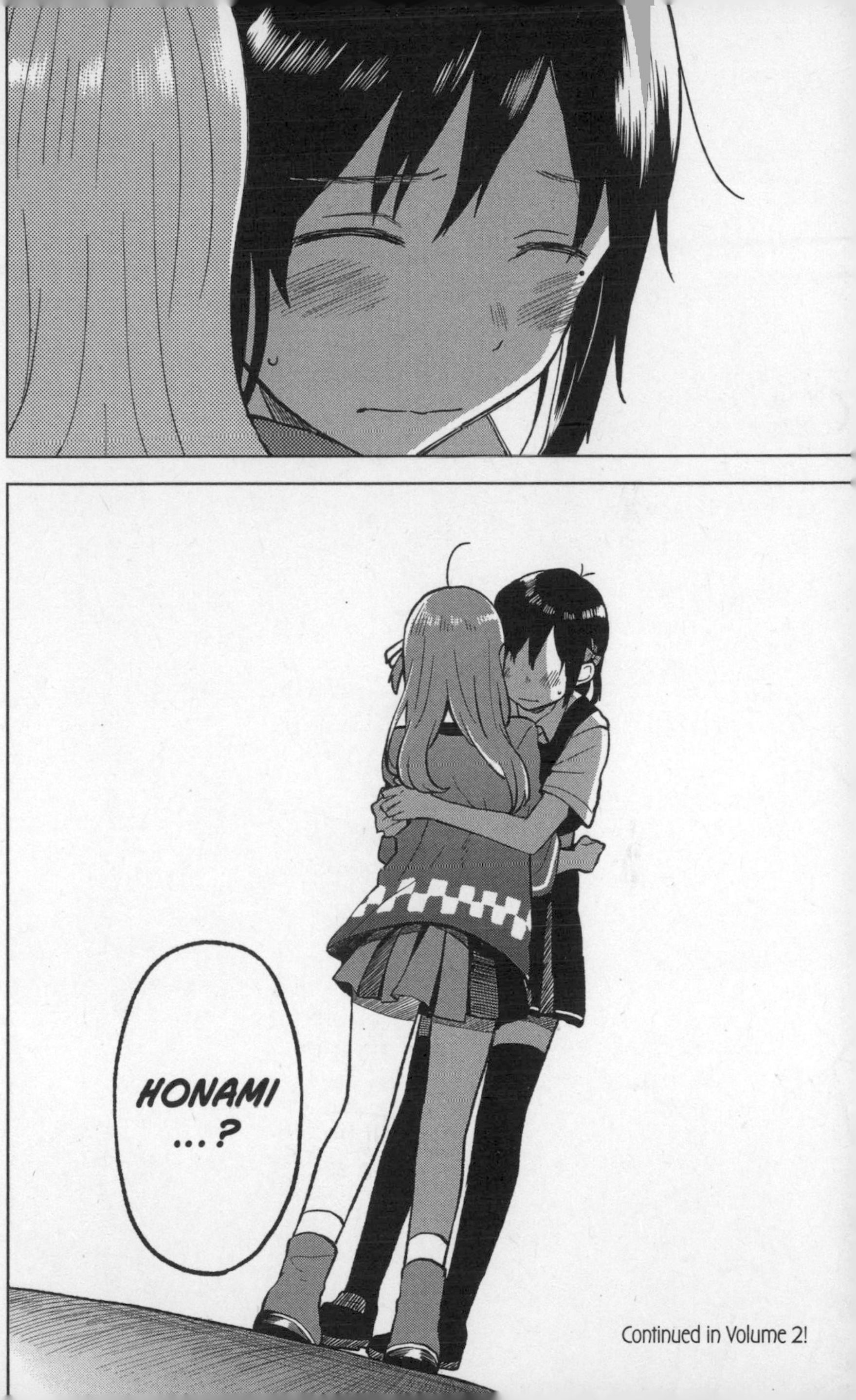
HONAMI ...?

Continued in Volume 2!

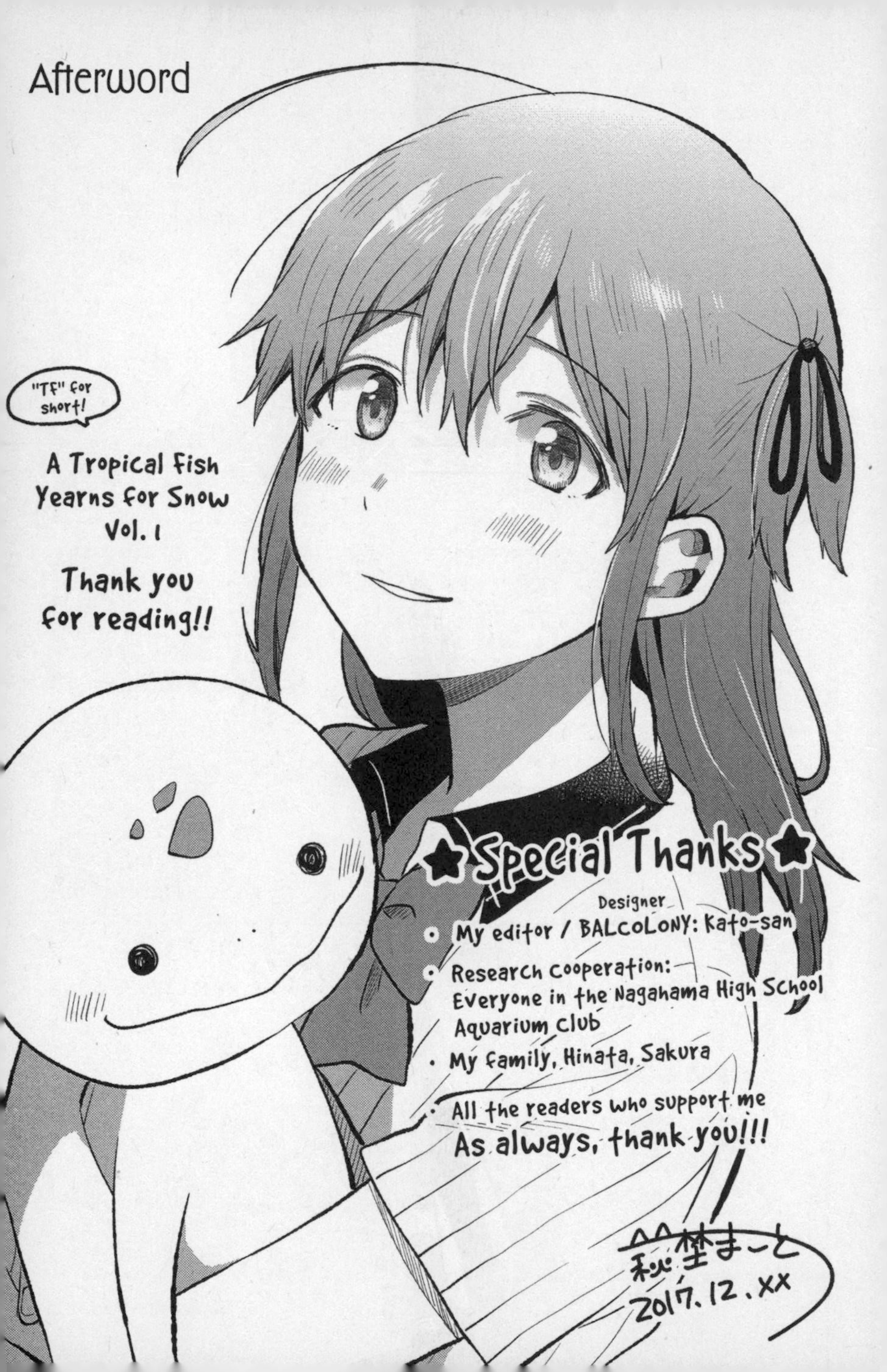
Afterword
"TF" for short!
A Tropical Fish Yearns for Snow Vol. 1
Thank you for reading!!
★Special Thanks★
• My editor / BALCOLONY: Kato-san
Designer
• Research cooperation: Everyone in the Nagahama High School Aquarium Club
• My family, Hinata, Sakura
• All the readers who support me
As always, thank you!!!
萩埜まこと
2017.12.XX

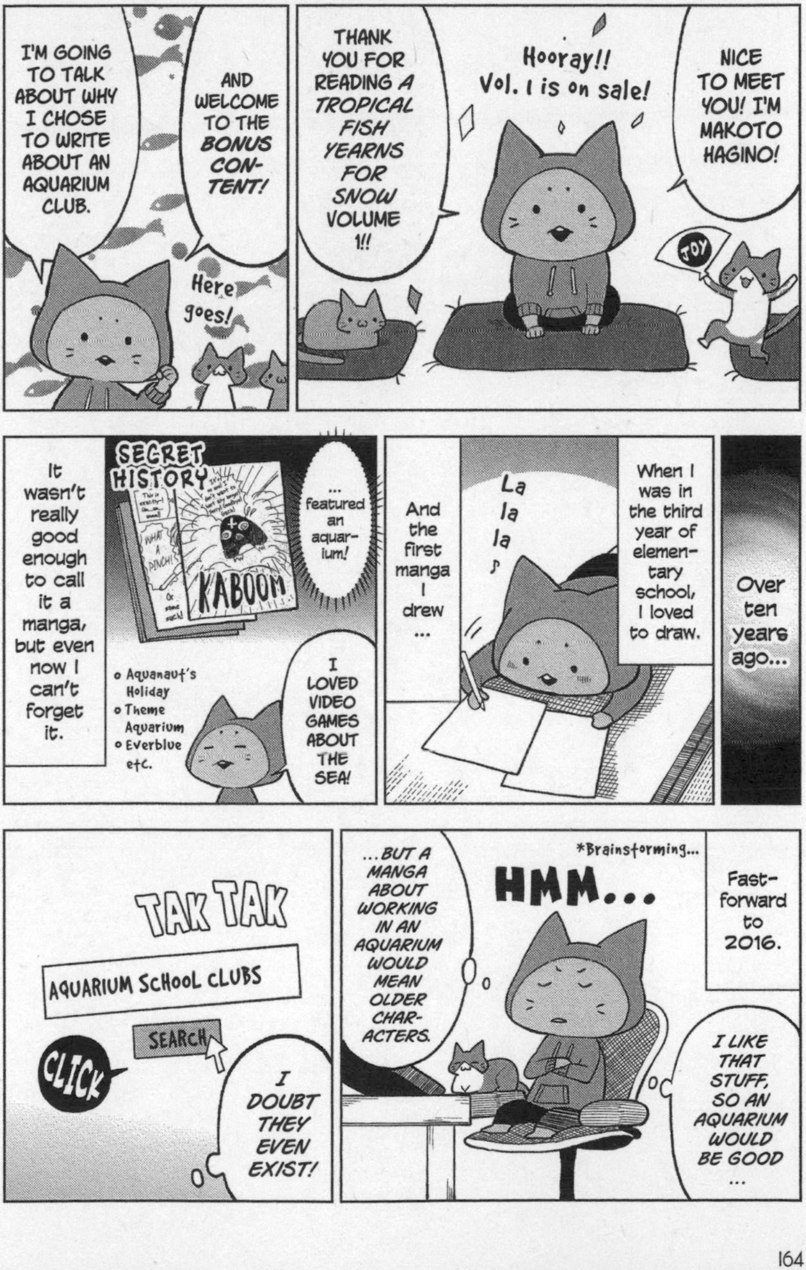
NICE TO MEET YOU! I'M MAKOTO HAGINO!
Hooray!! Vol. 1 is on sale!
JOY
THANK YOU FOR READING A TROPICAL FISH YEARNS FOR SNOW VOLUME 1!!
AND WELCOME TO THE BONUS CONTENT!
I'M GOING TO TALK ABOUT WHY I CHOSE TO WRITE ABOUT AN AQUARIUM CLUB.
Here goes!
Over ten years ago...
When I was in the third year of elementary school, I loved to draw.
La la la
And the first manga I drew ...
... featured an aquarium!
SECRET HISTORY
WHAT A PINCH!
Or some such!
KABOOM
I LOVED VIDEO GAMES ABOUT THE SEA!
Aquanaut's Holiday
Theme Aquarium
Everblue
etc.
It wasn't really good enough to call it a manga, but even now I can't forget it.
Fast-forward to 2016.
*Brainstorming...
HMM...
I LIKE THAT STUFF, SO AN AQUARIUM WOULD BE GOOD ...
...BUT A MANGA ABOUT WORKING IN AN AQUARIUM WOULD MEAN OLDER CHARACTERS.
TAK TAK
AQUARIUM SCHOOL CLUBS
SEARCH
CLICK
I DOUBT THEY EVEN EXIST!

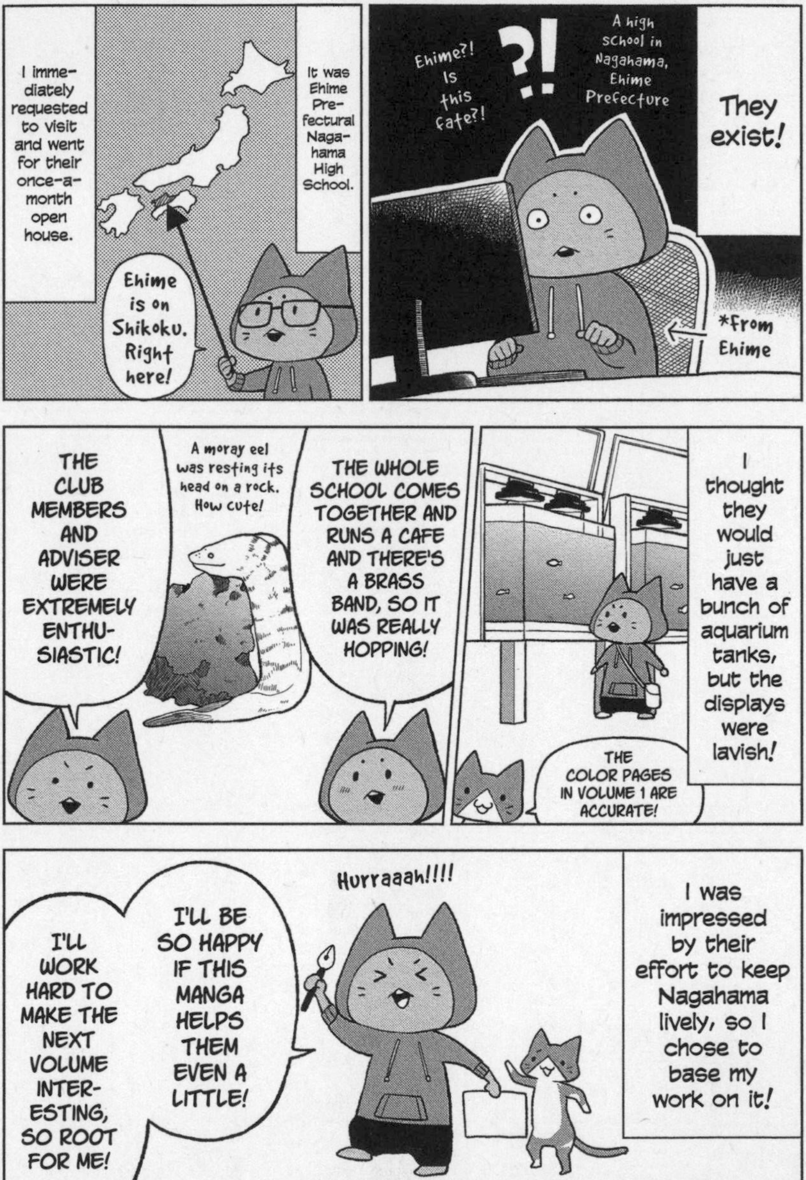
They exist!
A high school in Nagahama, Ehime Prefecture
?!
Ehime?! Is this fate?!
*From Ehime
It was Ehime Prefectural Nagahama High School.
I immediately requested to visit and went for their once-a-month open house.
Ehime is on Shikoku. Right here!
I thought they would just have a bunch of aquarium tanks, but the displays were lavish!
THE COLOR PAGES IN VOLUME 1 ARE ACCURATE!
THE WHOLE SCHOOL COMES TOGETHER AND RUNS A CAFE AND THERE'S A BRASS BAND, SO IT WAS REALLY HOPPING!
A moray eel was resting its head on a rock. How cute!
THE CLUB MEMBERS AND ADVISER WERE EXTREMELY ENTHUSIASTIC!
I was impressed by their effort to keep Nagahama lively, so I chose to base my work on it!
Hurraaah!!!!
I'LL BE SO HAPPY IF THIS MANGA HELPS THEM EVEN A LITTLE!
I'LL WORK HARD TO MAKE THE NEXT VOLUME INTERESTING, SO ROOT FOR ME!

A TROPICAL FISH YEARNS FOR SNOW
Vol. 1
VIZ Media Edition

STORY AND ART BY
MAKOTO HAGINO

English Translation & Adaptation/John Werry
Touch-Up Art & Lettering/Eve Grandt
Design/Yukiko Whitley
Editor/Pancha Diaz

NETTAIGYO WA YUKI NI KOGARERU Vol. 1
©MAKOTO HAGINO 2017
First published in Japan in 2017 by KADOKAWA CORPORATION, Tokyo.
English translation rights arranged with KADOKAWA CORPORATION, Tokyo.

Printed in the U.S.A.

Published by VIZ Media, LLC
P.O. Box 77010
San Francisco, CA 94107

10 9 8 7 6 5 4 3 2 1
First printing, November 2019

PARENTAL ADVISORY
A TROPICAL FISH YEARNS FOR SNOW is rated T
for Teen and is recommended for ages 13 and up.

A butterflies-in-your-stomach high school romance about two very different high school boys who find themselves unexpectedly falling for each other.

That Blue Sky Feeling

Story by **Okura**

Art by **Coma Hashii**

Outgoing high school student Noshiro finds himself drawn to Sanada, the school outcast, who is rumored to be gay. Rather than deter Noshiro, the rumor makes him even more determined to get close to Sanada, setting in motion a surprising tale of first love.

RATED TEEN

VIZ

A supernatural romance by the
creator of *Kiss of the Rose Princess*!

The DEMON PRINCE of MOMOCHI HOUSE

Story & Art by

Aya Shouoto

On her sixteenth birthday, orphan Himari Momochi inherits
her ancestral estate that she's never seen. Momochi House
exists on the barrier between the human and spiritual
realms, and Himari is meant to act as guardian between
the two worlds. But on the day she moves in, she finds
three handsome squatters already living in the house, and
one seems to have already taken over her role!

"Bloody" Mary, a vampire with a death wish, has spent the past 400 years chasing down a modern-day exorcist named Maria who is thought to have inherited "The Blood of Maria" and is the only one who can kill Mary. To Mary's dismay, Maria doesn't know how to kill vampires. Desperate to die, Mary agrees to become Maria's bodyguard until Maria can find a way to kill him.

Story and Art by
akaza samamiya

BLOODY MARY Volume 1 © Akaza SAMAMIYA 2014

Beautiful boy rebels using their fists to fall in love!

KENKA BANCHO
Otome
LOVE'S BATTLE ROYALE

FERVE

STORY & ART BY CHIE SHIMADA

Based on the game created by Spike Chunsoft

Hinako thought she didn't have any family, but on the day she starts high school, her twin brother Hikaru suddenly appears and tricks her into taking his place. But the new school Hinako attends in his stead is beyond unusual. Now she must fight her way to the top of Shishiku Academy, an all-boys school of delinquents!

This is the last page.

A Tropical Fish Yearns for Snow **has been printed in the original Japanese format to preserve the orientation of the artwork.**

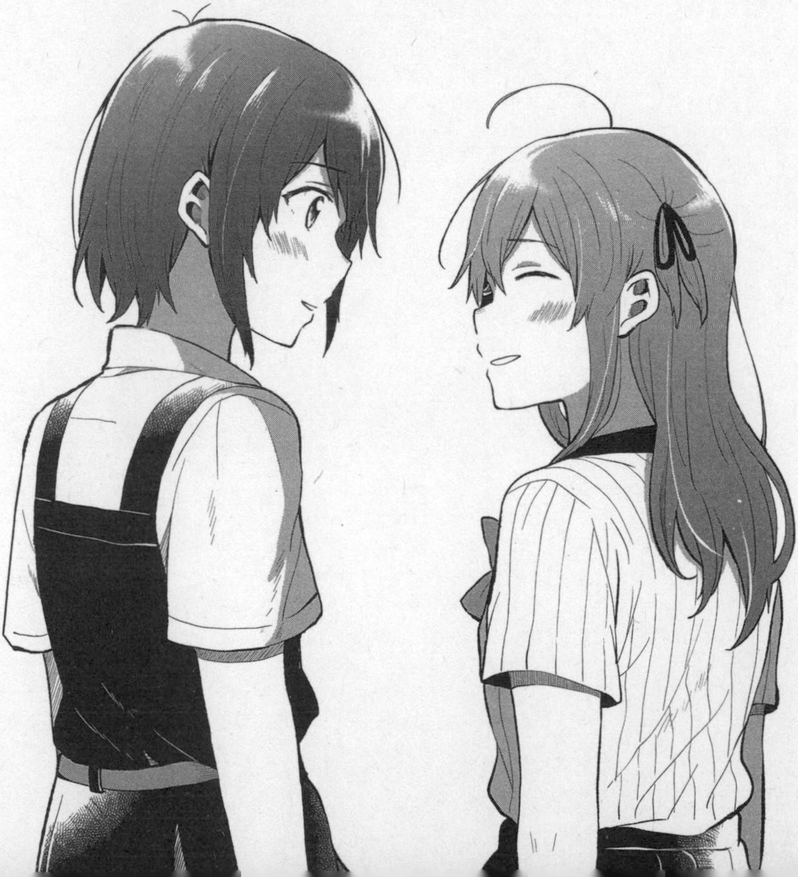

A Tropical Fish
Yearns for Snow

Story & Art by
Makoto Hagino

1

D0063648